D0445417

The Marriage of Sex and Spirit

Relationships at the Heart of Conscious Evolution

edited by
GERALYN GENDREAU, MFT
associate editors
Randy Peyser
Francesca Gentille
Courtney Arnold

www.MarriageOfSexAndSpirit.com

Elite Books
Santa Rosa, CA 95403
www.EliteBooksOnline.com

Library of Congress Cataloging-in-Publication Data:

The Marriage of Sex and Spirit : relationships at the heart of conscious evolution /edited by Geralyn Gendreau.

p. cm.

Includes bibliographical references.

ISNB 0-9710888-6-1

1. Human Sexuality. 2. Love. I. Gendreau, Geralyn

2006

128.46

Cover design by Vicki Valentine
Typesetting by Maria Ayala and Karin Kinsey
Copyedited by Melissa Mower, Laurie Masters, and Courtney Arnold
Typeset in Mona Lisa and Book Antiqua
Printed in USA by Bang Printing
First Edition

10 9 8 7 6 5 4 3 2 1

Contents

Section Five: Healing the Heart of Relationship

Section Six: Wonder in the Flesh

Section Seven: Daring Love's Risk

Section Eight: The Future of Relationship

Acknowledgments

I often quote Rebecca Wells who said, "It takes a village to write a book." With a project of this scope, it takes more than a village—it takes a cyber shire. Special thanks to Dawson Church for supporting my vision and seeing the new world stretch out before us. To Jeanne House, whose constant heart-streaming enthusiasm carried us through the ups and downs. To Courtney Arnold whose genuine brilliance continues to inspire and enlighten me. To Karin Kinsey, who stepped in at the last minute to save the day and typeset this tome. To Dawson's inner circle, especially Angela, Lionel, Alexander, and Jeff, who put up with all the hoopla that went into making this book happen. To Randy Peyser, whose previously published interviews with several of the authors in this book blossomed into beautiful chapters. To my associate editor, Francesca Gentille, who carried the dream in her heart for a solid year and who sparkles with feminine divinity. To Laurie Masters, a gem of a new friend, thorough copy editor, and brilliant mirror. To Dina, who pinch-hit polished the final version of "Meet the Beloved." To Rinaldo Brutico who rallied on my behalf in the final hours. To all the knights of the table round, you know who you are, and especially to Grant Kemp, my rock for some thirty-plus years, Tiger, whose instinctive genius guides me steadily into unmapped and unguarded regions of the heart, and to David Alexander English, whose life and art always reminds me that the universe is friendly. And special thanks to John Kalb for tending the mystic flame and having the courage to love without limits. Lastly, to my extended family—now rippling out into the world further than I ever would have imagined, thanks to Dawson and these visionary projects.

INTRODUCTION

When I first proposed *The Marriage of Sex and Spirit* as a title for a relationship anthology, the twinkle in my publisher's eyes began to dance. Dawson Church, one of the most pioneering publishers and erudite voices in the book market today, immediately sensed the potency of this seed. Last fall, at the hugely successful book release party for *Healing Our Planet, Healing Our Selves*—the anthology I edited with Dawson in 2004—I sensed that that book's title had struck a common chord. Some 800 people filled the Center for Spiritual Living in Santa Rosa, California, confirming that the book contains many seminal and timely ideas for which the time has come. Sacred sex is another idea whose time has come.

While working to compile this new collection, I attended San Francisco's now-famous Exotic Erotic Ball for the very first time. Stunned by the immense response to the event—some 7,000 people crowded into the Cow Palace to wander the halls, immersed in an ocean of bare flesh—it dawned on me that the overall sensibility was rather base. I had an energetic hangover from the intensity of that cattle call, and began to wonder what would happen if the Exotic Erotic got an upward spin. What I saw in my mind's eye was a wild, sacred dance—a springtime celebration of eros that would be called The Ecstatic Erotic Ball.

Ecstasy, in my mind, is the key. Let's face it, sex is everywhere and even has a huge cult following in the "reclaim it as human, powerful, and lots of fun" camp. What mainstream culture tends to miss, however, is the sacred component. Ecstasy, from the Greek root, *ekstasis* means *to stand outside of oneself.* The term comes to us, quite literally, by way of the Dionysian tradition, in which ritual ecstatic sex was practiced as a means of communing with God. Unfortunately, in the monotheistic, Judeo-Christian tradition, we have tended to see sex and spirituality as *polar opposites.* This is the disjuncture that is being healed by the work of the authors we have gathered together in this collection.

My treasured friend and mentor, Stuart Sovatsky, said it this way: "I believe we are creating the next wave of the sexual liberation that began in the sixties, but this time with concern for the spiritual dimensions of life in ways that will transform our understanding of both sex and religion/spirituality. We are the ones taking the baton from Masters and Johnson, Kinsey, D. H. Lawrence, and James Joyce and finding culmination in unmapped orgasms of the heart—where lovers are ablaze, melted into each other in an endless orgasm of mind and body."

Some say money makes the world go around. But what is money if it does not link with pleasure? In *The History of Sexuality,* Michel Foucault speaks to the role of pleasure as it relates to the truth of sex: "In the erotic art, truth is drawn from pleasure itself... in terms of its intensity, its specific quality, its duration, its reverberations in the body and the soul." He goes on to discuss the value of working with a master who "can transmit this art in an esoteric manner as the culmination of an initiation in which he [she] guides the disciple's progress with unfailing skill and severity. The effects of this masterful art... are said to transfigure the one fortunate enough to receive its privileges: an absolute mastery of the body, a singular bliss, obliviousness to time and limits, the elixir of life, the exile of death and its threats."

It was Teilhard de Chardin who said, so very succinctly: "After we have mastered the wind, the waves, the tides, and gravity, we shall harness the energies of love. Then, for the second time in the history of the world, man will have discovered fire."

Sacred sex is elemental, just like gold and fire. Will you help us spread the flame of this treasure?

Geralyn Gendreau
Ojai, California

Part One

The Great Marriage

When the Ocean comes to you as a lover,
marry, at once, quickly for God's sake!
Don't postpone it!
Existence has no better gift.
No amount of searching will find this.
~Rumi

Marry me moon, and I will never be lonely again.
~Blake More, *Honey Moon*

Deepak Chopra:

Sacred Marriage

People often think of relationship in terms of "convenience," but what could be more inconvenient than having every fiber in your body touched by the timeless gifts of passion and love? Passion is not only one of the greatest gifts of life, but one of the strongest bonds of a relationship. In the early stages of a relationship, we experience attraction and infatuation. The passion born out of those stages can be intoxicating. As Rumi said, "If infatuation is madness, then I want to be crazy."

In my book, *The Path to Love,* I invite you to make a soul bargain with love in order to align yourself with love. Far more than an emotion, love is a real force. And if love is attuned to who you are, love will respond. At the Chopra Center, we begin each day with meditation. Prior to meditating we ask people to still themselves, then gently and innocently ask the question: "What do I want?" As they answer this question, they place their intentions into their subconscious mind and soul. We ask ourselves this question in a romantic context, an emotional context, or a physical context, and embed these intentions like seeds in the fertile soil of the subconscious.

Vedic scripture reveals that we have total control over our actions and no control over the fruits of those actions. After placing our pure intentions so deeply within our souls, we let go of the outcome and leave it up to the universe. However, the seed has been planted. When we drift into that place of stillness and silence, which is referred to as

Deepak Chopra, M.D., has written some thirty books, which have been translated into thirty-five languages. He is also the author of more than one hundred audio- and videotape series, including five critically acclaimed programs on public television. In 1999 *Time* magazine selected Dr. Chopra as one of the Top 100 Icons and Heroes of the Century, describing him as "the poet-prophet of alternative medicine." Dr. Chopra currently serves as CEO and founder of The Chopra Center for Well Being in Carlsbad, California. For more information you can visit his web site at www.chopra.com.

the gap, the seeds of the subconscious speak directly to the universal consciousness. This exercise is incredibly powerful and allows individuals to truly manifest their deepest desires for love, relationship, and life.

Founded in ancient India, the 5,000-year-old science of life known as Ayurveda has as its cornerstone the oneness that exists within all things. It is by tapping into that wholeness, which is essential to the world, that we bring heaven to earth. We can achieve ecstasy within our relationships when we intuitively and innocently understand that we are all the same; we are simply wearing different disguises. The more we are willing to step into a universal consciousness with our partner, the more we can shift our attention from the "I/Me" to the "Us/We."

As a relationship unfolds from a point of oneness, the bounds of the ego, as well as possessiveness and fear, are replaced by selfless love, appreciation, and grace. Then each moment becomes an opportunity for ecstasy. Layers of our disguise naturally slip away and all we are left with is one soul consciousness communicating with another, acknowledging the sanctity of their oneness.

There is a difference between loneliness and aloneness. Being alone is a wonderful experience. It is a self-affirming action because it heralds our love of self, and therefore, our understanding of our purpose within the divine. The issue becomes one of conscious communication; it is restorative to our souls to spend time alone. Explore your intentions, desires, and how you can intuitively and spontaneously fulfill them. By working with your intentions and desires, you will be able to manifest an environment that contains the flexibility to meet your needs. In morning and evening meditations, as you drift into the stillness and silence, reconfirm not only your singleness, but also your universality.

-§-

Far more than an emotion, love is a real force.

-§-

When we bring ourselves into a state of present moment awareness, we allow the divine within us to establish an ecstasy that weaves through every moment of our waking life. Ecstasy is about bringing heaven to earth. Achieving ecstasy is not beyond our reach. If you tap into the divine energy of the present moment, you can live your entire life without regret or expectation. The ecstasy of meditation, which is restful awareness, is not achieved through meditation itself, but rather when you bring stillness and silence into your daily existence.

I often encourage couples to write sutras regarding what they've learned about love. Sutra is Sanskrit for "stitch" or "suture." As in medical science, a suture connects two things. We link these stitches by connecting them to a powerful affirmation. For example:

"From a pure heart anything can be accomplished. If you ask what the universe is doing, it is eavesdropping on your every desire."

This is a sutra in which you are actually communicating with the universe. This dialogue not only weaves healing and transformational threads, but also acts as a connector between our physical state and that of divine spirit. By writing sutras, you can learn to innocently blend your deepest intentions with the universal consciousness.

A question that is often overlooked when there seems to be discontent or stress in a relationship is, *"What actually just happened?"* So often, we find ourselves unable to solve or evolve in our current situation because we are steeped in blame, accusation, and defense of our position. Asking ourselves what just happened in a conversation or interaction allows us to look at a situation clearly and objectively, so as to pierce the drama and baggage that often accompany miscommunication.

Ninety-five percent of the problems in relationships exist because of lapses in communication. The communication between two people in a relationship can evolve and grow exponentially when both people make a commitment to communicate using the principles that Marshall Rosenberg offers in his book, *Non-Violent Communication.* The next time your partner has you at wit's end, simply ask yourself, "What happened here?" Then ask, "How can I selflessly, defenselessly, and compassionately take the relationship to a higher level?"

-§-

The seeds of the subconscious speak directly to the universal consciousness.

-§-

I consider relationships to be one of the most important aspects of being, as all relationships are mirrors of ourselves. Only when Shiva and Shakti are married within will you be able to enter a sacred marriage with someone else. Shiva is silence; Shakti is power. Shiva is creativity; Shakti is creation. Shiva is love; Shakti is love fully expressed. For union to be whole, these two energies must exist.

Many women come to the Chopra Center to explore their Shakti side and incorporate more of Shiva's energy in their souls. Through Vedic meditation and exercises, they learn to intuitively recognize the sacred marriage within them.

Power is complemented by graciousness.

Strength is complemented by ease.

Passion is complemented by creativity.

This union is the highest we can espouse in a holistic and universal context.

Gabriel Cousens:

Eros and Intimacy

Intimacy takes us into the mystery of life; it is not about safety or security. It is about the alchemical process of transformation. It takes us to the frontiers of human existence and brings us face-to-face with our angels and demons. It may activate our deepest thought forms—our issues with our family of origin, our personal patterns, who we are, our ability to express and receive love, and the essence of what spiritual life is about.

The sacred relationship is our journey into the unknown. Opening up to the risk of intimacy is part of the evolution of human consciousness. We are challenged to maintain and grow within a live, turned-on connection and love, and to free ourselves from old patterns of pain. In the process, we also need to create space for the other to exist and to grow.

At a high level of intimacy, we support each other to become the fullest expressions of that which we are meant to be—the wild female and the wild male. To become the original of whom we are meant to be. We, as partners, have the choice and ability to give space to the other to become their full, original self.

This is very different from the typical kind of relationship, in which we try to tame the other person into our idea of who he or she should be for us. In intimacy, our role is to help the other reach their

Gabriel Cousens, M.D., is founder of the Tree of Life Foundation and Rejuvenation Center in Patagonia, Arizona. Dr. Cousens is a holistic medical doctor, licensed psychiatrist, family therapist, and a licensed homeopathic physician. Dr. Cousens uses nutrition, naturopathy, Ayurveda, and homeopathy, blended with spiritual awareness. His bestselling books include *Rainbow Green Live-Food Cuisine* (North Atlantic, 2003), *Spiritual Nutrition* (North Atlantic, 2005), and *Conscious Eating* (North Atlantic, 2000), and *Depression-Free for Life* (Morrow, 2003). Dr. Cousens is known worldwide as an empowered spiritual teacher and the leading medical authority on vegan live-food nutrition. Find more information at www.treeoflife.nu.

full depth as a human being. Intimacy is an alchemical process of transformation. It invokes the presence of the divine. We call this the alchemical merging into the One.

The definition of intimacy is maintaining an open heart, in love, with the other over time. It is very personal. This is one of the differences between Eastern tantra, where the woman is the Goddess with no face, and what I am going to call Kabbalistic tantra, where the woman is the goddess we call the *Shekhinah,* which has a personal face. She has a name.

The concept of the name is very important when we talk about intimacy. The difference between the Temple Priestess, the Goddess, and the prostitute, who helps invoke the divine, but who is faceless, is that in a personal, intimate, ongoing relationship, the person has a face and has a history to which we are connected. This is an extremely important difference from Eastern Tantra, in which the experience is of the divine in all, but not necessarily in that person. The prophets were very much against the Temple prostitutes because they didn't have the personal quality. When a person has a name, that personal aspect links them to God.

-§-
When a person has a name, that personal aspect links them to God.
-§-

In intimacy, we have two essences that must be balanced. The female essence, which can be in a male or a female person, is the rainbow radiance of who we are—the full flow and dance of love. It wants to shine, to be seen, and needs to be recognized and to be known. The female essence is the flower and the joy of fullness. The male essence, which can also be in a male or a female person, is to die into the unknown—a total focus on oneness, dissolving into the Nothing. So, one is about emptiness and the other is about fullness. And these need to match for a relationship to really work.

Think of these two essences like a battery with sparks, a polarity that gives spark to the relationship. If you don't have that arc of energy between the two poles, it is hard to have a deep relationship. The female essence is everything that changes: light, colors, sound, feeling, and flow—the flow of the universe. The male essence is the part that never changes. It is the witness.

In the Hindu paradigm, it is Shiva and Shakti. Shakti is the play of consciousness in the world. Shiva is the nothing. It just sits there and witnesses the world, unchanging; it is absolute consciousness itself. These characteristics help us to understand the differences. When the male and female essences get together, there is a merging of light and consciousness. This alchemical energy is the essence of real, deep merging with God.

Now, let's talk about communication. The female essence needs one thing: to know it's loved. If the male essence does not communicate to the female that she is loved, things don't work so well. What the male essence needs is to know that it is succeeding and not failing. The difference in needs causes the male and female essences to communicate on different levels. All communication—in relationship, in lovemaking, and in everyday life—has to hold these messages. This is what we call meta-communication.

By understanding these essences, we can give and receive in a way that uplifts the other person and allows space for them to be their full, authentic self. In order for this to be possible, however, both people have to be operating from the same level of intention, or awareness.

There are levels of relationship along the spectrum of what we call, in the psychological world, undifferentiated to differentiated. The extremes of the undifferentiated woman and man have no boundaries.

The level-one relationship is the least differentiated and, therefore, co-dependent. It is like a business deal, in which getting ego needs taken care of is the primary goal. In terms of male and female, it has to do with raw sexuality versus sexuality as a way of sharing radiance. It is more like an exchange. In this kind of relationship, the female essence uses its sexuality to attract the male. This is not what happens at all levels, but at level one, this is what she is doing. That is what we see today in the marketplace, with the overtly sexual way women dress and so forth. The male essence attracts at level one by power and fame, which is what attracts that level of female essence, which is looking to be made whole by the male.

-§-
When the male and female essences get together, there is a merging of light and consciousness.
-§-

In a level-two relationship, people are working hard on their boundaries and have an equality. It is a separate-but-equal relationship, like when two people have separate bank accounts, and a way of relating as professionals. Both are equal, and both are denying their essence. The male denies his essence as meditator dying into the nothing. The female denies her radiance and walks around in her business suit, but isn't comfortable with that as her essence. When we are equal, everything is the same. At level two, the biggest struggle is to maintain boundaries and equality. Essence polarity is often lost.

The third level of relationship is where we talk about the alchemical merging into God. Here, the goal is supporting each other, with both giving their holy gift. The third-level female essence gives her holy gift not to attract a man, but simply to be the radiance of the divine. Her gift is to inspire everyone else to be that radiance. The third-level man sees a beautiful woman, or a beautiful horse, or beautiful nature, and he is inspired to give his gift of the Nothing. She inspires him, and he inspires her. That is the essence; it is bigger than we are.

Level one is about ego, and level two is about partnership—but at level three we go on into being beyond boundaries. We feel from the heart, without limitations. When we live by love, we are *lived by* liberation. The only thing that matters is God; God is the complete center of life. We go beyond the egocentric, ethnocentric, into the mystical experience of the One in all things. This level-three orientation is the joy of the culture of liberation. We are not living out of habits or following robotic preferences. We are being lived by love, and that is what relationship is all about.

-§-
When we live by love, we are *lived by* liberation.
-§-

At level two, we talk about cooperation, what is fair. We strive for vigorous independence, and are afraid to love too much because we might lose ourselves. But at level three a community of trust begins to unfold—everyone is being lived by something larger than themselves. The essential question becomes, "*How can love and light shine most fully?*" Even if we give up our personal preferences, it is for the sake of a deeper being—to be the expression of God. Level three is where we use sexuality to liberate love and open ourselves to the divine.

At level three of relationship, life expresses the deepest level of love, as we go beyond our personal boundaries (level one), and our partner's boundaries (level two), to what would most serve our partner and the world. It is important to remember that people actually operate in all three stages, but are predominately centered in one or another. This means that we revisit our goals and challenges as we grow toward the ideal.

At level three, the feminine is seeking the fullness of love, which, at level one, may have come out in terms of food, chocolate, shopping, and so on. The masculine essence, at level three, seeks emptiness, death, liberation, and meditation. In terms of sexual relationship, with ejaculation, a kind of emptiness is created—the kind of emptiness that is level one. At level three we are placing more focus on *non-ejaculatory sex*. This creates a kind of multi-level orgasm, for both men and women, in which we merge into each other and become one. This experience of merging within sexual love is described in the following level-three poems:

TANTRIC SUNRISE

Awaking from the exquisite bliss of sleep
Gently massaging your breast and succulent vortexes
Feeling the subtle heat increase as your nipples and this body pulse
with blood
Our lips lusciously touch, giving birth to our tongues
Which mate like ovum and sperm, giving birth to life.
In that moment, the light of a thousand suns explodes in my head.
What an awesome sunrise, which goes all day long,
Forever keeping this one awake!

The sexual alchemy brings an inner alchemy of light, which then keeps going all of the time. So, the relationship is always inspiring the light and love.

HOLY TOUCH

We lay together in object singular silent holy ecstasy
Draped over and within each other
Subtle, blazing love
Our skin succulent to the full body touch
Erotic, full chakra light show
Our sensuous bodies and quiet breath touch
Yoni to lingam, belly to belly, breath to breath
The light radiating the magic by touching skin
Into the singular divine wholeness
In the Holy Touch, all universes are healed
Creation smiles and laughs with the play of the radiance

This is about the merging again—the alchemical merging that is non-ejaculatory, because ejaculation shorts the circuit. In our Sacred Relationship workshop at the Tree of Life, we teach the basic Mantak Chia Taoist techniques to achieve this. Using this approach, it takes about half an hour to get to that merging, where boundaries dissolve and there is only one. These techniques are not just about sexuality and energy, but also about God.

BEING LOVE

We make love until every cell of the delicate centers membrane of our
physical body alchemically change to LOVE
Until our full sensuous lips and tongues become one embrace
Until our breath, the one exhale of the universe
Until we become the divine subtle nectar
I suckle from your incredible breasts
As our two bellies merge as one umbilical cord connected to
the Creator,
Until I thought as my burning lingam in the fire of your yoni
Which magical nectar forget their owners
And become the cosmic Shiva Lingam
We love until there is nothing left
With the Sublime One laughing in holy joy

Eros is the essence of sacred relationship, and sex in the level-three context is the unity of consciousness and light. It is experienced as an alchemical merging, as described in the poems. The female essence is looking for a male who can feel her depth—the depth of presence and intention. The most important thing, as we move into eros for the female essence, is for the male to be present. The male essence is looking for a range of female energetics. Because the male is into the One, he is looking for balance. The male has to offer his presence, and the female has to offer the full range of the female essence. This is the merging of heaven with earth of Chinese metaphor. At the level where sex between the male and female essences liberates the gifting of love, eros begins. Eros is the ability in a relationship to perceive the inner beauty of the other. It allows us to celebrate the divine essence of the other. But eros is bigger than just this—eros is seeing the divine in all of creation.

The essence of eros, in the Western Kabbalistic tradition, comes from the cherubim that were said to be on the Ark. The cherubim and the Ark on the Holy of Holies were magically making love. That is the center of spirituality in the Hebrew Kabbalistic tradition. In drawings of the Ark, the two angels are facing each other. In the primal myth, at the beginning of time, Abba and Ima, the male and female energies, were face to face. The vessels of creation were filled with light, but they could not hold the light and fractured. When the vessels fractured from so much light, Abba and Ima turned from facing each other to having their backs together. So Eros is connected to Abba and Ima returning to face one another.

The Holiest of Holies, which is the template for the level-three relationship, is made up of the tablet and the Ark. The tablet represents the phallus, and the Ark represents the vagina. So, we have the sense that eros is truly celebrating God in all of creation. In Kabbalistic terms, we call the experience of God in all of creation the Shekhinah.

-§-
When a man and a woman make love, they are invoking the Divine.
-§-

It is said that, in the time of the First Temple, people were having a problem with adultery. Eros and energy were getting out of hand, so priests fasted and prayed that eros would be taken out of the society. After three days, God answered their prayers, and a lion leaped out of the Ark between the two angels, the two cherubim. For the next three days the whole society shut down—chickens didn't lay eggs, artists stopped writing poetry, people didn't have the energy to go to work, and relationships started to fall apart.

The priests said, "I don't think we did this right." So, then, they prayed that just the positive side of eros should come back.

And God said, "No deal; you have a shadow side that goes with it."

So, God and the priests agreed that the lion would come back, the positive side of eros along with the negative side, but it just wouldn't be as strong.

From this story we see that eros runs all of society. It is the whole life force. Eros is seeing God in all things. Alchemical sexuality, and even level-one sexuality, activates some level of eros that appreciates God in all things. That becomes a path to the divine.

Eros in the time of the Temple was centered in the Holy of Holies. When the Temple fell (557 B.C.), eros went into exile. Eros has been exiled to sexuality, which only helps lead you to full love. Now, in our society, sex is even debased as a commodity, which is pornography. That is the exile of the exile.

What are we to do in order to reestablish sacred relationship as the center, as a key path to knowing the divine? In the Kabbalistic paradigm, it is "As Above so Below; so Below as Above." When a man and a woman make love, they are invoking the divine. When Abba and Ima face each other, there is a healing on the cosmic plane, which then becomes a healing on the physical plane.

In this way, when you are making love, it is making love with the whole universe—with breath and the whole being. We teach that it is not only for your sexual pleasure, or for the merging of two people, but that you make love to become a healed unit—a He-Adam and She-Adam becoming one, Abba and Ima facing each other. You are healing the whole universe as you heal the male/female split.

You are invoking all the power of God, and, in that way, it becomes a spiritual path.

Tikkun ha'nefesh means healing your personal self, and *tikkun ha'olam,* healing the Universal Self. Inhaling sends love downwards and within. When you exhale, you are sending love out to the whole universe. You are healing at microcosmic levels that heal at the macrocosmic level.

Erotic living is only a little bit about sexuality. There are five faces of eros, and one is being on the inside. What this means is that most of the time we aren't really on the inside of an experience; we are on the outside. Erotic living is really being there, taking part in the subjective reality of experience. To live in an erotic way is to be fully present on the inside.

-§-
Sexual union is the great mystical act that heals all the world.
-§-

The opposite of eros is alienation. It is emptiness or being on the outside. *Lif'nei,* to live on the inside of God's face, face-to-face with God, means that we feel the aspects of God in all of life as they manifest. When we are not feeling this, we have an emptiness. Everything comes from emptiness, but most people are uncomfortable with it. So, we have addiction and all the activities we do in order to avoid the emptiness: sex, food, public acclaim, drugs, work, gambling, whatever—that is called pseudo-eros.

True eros is the feeling of fullness in the other. Only when you can hold the emptiness can you be filled with eros. It is like in meditation, when you go into the Nothing. What is hard, of course, is holding the silence and emptiness in sex. The deep secret of the cherubim is that sex points to living our lives in a fuller way. It is experiencing the beauty and wonder of God in all of creation. Sexual union is the great mystical act that heals all the world.

To live erotically means to be and see God in all things. True eros is the key to living erotically in the non-sexual areas of our lives. That is the point! The erotic becomes the divine kiss that powers our desire for God, and at the same time is the result of God-merging.

This is the first face of Eros. The second face is the intense yearning that comes out of the divine kiss. It is the yearning for God. Experiencing eros is the one thing we can do on the physical plane that activates this yearning. Once the yearning starts, we are willing to take it to higher and higher levels, which, in my book, *Spiritual Nutrition: Six Foundations for Spiritual Life and the Awakening of Kundalini,* I call the Six Foundations:

1. Spiritual nutrition (food) and spiritual fasting

2. Building the life force (*prana*) with pranayama, yoga, sacred dance, etc.
3. Service and charity (when we give, we are connecting)
4. Being inspired by a spiritual teacher (*satsang*), support by a spiritual group, reading the great literature, jnana yoga
5. Silence, meditation, praying, mantra repetition, and chanting
6. *Shaktipat* and the awakening of Kundalini energy

The third face of eros is called presence. If we aren't present, we can't really experience eros. To be present we have to let go of the past, all of our baggage, and the future, which includes all of our fears. Female essence loves the male to be present. This is critical in relationship.

To be present is to be in the now, to let go of all control, all ideas of how the other person should be, and to let go of intense perfectionist consciousness. As Emerson said, "God made everything with a crack in it." It is important to understand that, when you are really present in your self, you create the space for the other to exist. If you are narcissistic there is no room, and the other only exists as a projection of your needs. They will only become what you are trying to shape them into. Both are trying to get the other to act in a certain way, but neither is trying to help the other to be his or her full essence, or full, original self.

-§-
When you are really present in your self, you create the space for the other to exist.
-§-

The key to presence is an inner state of letting go—of control and of the idea of how things "should be." There is a wonderful story:

> Rabbi Michael and his wife were very, very poor, always struggling to get by. Just before *Sukkot,* a man gave him a beautiful donation. He looked at it; it was so much money. He said, "Wow!" and he counted it. He'd been eyeing this esrog in town (a citrus fruit used in the festival of Sukkot). It came from Israel and it was worth a lot of money. He said, "I'm just gonna to do it," and he put it down and bought the esrog, which took all the money. He went home and told his wife how excited he was—this was the best, most beautiful esrog. She asked, "Where, where did you get the money?" He said, "Well, it was donated to me." She started to think about it, and it started to compute in her mind: *Now, wait a second – that money could have gone to supporting our kids and taking care of our household.* Her practical side linked in. She got angrier and angrier the happier he got—and finally, after she exploded at him and said, "How could you do this! We're so poor, and we

have no money, and you spent it on an esrog!" she took the esrog, bit off the tip, and smashed it against the wall.

Then there was a big silence. A minute or two passed. Reb Michael was stunned; his face turned red, and turned white, and he just didn't know what to do. And his wife was worrying, *Oh my God; look what I just did.*

And then he started to laugh. He said, "Before the money, there was no esrog. And now, with money, there's no money, and there's no esrog. We have only each other."

And so they danced the night in love.

What happened is that they gave up their positions. Her position was *We need money to do the practical things.* His position was *We're mystics and we need money for the rituals.* When they both gave up their positions regarding how the family should run, each against the will of the other, the gates of love opened. That is being in the presence.

The fourth face of eros is what we call the interconnectivity of all being. It is a celebration of the divine in all things. When you can celebrate the divine in your relationship, you make love and are turned on to seeing the divine in all things—not just other men and women, but all of life. Again, in this way, you are making love with the whole universe.

The fifth face of eros, seeing the other, depends on all the first four, and is the essence of what the female needs. If the man cannot see her, the relationship is missing the most important thing. It is also really important for the male to be seen: to be appreciated for his thoughts and ideas, for the Nothing, and for the willingness to have a purpose and direction in life. This seeing and being able to see the other person comes from being on the inside. It means connecting. It means having that sense of presence to allow each other to be who they are, and giving up control of how you believe they should be.

-§-
We are not our personalities; we are the deeper essence of God expressing.
-§-

In seeing the other's face, we must return to the power of naming. Our name is the face of God. We are that unique expression of God, expressed through us in our lives. In slavery there is no name. In the Torah, the slaves in Egypt are freed. It is then that they are named— in the book of *Shemot,* which means "names" (Exodus)—and therefore exist. Your name is a part of God, and you are a part of God! They who have names are holy.

We are not our personalities; we are that deeper essence of God expressing. Humans have been trying to be the expression of God, but it is really the other way around—God is trying to express through humans. The embracing cherubs represent the unity of the name. Another story comes to mind, about the importance of being seen.

> There once was a man who was a very spiritual person, but he had this emptiness. There was a harlot that lived by the sea. This harlot charged 400 gold pieces for sexual interactions. She had six silver beds and one golden bed. So when he came to her, she walked up the bed nude, up the different ladders, and he climbed up the bed after her. But then his ritual fringes magically climbed up the different ladders, and they slapped him in the face. He stopped and he said, "I cannot be in this relationship with you this way." He slid down the ladders, and she came down asking "What is my defect, why is it you cannot be with me?"
>
> "I never saw a woman as beautiful as you, but the fringes reminded me that there is a higher order or ethos. I can't be with you in this condition; if I am going to be with you, I have to be with you as a full human being," he replied.
>
> She said, "I won't let you go until you tell me the name of your teacher, your village, and your name." At that point, she broke the code, meaning, "You now have a face, I now have a face; we have become real people. We have become vulnerable and fragile and open to intimacy."
>
> So he went away, and she sold everything except her bed sheets. She kept a third of the money for herself, and she went looking for the man's master, Chaya. When she found him, she said, "You must help me, because I want to convert and marry this man." Master Chaya realized that this was a major transformation for her, so he converted her and married them. They sleep on the same bed sheets, now as husband and wife.

Here is a man caught in his struggle with emptiness, with pseudo-eros, who is not seeing the Shekhinah in all of life. He goes to the seaside, where there is passion, and he meets the harlot. He doesn't know a thing about intimacy or relationship. Meanwhile, she is just dealing with fantasy-world pseudo-eros, helping men with their emptiness by giving them their peak experiences. She is the example of the Shekhinah in exile. When he says, "I cannot be with you except to be with you fully," the whole field is shifted. She experiences being seen for the first time in her whole life. Then she asks him for his name.

At that point the harlot becomes authentic, real, and sacred. She is no longer naked of body, but of soul. At that eternal point, they are married for the sake of heaven. She has now claimed her name. She is married truly for the sake of the name.

To be seen is to be loved. Love is the perception of the beauty of the other. Life is about moving toward claiming our name—so, we manifest God's name when we personalize and live our story. The good news is that the harlot keeps the satin sheets, because she still remains as beautiful and as sexual as before; but her sexuality is upgraded by her spiritual transformation.

The story is about the redemption of the Shekhinah, the Sacred Feminine, through ethos. It is honoring the ethics of "I must know your name." The sheets of forbidden sex have transformed to sheets of erotic love. The essence of this is that when we link sexuality and expand it into full eros, it requires being seen. It requires us being present. It requires us having a connection to all creation. This is the idea of being on the inside, or being face-to-face with God. It requires intense yearning. When we link all of this together through sexuality, it brings us to experience and celebrate the divine in all things through eros. That is how sexuality and the divine are linked.

-§-
To be seen is to be loved.
-§-

In the Kabbalistic approach, the whole idea is that we be present, which also means we let go of all of our baggage. There is a Zen story about this:

> A Zen monk, after spending maybe forty years in a monastery, feels that It is not happening; he's not getting anywhere. The master of the monastery says, "Okay, I give you permission to go up the mountain and see what happens." And so he goes off, and he's very tired, worn, and confused, because nothing has seemed to work for forty years. As he walks up the hill, he sees a man coming down who's just glowing! The monk says, "Perhaps you can tell me about enlightenment." The man looks at him, smiles, and drops the bag, the bundle he's carrying. At that point, the monk becomes enlightened. The monk asks the man one other question: *"Now what do you do?"* The man picks up the bundle and keeps walking down the hill.

This story is also a little discussion of the idea about waking up in an instant. We can get it instantly—after we do possibly forty years of work *preparing* to get it instantly. As the monk walks down the mountain, he is in the presence of the divine without past, present, or future. We need to let our bundles fall, only to pick them up again, while remaining the witness, and walk down the mountain. That walk down the mountain, being totally in the presence of the divine, is the secret of eros. To drop the bundle is to let go of the past and future so we can be in the non-goal-directed present, where the dance and ecstasy of eros is in totality.

Eros, intimacy, and sacred relationship are all about the consciousness that you take into your sexuality. It is more about the living room than the bedroom. When we let go and allow intimacy to show us the way to Sacred relationship, the healing is expanded from the self to the world. Making love is a microcosm that heals the macrocosm.

Riane Eisler:

Changing Old Life Scripts

Although many of us may not think of it this way, the media modeling of uncaring and hurtful behaviors as "cool" sets a negative standard for all our relations—including romantic ones. When I watch music videos on TV I think of the blatantly contradictory messages directed at young people—and all of us—about how women and men should relate. On the one hand, we hear a lot about equality, nonviolence, and caring. But on the street and in much of popular music and TV, we hear and see precisely the reverse. Here relations of domination, humiliation, inequality, and violence are made to seem sexy; glamorous, desirable—things the superstars who are young people's icons do and enjoy.

Again, the problem isn't just the mass media. We have deeply ingrained cultural scripts that insist on the dominance of men and the submission of women. According to these scripts, which are all around us and in us, women want to be dominated and humiliated, and think men who dominate them are sexy; These messages tell us that everyone in these unequal relations has a great time.

In reality, there is no scientific evidence that women have an innate desire to be dominated. Nor is there any evidence that men have an innate desire to dominate. Men and women have just been trained that way. Given half a chance, women want to be treated with respect, consideration, gentleness, and caring. And when men treat

Riane Eisler, Ph.D., is an internationally renowned cultural historian and evolutionary theorist. She is the author of several groundbreaking books, including *The Chalice and the Blade* (Harper & Row, 1987) and *Sacred Pleasure* (HarperSanFrancisco, 1996). She is a charismatic speaker who keynotes conferences worldwide, and president of the Center for Partnership Studies in Tucson, Arizona. Dr. Eisler was born in Vienna, fled from the Nazis with her parents, and later emigrated to the United States. She obtained degrees in sociology and law from the University of California. She lives in Pacific Grove, California, with her husband, writer David Loye.

women in this way, they find greater self-respect and pleasure in their own lives.[1]

Then there are cultural scripts telling women to invest themselves primarily in their relations with men, but telling men to invest themselves primarily in their individual pursuits and careers rather than their relationships with women. These are obviously contradictory scripts, and they make for a lose-lose situation for both women and men. Women don't get the close intimate relations they are taught are primary. And men can't figure out why women are so dissatisfied, since men have been taught that their careers are the main thing in life and the main thing women should do in their lives is to support men's goals.

-§-

We hear a lot about equality, nonviolence, and caring. But in much of popular music and TV, we hear and see precisely the reverse.

-§-

All these scripts are variations of one basic dominator idea: men must always be in control. One outcome of this notion is violence against women. Another is a suspicion in men that women are trying to manipulate them. And people who are not supposed to exercise power often do manipulate: this is the only way they can get what they want. Small wonder that so many people are flocking to counselors, workshops, conferences, and retreats that promise them new relational skills.

But no matter how many new techniques we learn, or how skillful we become at them, as long as we remain within the trap of dominator relations, we're not going to get what we want. We won't satisfy our needs for trust and safety, for respect and consideration, for being recognized and loved for who we really are. Nor will books like *The Rules,* which advise women how to better manipulate men, do more than drive us further into the dead-end trap of traditional relations based on domination and submission.

Dysfunctional old ideas about women and men are a major obstacle to change. I can speak to this from personal experience. I spent many unhappy years totally unaware of the impact on my life of stereotyped gender roles and relations. I thought our marital problems were unique to me and my former husband.

When I woke up to the connection between the culturally prescribed life scripts hammering at me and my personal problems, my consciousness and my life were transformed. This was during the 1960s. Women were coming together in the second wave of the modern feminist movement the women's liberation movement that took up where the nineteenth-century movement for the vote and education left off. For some of us, this awakening was gradual. For me, it was dramatic and sudden.

Before then, I had already begun to make big changes in my life. I had quit my job at a Beverly Hills entertainment law firm, my marriage, and smoking, all within three months. Clearly, I was ready for a major change of direction.

One day, I found myself reading the want ads, not quite sure what I was searching for. But when I saw this one ad, I knew instantly it was what I had been looking for. It was an ad for a volunteer attorney to help found the first Women's Center on the West Coast, the second, after New York, in the United States.

I answered the ad, and that was the beginning of a whole new career as an organizer, human rights advocate, and lecturer. I founded the first legal program in the United States dealing with what was then the novel concept of women and the law. I wrote a Friend of the Court brief to the United States Supreme Court arguing what was then also a novel concept: that women should be defined as "persons" under the Equal Protection clause of the Fourteenth Amendment. I marched in demonstrations, spoke on women's rights at universities and other places, read everything I could find on women's history, feminism, and the dynamics of social change, and taught the first courses at UCLA in what was later known as Women's Studies.

Because I had very little external or internal support for my newfound independence, and because I was still in the dominator mode when it came to relations with myself, I pushed myself so hard I became very ill. But that illness was the time of greatest transformation. It gave me the space and time to reassess the overall direction of my life.

-§-

I came face to face with a tape in my head telling me I was a horrible, selfish person because I was pursuing my own development and creativity.

-§-

When I did, I came face to face with a tape in my head I hadn't even known was playing—a tape that kept telling me I was a horrible, selfish person because I was pursuing my own development and creativity. I also realized there was another tape telling me I was a bad person because I wasn't working to help others, as I had before, but to help those of my kind—girls and women. These tapes played so often and so loud that I had to keep telling myself almost daily that nothing terrible would happen if I got what I wanted.

This went on for a long time, until finally I began to do what I had always wanted to do: seriously devote myself to research and writing. While this shift in direction didn't stop the tapes, I found after a while that I could ignore them, and move on with my life.

It was an exciting time, a time of intense changes, changes that were vastly accelerated when, after writing two published books—one on women and no-fault divorce, the other on the proposed Equal Rights Amendment [2]—I embarked on the research that eventually led to publication of *The Chalice and the Blade* and many other books and articles.

In the process of changing so many old habits of thinking, feeling, and behaving, my relationships with men also radically changed. As I was no longer willing to play the conventional "feminine" role, the kinds of men I began to date were quite different from those I had known earlier, who were themselves still immersed in stereotyped gender roles.

Then I met David. And because I was able to leave behind much of my old gender programming, I now have—and have had for more than twenty years—a true partnership with a man who has also left much of his gender programming behind.

Of course we quarrel, of course there are times when we don't get along, times when we get angry and upset. Some issues we've never resolved, and probably never will. But most of the time we are exuberantly grateful that we found each other—and grateful that we live in a time when both women and men can be more completely realized as human beings, loving and nurturing, assertive and creative, fully human and fully alive.

-§-
In the process of changing so many old habits of thinking, feeling, and behaving, my relationships with men also radically changed.
-§-

Because neither of us expects the other to fit into a particular mold, David and I have grown a great deal together. We are able to support each other's personal and creative growth. Some of our creativity has been channeled into inventing new ways of relating, ways to help us keep an even keel when we're not getting along.

So I speak from experience when I say partnership works. Like a growing number of others who've struggled to leave their dominator psychic baggage behind, I've been blessed to find what I had almost despaired of finding: a true partner with whom to share my life and my love.

Sex, Pleasure, and Love

More than anything else, we humans want meaningful connections. We want love and we want pleasure. When we don't have these, we become distressed, out of touch with ourselves and others, and all too often distorted—mean and mean-spirited, insensitive and cruel, angry, even violent. This then spills over from intimate relations to other relations—to insensitivity to the pain of others, to social and economic policies that perpetuate inequality and inequity, to crime, terrorism, and war. Dominator intimate relations are at the base of the entire dominator pyramid. To build a better world, shifting intimate relations away from the pain, fear, and rage inherent in the domination model is foundational. Relations of domination and submission are not conducive to either real love or real pleasure. They even get in the way of the pleasure that comes through our unique human sexuality.

Although sexuality has been reviled as part of our "animal nature," human sexuality is very different from the sexuality of other species. In humans, sex can be purely for pleasure rather than just for procreation. Females can be sexually active throughout the year, rather than only during certain periods. Humans also have the capacity for much longer and more intense sexual pleasure. For us, sex can provide what Masters and Johnson called "the pleasure bond," a sense of well-being and togetherness.[3] But having sex that gives us this pleasure bond is not easy in relations where tension, mistrust, fear, contempt, guilt, and other negative emotions keep getting in the way.

-§-
Relations of domination and submission are not conducive to either real love or real pleasure.
-§-

When for men sex means sexual conquest, when it's associated with "scoring" and control, it becomes difficult for men to let go in the way that is most conducive to prolonged and deep orgasmic experiences. When men view women as sexual objects rather than full-fledged human beings, it's difficult for them to experience the caring connection that makes sex a wondrous experience rather than a mere release of tension.

When women's sexuality is under strict male control, you find practices ranging from the sexual mutilation of girls to the stoning to death of "immoral" women, all of which numb and terrorize women in ways that make it impossible for them to be in touch with their natural, joyful sexuality. And when women are deprived of reproductive choice, as they are in rigid dominator societies, sex can become bondage rather than bonding.

I believe that it is immoral to deprive people of family planning methods. I say this not only because of what it does to women, but because of what it does to children. I believe every child has a right to be born wanted. I also believe it is immoral to deprive people of knowledge about human sexuality. Of course, depriving people of knowledge is a way to maintain domination. So it shouldn't surprise us that wider knowledge about sexuality, including information about

contraception, has gone hand in hand with the movement toward partnership.

When I was growing up, talking about sex was completely taboo, not just in polite company but even among close friends and family. My mother never explained anything about sex to me. She was simply too embarrassed and had no clue as to how to broach the subject. Even pregnancy was considered unfit for children to see or know anything about. We were told that the stork delivers babies—an absurd story that lingers on.

Because of the cultural movement toward partnership, much has changed. Today, many parents explain human sexuality to their children as soon as they ask about it. Childbirth is shown on the Internet, and children are often present when younger siblings are born. More and more of us are recognizing that there is nothing wrong with our bodies (we all get one), that sex is not dirty (everyone has sexual urges), that sex is not evil or sinful (though sexual violence and domination are), that women as well as men have sexual urges and a great capacity for sexual pleasure (including the capacity for multiple orgasms), that some people are homosexual or bisexual (and that this shouldn't be a reason for discrimination or persecution), that we're all entitled to education about sexuality (including education about family planning), and that there is a spiritual dimension to human sexuality.

This is all part of the movement toward the kind of sexuality that goes with a partnership rather than domination model. However, these healthy trends are only part of the story.

There is, at the same time, a great deal pulling us back toward the kind of sexuality appropriate for dominator relations. In the name of sexual liberalism, violence and domination are graphically sexualized in movies, CDs, and video games, so that a natural act designed to give us pleasure is linked with pain, humiliation, and violence. In the name of religion, there is a push to again deny women reproductive choice, to maintain rigid male control over women's sexuality, and to demonize homosexuality. There is also the constant association of sex with preadolescent dirty talk, of slang sexual insults and swear words, of sex as something we hold in contempt, something we're angry about.

-§-
It is immoral to deprive people of knowledge about human sexuality.
-§-

Using the lenses of the partnership and domination models helps us sort these messages into the point-counterpoint of two very different views of our bodies and sexuality. But it does more than that: It helps us become aware of what makes for more fulfilling sexual lives, for more pleasure and less pain, and for the more meaningful and loving relationships we all want.

One of the most interesting, though not widely known, facts about sexuality is that orgasmic states have some of the same characteristics as mystical experiences.[4] Both involve altered states of consciousness.

This linking of sexuality and spirituality actually goes back to ancient times. Religions from more partnership-oriented ancient societies celebrated the sacred marriage of a female divinity or Goddess with her divine lover.[5] In archeological findings, we see indications of a veneration of this act that gives us life and pleasure. For example, the explicitly sexual sculpture of the "Gumelnita lovers," excavated in Romania, dates back more than six thousand years.

-§-
Orgasmic states have some of the same characteristics as mystical experiences.
-§-

Mystical literature, both Western and Eastern, has many clues to an earlier spiritual tradition in which woman's body, man's body, and sexuality were sacred. We read of spirituality in erotic terms—of passion, of intense feelings, and in some mystical writings such as tantric yoga, of sexual union between woman and man as a path to the divine.

Can you imagine a spirituality in which sex and the human body are part of the sacred? Can you imagine a world where our most intimate bodily relations—sexual relations and birth-giving—are seen as part of the miracle of life and nature?

You and I can begin moving toward this world by liberating ourselves from centuries of the wrong tapes. As we leave behind dominator habits we've inherited, as we move toward a partnership view of love, pleasure, and sex, we move closer to a world where our deep human yearning for love, pleasure, and caring connection can be fulfilled.

---

1 A good video on this point is *Tough Guise: Violence, Media & the Crisis in Masculinity,* featuring Jackson Katz, produced by the Media Education Foundation [phone: (8oo) 897-0089; www.xnediaed.org].

2 Riane Eisler. *Dissolution: No-Fault Divorce, Marriage, and the Future of Women* (New York: McGraw-Hill, 1977) and Riane Eisler. *The Equal Rights Handbook What ERA Means to Your Life, Your Rights, and the Future* (New York: Avon, 1978). Both books are flow available from www.iUniverse.com.

3 William H. Masters and Virginia E. Johnson, *The Pleasure Bond* (New York: Bantam Books, 1976).

4 Julian N. Davidson, "The Psychobiology of Sexual Experience," in *The Psychobiology of Consciousness,* CD. Julian N. Davidson and Richard J. Davidson (New York: Plenum Press, 1980).

5 See Eisler, *Sacred Pleasure.*

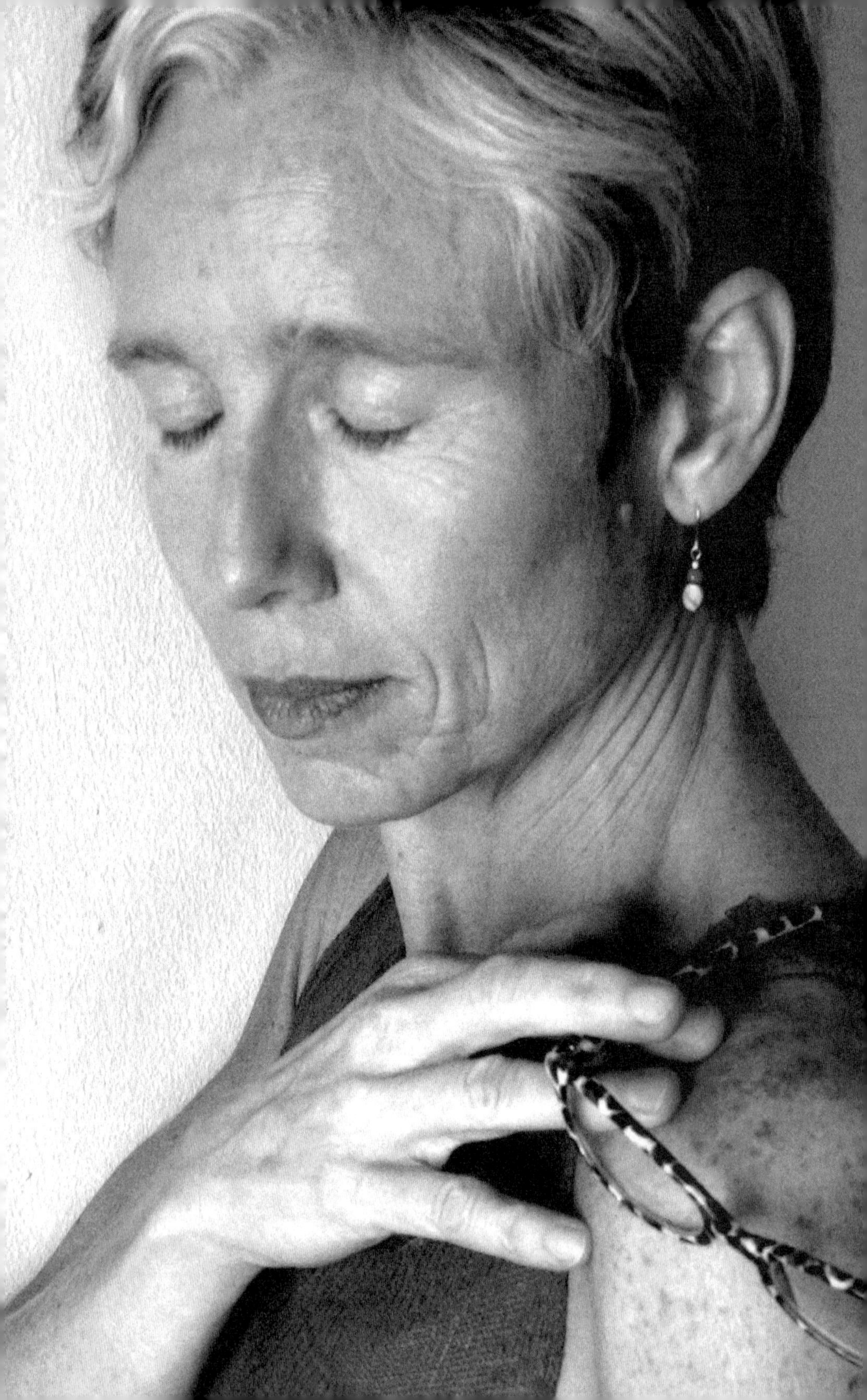

Janna Wissler:

The Fire

Your body *is* an object.

Ask any cadaver.

Ask any rape victim.

Your lover's body, too. Object.

Edges, curves, light and shadow, soft and hard—your body, my body: separate. Slam dancing does not unite them. "Eating each other" is metaphor. Kissing, sexing, our bodies truly merge only in rivulets we try to keep from the sheets. Or in a child.

We *feel* so united. We really, really do.

But when your lover makes other plans? When he "eats" another? When your husband or wife "just looks"?

OOOOOOhhhh, the pain. The separation. The lonely, pitted, aching, longing. Rage. Indignity. Burn.

Anyone who ventures in, anyone who loves, feels this possibility of separation, of heartache, always in the wings. Fears, jealousies, accidents, death.

Madness. It's enough to drive a soul to drink, vow fidelity, start a war, fast, eat, flip on the tube, try to lose just ten more pounds.

But love we must. There is no escape. The desire for union does not go away. Think you've stifled it, satisfied it, or that love has

Janna Wissler, MFT, founder of the Institute for Being Human, has practiced psychotherapy in San Francisco for the past 20 years. She helps individuals and couples find and walk their true path—in relationship, right work, daily habits, sense of self, and all other matters both human and divine. Her work has expanded body-ward with co-author and muse Jeffrey MacMullen of Therapeutic Body Care. Together, they are developing a homegrown tantric practice using touch, talk, and dance to weave life energies into greater awareness, vibrance, and conversation. DVDs and CDs of Janna reading her chapter are available on her website, www.BeingHuman.us.

deserted you, and you fall for the blond frothing your cappuccino, the hunk sawing two-by-fours out back, the nurse changing your catheter bag. The Porsche.

They all go home and sleep without you. The Porsche is beyond your means. Your heart is on fire.

This is love on the physical plane. This is our endeavor. This is the deal. We are objects, living among objects, particles separate in time and space.

The conundrum being: We *do* experience union, the wave. And when we do, we know it to be the very bedrock of our lives. We make our vows: To the magnificent leap of spirit through flesh. To the presence inside touch. To the look with no beginning or end: Your eyes, my eyes, Spirit penetrating…all…the…way to…Beyond. Trinity. Unity. Entering. Opening. Yielding to the moment, ecstasy of the dance. With your lover, your child, your cat. Yea, even with your bowl and spoon. Yes, yes, yes… Your love of this life, its form and abiding spirit.

-§-
We are spirit, uniting. We are objects, separating.
-§-

It is to live for. It is to die for.

And inevitably, something is gonna hurt like hell. The lover loves another, the child grows and moves away, the bowl is broken, the spoon lost.

We are spirit, uniting. We are objects, separating. Unavoidable, irresistible, we are helpless in this reality. Pursue ecstatic union, and you cannot escape hell.

We attempt to lessen the pain:

By downsizing appetite: I won't hurt so much if I don't want so much. Fierce, childish desires must be tamed. For a while, this seems a small price to pay for avoiding the searing flames. But downsizing sickens. Desire smolders—and erupts. Your tears call you by name. You must live this life.

Some try to lessen the pain by residing in spirit alone—circumvent the whole bloody mess. Spiritual path, heaven on Earth. Now I have the key: if I just love everything and everyone, I'll always be happy. Then you criticize your sister who is "not on a spiritual path," and you tell your lover, "You need to get some therapy, man."

It's tempting to take up residence in matter alone, being "realistic" day to day: Bread and butter, pay the bills, fulfillment slips from mind, deferred. I'll meditate tomorrow, when I start losing weight. Meanwhile, late into the evening, ease the loneliness through consumption, dependence, and violation. No matter that we call it "relaxation," "love," "erotica." Ever-present objectification: seductive, empty, scary, banal.

Or what about that *other* hell, when you simply Must Get Away: Solitude, Solitude, I must have Solitude. Avoid union to avoid *that* hell, eh?

The list goes on, the ways we miss it.

Lucky for us, none of them work. We are coaxed by life into finding a real way. Propelled by desire, molded by disappointment, we are ushered into our full-blooded humanity: souls big enough to contain it all, strong enough to love it all—particle and wave, union and separation, life and death. Orgasm.

§ § §

My lover laughed—lying on the bed in his den—when I told him about the workshop on "seven types of orgasm." At first, I thought his laugh said, "She forgot the higher four." Then his laugh penetrated deeper, and I heard, "Categorizing: Yeow!" Deeper still, his laugh teased, "The number is infinite, surely." Subtle golden orgasm standing in afternoon sun. Dripping, hungry mouth munches salty, greasy noodles—god, you should see his hands dart and weave above the stove. The crisper "aaaaaahh" of juicy, red, evil apple—bite, drip, bite, suck. Infinite orgasm, the spark of sensual encounter.

-§-
I had to surrender, of course. It doesn't "just happen."
-§-

I used to worry about orgasm of one type only: the one I was unable to have. Sexually active at age fourteen, I didn't orgasm for another fourteen years. He would come, I saw the glory of it, and me we pleased as best we could. Sex inevitably got repetitive; it was "for him." My shame quietly haunted me—dysfunction. Not a "real woman."

I experienced my first orgasm with a vibrator at twenty-eight. With my hand at thirty-eight. His hand, age forty. Him inside me, age forty-five. Him in my mouth, age fifty. Now I orgasm on the dance floor fully clothed, or standing next to real presence. Permission is granted, the gates open, energy flows, deliciousness ensues.

Orgasm…feh. A word. An accomplishment. I am now sexually "normal."

I used to worry, you know? Worry?

I don't worry so much these days, and ease is related to orgasm.

The stamp of "normal" doesn't hurt: one *does* want to be human. But that young preoccupation with "inadequacy"—oh, sweetie—has slipped in the balance; it no longer holds sway.

Orgasm still matters, but ever so much differently. No longer an unattainable "prize," it now enters my body and being as grace. Its gentle pulsing aerates my soul. Not just in sexing, but in all of life.

§ § §

The life-giving power of orgasm came to me under the madrones. Afternoon sun. Quiet: we left the stream behind the ridge. Just him and me, together, moving. Soft clothes. Rustle of leaves. Bare feet. Breath. And keen attention. Keen.

As the gossamer gates opened and the juice began to flow, I knew: This is me issuing forth from hidden depths. Up and outward in gentle waves, through channels of biology, energy, and being. One more rivulet of *me,* now free to move through, between, within, among. Next time I speak, my words will ring with a bit more clarity and depth. When next I decide how to spend a quiet evening, I will be more sure and rich in my choice. When I return to my desk, to my bank balance, the list of what to do and who to call, I will not be such a stranger in this world. New life, new energy, new consciousness, conceived and born of this fleeting union in the glow of afternoon.

I had to surrender, of course. It doesn't "just happen," not for me anyway. There is a decision to be made, standing fully clothed under strips of red bark, with a man I've met before only twice. *Am I going to let him know how delicious his presence is to me? His arm brushing mine, his leg pressing ever so gently, firmly, there. This stretching together, this tension, stillness, presence, stillness, rising, rising… Am I going to let it show? Dare I? Can I? Will I?*

Aaaaahhhh. Yes. Yes. We will taste the suchness of desire, the sweetness of fulfilling over-spilling. Yes, yes, yes, wave, gentle wave, sea creature, I. Inside and outside merge. Undulation. I am animal, plant, prima materia, and more human than ever before.

§ § §

My desire… Sweet God Almighty, it feels so hard won. This simple, sweet, naked desire I claim at last as mine.

We know, those of us who are 40, 50—oh, and beyond—how hard won this simple pleasure of being in flesh. What fires must be traversed, sat within, endured—nights, years, decades in prayer.

Ripening fruit, we are.

Desire. Do you want him? Does she call to you? How deeply will you let yourself ache? Be torn open?

It can feel humiliating, in our culture of "self-love," to be ravaged with desire for another.

But what feels so impossible is that it simply *hurts.* The cells cry. The sex aches. The heart does indeed break. Split to the core, you are bleeding and bare, and you cannot comprehend.

The mind frenzies to find an answer that will make…it…stop… "I deserve better." "It's time to move on." "I must learn to love myself."

The spirit life is truncated just there, with the mind's easy solutions. The mind's coveted prize to become a reasonable, well-adjusted person who will not embarrass herself one more time—who will, in the future and for all time, steer clear of inchoate, self-confounding intensity. Whee and double-whee: the aspirations of the mind.

But underneath it all, the Wild Master will not let you rest. It is your destiny to come Home. He will call and you will come—sooner or…later.

§ § §

I have many lovers at this time in my life. I am fifty. Childless. A life of serial monogamy, until now.

Sitting by this window—the window *he* built over fern-draped wall of stream—I declare "yes" to each gateway that whispers of the trinity: me, him, love. Life.

I will be challenged, of course. Subtler "nos" will lift their heads. Expectations will be dashed, mind-pictures torn to shreds. Loss, loss, humiliation and loss. The burning, refining surrender never ends. But now I know the dance of kinship between searing flames and our most exalted turn-ons—a never-ending conversation that deepens and ripens every elder ever molded from the hotbed of human potential.

Some lovers we love through clothes—the dance floor our marriage bed. Women, too—god, are we luscious or what?

Other lovers, we love across bistro tables, check-out counters, or walking along an urban street: conversation, intimation, insinuation, a glance.

With one or two, we are skin to skin. Penetration. Wet spots and mess. Sweet merging of life's rivers, the river's mouth, the sea.

And with each moment of true encounter, something new is conceived.

When I want to come Home, a lover rises from the world to guide me gently and firmly into my belly and hips. I now know Hara; my dance knows center.

When I long for a bigger life, for more movement and flow, a world player shows up, forward motion and tender flash. He talks to me, teaches me, and touches me…there.

Transmissions of energy and intelligence from The Other. I open. I flow. And it is no longer just *my* energy, but *our* energy running through the veins. He knows it. I know it. It is sexy. It is alive—the more fiercely and playfully, the closer we embrace death.

This is power, honey. This is richness, true life. After decades of longing, I am prepared to savor the taste of strength, mastery, freedom, abundance. Spirit leaps and seeps through matter and over time, the Lover appears, the Beloved is known.

I don't know quite what I will do with the sensation when sometimes, sitting with a client, I know: "We can no longer just sit here, you and me. We must move. We must touch. We must leap through substance and mess. We must eat together, raise children, grow vegetables, brush the cat and weave his old yellow fur into sparkling fishing lures." The myriad forms of separation and union. Infinite orgasm. Love: It is to live within; it is to die within. It is all there is, whether we know it or not.

§ § §

One more thing, before his hands serve dinner. This business of the refining fire…

Our culture, so "healthy," so averse to real suffering.

I want to say a few words to the one who asks, "How?"

There is an alchemical operation called *Calcinatio:* sitting in the refining fires when desire is frustrated by God. By him-her. By life.

There are two poles between which the fire will burn: desire and frustration. Drop either pole, and you will miss it. Once again.

Tell the truth about what you want. Truth will change as the ash turns to white. But you must keep telling it straight and clear: What do you *truly* desire?

And suffer the burning of your refining defeats. Suffer in the tender arms of God—Innermost, True Beloved.

I won't say more about it just now. This is the measure for today.

But pray. If you pray you will be shown how to burn. The Way will open, pain become portal. Life is trustworthy. Your desires your very Own.

Jeanne House:

It's Not Eve's Fault That Adam Ate the Apple

Entering through an opening in a flowering hedge, I step into a garden of heavenly beauty. I take in the fragrance of rose and lilac, and then the subtle scent of lily-of-the-valley. The gentle breeze touches my cheek with the softness of a kiss. My gaze rests upon the delicate flowers lining the meandering walkway, and then lifts to absorb the blooming springtime surrounding me.

A young doe and fawn watch calmly from a distant resting place. A furry cottontail stops to notice my presence. Birds welcome me with chirps and songs as they flutter from tree to bush. I notice a stream flowing over smooth rocks in a quiet pool with water lilies and flecks of tiny golden fish. The sound of the trickling water soothes my mind.

To my right, I gradually sense the gentle presence of my Father and soon feel the pressure of his hand holding mine. Then my smiling Mother appears, softly, to take the other hand. I feel the radiance that spreads though me. My heart is burning and the fire expands – outward and upward, blurring the boundaries of my being. I drink in their words of love and joy.

Suddenly, I wake up to find myself on an airplane, flying to Washington D.C. I love plane trips; no one can reach me here, and I can look out the window, through the clouds, to see snowy mountain peaks that remind me of Shangri-La.

I am very excited because I am on my way to meet an agent, who will be representing my book, *It Wasn't Eve's Fault that Adam*

Jeanne House, M.A., has headed up the marketing and sales efforts of two book distributors, Summit Beacon and Associated Publishers Group, as well as holding prior positions with NBC-TV and Miami University. She has a postgraduate degree in Consciousness Studies, and is completing a second degree in Transformational Psychology. She is currently the Marketing and Sales Director of Elite Books. Her passion and specialty is Soul Communication–communicating directly to the soul needs of the reader. Her website is www.SolCommunication.com. The first three paragraphs above are used with permission from The Hearts Center and Anita Wolberd, www.joyinthenow.com.

Ate the Apple: Finding the Masculine and Feminine Balance Within. After all the work I have been doing on my manuscript, I am steeped in the symbolism of the story of Adam and Eve. I am also completely exhausted.

Nodding off, I close my eyes once again... and I am in a classroom. "Congratulations!" the instructor says. "We now graduate you from the school of Being Overly Organized and Orderly. You are an expert at being responsible and in your head. Now we enroll you in the next class, on a subject of which you are woefully ignorant—How to be In Your Body, In the Moment, and In JOY. We regret to inform you that this class is very different than the one you just completed. All of the things that you have learned about being responsible and in your head will be of no use to you whatsoever. Attempting to approach the lessons ahead with the tools, skills, and wisdom of the past will not work. But rest assured that all you have learned and established is not lost as you move into this *new way of being;* in fact, it is only enhanced. Only by letting go of all of that, however, can you freely move into this *new way of joy.* The old way was the *Via Dolorosa,* the way of struggle and strife. The joyous way is that of surrendering to the natural flow within. In order to do this, we must get over self-blame and embrace the notion that we are one with the flow and joy of the universe."

-§-
The joyous way is that of surrendering to the natural flow within.
-§-

I know that I am dreaming, and simultaneously witnessing this dream. Somehow, this *new way of being* sounds familiar to me. But where have I experienced this before? As I am asking this question a screen comes up in the classroom, and on the screen are two beautiful souls, both naked and transparent. Their bodies have an etheric quality, and rays of rainbow-colored light show through them. I feel an immediate affinity with them, as if they are naturally a part of me.

These two *innocents* are in a garden: a place where things grow, where there is beauty to the eye, the ear, the touch. Fragrances delight and the palate is satisfied. The garden is called Eden, which means *a place of happiness.* Adam and Eve are here to guide us in being in our bodies and hearts, with the pressure of spirit fully inhabiting, inspiring, and filling us with wisdom, love, and joy.

Then, I see two radiant beings telling Adam and Eve to go out into the material world in order to co-create with God the beauty and abundance that they have experienced in Eden, and to show mankind the colors of the seven rays of light descending through them. They look like opals, and the earth behind them is light, with the same opalescent qualities.

I wonder where I have heard of the concept of *being radiant.* Then I remember the chapter that Donna Eden and David Feinstein wrote for this book. Donna, a renowned energy practitioner, tells us that we have inner, radiant circuits that exude a *radiant glow* whenever they are activated. Radiant energies are activated when we feel exhilaration, love, orgasm, hope, gratitude, rapture, and spiritual ecstasy. Our brains are wired for joy. In their chapter, David and Donna show us how to increase the joyful energy throughout our bodies. They teach us that we create energy patterns (habits) that inhibit our feelings of joy from easily flowing through our bodies. Our stress-filled lifestyles contribute to our diminished levels of joy, and this diminished capacity gets wired into our energy systems.

-§-
Allow the natural energy of spirit to flow through the container of your relationship.
-§-

Since we are all capable of experiencing childlike joy, increasing the capacity for joy is just a matter of opening natural channels that have been shut down. Energy follows habit, and we simply need to make a habit of nurturing our radiant circuits, which are in gear whenever we feel the joy and wonderment of our beloved. When we allow the natural energy of spirit to flow through the container of our relationship, as Adam and Eve did, we are co-creating with the universe.

Suddenly, the plane hits a pocket of turbulence and I am awakened from this sojourn. I realize that if we can look at each moment as a new beginning, we can let go of condemnation. We must be willing to see the *innocence in each other;* in this way, we can directly experience a fresh opportunity for mutual happiness.

Adam and Eve's story is our story. We all were born innocent and naked. As we grew up, we added, layer-by-layer, the clothes of cultural norms and attitudes that weren't originally ours. This is the fallen serpentine consciousness, and not the exalted serpent of wholeness. The fallen serpentine consciousness, then, is merely the *devil*—which is *lived* inverted—in disguise. We all have the full radiance of Eden within, but we have put layers and layers of clothing over our natural, inner radiance.

We banish ourselves from Eden with our own thoughts. Many of us feel that we are trapped in the world we see. But, if we remember that our thoughts make up the world, then we can begin to change them. Our beliefs set up a cause and effect pattern that keeps us enmeshed in our situation. If our past belief system does not give us the *fruits of joy* that we desire, then we have a choice to assume responsibility for our thoughts, feelings, and reactions—and we can choose to change our beliefs. If we are "naked" and transparent to ourselves, and realize that our outside world is a direct result of the way we think and perceive on the inside, then we can *choose* a different reality. That is precisely what Adam and Eve did—*they both chose freely to experiment with energy.* They both chose to shift from their previous reality of unity and wholeness (the serpent biting its tail), to a reality experienced as two separate halves (the fallen serpent, with the energy circuit disconnected). This is what most of us experience today. This is the greater symbolism of the serpent of wholeness—with the tail and the head united in oneness.

-§-
As we reach out towards another, have we lost our grip on the Tree of Life, that original symbol of oneness?
-§-

The screen comes down once again and I see that, at the beginning of creation, Adam blames Eve for the fall; and Eve, in turn, blames the serpent. I see that Eve, having closer affinities to matter than Adam, is more susceptible to the wiles of the serpent. And Adam, who truly loves Eve, makes a free will choice to follow her, because of his passion, or Eros. I realize that *it isn't Eve's fault* that Adam ate the apple!

Anodea Judith writes, in *Waking the Global Heart,* that desire is both sweet and dangerous when we first explore the world through our senses. Desire, passion, and sexuality are the perfect seduction, separating us from the original oneness of our beloved. She says that the realm of Eros brings us into our duality. *"Through evolution's innate wisdom, it is pleasure that urges the inner current of the soul to connect and bond with another."*

We all have a yearning for Eden within—a memory that we have never lost. It is this innermost yearning that lets us know there is something not quite right in our lives. How do we know this? Our unconscious memory of Eden reminds us of the passion, and *joie de vivre* of the spirit, goading us ever onward and upward, beyond our current circumstances. This is the part of us that wants to merge with the other.

The question, then, is: As we reach out towards another, have we lost our grip on the *Tree of Life,* that original symbol of oneness? We can find out by looking at the *fruits* of our actions. If we are ready to accept responsibility for our own choices and not blame others—Adam, Eve, or God—then it will be easier for us to forgive our partners; this will dissolve our sense of separation. One way to do this is to observe ourselves, within our own relationships, with a sense of non-attachment.

The first step in this process requires that we notice when we are operating from the *Fallen Eve Consciousness,* clinging to the idea that we know exactly what our beloved is going to think, do, and say. This clinging puts a kind of relational hex on our partners—they may never break out of the evil, or *veiled,* idea that we have envisioned for them! This keeps us enmeshed so deeply in the relationship that we cannot see the whole reality.

Next, we must notice when we are operating from the *Fallen Adam Consciousness,* in which we judge, shame, and blame our beloved, expecting them to do or be something that they are not. In this consciousness state we are aloof, cold-hearted, and distant because we feel that others deserve to be banished from paradise!

When Adam and Eve became enmeshed in their senses, they lost their inner sense, the ability to tune in to the upward flow of energy. When we become fixed on our outer reality, or on another person, the pull of gravity keeps our energies grounded. But when we *let go* and let the *spirit flow* through all of our exchanges, we make room for the return current of energy from above. If we become self-absorbed and our energies are tied up in self-gratification and selfish pursuits, energy doesn't go anywhere—the circuit cannot complete.

The main question that we can ask ourselves is: Am I experiencing my life *my* way, or am I choosing the *high(er)* way of cooperation?

Today We Have an Energy Crisis

When we choose to get enmeshed in the sensual portion of our being alone, our energies descend into our lower extremities and get stuck there. The "fall," then, is merely a *fallen energetic state.* While in the Garden of Eden, I notice that the majority of Adam and Eve's energies are concentrated in the centers above their hearts. In today's world, our energy equation has reversed; most of us carry the majority of our energy in the lower portion of our beings, with just a small amount of energy circulating upward. We are energy conduits, and must make the simple choice of balance or energy conservation. In order to change the flow of energy, we have to change our habit patterns from those of lowering energy to raising it. This is the figure eight flow of Alpha and Omega. It is the exalted serpent, swallowing its tail. It is possible to keep the energy flowing freely between the inner Eden and our day-to-day consciousness. To do this, we must weave light in and through our being, and move energy within our auras. This is the tai chi flow of matter and spirit.

-§-
We create Eden, literally, within ourselves.
-§-

The goal, then, is to keep energy moving from the lower portion to the higher portion of our being. If we follow the serpent of our sensuality alone, which lacks the flame of the Spirit, or if we choose the Spirit, but do not wed it to matter, our energy gets stuck, rather than flowing up and down. This is not sin, but merely cause and effect. What comes around goes around. The effect is that we don't have wholeness, but rounds and rounds of chasing our tail. All things come into position within the perspective that *we ourselves create*—and what we create is a matter of choice. So, the way to back to Eden is found by going within.

I am once again in the classroom. The instructor begins his lesson:

> Adam (atom) and Eve (electron) are in each cell of our being. The atom, without the electron, is incomplete; and the electron, without the atom, cannot fulfill its destiny. Adam and Eve are parts of one another, just as they are parts of us. And as we think, feel, and act towards one another on the outer level, our atoms and electrons respond accordingly on the inner. So we create Eden, literally, within ourselves. The choice is always there. We create Eden with each thought, with each feeling, and with each act. We also create Eden *within* each act, if this is what we choose. This means that the choice between sin and sacrament is a matter of intention.

For instance, if sex is nothing more, nor less, than sacred energy in motion, then we should be careful with whom we exchange our energies. These decisions should be based upon a heart connection, rather than just a sensual one. We are continually required to choose between the ways of the fallen serpent and the ways of Eden. If our sexual connections are to be exalted, we need to meet our partners in the pull of a spiritual flame, which is a common devotion to the source of spiritual light. This is what endures, when sexual satisfactions slips away and eventually drains us of the very light we seek. When energy is sanctified, sexual fusion enhances the positive qualities of each partner—and creative flow raises both energies upwards, reinforcing their original divine identity and reflecting *Adam and Eve in the beginning of time.* This is the energy of a union consecrated to the love of the divine light within, forming a harmonious interchange of the male and female energies—which can then yield the offspring of a child, a higher inspiration, or a work of art. This is the serpent biting its tail, and the result is *wholeness* rather than *separateness.*

-§-
The energy of our union is consecrated to the love of the divine light within.
-§-

Adam and Eve represent the undifferentiated whole within each of us: male and female, without boundaries. They are innocent and naked without knowing it. They are as simple as children who are living without toil, without fear of the future, and without regret for the past. If we surrender attachment, control, and judgment of our beloved, and instead believe in their innate capacity to out-picture paradise, then Eden will no longer be a notion—it will become a reality. The way back to Eden is to become our natural selves. We can spend our whole lives thinking and writing about the symbolism of Adam and Eve, trying to decipher their secrets through the force of our minds, but it isn't until we relax into the garden of our hearts that their true story unfolds. The dream movie I have just seen revealed that the Garden of Eden is a lost paradise only if we reject its joy. We are expelled only if we choose misery and gloom. The garden is within, quietly waiting.

As the plane descends toward Dulles airport, I realize that I have been searching for Eden by escaping my daily life when, in fact, it is fused within my heart. We touch ground, and this city I have never visited feels reassuringly familiar. Eden is never actually lost—no matter how far I roam from home.

Part Two

Reconceiving Sex as Sacred

Call it many things, give your desires polite names
If you must; mask the primal instinct from your
Reality if you cannot bear that sacred edge...
Among strong men in the tavern I can speak a truth no one will laugh at:
My heart is like a wild alley cat, in heat; in every possible way
we conspire to know Freedom and love.

There is something holy deep inside you that is so ardent and awake it
needs to lie down naked next to God.
~Hafiz

David Deida:

Finding God Through Sex

For many men, most of their lives, sex is their actual religion. In church, their attention is occupied not by the sermon, but by the exotic woman with the nice legs two pews over. They spend more time watching women's bodies on the street and bikinied actresses on TV than contemplating the glory of God.

At a strip joint, they may shout their praises, "Oh, my God! You're unbelievable! Yes! You're fantastic!" And in bed, too, orgasming with their woman, "Oh, my God! My God, I love you." Yet, outside of the sexual realm, most men remain uncommitted in their praise of the divine mystery alive as all.

Divine praise during sex is not an accident. Our bodies are built so that sex stimulates our energies and opens our hearts. Our sense of aliveness is heightened, our perception of beauty and perfection is glorified. Sexual exultation is as close as most of us get to religious awe.

If we are too obstructed physically or are afraid of deep love in relationship, then money may become our religion. But sex is a more primal possibility for the bliss we hope our lives can give us. Sex affords us the opportunity for letting go of ourselves without reservation and merging with our lover in pleasure and love.

Acknowledged as one of the world's most insightful and provocative teachers of our time, best-selling author David Deida continues to revolutionize the way that men and women grow spiritually and sexually. His teachings and writings have been hailed as among the most original and authentic contributions to personal and spiritual growth currently available. His books are published in more than twenty languages and include several practical texts on authentic sexual spirituality, including *Finding God through Sex* (Sounds True, 2005), the autobiographical novel *Wild Nights* (Sounds True, 2005); and the classic, *The Way of the Superior Man* (Sounds True, 2004). More at www.deida.info.

The Bliss of Spiritual Depth

This feeling of two merging into one is the epitome of sacred and secular pleasure. As babies we merged with our mothers. As children we merged with our toys and friends. As teenagers we merged with our thoughts, drugs, cars, and music. As adults we merge with the slope we ski, with the coffee we drink, with our children while we hold them, with the TV while we relax, and with new clothing as we shop. But few of us experience the intensity of pleasure and love anywhere else as consistently as we do during good sex.

Because sex and its pleasures are so intense, some people substitute the communion afforded by sex for divine communion. As long as genital stimulation or emotional flow is more pleasurable than our experience of deep being, our sex lives will take precedence over our spiritual lives. We will devote more energy to sexual pleasure than to the bliss of spiritual depth.

You can suck your lover's breast and feel blissful, like a baby merging with his mother. This is comfortable and safe but not very deep. You can merge with your lover's waves of orgasmic delight and feel the same kind of bliss you would while surfing the ocean or getting a great massage, but it doesn't last too long. You can merge emotionally with your lover, relishing each other's feelings in a kind of emotional telepath of vulnerable sharing. The pleasure of this openness and trust can be truly sublime, but it is difficult to enjoy this merger while at the office the next day.

-§-

Sex affords us the opportunity for letting go of ourselves without reservation.

-§-

Merging with the divine—the mystery and depth of open being—has very little to do with infantile oneness, losing yourself in athletic flow, or merging with your lover emotionally. Whereas all these mergers are with a particular state of pleasure, excitement, or empathy, divine merger is not with any particular state at all, but with the deep openness of *all* states.

The Fury of Love's Light

She was very wet, I was deep inside of her, and she was bucking like a wild goat. She grabbed my ass and pulled me as if to bring me yet deeper. But deeper I could not go. I was pressed against her, and she was grinding against me…

Her wild sexual abandon was about to make me come. It wasn't just the physical stimulation; her feminine bestiality was drawing the savage mammal out of me… I began pumping like a wild man, feeling like I would, in moments, pump gallons of semen deep into her hungry body. And then, suddenly, I noticed that we were both merely animals. Humping happily. Lost in the sweat of the moment. Heart eclipsed by fervor.

Recognizing this, I practiced to reclaim my heart. I remembered love and breathed love. I slowed down for a moment and allowed my body to be pervaded by the love emanating form my heart and hers. Our rampant thrust and clutch were eased of vicious zeal and rejuvenated by the steady force of love, circulated by our breath.

Hearts resurrected, breathing wide, our bodies opened, we now loosed our love through the animal of our desire. Her disposition, as well as mine, changed instantly. We were still wild. But now, we were open and loving. We still clawed and rammed. Our bodies continued flailing and our sweat continued flying, but the wild force of our surrender was moved by love. Even while clawing each other, our hearts communed and our bodies relaxed in the thick spread of love.

Know the difference between surrendering to animal lust and surrendering as love through the play of desire. Lusty abandon is fine. There are times when all you want is the fun of wild sex. But this is a very different way to have sex than giving love *through* the wildness of your sexing.

-§-
Know the difference between surrendering to animal lust and surrendering as love through the play of desire.
-§-

When you are in the throes of crazed coupling, locate your deepest core of love, and offer this gift through your animal zing. The masculine partner transforms the static electricity of chaotic excitement into a heart-focused thunderbolt of love. The feminine partner opens as large as the universe, devouring all lesser forces in the fury of love's light.

Masculine Direction and Feminine Energy—The Fully Polarized Sexual Dynamic

Sexually speaking, the masculine is the force of direction and the feminine is the force of energy. That is, the masculine provides the form in which the feminine can freely flow, like the structure of the riverbank guides the energetic flow of water. Less obvious is the fact that the force of the river's water carves the shape of the riverbank that guides it.

Neither masculine nor feminine is superior or inferior. Both are part of the same process, whereby men and women learn to recognize their oneness and love their twoness. Masculine and feminine are both necessary for the fully polarized sexual dynamic. Whether homosexual,

heterosexual, or bisexual, in any given moment, one partner must be more like the water and one partner more like the riverbank, or else the flow of sexual energy will become shallow or dry up.

For instance, if neither partner is willing to take the masculine lead and direct the moment, then the immense feminine power of sexual energy will go all over the place, never stabilizing in the deepest gorges of love. Sex may be fun, intensely pleasurable, and wild, but it will tend toward the superficial, repeating the same pleasurable patterns over and over without growth in depth.

On the other hand, if both partners insist on taking the lead, there will be no flow of water, no force of sexual energy, no abundant liquid ecstasy in which to dive and commune. The rigid stance of control will predominate if both partners are willing to be the riverbank, but neither is willing to let go and flow freely in the pleasure of love.

Every man and every woman should be able to enjoy both aspects of sexuality, masculine and feminine, deepening the sex as well as widening the energy of ecstasy, directing the flow as well as creating the energy of the flow. Although both aspects of sexuality can be accessed and enjoyed by every man and woman, each individual will have a preference dictated by his or her sexual essence.

Heterosexual or homosexual, each person will find a sexual complement in a partner who most enjoys playing the reciprocal sexual force to their own, and this masculine-feminine play can flip and shift between partners moment by moment. Therefore, it is important that each person understand and be willing to embrace the fullness of both masculine and feminine forces without denigrating or shying away from either.

For Him—or the Masculine-Playing Partner

It's not a nice thing to consider. Certainly, it isn't a politically correct thing to say. But it seems apparent: for many men, their "purpose" comes before their intimacy. Some men's purpose is financial: work first, love second. Some men's purpose is artistic: painting first, relationship second. Some men's purpose is political: fight for the country first, spend time with the family second. Some men's purpose is spiritual: meditate first, make love second.

Because the masculine is oriented toward the freedom of consciousness (rather than the flow of love), it chooses purpose over relationship. "Purpose," in this sense, is whatever a man (or woman) feels is their reason for being alive, the center or guiding principle of their life. It doesn't matter what a man says, his purpose is revealed in what he does. He may say that his intimate relationship means more to him than anything, but when he spends 70 hours a week working and most of the rest of the time recovering from working, you know where his priority lies. You know the guiding force of his life. You know his purpose: work, and whatever type of freedom he feels work will give him— financial, artistic, political, spiritual, and so on.

The masculine (in men and women) seeks freedom through accomplishing a mission. Ultimately, this is the blissful freedom of open consciousness, but most men only approximate this sense of freedom through large bank accounts or a corner office with windows. If you are a man with a masculine essence, the freedom—expressed through your devotion to your purpose—is your ultimate concern. Your intimate relationship comes second.

Your woman may be the most important person in your life. You may truly love her. But if you deny your deepest purpose to spend time with her, your resentment will grow despite your love.

Men don't buy as many "relationship books" as women do, because many men don't care as much about relationships. Or, a better way of putting it is that many men care more about something else: Freedom.

You have probably had one or more intimate relationships in your life. You have probably had your heart ripped to shreds by a woman. You have probably also felt like your woman was an angel, a saint, a lover beyond compare. She probably has given you more love than you ever imagined possible, and you have probably felt like you would do anything for her, even give your life for her, if necessary.

But if your woman could have a videotape of what went on in your head all day, she would probably be startled. No matter how much you love your woman, your attention is mostly occupied by concerns about your work, your art, your mission, your quest, your money—not to mention plenty of moments of distraction by other women throughout the day.

-§-
Give your deepest gifts to your woman, and you give your deepest gifts to the world.
-§-

Which leads to this conclusion: most men aren't motivated to improve their intimacy or sex skills until they realize that in doing so they are actually advancing their true purpose. Your capacity to make love to your woman is your capacity to make love to the world. If you can enter your woman with love in spite of her resistances, if you can bloom her heart in happiness, if you can bring her depth when she is superficial, align her life when she feels lost, brighten her with humor when she is dark—if you can learn to give your deepest gifts to your

woman, then by doing so you are also learning to give your deepest gifts to the world.

For Her—or the Feminine-Playing Partner

Unfortunately, most men are sexual dorks. The height of sexual experience in many men's minds is being able to give a woman multiple orgasms through oral sex. There's nothing wrong with multiple orgasms or oral sex. But for most women, in addition to physical pleasure, sex is a doorway to profound emotional fulfillment and spiritual surrender—and most men just don't know how to open this door completely.

The way somebody dances tells you a lot about how they make love. The ease with which they move their hips, their capacity to express musical rhythm from toes to nose, their connectedness or obliviousness to their dance partner, all reveal aspects of their sexual capacity.

A woman who is married to a man who can't dance often longs for a partner who could glide her across the dance floor. This reveals more than her predilections about dance; it shows what she is lacking in bed. If a man can dance well, it means he can enjoy his body, feel the energy of the music, and match his partner's rhythm. If he is a really good dancer, it means he could move her *beyond* what she might do on her own. Most women are turned on by a man who can take them to new places, not only on the dance floor but in bed and throughout life.

However, there is a big difference between energy and consciousness: a man could be a great dancer—with all the right moves—and yet not be very deep in his daily life. That is, a man could be good at moving energy but not be very conscious; he can take you to new places of physical pleasure, but not to greater spiritual depths and emotional fullness.

The deeper or more conscious a man is, the more trustable he is. You can feel his commitment to truth. You can trust what he says. His life is aligned by a profound sense of purpose that you can count on. Yet he may still be a lousy dancer.

A good dancer may be able to sweep you off your feet physically, but in day-to-day life he may appall you. He may lack a sense of purpose, flit from one woman to another without commitment, and orient his life around having fun, disregarding the daily cultivation of depth and meaning. Yet his smooth moves might trick you into lust.

Ideally, a man embodies both depth of consciousness and physical grace. He is guided by true purpose and is also able to move spontaneously with energy. He is a man of integrity and style. But, if you have to make a choice, a deep man is a much better intimate partner in the long run than a superficial fancy dancer, a Mr. Suave.

If you happen to be with a good man who can't dance—who is, therefore, probably somewhat of a dork in bed—don't despair. He can practice "dancing" with you in bed or on the dance floor. It is much more likely that a deep man will become better at dancing than a superficial man will develop depth. But even if your man remains a clunky lover, you can continue to open.

Allow love to enter your body with or without your man's expertise. This is a crucial practice. You are built to grow spiritually by receiving and opening to the force of love-consciousness in your body, and you don't need a man to do so.

Everyday, whether you are alone lying in the grass or in bed making love with your man, practice allowing yourself to be "taken" by the deepest, most loving masculine force you can imagine. As a young girl, you may have fantasized about unicorns and horses. As an adolescent you probably dreamed of the high-school quarterback or the motorcycle bad boy. In your early adulthood, you may have pined for a professor, a "genius" type, or a therapist/teacher who could save you and take you to a new place of understanding and happiness. As a grown woman, you have probably sought for a lover whose strength and integrity you could depend on and trust—and who would also ravish you into bliss.

-§-

You are love. You live as love. And when you find you heart yearning still, practice surrendering more deeply as love.

-§-

Now, it may be time to practice opening directly—to be lived *by* and *as* the love-force you hoped for in previous forms. Your exquisite permeability to your lover's sexual flesh and emotional needs is but an innuendo of your divine permeability—your openness to, communion with, and surrender as the force of unbounded love.

You neither are possessed by your lover's needs nor by your own. You *are* love. You live *as* love. And when you find your heart yearning still, practice surrendering more deeply as love. While washing the dishes, picking your child up from school, or firing an employee, practice allowing love to flow through your every gesture, word, and breath. In every moment, practice receiving love deeply into your body and giving love from every cell. You are thus transfigured, breath by breath, from a needy woman looking for love, to a self-sufficient woman who loves herself, to a woman always and already full of love's bliss and blessing power.

A Bright Immensity of Joy

Learning to surrender directly to love is often an agonizing process. You will be disillusioned of your dreams of comfort, security, and romance. Every emotion that you have stuffed into your body without feeling fully will emerge for you to re-experience. Years of loneliness and ache will be exposed as your heart unfolds. Yet, when the time comes, you have no choice but to go through this process and learn to surrender as love, receiving and giving the bliss of deep openness with every breath.

-§-
Bliss is born of your true nature—an eternal love that cannot be lost.
-§-

This bliss is born of your true nature—an eternal love that cannot be lost. The force of this love cannot be beaten or victimized. This love fills your body and heart with a pleasure so deep that even your own thoughts and emotions cannot sway your fundamental happiness. Your loneliness is filled with a bright immensity of joy. This love-energy flows from your heart through your body and out your feet, hands, and eyes like beams of beauty. You live in love's rapture, even as your day-to-day life continues in the form that you choose.

Sex becomes literally making love, magnifying love—from the boundless depth of your heart, through every inch of your body, and in merger with your lover. You are so full of love and pleasure that it is impossible to give it up in an effort to please your partner. You are so open in bliss that you no longer need to guard your heart for fear of being hurt or taken advantage of. Your love is larger than both of you. You have nothing to fear or protect. Love has already worked its way through your secret hopes and dreads and opened every speck of you as light.

From Lust to Love and Beyond

There are three basic steps to converting conventional sexuality into a means of communion.

1. Feel your own sensations fully.

Whatever you are feeling, feel it completely. Feel the sensations on your skin and the energy moving through the inside of your body. Feel your emotions and thoughts come and go, without adding anything to their natural flow. Feel your body, mind, and emotions completely, without distraction.

2. Feel into your lover's sensations fully.

Feel through your own sensations, and feel into your partner fully. Feel your partner's breath. Feel the energy moving through your partner's body. Feel what your partner is feeling on every surface of skin, mouth, vagina, penis, anus, and even between his or her toes. Feel your partner's heart, emotions, and desires. This will take practice, but eventually you may be able to feel your partner's entire body, emotions, and thoughts almost as clearly as you can feel your own.

-§-
Feel your body, mind, and emotions completely, without distraction.
-§-

3. Feel *through* your lover into the divine.

Feel even through your partner's sensations, feeling beyond them, until you can feel the nature of feeling itself. This isn't about trying to understand something intellectually, but is actually a matter of feeling, like when you feel the soul of a great musician through his or her music—you don't just hear the music, but commune with a quality that lies through and beyond every note and pause.

Feeling through your own sensations, feeling through your partner's sensations, you become aware of the spacious quality of feeling itself. Within this spaciousness all things transpire. Every thought moves. Your lover's flesh glistens. Sweet and sour tastes fleet. Every inch and dread and succulent delectation is self-manifesting, spontaneous, evanescent, and alive. Full yet empty. Glorious yet gone as it arises.

You'll know when you are feeling *through* experience in this way, sexual and otherwise, because you will cease adding tension, fear, or closure to the present moment that is openness itself. Sex will drop through the hole of the moment suffused as the oneness it is trying to achieve. All urgency for sensation and pleasure will be reversed in a bodily utterance of fullness. The moment will consume itself in love and the remainder stands without time.

Deep in our hearts, we are all searching for ways to give and receive love, forever and for real. To open as love, to live as this freedom, is our deepest calling. Each of us must find our own unique way of living true to our deep being. But whatever way we find, we will discover that love is the only way to live that is not less than God, less that truth, less than our deepest need and divine potential.

Margot Anand:

Truth Is Erotic

The very first time I made love, I was thrown into a remarkable encounter with the truth of my being, as consciousness expanded beyond my body, beyond my mind, and beyond the normal boundaries of time. I connected with the eternal Self—with what existed before I was born and will continue to exist after I die. I had never heard the word *tantra,* and yet I knew that sexuality was my path to awakening, for I had realized the light of spirit in my first lover's arms.

Orgasm brings us closer to the divine than any other experience. In the moment of orgasm, a bonding happens between the right and left hemispheres of the brain. When the artistic, feeling, intuitive right side of the brain fuses with the center of thinking and logic on the left side, a zero point of total connection can be touched. The ego disappears, time and space cease to exist, and you become one with energy and consciousness. This is the sacred dimension of sex.

Sex lies at the root of life, and it is crucial that we learn reverence for it. We need training in the art of love. Sexuality is a very natural instinct, and a powerfully creative force. Each of us can put that force to work in the service of healing, transformation, and the realization of our dreams. And yet many ideas we have about sex keep us confused. Either we view sexuality as a natural impulse that ought not be interfered with, or we perceive it as something hidden, dirty, and forbidden. Of course, the latter is what makes it so interesting and brings

Margot Anand is an internationally acclaimed seminar leader and public speaker. Her best-selling books *The Art of Sexual Ecstasy* (Tarcher, 1989), *The Art of Sexual Magic* (Putnam, 1995), and *Sexual Ecstasy: The Art of Orgasm* (Tarcher, 2000), and her latest book, *The Sexual Ecstasy Workbook* (Tarcher, 2005), have each sold over a million copies. She has extensive training in Gestalt Therapy, Hindu and Buddhist Tantra, bioenergetics, massage, meditation, Arica, and Integral Yoga. Anand developed the Love and Ecstasy Training, a method of healing and enhancing sexuality to its ultimate potential. She is the founder of SkyDancing Tantra Institutes.

violence and exploitation into sex. In this country it is difficult to talk about sex and maintain a sense of dignity. We have to fight through all the cultural taboos to have a good time.

The damage to human society caused by the condemnation of sex is incalculable. Instead of celebrating sex as a creative force, we turn it into a furtive, guilt-ridden affair. Religion has always tried to control human sexuality—because when people become ecstatic, they are free. People are led to believe that a priest is necessary in order to have a relationship with the divine. They do not believe it is possible to go direct and have an experience of God on their own. I call this the Anti-Ecstatic Conspiracy. The system does not want us to wake up to our natural ecstasy. The moment a person does wake up, they become a free thinker. For the power elite, that is considered dangerous. Tantra arose in rebellion against the repressive orthodoxy of the Brahmins, the Hindu priesthood, and against the idea that one had to be celibate to gain enlightenment.

Tantra, in essence, is the path of acceptance, of including the higher and the lower, the earthly and the spiritual. It allows God and the Devil to hold hands, as two poles, or two aspects of a single energy. Tantra is the art of choosing with awareness what brings you joy, and it is the art of weaving contradictory aspects of your personality into one whole for the purpose of expanding your consciousness.

-§-

I knew that sexuality was my path to awakening, for I had realized the light of spirit in my first lover's arms.

-§-

For example, let's say you're on a date. Your heart says, "I want to open up…this could be the one." But your mind says, "Absolutely not…remember what happened last time." And your body says, "I'm turned on. I want sex." All the different aspects of you are contradicting one another. You are out of harmony and you're in pain. Tantra works with the chakras to harmonize your energy and your consciousness into one entity. This is the marriage of Shakti—pure energy—and Shiva—pure consciousness. When these two marry, the world is born. That is the cosmology of tantra. The goddess Shakti and the god Shiva are the two aspects of the divine. When they are joined as one, their fusion gives birth to the cosmos. From the tantric perspective, the cosmos is born out of erotic union between the essences of male and female.

Tantra acknowledges that sex is the basis of all life. To make human sexuality and erotic union a form of worship and meditation is to practice reverence for life. When pleasure is taken up as a spiritual discipline, it leads to liberation. I have come to believe that all suffering is rooted in the loss of access to our natural ecstasy, and that reclaiming our natural ecstasy holds the key to our liberation. This is where SkyDancing Tantra and high sex comes in. Sex is a practice that releases endorphins, that expands our brain, and releases natural opiates that relieve pain. I've discovered that if you have one long orgasm a day, your whole life will change. Creativity increases, as does magnetism, your ability to handle crisis—even your finances improve. Sex is the shortest and best way to access a naturally high state of being.

Ordinary sex is a matter of instinctual impulse, conditioned by family values, by what we learn in school, and by what the culture teaches us. Often, that conditioning gets in the way of our ability to be totally natural and allow our real responses to emerge. A whole crowd is in the bedroom with us—mother, father, aunts, uncles, grandmother, and grandfather—all with their opinions about how it should go, what is honorable, and what is not. As a result, ordinary sex is rather limited.

-§-

Religion has always tried to control human sexuality—because when people become ecstatic, they are free.

-§-

High sex allows us to move into sex with full awareness, responding moment to moment with the rising energy, being in the present without dragging in the past or projecting into the future. You cannot have good sex unless you drop the past and the future, and become totally present. Often, when lovers get excited, they have to have a quarrel first because they are about to drop their defenses. When those defenses drop, all the little demons of frustration and resentment they have been avoiding suddenly emerge. The quarrel is a catharsis to release all the charged energy. When lovers are able to navigate this negative energy, to forgive, surrender, and refocus on having a good orgasm together, they arrive at a new place and are healed.

The word surrender includes the root verb *render,* which means, among other things, to melt. In terms of SkyDancing tantra, surrender means seeing and feeling the highest potential of the divine in your lover and melting into that energy. This is the consciousness of *namaste* in yoga. When you open to that reality, all differences between you disappear. You are both divine. If you approach sex in that way, miracles take place.

Historically speaking, SkyDancers were the wild, free, ecstatic dakinis—also called female awakeners. The word dakini means "woman who revels in the freedom of emptiness." SkyDancers were, and are, women of passion who were profoundly devoted to spiritual awakening. The path of the SkyDancer is a path of spiritual partnership that teaches the complete reciprocity of male and female practitioners as they learn the art of integrating ecstatic states into everyday life. In traditional yoga, you control and purify yourself in order to realize enlightenment, but the tantric perspective says that you are already divine exactly as you are. Tantra tells you to completely let go and dive deeply into your nature as it is. Tantra is the yoga of love.

Tantric philosophy teaches that we all have aspects of both the masculine and the feminine within us. Jung called these two aspects the animus and the anima. We all have the hormones of both, which allow us to experience the polarity. It is culture that imposes designated male and female attitudes and roles. Of course, there are differences between men and women, physiologically speaking. There is a different psychology and timing in the way a woman's body responds as compared to a man's. When the man is excited, when he sees the beauty of a certain type of woman, his penis responds automatically. It is a brain/sex reflex that he has very little control over, and it can happen in seconds. Once he is inside a woman, then he can relax—that is when he opens his heart. This may take all of ten minutes. The erect penis just wants to be in the garden.

-§-
Tantra is the yoga of love.
-§-

The woman is very different. Where the man starts with his sex and then moves to the heart, for the woman it is the other way around. She needs more time. Her heart must warm to him first, and she needs to feel safe and protected. Then she can open and trust her man. When all of that is given, she relaxes, her juices flow, and then her sex opens. This may take half an hour, or half a year—so he is ready long before she is. Confusion results if she lets him have his way and he lands before she has time to take off. She may be unable to have an orgasm and become frustrated. If she doesn't talk about it, the whole situation can escalate. This is why, as I always say, truth is erotic. When you tell the truth you take a risk. If love is there and you are willing to grow together, there is plenty to explore. The only wrong way to have sex is without awareness and communication. The most beautiful way is to have sex in a sacred space, as I explain in my book, *The Art of Sexual Ecstasy,* and now in my extraordinary DVD series, *Margot Anand's Secret Keys to the Ultimate Love Life.*

We seek comfort, pleasure, and ecstasy from the moment we are born. Comfort is a natural state of wellbeing and absence of pain. Pleasure comes from gratification of our physical needs and emotional desires. Sexual ecstasy is an experience of intense fulfillment, contentment, and inner joy. In most cases, ecstasy is discontinuous—it happens, it peaks, and then it's gone. Back in our ordinary consciousness, we are left with the intuitive insight of an expanded wholeness. Such moments motivate us to grow. Patient inner work is needed to recognize and transform the behaviors that sabotage our ability to live in joy and be "self-actualized." As we become increasingly aware and stable in this potential, we discover ecstasy as an intense state of contentment that allows us to freely choose what is pleasing—both for us and for others.

I had the very good fortune to work quite intensively for several years with a tantra teacher who taught me sex magic. He would visit me unexpectedly in the secret hours of the night, and we'd engage in intense breathing exercises that would generate a fiery energy in my body. Then, making love in a very slow, conscious way, he would direct me to focus this fiery energy into my heart. After a while, I had powerful visions. In one I was a Buddha, a spirit being, sitting blissfully in a cave. As I watched, the cave became red in color and started to pulsate. Soon, I became aware that my Buddha-being was sitting inside the cave of my own heart. My bliss began to expand with the size of the cave, growing bigger until it filled the entire universe. From there, I was able to radiate unconditional love to all living beings. My teacher later described the transmission as the "wisdom of the heart."

-§-
I became aware that my Buddha-being was sitting inside the cave of my own heart.
-§-

The emphasis in transmitted tantric teachings such as this tends to be mystical rather than magical, but the same approach is used in both arts. The adept has a choice: to reside in a state of mystical union with the universe, or to harness the universal powers derived from that union and channel them into manifesting on the physical plane. In the tantric tradition of Tibet, mysticism and magic flourished side by side. It was left to the initiate to decide how to use such powers as a matter of personal integrity and responsibility—as it is for us today.

Recently, upon my return from a twenty-one-day enlightenment process at the Oneness University near Chennai in India, where I received energy transference (deeksha) from Bhagwan Kalki and his wife, Amma, a friend asked, "So, are you enlightened?"

I laughed, and said, "Enlightenment is a process that begins and never ends."

In my work over the years, I have moved more and more in the direction of meditation, focusing on the ecstasy of emptiness, which I find can sometimes be a better orgasm than sex. Ideally, of course, we want to connect the two. To go to your lover and remain desireless at the height of desire is the ultimate.

Let me explain. To be desireless in any action means being fully present in one given moment, accepting that I don't know what the next moment will bring, staying present to emptiness without bringing in the past or projecting into the future, and deeply accepting that

I am in the mystery and God is guiding the wheel. Now, imagine bringing this frame of mind into the arms of the beloved, making love in a space of emptiness and presence. Desire is present, you feel it, you feel in love, and yet you do not want anything. You have no expectations that your lover has to love you this way, move that way, keep his erection for this amount of time, etc. No. You accept what is, not knowing what the next moment will bring because you are only conscious now, and now, and now...and you desire nothing more than what is in the moment. That aspect of detachment and witnessing generates emptiness in sex, emptiness in love—living ecstasy with detachment—this is sexual enlightenment.

You were conceived in the act of pleasure. Ecstasy was programmed into you the moment the sperm met the egg in your mother's womb. It exists inside you right now. It is possible to live from that joy, to live a life cut like a precious jewel. Who you truly are radiates an energy that is healing and enchanting. And every step you take carries the possibility of that awakening.

Charlotte Kasl:

The Zen of Lovemaking

To make love in the arms of the Beloved is to cross the chasm between the false self of constructed images to the state of "I Am," the state of no labels—simply the breath and being of our momentary experience.

Rumi writes, "The sky bares its neck so beautifully. We're here again with the Beloved. This air, a shout. These meadow sounds, an astonishing myth. Inside this globe the soul roars like thunder, And now Silence." Sexuality in the heart of the beloved is a natural, free-flowing coming together of two committed people—heart, mind, spirit, and body. When we empty our minds and welcome the meadow sounds, thunder, silence, and air into our lovemaking, we dissolve into the experience, into union.

This union of mystic lovers is grounded in truth, connection, and a willingness to crack open our shells—to know and be known. It is earthy yet transcendent. We dare to keep our eyes open to each other as we edge into the vast knowing of our bodies and hearts. We surrender into each other, willing to have our hiding places revealed.

When sexuality is not married to spirit and heartfelt relationship, it risks being a superficial experience driven by ego and biology, with the all-too-common qualities of owning, acquiring, controlling, acquiescing, possessing, and self satisfaction, with scant concern for one's partner. The undercurrent is one of disconnection from our self and

Charlotte Kasl, M.A., Ph.D., has been a psychotherapist and workshop leader for twenty-nine years. Author of *Women, Sex, and Addiction* (Houghton Mifflin, 1989), *Many Roads, One Journey: Moving Beyond the Twelve Steps* (Harper, 1992), *Finding Joy* (Harper, 1994), *A Home for the Heart* (HarperCollins, 1997), and the popular series, *If the Buddha Dated/Married/Got Stuck* (Penguin, 1999/2001/2005), she also pioneered an international 16-step empowerment model for overcoming trauma and addiction. *If the Buddha Dated* was a finalist for the National Book Award. *Women, Sex, and Addiction* resulted in a Lifetime Achievement Award. More at www.charlottekasl.com.

our partner, an experience often submerged in guilt and shame. From a spiritual perspective, however, sexuality becomes a rich interpenetration of energies, an all-over experience that is subtle, tender, strong, and lasting. It becomes an exploration: a gentle stroke on the cheek while looking each other in the eyes, whispering from the heart, slow kisses, movement from deep inside that aligns into a single dance—all these are part of the mosaic of making love because they are all about connection.

-§-
"Ishq Allah, Mahbud Li'llah"—"God is Love, Lover and Beloved"
-§-

Sexual energy is powerful. It can draw us together or tear us apart; it can sooth or wound; it can be objectified or enter a flow of giving and receiving that merges into an experience of oneness and deep ease with another human being. Sexuality can include opening our tender selves or closing down in fear, telling half lies or reaching for the truth. Sexuality can become routine, predictable, and empty if we say yes when we mean no, fear asking for what we want, or are too ashamed to explore the passionate depths of our unknown bodies.

When sexuality is grounded in spirituality, embedded in a commitment to truth and understanding, it becomes an ongoing exploration, a deepening of knowing. This takes people to that mystical "us" place, where the unique alchemy of two becomes as one. As Martin Buber says in *I and Thou,* it's not about the blood that circulates in my veins or yours, it's about the air that moves between us.

When I asked couples what opened the path to free-flowing sexuality, the most frequent word they mentioned was trust—trust that one's partner will be responsive, reliable, willing to talk, and respect a yes or a no. People wanted a relationship that was steadfast *and* passionate, committed *and* flexible. They wanted a connection grounded in respect, sensitivity, understanding, honored agreements, and being held in their partner's heart at all times.

When we make love to our partner as the Beloved, conditioned thoughts and fears of the past or future become stilled. It could be called Zen love—a complete experience of body, mind, and spirit, in which the concepts of giving and receiving dissolve into a sacred dance that is playful, deep, intuitive, and honest. It is the oneness of the universe played out in the unity of our physical and emotional relationship. The censors, fears, and deeply held conditioning slip away over time as trust, safety, and kindness deepen the relationship at every level. We feel free to allow our senses to be alive; our hearts and bodies become willing to engage, to struggle, to be known, and to feel pleasure. If we slip away into worry or thought, we can say so openly without fear, accepting our humanness as part of the ebb and flow of coming together, slipping into self, and surrendering again to the power of the moment. The honesty of revealing such moments opens the possibility of being allies in the "us" place. Instead of pretending to be present—which creates separateness—one can say, "I seem to have shut down. Can you just hold me for a moment?" The partner might ask, "What would you like?" Everything that happens is included in the lovemaking dance. Zen is now, simply being real.

Commitment is core to experiencing both self and other as the Beloved because, for most people, the vulnerability of intimate sexuality requires security and safety. To open ourselves deeply, we need assurance that our beloved will still be with us tomorrow, and the next day, and the next. The fear that our beloved may momentarily leave creates tension in the body, which is counter to the physical and emotional ease that underlies a ripening sexuality.

It is a challenge to get to this state of ease when we've been brought up in a culture of sexual objectification, in which a superficial politeness often supercedes speaking our truths; in which sex has routinely been associated with the ego—how much, how often, and how high; in which sex is about proof of being powerful, loved, important, wanted, or desirable; in which sex becomes relegated to superficial concepts of stimulation, rather than connecting emotionally and deeply pleasuring each other; in which sex is a high that can be bought, taken, or coerced. Moreover, many of us have echoes in our mind saying that celibacy is somehow more enlightened, holy, and pure than physical sexuality and passion. How does one translate those beliefs into feeling free and innocent about sexual intimacy?

In the absence of deep connection, passion fades; we become restless and seek new forms of external stimulation. This restlessness can pervade our lives, taking the form of seeking out new sexual techniques, flirtation, new partners, and it can spill over to other areas of acquisition as well—more money, status, spending, and innumerable external diversions. This is not to deny that bringing creativity to life and to lovemaking is a wonderful part of the ongoing evolution of a relationship. It's to say that we either go deeply into our core passions and truths, or we get restless and seek out stimulation that will never satisfy in the long run.

-§-
As we allow our coverings and masks to slip away, so does our shame.
-§-

Most of us have a bridge to cross, constructed of commitment to ourselves, to honesty, to integrity, to truth, and to healing whatever creates shame. As we allow our coverings and masks to slip away, so does our shame. Passion evolves as we learn to go deeply with each other, into those vulnerable realms that feel breathtakingly tender.

We also make friends with our physical nature. If we are to merge sexuality with spirituality, then we need to re-kindle a childlike bodily innocence and feel at ease with the sensations that arise from touch, exploration, and connection. While sex can be a transcendent experience, it is also about flesh, smells, taste, fluids, writhing in pleasure, and all the sounds of sexual arousal and excitement. Sexuality creates a torrent of energy in the body that can expose our hiding places and rip loose our fears, anger, shame, and grief, along with our joy, delight, and tenderness. To be open to sexuality as a life-giving experience is to invite all human emotions to join us in bed.

-§-
I, you, he, she we
In the garden of
mystic lovers,
These are not true
distinctions
—Rumi, from *Say I Am You.*
-§-

Emotional ease, honesty, and truth telling translate into a physical ease, primarily because we move from objectification of another to seeing each other as mirrors of ourselves. I see your hurt, and I know it in myself. When I see your joy in breaking through a fear it echoes in my solar plexus. I celebrate with you. We are here to care for each other—not to use or be used, but to know each other, to love with an open hand and find our special dance. I feel you emotionally. I know you.

When we move beyond sex-role stereotypes, we meet each other in the richness of being human, not as caricatures of men or women. When we are both giving and receptive, wild and tender, playful and still, we are not constricted by concepts of male and female; rather, we are two people flowing from essence, embracing through our physical bodies. Whether we are a heterosexual or a same sex couple, we are two lives merging with one another, inviting sexuality to spark our deepest passion and the bond between us.

Pure love resides beneath notions of objectification, and love opens the field where sexuality naturally merges with spirituality. We don't "work" at having spiritual sex, whatever that is; rather, we commit to integrity, truth, and revealing ourselves. We can then experience physical love as a subtle interpenetration of energy that flows throughout our bodies—from our fingertips to our legs, through our genitals and our emotional body. It becomes a single experience of making love with our partner, with life, and with the Beloved. We become generous with touch, laughter, pleasing, giving, creativity, receiving, and exploring together. It is all possibility happening between the two of us. When it feels like we're losing a part of ourselves, or that it's hard to give, it's a signal that we are protecting our constructed or conditioned self, which the ego thinks is real. From a Zen perspective, there is no identity to lose because we are part of a greater flow of energy. But we also need to address the momentary fears the ego creates. This is when, once again, we reveal our momentary experience, realizing it is part of human experience—not to be regarded as good or bad, better or worse. It's just what's happening in the moment.

We often hear that sexual passion quiets with time, yet when I interviewed long-term couples for *If the Buddha Married,* I found couples whose sexual passion had truly deepened and ripened. Ruth glowed as she spoke of her marriage of 42 years.

"With sexuality, there is something that goes on between the spirit and the soul and the physical—an element that wants to give and take, to understand. The sexual relationship happens because of love. Real love that comes from giving, knowing, and sharing. It's not an emotional, sentimental thing. Love follows when you show care, respect, and kindness. Sexuality is like a circle: the sexual union builds the love, and the love builds the sexual desire. Sexuality binds us together. With a successful sexual relationship, there is a delight in each other that filters through the day. It's an incredible superglue.

"There is something magical in the commitment to leave our father and mother and cleave to our partner. To truly become as one. When you have a commitment that is for life, and there is a backing of spirituality, love is patient, kind, and forgiving; you have an ointment that soothes. Without commitment, sex is like opening up a box of chocolates—a sweet taste but no meaning. With dissatisfaction in a sexual relationship, something wears away; the relationship rusts and the harmony fades. With ongoing commitment and love, the sexual union becomes an experience a teenager couldn't even dream of."

-§-

The power of Love came
into me
And I became fierce like
a lion,
then tender like the
evening star

—Rumi, from *Like This*

-§-

Enduring passion requires couples to move beyond much of our Western sexual conditioning. As Renata Stehdahl writes in *True Secrets of Lesbian Desire,* one of the most tender, permission-giving books for any woman or man, "Intimate passion is a process in which the individual couple works together to undo inhibitions patiently and increasingly, over time. Bodies take time to reveal their secrets, longings, fears, and pleasures. This is what we mean by intimacy—the tender and empathic search for each other with its subtle discovering and revelations."

Spiritually grounded sexuality thus becomes one with truth. We ebb into a safety zone where our longings and desires are not censored by thoughts such as *"That's weird," "What would she think of me?"* To quote Stendhal again, "With truth as the aphrodisiac, the lovers' bed would no longer be the place of mute misery, faked orgasm, and

other lies to get it over with—the place of silent mutiny and refusal, of self-violation in order to overcome disgust, of the mechanical race to orgasm... With truth's aphrodisiac, the lovers' bed need no longer hold a hundred years of solitude."

Ponder making love with a Zen beginner's mind. When you take off your clothes you also remove your mental coverings, slip into your body, and allow your intuitive, creative side to awaken. The wonder of creation comes alive in your moment-to-moment experience as your touch vibrates through you and into your beloved—as if you were discovering each other for the first time. Imagine making love with a completely empty mind; or, if you have thoughts, may they be a wish that you both know love and the source of all love. Imagine, slowly, while gazing softly into each other's eyes, stroking and touching as your body awakens and draws you into a sensuous dance. When you are exquisitely attuned to the responses of your beloved, you notice the smallest ripple of response either rising to meet you or pulling back. This becomes your special composition, the momentary expression of both your bodies. There is only this touch, and this moment. You allow the energy that arises to fill your body and expand, like a wave washing through you, like fire and thunder, or the softness of a spring rain. You eyes return to each other, taking you to a knowing, vulnerable place. Ultimately, you allow your bodies to do what they want to do as they attune to each other, creating a new composition with its own rhythm and harmony. The flames and ether come into your veins. Pleasure. Ecstasy. Then stillness, as you rest in the arms of the Beloved. Soft, joyful, powerful, sweet. Natural.

-§-

Is this then a touch?...
quivering me
to a new identity,
Flames and ether
making a rush
for my veins...
My flesh and blood
playing out lightning
to strike what is hardly
different from myself
—Walt Whitman,
Leaves of Grass

-§-

Angela Le:

Angels in Disguise

Legend has it that a notorious outlaw once roamed the Northern plains of Tibet, whose crimes included murder, robbery, and rape. His reputation spread far and wide, instilling fear in all those who crossed the Tibetan Plateau. This fierce and fearless bandit thought nothing of assailing groups of travelers and taking what he liked. Then, one day, he came upon a caravan that included a certain woman who was the consort of a revered guru. This particular guru was known for his ability to appear to any being in a form that would benefit them according to their personal karma. Apparently, the woman also had this gift. The bandit kidnapped and brutally raped her over and over again. It was not long after that summer day that the bandit renounced his life of violence and took up the path of a wandering monk. Over the years, he became a great healer and some say even a saint.

When the man was old and dying, someone asked him what had changed him all those years ago. He grew quiet for a moment and thought back to the rape, remembering how the woman had looked at him, how much tenderness and understanding. He leaned back on his bed, closed his eyes for the last time and answered, "It was her absolute compassion that changed me."

When I first heard of this legend many years ago, its message spoke directly to my soul. As a war child who carried a legacy of

Angela Le, L.Ac., is a licensed acupuncturist who has established successful practices in California and New York City. Known for her passionate, vibrant, and nurturing teaching style, she conducts workshops, retreats, and lectures nationally and internationally. Angela graduated with honors from Yo San University in Los Angeles, and has created remarkable synergistic alliances with Western medical providers, partnering with Daniel Andrews, M.D., a cardiologist, to establish the Natural Healing Center in Napa, California. She specializes in women's health, and believes in maintaining a strong spiritual practice despite her professional commitments. She is writing an upcoming book based on her work.

tremendous abuse and violence, I knew the story had something to teach me about the curative power of compassion.

The daughter of a U.S. soldier who took a Vietnamese woman as his wife, I am one of twenty-five thousand Amerasian children born as a direct result of this country's involvement in the Vietnam War. My mother and I immigrated to this country when I was eight months old. The year was 1974. The war was nearing an end, and my father dropped us off in Long Beach, California. Then he went on to fulfill his tour of duty. My mother had no money, no family, no way of going home, and a new baby in her arms. With little more than a third-grade education, she worked seven nights a week to support us.

I will never forget the excitement I felt years later when Mother announced she had hired a woman named Gloria to take care of me. As a child often left alone to fend for myself, a babysitter was like a guardian angel in the flesh—a gift, pure and simple. Nothing could have prepared me for what would actually come my way.

-§-
Even when I look back at some of my worst experiences, I can see beauty, love—even innocence.
-§-

My world suddenly turned dirty and terrifying. For the next three years—at the hands of my caretaker—I became the victim of daily sexual perversion and brutality. I had no power over my own body, felt no feelings save anger, and endured a near-fatal wounding of my soul. My pain and ignorance made self-destruction and abuse seem normal, even intriguing at times. Gloria made it so easy—I was the center of her universe and, in truth, she was the center of mine. I wanted love, even if I had to pay the devil in secrets. My head swirled with contradictory feelings as love became entwined with feeling bad, dirty, and shameful. I learned to leave my body during those twisted nights; it was the only way to survive.

By the time I entered puberty, rape, violence, and seduction were the ordinary components of intimacy. At fourteen, I followed the siren call of love again. I went with John, an eighteen-year-old crush, to his house and was violently raped. Why would I, a victim of long-term sexual abuse, enter such a dangerous situation? Perhaps I was destructively repeating the pattern Gloria had started. I only remember being excited to be going home with John, hoping like any naïve fourteen-year-old to hold his hand or be kissed. Perhaps I was disassociating like an ostrich with her head in the sand, unafraid as long as I did not actually see what might hurt me. Or perhaps I was truly innocent of the risk. I had no idea that sexual terror came in the shape of men as well as women. Now that I had reason to be afraid of everybody, regardless of gender, I became afraid of no one and nothing. Disassociation had helped me get through the first traumatic abuse, and it worked again—ultimately leading me to feel nothing at all, not during the rape, and not after. Not for a long, long time.

I handled major traumas like sexual abuse, being chased by a gang member with a gun, or watching my neighborhood go up in flames when the Rodney King verdict sparked the Los Angeles riots, with surprising ease. No one could hurt me; I could walk away from any person or situation and feel nothing. In fact, I became the hunter. I was attractive and men were everywhere. If a man had money, respect, and an impressive pedigree—all of which I lacked and believed would keep me safe—he became my prey. A few times, I felt something I thought of as love, but not for long. Sex, money, alcohol, and lies always tied me up into a suicidal knot of loneliness and despair. No matter who or how much I got, I was never satisfied. Buddhists call this the realm of the hungry ghost.

I saw my life in terms of absolutes: situations were always either good or bad. But life isn't really that way. Most moments generally contain a little of both. Even when I look back at some of my worst experiences, I can see beauty, love—even innocence. The universe had been blessing me all along. Some blessings were obvious, like summers spent with my sister, Diana, and her family, or Mother bringing home our first puppy. Even my brother, Tim, brought an unexpected gift when he led me to believe that meditation could give me the power to levitate. In a funny way, he turned out to be right.

-§-

Suffering does not belong to me alone, and any healing forged in me is a healing for the whole.

-§-

I started to meditate, and slowly my spirit began to lift. I did not see flashing lights, but I did feel moments of pure joy, a flicker of hope that life could be different. I had a new secret, only this was a good one. Little by little, the rock of shame I carried inside me began to dissolve.

Then, at the age of nineteen, I met a wise and gentle woman. We talked for hours about my life and my suffering. She told me of a Tibetan prophecy that predicted a dark age of chaos, suffering, and ignorance. The prophecy stated that out of this darkness, an equal amount of light would come into the world in the form of healers.

"Such a healer is a Bodhisattva," she said, "one who lives for the benefit of all other beings."

Her words were like a lighting strike to my soul. Could this painful journey of mine have been about karma all along? Could my karma be linked with the karma of all sentient beings? Did my sufferings contribute in some way to the evolution of the planet? I couldn't

decide what to believe, but her words offered me a new way of seeing my life. I opened to the possibility that my suffering could actually be a gift. That the harshness of the journey was proportional to the learning I could gain, and that my greatest tormentors were also my greatest teachers. And in this I found forgiveness—for them, and for my own transgressions.

Not only did this perspective help me understand and accept my past, it opened a path to an unforeseen future. Like the bandit on the plains of Tibet, my life took a deep banking turn toward a life of healing and service. My first lesson was to realize that my tendency to be judgmental, impatient, and angry perpetuated my suffering and sent a ripple effect of suffering into the lives of others. Understanding this made my personal healing a high priority, and eventually a gift to me and others who were thus freed from the burden of my unhappiness. Healing came full circle when I realized this essential truth: *suffering does not belong to me alone, and any healing forged in me is a healing for the whole.*

-§-
Each phase of healing has its own intrinsic wisdom that cannot be rushed or skipped to reach an arbitrary goal.
-§-

Mindfulness practice—specifically Vipassana meditation—has been a great resource in my healing. When the mind and senses become still, our body-being has a chance to come into harmony with nature as the essential self emerges. The embodiment of this quality can clearly be seen in the woman who met the bandit's savagery with compassion. Her behavior suggests a full realization of Buddhism's basic teaching: suffering exists when we attempt to secure our relationship with the "world out there" instead of with the "world home here."

According to this teaching, when we relinquish attachment to body, mind, and emotions, we lose the fear of death and thus transcend the primary cause of suffering and pain. Mindfulness practice reveals the essential emptiness beneath emotions, and the impermanence of mental constructs and concepts. Freedom from misery follows as our higher nature—blooming with compassion for the human condition—begins to flower.

Healing is an organic stage-wise process, meaning that each phase of healing has its own intrinsic wisdom that cannot be rushed or skipped to reach an arbitrary goal. As Mary Antin said, "We are not born all at once, but by bits. The birth and growth of the spirit, in those who are attentive to their own inner life, are slow and exceedingly painful. Our mothers are racked with the pains of our physical birth; we ourselves suffer the longer pains of our spiritual growth." Healing is, in a very real sense, a second birth, an awakening we engage in *consciously* by going after the truth that sets us free. When I began to see my early traumas as the path of a healer in the making, a second life began.

When we re-conceive suffering as the contractions of the soul giving birth to a spiritual path and higher purpose, pain becomes a guide—a signal alerting us to what needs attention. If we don't listen to pain for what it's telling us, we run the risk of going numb and distracting ourselves in any of the myriad ways readily available. In *The Power of Now,* Eckhart Tolle writes, "...It is easier to wake up from a nightmare than an ordinary dream." In other words, extreme suffering provides an alarm that can awaken us from the nightmarish state in which we are separate from God. What we become present to is a deep reservoir of wholeness that stretches far beyond what we normally see as ourselves. To realize that fullness, we need to let go of many notions and convictions, to literally die to our old concept of who we are. The fire of our suffering can burn through to this deeper discovery.

Likewise, the fire of desire and the deep pleasure of sex can draw us closer to the present moment where old wounds can be released. Years of mindfulness practice taught me how to stay present and breathe through whatever arose on the meditation pillow—be it excruciating knee pain, extreme boredom, or angry frustration. In time, I brought this same mindfulness to lovemaking. Sex became a meditation.

In so many ways, this practice is what finally brought me home to my body and to a healed sexual life, closing the gap in self-connection that disassociative processes had carved. I no longer had to abandon my own pleasure to an old reactive pattern. Breathing my way through it all, I discovered that awareness heals.

-§-

Suffering powerfully points us toward God by challenging us to stay open.

-§-

I had always paid a price for my disconnection. Or as I see it now, I did not really pay any price but was repeatedly and lovingly reminded that I could not be free of sexual suffering, of any suffering, by trying to escape it. I would need to integrate and receive my sexual self in full, all of it—the pain, the learning, Gloria, and the glory.

For more than a decade I struggled with health complications all centered in my sexual and reproductive organs. As I moved toward greater compassion and gratitude for *all* my lovers, even the Glorias, I found my medical symptoms disappearing as if by magic. One after another I let go of my painful experiences, of the anger and guilt, of proclaiming myself Victim or Perpetrator. When I stopped coupling

alcohol, even one glass of wine, with sex, I stopped getting the yeast infections that had plagued my relationships.

Since then my single purpose in sexual relationship has been to unite spirit with body, to find pleasure in consciousness and consciousness in pleasure. I no longer have to abandon my sexual response or my sexual health to the old reactive patterns of seduction, fear, power, and control, of juggling who would be hunter and who hunted. Breathing my way through it all, I could love and be loved in safety, feeling ecstasy and ultimate surrender with my eyes wide open.

My sexual suffering came to me in many forms. I've been sexually attacked by women and men, humans and microorganisms, family, strangers, myself, and my own body. Each of these has been a spiritual signpost saying, "Turn here; look here; walk here." Suffering powerfully points us toward God by challenging us to open and stay open—to override the impulse to shut down. Vital to the healing process is an attitude of surrender and acceptance, a stance of showing up for our experience as it is in the moment. Indeed, suffering itself is often a signal that we have shut down with blame, self-condemnation, and guilt—popular detours thoroughly modeled on daytime television. When we understand the signal and trust enough to open to our experience again, then we can truly begin to face the *actual* in-the-moment pain. This is when we begin to heal.

This, then, is the great gift that suffering offers us: a challenge to dig deeply, to find within us an untouchable state of well-being, a place of wholeness and joy that exists independent of changing circumstances and the actions of others. This is what I call using suffering to know God. As Karlfried von Durkheim said,

> The person who, being really on the Way, falls upon hard times in the world, will not, as a consequence, turn to that friend who offers him refuge and comfort and encourages their old self to survive. Rather, he will seek out someone who will faithfully and inexorably help him to risk himself, so that he may endure the difficulty and pass courageously through it. Only to the extent that a person exposes himself over and over again to annihilation, can that which is indestructible be found within him. In this daring…[we find] the dignity and the spirit of true awakening.

Suffering has a way of pointing us *Home* and inviting us to let go and discover the grace and wholeness underlying it all. Seeing this again and again builds a deeply lived faith that embraces fully the process of life.

Rather than looking to get what I want, I now look to see how much more I can accept and give. Rather than shutting down and disassociating in situations that are difficult, I subtly move toward the abyss of letting go. And in that moment, I feel more connected to God and to Truth. As Rumi said, "Your task is not to seek for love, but merely to seek and find all the barriers within yourself that you have built against it."

Even the most painful experience can be transformed into understanding with the eyes of compassion. Seeing through the disguise of our suffering, we realize that only angels surround us.

Lori Grace:

The Full Embrace

Susan and Alan came to me with the question that puzzles so many couples: if we love each other so much, why aren't we having more sex? *Newsweek* highlighted this dilemma in 2003 with its June cover article, "No Sex, Please, We're Married." In Susan and Alan's case, the problem was not "no sex" so much as a constant squabble about *when*. More than once a week, the two of them would argue about whether to have sex in the morning or the evening, and often the resulting tension found them skipping it altogether. After eight years of marriage, they both wished to find a way to relieve the ongoing tension between them.

Before the couple came to me for counseling, Alan was wondering where the passion in his relationship had gone. He was feeling concerned that somehow he was at fault. "We started out so passionate," he said. "What happened?" Susan, on the other hand, was longing for more attention and wanted her need for privacy respected. "He's all over me," she said. "And he's not listening to what I need!"

Alan felt hurt and angry. He wanted to wake up in the morning and reach out right away to the woman he loved. He delighted in the relaxed and dream-like feeling that accompanied early morning lovemaking and the ease with which he got an erection at that time of day. Susan preferred to make love in the evening. She wanted to spend more time in their lovemaking sessions looking into one another's

Lori Grace Star, M.A., has been a student and teacher of tantra yoga and sacred sexuality for over twenty years. She has also been teaching approaches to communication and conflict resolution for eleven years, and Compassionate Communication (NVC) for the past five. As the originator of Sexual Energetics, Lori combines elements from Bioenergetics, Reichian work, and movement therapy to help people unlock the vast potential of their sexual energy and to use it to greatly enrich their intimate relationships with others and with themselves. For further information, and details about her workshops and private practice, go to www.celebrationsoflove.com.

eyes, talking, and caressing one another. As the years went by, she needed more time to get aroused, and Alan's pace seemed rushed to her. She had begun to feel sad and irritated about their sex life.

Can Tantra Save This Marriage?

Susan and Alan were fortunate to have sought couples coaching from me at this time in my life and not thirty years ago. When I first started teaching Tantra, I was not aware of the effect of aging on the sex hormones of the body, nor had I grasped the power of empathy to transform negative communication patterns. In my early explorations of tantra, my sexual experiences and those of my students kept getting more and more remarkable in terms of passion and orgasm. And yet few of those relationships endured over the years. We could talk about what we wanted in bed, enjoy plenty of multiple orgasms, but sadly, a large percentage of these unions devolved into high drama and break-ups.

-§-
When either arousal or connection is missing, relationships begin to break down.
-§-

Today, I teach All-Embracing Tantra, which combines conscious communication techniques, heart-centered spiritual practices, Sexual Energetics, movement therapy, and the latest medical information on anti-aging.

The meaning of the word tantra comes from the Sanskrit word *tandere*: "to weave." We humans live in a complex, interwoven tapestry of thoughts, feelings, needs, memories, biochemistry, hormones, biomechanics, and spirit. If one piece of our being is out of balance, warning signals go off, producing physical or emotional pain within us. When we are in such pain, feeling sexually aroused or emotionally connected to our beloved can be a challenge. When either arousal or connection is missing, relationships begin to break down, and they may ultimately break up.

Over the next few months, Alan and Susan took up the task of addressing two specific aspects of a successful love relationship: mutual deepening of empathic understanding and vibrant sexual connection.

The Creative Power of Compassion

Initially, I worked with Alan and Susan in communication training, so that both of them could gain a deeper understanding of each other's unmet needs. Generally speaking, when a couple enters coaching, I recommend they read *Nonviolent Communication: A Language of*

Life by Marshall B. Rosenberg, Ph.D., or one of his shorter manuals. Even if a couple initially feels at ease with each other, familiarity with this system will be of significant benefit when communication issues arise as they explore new areas of sexual expression in their relationship.

Although I had studied a variety of communication techniques for more than twenty years, it wasn't until I found Nonviolent Communication (NVC) that I started experiencing much greater ease in all of my relationships. Even while interacting with my teenage son, I notice more connection and empathy between us when discussing difficult topics.

With NVC, also called Compassionate Communication (www.cnvc.org), we shift away from using complaint and criticism to get our needs met, and learn, instead, to express our feelings, wants, and needs directly. The NVC model facilitates judgment-free expressions that allow partners to melt into an experience of deep empathy. From this new place of empathic connection, an energetic field emerges, which I call the "creative power of compassion." In this shared space, the couple discovers ways to meet both parties' needs. New solutions arise not through compromise, but through understanding and empathizing with each other's needs.

In our first session, I requested that Susan and Alan each state how they were feeling and what they were wanting. Both were clearly feeling degrees of sadness, anger, disappointment, and resentment; both wanted improved communication, ease, harmony, and connection in their relationship. Then, I had them each express their more individual needs and then repeat back to each other what they heard. Alan reflected accurately Susan's need to connect with herself, and Susan—after a try or two—reflected for Alan his need for the relaxation and ease of morning sexual encounters.

-§-
New solutions arise not through compromise, but through understanding and empathizing with each other's needs.
-§-

Predictably, after they focused on each other's needs, the creative power of compassion took over, allowing Alan and Susan to brainstorm strategies for meeting both of their needs. With a shared understanding of Susan's need for self-connection in the morning and Alan's need for deep relaxation and ease as a prelude to sexuality, the couple came up with a new plan: Susan would wake up a half an hour earlier and take time for herself in yoga and meditation, and then she would return to bed to share sensual touch with Alan—which might well evolve into sexual play. This turned out to be an effective solution for both of them, and brought them to the next stage of our work together.

Optimizing the Aging Process

When Alan and Susan returned for their next session, they were feeling much more emotional ease and connection. However, at age fifty-four, Susan mentioned that she did not have much desire for sex and missed the erotic appetite she had enjoyed before menopause. She was dismayed at her vaginal dryness, which necessitated use of a lubricant. Alan reported that, although erections still came quite easily to him at age fifty-one, he was having trouble maintaining them as long as he would like.

I now turned my focus toward a hormonal approach to their situation, asking them a series of in-depth questions about desire level, ease of arousal, lubrication, sexual stamina, and patterns of ejaculation and orgasm. I recommended they both undergo a full hormonal review with an anti-aging physician or other healthcare professional (a suggestion I often make to younger people, as well).

Some people have hormonal imbalances from birth. For others, they arise due to stress, trauma, illness, or aging. Hormone imbalances can affect our mood, energy level, and sense of well-being. They can also affect either partner's ability to become aroused or reach climax, as well as the man's ability to maintain an erection. As men and women get older, hormonal output decreases, with the exception, generally, of cortisol.

We call this hormonal decline, or "change of life," *menopause* in women and *andropause* in men. Andropause often starts around forty or forty-five and usually occurs gradually, over a period of about twenty years. Menopause happens more abruptly, completing at the average age of fifty-two. It is usually preceded by an almost ten-year period called perimenopause. These downward shifts in hormone production can result in sexual dysfunction, wrinkled skin, hair and bone loss, fatigue, and increased risk of heart disease for both men and women.

Based on Susan's report that her sex drive was low, and Alan's statement that he had difficulty maintaining his erections at times, I recommended both get their free testosterone and DHEA sulfate measured in addition to a number of other hormones. Free testosterone and DHEA are the two major hormones that support sexual libido in both men and women. Too little of either can extinguish our sexual spark. I also recommended that Susan have—among other hormones—her estrogen level tested, as estrogen supports general tissue health and lubrication in the vaginal canal. For Alan's difficulty maintaining his erections, I suggested he have his estrogen, thyroid hormone, and blood lipid levels checked in addition to his free testosterone. For further information on suggested hormone tests and laboratories, please consult www.celebrationsoflove.com under hormone information.

Within two weeks, Alan and Susan had visited a holistic physician I recommended and brought their test results back to share with me. I examined the reports and discussed with them the hormones and levels each had been prescribed; I thought well of the recommendations they'd received.

Susan's estrogen level proved to be low, as I had suspected. She began using a vaginal cream made of estriol, a bioidentical form of estrogen. Her vaginal lubrication increased within days. Susan was delighted with this change, but she still longed to have more desire for sex, and to feel more relaxed about her sexuality. I reassured her that the testosterone and DHEA would likely increase her level of desire, which it did within two weeks. Alan also reported increased desire within a two-week period after taking DHEA and testosterone. He also noticed his erections becoming firmer and lasting longer.

To find an anti-aging physician or holistic health professional in your area, you can access the Life Extension Foundation's *Directory of Innovative Doctors* at www.lef.org.

Awakening More and More

With all the changes going on—positive though they were—both Alan and Susan wanted even more ease and joy in their sexual connection. I recommended sensate focus work, an approach pioneered by Masters and Johnson. Arousal almost always occurs when we are relaxed. That is why sensate focus, which allows each partner to give and receive non-demanding touch, is so effective.

I asked Susan and Alan to lie down side by side, facing one another, and instructed them to look gently into each other's eyes and relax their breathing. As Alan sensually brushed her body without expectation, Susan began to feel received as a whole person. She virtually blossomed like a flower, opening to welcome even more pleasure from his loving touch. Then Susan stroked Alan's chest, arms, abdomen, and penis with light caresses. He felt greater awareness of his body as she touched him. They found sensate focus work a real contribution to their newfound sense of connection; both partners were able to let go of performance concerns. Alan noticed that the more relaxed he became, the more easily he became erect.

After six weeks, the couple was more at ease and more connected to each other than they had been in months. At this point in their sessions, I introduced Susan and Alan to Sexual Energetics, a

body of work I developed while studying Bioenergetics and Reichian work in the seventies. Wilhelm Reich, M.D. charted and named the "orgasm reflex" in the 1930s in his book *The Function of the Orgasm.* As I describe below, the orgasm reflex can help people to feel their emotions more deeply, be more in touch with their body, expand their connection with their own sexual energy, and experience a much deeper release in orgasm.

An important aspect of Reichian therapy includes working with the orgasm reflex to uncover buried emotions and sensations—often sexual ones—that arise as one breathes and utters sounds. The basis of the orgasm reflex is breath, relaxation, and wave-like undulations that lead to a full orgasmic response and full-bodied orgasms through breathing alone. Reich discovered that the orgasm reflex could be used to increase erotic sensation, prolong arousal, spread sexual energy throughout the body, and profoundly increase surrender and release in orgasm.

I invited Alan and Susan to learn abdominal breathing by placing a hand on their own belly and feeling the rise and fall of their lower abdomen as they inhaled and exhaled in long, deep breaths. Breathing deeply into the abdomen pushes on the pelvic floor, subtly massaging the genitals from the inside.

Next, we moved to what I call the Self-Stimulating Breath, where a person actually uses abdominal breathing to create engorgement in the pelvic floor. The vagina engorges for the woman, and the area around the prostate engorges and pulses for the man. This feels sexual in a very internal way. A woman often finds herself becoming engorged and lubricated through breathing alone, if she has normal estrogen levels. Sometimes a person has to work through emotional blocks to become this open, if he or she has experienced trauma in the past.

Susan and Alan learned to relax their pelvic floors and their anuses as they inhaled, allowing the whole pelvic floor to expand. I taught them to let their pelvic floor relax back or even very gently contract as they exhaled. As they practiced this during our session, Susan noticed that her lubrication was increasing even without oral or manual stimulation. She and Alan practiced this breath both separately, and then together when they were sexually joined. She enjoyed expressing her love for Alan as she gently squeezed his penis on each exhale. I call this the Loving Squeeze. Susan felt as though she was gently milking Alan. She relaxed her vagina and anus totally as she inhaled, opening her vagina fully to receive his thrust, and then she squeezed him gently as she exhaled. Alan felt deeply received by Susan and very excited by this added stimulation to his penis.

We then turned our attention to learning the orgasm reflex, most particularly the undulation, or body wave, which allows energy and arousal to travel and spread more readily and completely throughout the body. When lovers combine this undulation with breathing and relaxation exercises, they often experience spontaneous, full-body shuddering and feelings of bliss. This kind of release often occurs separately from ejaculation or climax. It allows lovers to feel intense sexual energy throughout their bodies and prolong high states of arousal without detracting from eventual genital orgasm or male ejaculation.

Undulation begins with breathing in. Lying down, one first draws the pelvis back, making a little arch in the lower back as one inhales, filling the belly with breath. The chin tucks in slightly, as the curve in the small of the back appears. Exhaling, one gently brings the hips and pubic mound forward, flattening the small of the back and then tilting the pelvis forward slightly. When doing this with a partner, each lover's genitals and lips come closer to each other as they exhale.

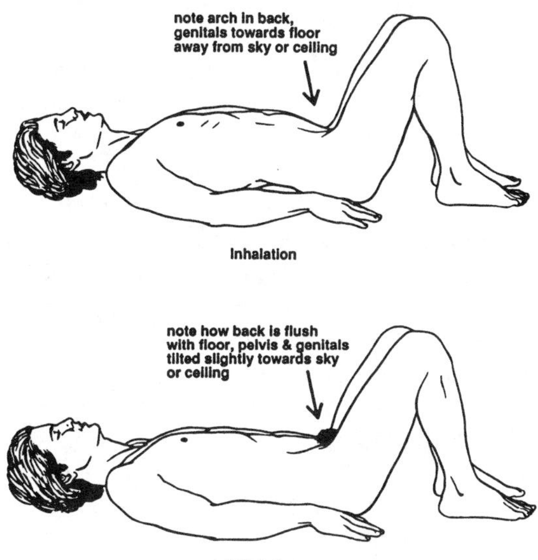

The Orgasm Reflex exercise

Alan and Susan also learned how to regulate their own passion using the breath. They learned how to use rapid breathing to build passion and move quickly to orgasm, as well as how to use long, deep breathing to slow down and contain sexual energy. Alan also learned additional, stronger methods for ejaculatory control. For example, I taught him to contract the muscles around his anus and genitals when

he felt fairly close to ejaculation and then to take a breath in, hold it, and visualize energy moving up his spine and finally allow himself a very long, slow exhale.

One benefit of increasing foreplay is that the longer we extend our arousal, the more testosterone and other hormones circulate through our bloodstream. Therefore, *especially as we get older, extended foreplay is good for our health!* After just fifteen minutes of extended foreplay, testosterone can remain heightened for a significant period of time.

The opportunity in tantric lovemaking is that most people can extend high levels of arousal for as long as they want—often hours at a time. Orgasm ceases to be an event; it becomes a state of being. This state of being affects our brainwaves in very positive, helpful ways.

-§-
In tantric lovemaking, orgasm ceases to be an event; it becomes a state of being.
-§-

Brain wave studies I conducted in 1993, with state-of-the-art biofeedback equipment, revealed that the state of extended arousal greatly expands brain wave amplitudes in meditative (alpha and theta) frequency ranges. From the point of view of the lover, this high-amplitude state feels like an extended experience of great present-mindedness and focus, which can be used to strengthen the power of visualization and prayer, or to facilitate deeper levels of intimacy—clearly terrific secondary gains. (You can learn more about this topic in an expanded version of this article by clicking "The Full Embrace" expanded version on our website.)

The week after Alan and Susan completed their instruction in these techniques, they e-mailed me saying they were feeling very connected with each other, and, at times, were experiencing what they called altered states of consciousness, as well as regular rushes of energy accompanied by delicious body spasms. For Alan, learning to circulate sexual energy throughout his body also became a step toward his experiencing multiple orgasms without ejaculation—another benefit of tantric practice. He reported his first experience of this kind within two weeks of beginning to work with the technique.

Sacred Tantric Ritual

East Indian sexual secrets from the *Kama Sutra* teach that a woman's heart chakra is the portal to her vagina. As the heart is opened and her nipples—which are extensions of the heart chakra—are manipulated, she becomes aroused. Conversely, a man's penis, the *Kama Sutra* notes, is the portal to his heart. As the penis is appreciated and aroused, *his* heart opens. Nipple play can then become erotic for him as well. This tantric view of our opposite energy poles also helped Susan and Alan feel more understanding of each other

The couple had now spent many hours in sensual play and delighted at the energy and passion they felt in their bodies. They had learned about the heightened states of consciousness available through the practice of tantra, states in which the mind lets go and surrenders to the energy of love. In such a state, we can merge with another and then return to ourselves even more "connected" than before.

More and more, states of mental, physical, and sexual bliss poured through Alan and Susan when they were connecting with each other. During high states of sexual arousal, they combined tantric meditation, relaxation, chanting, and prayer. They felt very, very close to each other.

Susan and Alan asked to learn more about tantric ritual so that they could set a more sacred context for the experiences and the new path to which they were committed. I prepared a special space for them and encouraged them to do the same in their own home. We created an altar with pictures of their spiritual guides and masters, including icons symbolic of the spiritual energy that they hold most dear. Such an altar might include pictures of Buddha, Krishna, the Earth Mother, a shamanic symbol, or even Jesus and Mary, as tantra embraces all faiths.

I showed Alan and Susan a Hindu sculpture of a phallus, called a *shivalingam,* and one of a *yoni,* the Sanskrit word for vulva. In contrast to Western culture, Asian traditions view the sex organs as God-given and sacred; it is not unusual to see these as altar pieces. Sexual energy—also referred to as *kundalini, ki,* or *chi*—is also seen as sacred. From an Asian point of view, practicing tantric lovemaking in front of an altar is celebrated.

-§-
In contrast to Western culture, Asian traditions view the sex organs as God-given and sacred.
-§-

I explained and guided them through a full tantric ritual, which they decided to incorporate into a special evening at home. Alan and Susan also set up a permanent altar in their bedroom at home, which became a focus for their own practice of tantra.

Alan and Susan also learned how to pray together by sitting facing each other in a position known as *yab-yum,* and putting their foreheads together at the third eye point—the visioning chakra—while toning and then sharing their tender prayers with each other.

In their practice at home, Susan and Alan included other aspects of tantric ritual, including taking time to bathe together, and anoint and bless each other's chakras with special oils. Lighting candles adds another dimension, as does burning incense in the room. Playing special music and chants—even singing and chanting along with them—adds to the mood. Erotic dance is yet another of the many forms of play that contributes to celebration and arousal.

In tantra, the eyes are considered to be the windows into the temple of the soul. As a result, the body is treated with a great deal of respect and care. Tantric practitioners—or tantrikas, as they are called—often gaze into the eyes of their beloved with a focus on the left, receptive, eye.

Susan and Alan learned that the purpose of eye gazing is to perceive each other as separate from the pictures each holds about the other in the form of memories, impressions, unresolved resentments, projections, and thoughts. As they looked into each other's eyes, they embraced the opportunity to look beyond the face of the personality, or ego, and into the core of each other's being. Through their own experience, they learned to value this level of connection and carry it into sexual arousal and even orgasm.

Six months later, during our last session together, Alan, Susan, and I reviewed their accomplishments. They had much to cherish. I was happy to see that they were committed to maintaining both their new health practices and their new style of communication, knowing these were key ingredients in their ability to support their results for a long time. I was also happy to see that they had fully integrated their Sexual Energetics work and were able to use it as a base for their deeply satisfying tantra practice. With great delight, I celebrated with them the new pleasures and heartfelt connection they had established.

MUKUNDA STILES:

The Nectar of Tantrik Love

"*Each was in their respective incubator... One [of the twins] was not expected to live. A nurse fought against hospital rules and placed the babies in one incubator. When they were placed together, the healthier of the two threw an arm over the other in an endearing embrace. The smaller baby's heart rate stabilized and her temperature rose to normal. Let us remember to embrace those who we love.*"

One tiny human embraces another in the midst of a difficult ordeal. This most basic gesture of human bonding is not only natural, it has a healing and rejuvenating effect. This article about two prematurely born infants, which my mother sent to me recently, beautifully expresses this most basic human need.

Love is a natural expression that arises when we are spontaneous. The challenge of human existence is to learn to be unconditional lovers. Like the man in Paul Sutherland's book, *Agnostic Prayer,* many of us are searching for freedom from the oppressive and critical aspects of the mind. Sutherland writes:

Love

Just Love

Let Love guide you

Love with joy

Love when happy

Love when sad

Trust and let Love teach you how to express Love

Mukunda Stiles, one of the American pioneers in Yoga Therapy, created his Structural Yoga Therapy system in 1976 following training in Krishnamacharya's lineage of teachers; most notably Rama Jyoti Vernon, B. K. S. Iyengar, and Indra Devi. He has a B.A. in religious studies, and did graduate study in kinesiology and therapeutic exercise. He trains spiritual mentors with the Claritas Institute, headed by Joan Borysenko. He is the author of the best-selling *Structural Yoga Therapy* (Weiser, 2001), and the *Yoga Sutras of Patanjali* (Weiser, 2001). His trainings in the U.S. and Europe are described at www.yogatherapycenter.org.

In tantrik yoga, this natural expression of care and compassion is prolonged during lovemaking, to help lovers stabilize their emotions while deeper underlying spiritual forces move and seek expression. As a woman opens to her true nature as Shakti—the feminine face of God—she is likely to cry. Tears are a natural expression of the Ayurvedic yoga principle called *kapha.* Kapha is the nurturing water element that manifests in several forms—as health promoting lymph substances of the immune system, and as the nectar of love in a mother's breast milk. When kapha evolves from these expressions into those of romantic or spiritual love, it becomes what is called *ojas* in Ayurveda—the juice of love.

-§-
The challenge of human existence is to learn to be unconditional lovers.
-§-

We see the natural, free flow of ojas when tears of joy flow profusely during true moments of lovemaking. When sexual or spiritual love is being made, the body naturally produces byproducts that are the essence of kapha; this is where women get their "juiciness." The salivary glands moisten the mouth, breasts swell to resemble those of a nursing mother, the sexual organs flow with their own unique nectar, or *amrita,* and our eyes flood with tears of pleasure, gratitude, and ecstasy. The practitioner of yoga (yogi, or yogini — feminine) also experiences this ojas as *kechari,* a nectar that flows from a secret energy center behind the third eye above the palate, eventually falling downward to be burned up in the digestive fire center. Specific techniques such as *Kechari Mudra,* in which the tongue goes upward and reaches back, allow what would ordinarily be lost to be tasted—revealing that the nectar of love originates within and, with its conscious cultivation, will evolve into supreme love. When love evolves to this point, it is no longer experienced as personal, but divine, spreading equally to all that come into your consciousness. In truth, it is consciousness that is bliss. Experiencing that, we are quite naturally filled with tears of love. All these are signs of ojas, which is liquid love.

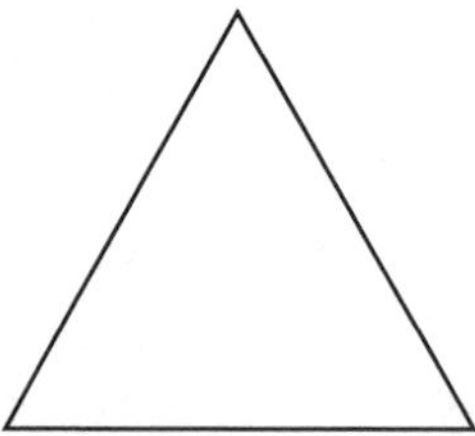

Yoni Mudra Rejuvenation

In the tantrik view, we have four subtle bodies in addition to our physical body. The first two contain six spinning (chakra) energy centers. The lowest of these is located at the pelvic floor; while the position of the second varies, being at the pubic region for men and the cervix for women. The close proximity of the first two chakras makes it challenging for us to distinguish the resulting intuitive perceptions from emotions, which is crucial for bodily-generated sensations to evolve into wisdom. Creativity and sensuality in the first chakra become abundance and sexual energy in the second chakra. When we experience a higher state of consciousness, such as a spiritual awakening, or the tsunamis of sexual arousal, spirituality and sexuality can become indistinguishable. One can easily become confused if not obsessed with spirituality, denying natural sexual expression—or infatuated with sex, losing the passion for spiritual fulfillment.

The *Yoni Mudra* is a helpful exercise that can lead to clarity when emotions, spiritual energies, and bodily sensations arise and cause us to become confused. To do this simple hand gesture, place your palms downward, flat on your lower abdomen. The thumbs align straight across, fingers together, so that when your forefingers touch a downward triangular space is created between your hands. *Mudras* are energetic gestures that have a unique property of helping one to retain elevated states of consciousness and increased life force.

For self-healing, and as a foundation for both connecting with and building *prana,* I recommend placing your hands frequently in the Yoni Mudra. This is especially beneficial after yoga or meditation practice. Using this mudra will develop the nurturing and healing energies that spiritual disciplines generate. Focus on directing your bodily sensations of prana to come home towards the pelvic cavity, located just where the abdomen ends. Direct the currents of sensation from the extremities to this sacred shape (yoni means "source") beneath your hands. This shape is the archetype of the feminine energy of receptivity.

-§-
The Yoni Mudra facilitates the release of the unconscious mind, so that what has been suppressed is allowed to surface into awareness.
-§-

Follow your currents of energy for some time, connecting to your energy until it feels steady, then lower your hands to your four pelvic bones (the two iliac bones at the outer upper pelvis, and the two pubic bones at the lower center) with a moderate pressure to receive the rejuvenated energy and store it into your pelvic bones and cavity. The optimal time for this practice is at the beginning or end of your day, just upon awakening or getting into bed. It can be done seated in bed or lying down. The morning practice will charge you up for an active day, and the evening practice will help you dive into a deeper state of rest to rejuvenate you more thoroughly. It is especially beneficial at night if you have had fatigue or difficulty getting continuous, nurturing sleep. As you persist with the Yoni Mudra

you can release the unconscious mind, so that what has been suppressed is allowed to surface into awareness. When the underlying pranic energy that creates healthy emotional and sensual expression is freed, your heart will naturally open. Often what happens over time is a transformation of the heart into an organ of sensate intelligence that literally *makes love.*

-§-
A male tantrik realizes that his partner is the doorway to a higher level of presence.
-§-

While with our partner, it is natural for us to move toward spontaneous love like that we thrived on as infants. Holding each other in the tantrik embrace called *yab-yum,* wherein one partners sits atop the other "Indian style," we discover the energetic goodness of both our partner's heart and our own. This exchange, in turn, allows subtle body pathways to open beyond the level of emotions, generating spiritual experience—direct contact with pure consciousness and bliss.

Partners exchange energies, making experiences available that neither can attain alone.

Emotional releases naturally arise when a man or a woman feels safe enough to be vulnerable. Therefore, safety and trust are essential cornerstones of any tantrik relationship. And yet, the release of suppressed emotions, or those overly expressed, can lead to the non-acceptance of these energies. As a result, one may not know how to act appropriately when feelings of sexuality, love, and spirituality emerge. With sustained discretion, we can find our true spiritual place in life with our tantrik partners. Deep tantra requires that we practice discernment, and focus attention on the development of love rather than self-centered hedonism, or suppression of natural function.

Communion with Your Partner

Ideal partners are grounded in their individual spiritual practices, and committed to the intention of tantrik practice as a process of spiritual transformation. Before proceeding with deep tantra practice, be sure that you both agree to encourage all energetic responses (including sexual energy) as long as they naturally arise. This ensures that the practice is experienced not only as sexual, but also as a sacred energetic ritual that connects you to the divine in a personal way. As the energy increases for both partners, it will quite naturally create *kriyas,* spontaneous movements and energy rushes. When your partner is having these, do not stimulate them, but rather keep your hands and body motionless to allow them to process the release into a spiritual opening. In this way your partner will be more likely to retain the elevated levels of *Shakti*—or pure energy.

On a practical note, the feminine partner, or *devi* as she is called in tantra, is encouraged to slow down and receive pleasure. Otherwise, she may quickly over-stimulate her masculine partner to the "point of no return." Once an untrained man has ejaculated, his energy will drop immediately—which is likely to spell the end of communion. A man can prolong the communion by letting his partner know if he is feeling close to that point. This is true both for preparatory practice with clothes on and intimate communion without clothes.

The secret men need to master for deep tantra is *karezza*—prolonged intercourse. From a tantrik perspective, it is far better to postpone ejaculation until the woman is completely satiated and filled with her devi energy, Shakti. Then, and only then, can her masculine tantrik partner do as he wishes. When the masculine partner keeps his attention on what brings pleasure and ecstasy to the woman, it will increase the energy level for both.

From this, the man learns to manifest more of his dispassion (Shiva-nature) through patience and persistence, as his devi becomes transformed into a living presence of Shakti. Both need to learn to be with the energy and with themselves. It is enough to stay steady in the Self. This practice needs to be free of time constraints. The more adept you are at being with the Prana Shakti, the more it will guide you to experiences beyond what can be described in words. And so, surrender to that One.

An important reminder for the masculine partner is to focus on maintaining a powerful role of protecting the feminine partner from any overpowering emotions, and providing for her comfort so that joy and Spirit will arise naturally and effortlessly. A male tantrik will do anything that will increase his partner's passion, as he realizes that she

is the doorway to a higher level of presence. She is perceived as Yoni Devi, "the Source of light," and she in turn sees him as a reflection of her own constant True Self. Devi is the source of pleasure. The role for a tantrik woman is to increase her energy level and be rejuvenated by her communion practice. This will naturally increase her femininity as it heightens her innate nurturing nature.

In tantrik yoga we say that the highest place in the body is not the head or the crown chakra, but the secret third dimension of the heart. Not the physical heart, nor the heart chakra, but what is called the spiritual heart; it is a secret "cave within the heart of hearts." To find this place of union with God/dess, one needs to understand the essence of tantrik yoga training. *Vasistha's Yoga,* (tr. Swami Venkatesananda), one of the most detailed yogic texts, provides guidelines for spiritual illumination. In this text, the sage Vasistha clarifies the mindfulness necessary for communion:

> When the mind does not crave for pleasure it is absorbed into the Self, along with the life force of prana. If the mind remains absorbed even for a quarter of an hour it undergoes a complete change, for it tastes the supreme state of self-knowledge and will not abandon it. Even if the mind tasted it for a second, it does not return to this worldly state. The very seeds of the illusion of the world and the cycle of birth and death are fried. With them, ignorance is dispelled and the unstable mind is utterly pacified; one who has reached this is rooted in truth. He beholds the inner life and rests in supreme peace.

The mind loves to embrace ideas and because of this is constantly active, searching for satiation. It will never be content without finding the True Self. Similarly, a lover seeks this state of absorption in the embrace of another, knowing and trusting that when the Beloved is found, the embrace will reveal the goal of his or her spiritual love quest. So, we continue to embrace others until we find that One. The true consort is the one with whom this quest for the True Self can be shared. Both support each other in their quests, selflessly seeking what is as naturally arising as the prolonged love embrace of their consort.

-§-
It is the dispassionate mind that will generate compassion and spiritual love.
-§-

The process of seeking your spiritual energy and letting it guide you to the place of communion is now to be shared in the most intimate fashion with your partner. When you or your partner fully express negative emotions such as guilt, fear, or self-doubt, it is crucial for mental and emotional wellbeing to be held in a very harmonious place. When embracing your emoting partner with tenderness and loving affection, disregard your own emotional reactions. It is the dispassionate mind that will generate true compassionate love that is healing, nurturing, and transforming for both of you. Being in the energy of transformation is what tantra is all about. This unconditional love is the essence of tantrik communion practice.

Sadhana is the yogic term for daily physical, energetic, and spiritual practice. When practice enters the context of lovemaking, this loving sadhana enhances the currents of your life force to such a powerful level that whatever feelings of guilt, fear, or hurt present themselves will be transformed by the greater waves of unconditional love. Fear is considered a *vata* imbalance in Ayurveda, and when surrendered and elevated, it becomes serenity. If the tantrik couple persists, whatever started as a negative thought or emotion will become supreme peace. With the blessing of a committed, motivated partnership, the two of you can surrender to this elevated energy, trusting that it knows its way to the spiritual heart regardless of the complexity of the journey through all the "subtle bodies." This turns lovemaking into a rejuvenating, uplifting, and heart-expanding process.

The Tibetan tantrik tradition is full of stories about masters who had consorts assist them in the final production of co-emergent bliss and the wisdom of enlightenment. Wherever the master finds his consort, his great bliss awakens her natural insight. Saraha, after a long tenure at Nalanda University, took an arrow-smith's daughter as his consort, and said, *"Only now am I a truly pure being."* (*The Divine Madman – The Sublime Life and Songs of Drukpa Kunley,* tr. Keith Dowman). We see the divine play between the lovers in this excerpt:

> The madman Drukpa Kunley encountered the demons of Bhutan, and like his predecessor Padmasambhava, rid the country of them. One Demoness had the capacity to change forms and she became a beautiful and seductive woman seeking his assistance. She said "I beg you to lead me to a blissful release. Am I not a celestial ornament? Above my waist my form is entrancing while below my waist in my Mandala of Bliss. My muscles are strong, and my up thrust is skillful—I offer you my art in milking! For you who delight in love-making, and I a serpent with fervent lust, this meeting today offers great joy. Please stay with me here and I'll offer you my body in devotion, I beg you to grant me your godly favor!" Then she promised to serve the tantrik spiritual tradition thereafter and vowed never to harm living beings. Finally to prepare her as a suitable candidate for instruction on higher spiritual union, he purified her through divine sexual play.

Looking deeper into this tradition, Tsultrim Allione, author of *Women of Wisdom,* writes:

> The Tibetans recognize the importance of sexual yoga in opening up further fields of awareness and insight, and in bestowing the blessing of long life on the tantrika. Besides the sexual contact, living with a Wisdom Dakini consort brings intuitive insights in daily life situations… It should be noted that this contact with a consort does not come at the beginning of the training when the passions are still out of control and distraction is rampant. Rather, the taking of a consort is suggested as one of the final measures for complete enlightenment. Emotions are very powerful, and unless we can truly use them for further depth of awareness, intimate relationships can become an insurmountable obstacle instead of a boon to the practitioner... All tantrikas must be tuned into the energy of their own bodies and that of the world around them. This means they must have a positive relationship to the Dakini, who is energy in all of its forms. She acts as a spiritual midwife helping the tantrika to give birth to the wisdom, which she embodies by cutting through conceptualization and working directly with the life force.

God/dess Consciousness

From where does spiritual wisdom arise? The classical yogic and tantrik texts agree that it arises from three factors: persistent personal discipline, scriptural knowledge as expressed in living teachers, and devotion to Spirit. These three factors all rest on meditation as the foundational practice. tantrik meditation consists of stilling the mind, emotions, and life force (prana), and detaching yourself from the tendency to identify with and react to your thoughts and feelings. Just feel your feelings and know that they are there; they are not you. To raise the efficiency of spiritual practice, dedicate your actions to be of service to others, as manifestations of the One Being. One who is given over to this selfless service attains that path in a gradual way; for, by seeking to be of service to others, your life force is gradually given over to thoughts of others first, and considerations for yourself second. When one fully gives him- or herself to the Divine Presence, no thoughts of *what comes for me?* remain. All is done as a force of nature expressing service to itself. Finding the path of your unique service—whatever it is—will increase your life force.

-§-
Finding the path of your unique service to others will increase your life force.
-§-

The original yogic text is the *Yoga Sutras of Patanjali,* my interpretation of which is available on my website. In chapter 1, sutra 23 states: "The end of spiritual practice is only attained by placing yourself in the Lord (Isvara)." This frank command means that devotion is the only path for those who seek the highest illumination. For them, the primary attainment is devotional surrender to the One Being. The highest practice is constant submission. My last teacher recommended that attitudes of gratefulness and gratitude be given priority. He showed me that by cultivating these attitudes, I could attain true humility. Although spiritual experiences may come uninvited, it requires many years to perfect the process of illumination that comes with these gifts. In the meantime, here is some practical advice from *Vasistha's Yoga*:

> The Lord should be worshipped with everything that is obtained without effort. One should never make the least effort to attain that which one does not possess. The Lord should be worshipped by means of all the enjoyments that the body enjoys, through eating, drinking, being with one's consort, and other such pleasures. The Lord should be worshipped with the illnesses one experiences and with every sort of unhappiness or suffering one experiences… The realization of this infinite consciousness (which is totally effortless) is alone the best form of worship.

Regardless of whether situations are pleasant or unpleasant, the divine consciousness shines within them all. How do we find that One? The *Yoga Sutras 1,* 12 state that success in all of the paths to yoga is attained by consistent, earnest practice over a long period of time, coupled with dispassionate nonattachment from the result of that practice. Effort and surrender are the keys to knowing that One.

Paul Brunton was a central figure in bringing to light the messages of the spiritual masters of India. His first book, published in 1934 and still in print, is entitled *A Search in Secret India.* Brunton wandered the length and breadth of India, searching for an illumined master. His search led him to the twentieth century's greatest sage, Ramana Maharshi. The book *Day by Day with Bhagavan,* by Devaraja Mudaliar, quotes Paul Brunton as saying, "Divine Grace descends and acts only when it is invoked by total self-surrender. It acts from within, because God resides in the heart of all beings. Its whisper can be heard only in a mind purified by self surrender and prayer."

One of the most dramatically effective prayers I have found is used to reinforce the third step of the Twelve Step program for overcoming self centeredness and addictive behaviors:

> *Divine Mother* [or God/dess of my understanding], *I offer myself unto you – to build with me and to do with me as you will. Release me from the bondage of self, that I may better do your will. Take away my difficulties, that victory over them will bear witness*

to those I would help of your Power, your Love and your Way of life. May I do your will always! —from *The Big Book*

I begin my morning sadhana by lying flat on my belly facing my altar, which is covered with relics from my teachers. In that submissive position I say this prayer three times, or until I feel taken over by that One who is the object of my prayer. The Presence comes in Her time and Her way, though She comes consistently to me and to all who seek Her. There is nothing that She cannot create or destroy. Nothing is impossible for Her. All prosperity and all adversity, all ages of the lifespan, all happiness and suffering—all these are nothing but the play of God/dess as pure consciousness. Seeing this, fear and illusion dissolve and peace begins to arise naturally and spontaneously of their own accord. Resting in your own relaxed self is the most natural act. Being that One, one knows the purity of the True Self.

Remember that when sexual or emotional energy is allowed to build, it will naturally become neutral energy. And, if you persist, the lower self—the emotional energies and energies of self-centeredness—is transformed into the qualities of your True Self.

What more grounded way can there be to come to love the world than through your capacity to unconditionally love your most intimate partner? When you open yourself to the sensations that are Love, allow those sensations to be felt as Shakti leading you into a loving, contemplative state with stillness, your innate Shiva. The following sutras are from what are considered to be the highest teachings of Tantra—from a non-dual tradition that later blossomed into Kashmir Shaivism. There are 112 meditations in the *Vijnana Bhairava Tantra* that deepen the intimate expression of yoga as communion with the True Self. Out of these, however, only three are born out of communion with your tantrik consort. Here are adaptations of those verses from versions found in *Zen Flesh, Zen Bones* by Paul Reps and Nyogen Senzaki, and *Yoga Spandakarika,* by Daniel Odier:

> 43. At the beginning of sexual passion, be in the fire, absorbed into her by the flames of passion. Allow the burning, persisting with the nectar of intimacy, then merge into Spirit.
>
> 44. When, in such an embrace, your senses are shaken as leaves in the wind, enter this shaking as you merge with the celestial bliss of ecstatic love.
>
> 45. O Goddess! Even from remembering the intimate bliss of sexual communion, without Shakti's embrace, the radiant pleasures of kissing, hugging, and embracing again swell into a flood of delight.

Part Three

Loving the Broken Pieces

Yes, we will melt back into the stars
but first, let us moisten the ground with our tears.
~Blake More

Parts of me see and hear quite clearly,
While other parts are stone deaf and blind.
~Geralyn Gendreau

Harriet Lerner:

12

Love Can Make You Stupid

A friend confessed to me recently that she wasted a full hour before her date arrived with the inane activity of arranging and rearranging the magazines on her coffee table to make just the right impression. Then she camped out by the front window awaiting his approach, so that she could dash to the CD player to ensure that a particular song would be playing as she opened the door. Later they went to a movie that she found so offensive that she could hardly stay in her seat, but when he left the theater raving about it, she didn't share an honest response.

We can act like this in the beginning, but we can't sustain it for too long if the relationship is to move forward. Over time, we must move in the direction of greater authenticity, especially when we feel the relationship is significant and we want it to endure. The more intimate the relationship, the greater both the possibility and the longing to share ourselves—and the bigger the emotional consequences of not telling, of not being real, of not bringing our full self and true voice into it.

After all, if a potential partner doesn't want to stick around after a well-meaning revelation that we had an abortion, a mastectomy, two previous marriages, or a recent Nobel Prize nomination, we're better off without that person. We may also be better off without him if he doesn't especially like hearing our exuberance, expansiveness, and

Harriet Lerner, Ph.D., is best known for her work on the psychology of women and family relationships. She has dedicated her writing life to translating complex theory into accessible and useful prose, and has become one of our nation's most trusted and respected relationship experts. She is the author of many books, including a feminist revision of psychoanalytic theory and practice, entitled *Women in Therapy* (Harper, 1989), *The Dance of Anger* (HarperCollins, 1985), *The Dance of Intimacy* (HarperCollins, 1989), *The Dance of Connection* (HarperCollins, 2001), and her latest book, *The Dance of Fear* (HarperCollins, 2004). Learn more at www.harrietlerner.com.

ambitions, or if she shuts down when we voice our insecurities, fears, or a painful story from the past. Likewise, the other person has a right to know us accurately, to consider the relationship and make plans for the future based on facts, not fantasies or projections. Intimacy—and our judgment about the relationship—suffers in the shadow of silence and pretending, which does not allow us to know the other person or to be fully known.

-§-
The more intimate the relationship, the bigger the emotional consequences of not being real.
-§-

We've seen how some kinds of pretending can be brave and enhancing, but that's not the sort of pretending I was raised on. When I was growing up in the 1950s, before modern feminism, we were taught to "play dumb," let the man win, pretend he's boss, and listen wide-eyed to his ideas, no matter how boring, gracefully adding a footnote from time to time. Anything to get and keep a man. Grown women behaved like female impersonators, to use Gloria Steinem's wonderful phrase.

Today we're bombarded with messages everywhere encouraging us to speak authentically and truly. Columnist Ellen Goodman has a friend who wisely encourages each of her three little girls to "Speak up, speak up, speak up," with the frank explanation, "the only person you'll scare off is your future ex-husband!" That's a fairly radical lesson—that having a man shouldn't occur at the expense of having a self. But despite lots of good advice out there, love and romance do not tend to foster the expression of a clear and strong voice. As my friend, the cartoonist Jennifer Bern, notes, pairing up is more likely to reduce the "judgment lobe" of our brain to the size of a pinto bean.

Falling In Love Tells Us Nothing

Falling in love tells us absolutely nothing about whether a particular relationship is healthy or good for us. Steamy starts are compelling, but intense emotions can block our objectivity and blur our capacity for clear thinking and clear speaking.

A friend, Amy, fell in love with a woman at a weekend workshop on gay activism, and she's already reorganizing her whole life to be with her. Amy has known this person for only three weeks, yet she's planning to give away her beloved cat because of her new girlfriend's allergies. Amy's friends are skeptical and want her to slow down, but she's convinced she's found true love.

And maybe she has. Love means something different to every person who feels it, and it has no God-given definition. After all, if Amy feels in love, well, then she's in love—no matter what anyone tells her. Some people do experience a profound and immediate connection to another person that proves to be enduring. But intense feelings, no matter how consuming, are hardly a measure of true and enduring closeness. Intensity and intimacy are not the same thing, although many people confuse the two.

It doesn't matter whether Amy calls it *love* or *sauerkraut.* The most important question is not the intensity of the love we feel, but whether the relationship is good for us and whether we are navigating our part of it in a solid way. Time and conversation help to size this up. Is there a sense of safety, ease, and comfort in the relationship that makes authenticity and self-disclosure possible? Does the person we love enlarge (rather than diminish) our sense of our self and our capacity to speak our own truths? Is the connection based on mutuality; including mutual respect, mutual empathy, mutual nurturance and caretaking? Are we able to voice our differences to bring conflict out in the open and resolve it?

Only when we stay in a relationship over time and evaluate it with both our head and our heart can we begin to put it to the test. This involves lots of talking so that hot spots—whatever they may be—can be spoken to openly. Discussing differences up front is no guarantee against future problems, but it can help both partners assess their ability to negotiate, consider each other's feelings, and compromise when appropriate. Dealing with differences will put the clarity of your voice—and your capacity to listen to the different voice of the other—to the test.

The Dilemma of Differences

While listening to National Public Radio on the way to work one day, I happened to catch the tail end of a truly chilling interview with a white supremacist. I told myself that he too was one of God's children, and that he surely possessed some good qualities along with his very bad ones. I reminded myself that he was once a cute little baby boy, and that he didn't nurse at his mother's breast or roll down the street in his little stroller plotting how to keep America pure and white. I pictured him giving a great big smile to the nice African-American or Jewish woman who stopped to coo at him, just as he smiled at the nice, white Christian lady. But something happened to this poor little guy along the way to growing up.

-§-
Intimacy suffers in the shadow of silence and pretending.
-§-

Something happens to almost all of us, although, thank goodness, not to the extreme of preaching hate. Humans don't tend to do well with differences. We learn to hate a difference, glorify a difference, exaggerate a difference, deny, minimize, or eradicate a difference. We may engage in nonproductive efforts to change, fix, or shape up the person who isn't doing or seeing things our way. In the history of nations, families, or couples, folks find it hard to discuss their differences in a mature and thoughtful way.

Reassuring Sameness

Of course, there's something to be said for huddling together with folks who are just like us. It's easy to voice your thoughts and feelings to someone who already agrees with your every word and is going to nod vigorously with approval as you speak. Tempers are less likely to flare when two people think, react, believe, and vote exactly the same way.

-§-

Falling in love tells us absolutely nothing about whether a particular relationship is healthy or good for us.

-§-

In contrast, differences—even minor ones—can drive a wedge between people. But like it or not, differences will inevitably emerge in any close relationship, and thank goodness for that. What could be more boring than hanging around with folks exactly like ourselves? Differences don't just threaten and divide us. They also inform, enrich, and enliven us. Indeed, differences are the only way we learn. If our intimate relationships were composed only of people identical to ourselves, our personal growth would come to an abrupt halt.

Getting Past the Velcro Stage of Intimacy

In the early stages of a relationship, partners tend to overlook, excuse, or submerge their differences, or they're taken by the novelty and find the differences exciting or appealing. If you just happen to be in the Velcro stage of a romantic relationship, you're probably in a trance. As a French proverb tells us, "All beginnings are lovely."

When you're overly eager for a relationship to work, you will resist getting differences out in the open, looking them straight in the eye, and having a good fight when necessary. Instead, you may ride the relationship like a two-person bicycle that will topple over if there's not perfect agreement and togetherness. The urge to merge is very strong, and if you're in the grip of it, you'll submerge the clarity of your voice in order to preserve a positive picture of the other person and the relationship.

Intimate beginnings pull for a pseudo-harmonious togetherness. That said, I encourage you to resist that pull and to be as clear-eyed and awake as possible. Do as much talking and listening as you can before you entwine your emotional and financial futures. You can't choose your kids, parents, or relatives, but you can choose your partner, preferably after a courtship (to use an old-fashioned word) that allows you to enlarge and deepen the conversation.

Intimacy usually develops among people who share deeply held belief and core values. But closeness should not be confused with sameness, and relationships go best when we get past glorying or devaluing differences and face them with curiosity and respect. Dealing with differences is the perfect training ground for making choices about how we speak and how we listen. A relationship built on silence, on the shedding, or suppression of differences, doesn't have a strong foundation. Nor does it help for two people to get polarized around differences and divide into opposing camps.

When Friends Become Roommates

Close friends tend to voice differences and negotiate solutions more easily than partners or mates. After all, friends can retreat to separate spheres and adopt a "live and let live" attitude. Also, friendship rarely becomes a nest of extreme pathology; if we consistently feel diminished, silenced, or unheard, we don't just dream of escape—we get out.

Once under the same roof with a partner—hearts, finances, and futures intertwined—it's harder to clarify where we can compromise, give in, and go along—and where we can't. So let's start with friendship for a model of how to speak to differences and negotiate them.

-§-
Intensity and intimacy are not the same thing.
-§-

An incident with my longtime friend, Judy Margulis, comes to mind. As college freshmen, Judy and I lived in the same dorm (actually, a big old house) when we both arrived in Madison, Wisconsin. Judy was neat and orderly, while I was messy. This difference wasn't a problem until I asked Judy to room with me the following year.

You won't be surprised to learn that Judy's neatness didn't pose a problem for me. I would never have taken offense even if she wanted to spend all her spare time tidying up after me. But my habits did pose a problem for her, which, you may have noticed, is how this particular difference generally works out. I've yet to hear the messy person complain, "I'm so upset! I throw my clothes on the floor, and when I come home that inconsiderate partner of mine has picked them up, folded them, and put them neatly away!" Nope. Instead, it's the neat person who tends to get grumpy and irritable.

Actually, that's not true 100 percent of the time. My friend Marcia was not pleased when her college roommate rearranged her books by size and color. Similarly, many of us would feel outraged if a partner tidied up our out-of-control study or work space without our permission. There's the matter of privacy, personal space, and our right to have others stay out of what we take to be "ours." That said, I've been a therapist long enough to know that it's usually the person who messes up the shared space who is viewed as the problem.

-§-

If you just happen to be in the Velcro stage of a romantic relationship, you're probably in a trance.

-§-

Judy handled her dilemma about rooming with me in an exemplary way. She told me that she'd room with me only if I would agree to keep the room neat on a daily basis. She didn't ask me to sign a written contract, but she was that clear. She wasn't just sharing her thoughts and feelings. She really meant it. I negotiated one loophole, which was that I could throw stuff on my bed if I kept everything else neat. Judy agreed, and we remained together happily the following year.

Judy just naturally followed all the rules of good communication. She didn't criticize me or put me down. She didn't imply that her neatness was a virtue (although she may well have believed that) or that my disorganization was a sign of personal failure. She didn't talk about our differences in terms of good or bad, right or wrong, or better or worse. She appeared uninvested in changing or fixing me, nor did she take it personally that my belongings usually landed first on the floor. She simply clarified that she wouldn't live in a messy room, and she let me know specifically what she needed from me in order for us to be roommates.

Part of the reason Judy was able to express herself so clearly, is that it was a low-pressure situation. If we hadn't been able to come to an agreement, we'd have remained friends but we would not have shared a room. Let's look at this same challenge for an intimate couple where the stakes are higher and the emotional field more intense.

I'm Neat, He's a Slob

Mona sought my advice because she was "a total neatness freak" and her boyfriend, Dan, was an incredible slob. She was the sort of person who lined up her shoes in a perfect row and never went to bed with even one dirty spoon in the sink. In contrast, Dan messed up every room he walked into and failed to notice that anything needed to be picked up. Mona put the problem this way: "We're discussing marriage, and he says he can't change. It doesn't make sense to leave him over this one issue, but I'll go nuts if we're living in the same apartment and I'm always picking up after him." She wanted my advice and was curious about what I'd do and say in her situation. Of course, both Mona and Dan might benefit by becoming more like each other. It would be great if she could loosen up and become less of a "neatness freak," and if Dan could do a better job of picking up after himself. After all, two mature, kind-hearted friends, forced to share a common space, would likely accommodate each other. Why should two people who presumably love each other do any less? Unfortunately, the challenge of intimacy tends not to evoke our most mature selves. Instead, she anxiously pursues him to change, and he stubbornly digs in his heels in response to her efforts to change him. So nothing changes at all.

What To Do?

What can Mona do? First, she needs to be clear about who owns the problem. Dan is as happy as a lark with his customary ways and can easily ignore Mona's neatness. Mona, for her part, is upset by his behavior. Quite simply, she has the problem, which isn't to imply that she's wrong, to blame, or at fault in any way. Mona needs to resolve her current dilemma herself, because no one else will do this for her.

Mona needs to keep talking to Dan about her problem ("I'm a neatness freak") without acting like it's her job to change him. It will help matters if she can avoid the usual communication stoppers, such as criticizing, lecturing, admonishing, threatening, analyzing, and blaming. She can stick to "I-language" (non-blaming statements about the self) as she tells Dan what she's feeling and what she wants from him. For example, "Dan, I need to tell you something about myself. I'm a neatness freak. I get really anxious when things around me get out of order. I can't handle it. My nervous system starts twitching. If we're going to live together, we have to make a plan, or I'll go nuts."

-§-

Close friends tend to voice differences and negotiate solutions more easily than partners or mates.

-§-

Making a relationship work obviously requires good humor, generosity, a tolerance for differences, and a willingness for give-and-take. Slobs deserve a room of their own (or a corner or a big armchair, depending on what space permits) where they can dump stuff in a big heap. Every neatness freak deserves to have some rules about public space. There is always room to negotiate in a relationship—and if there isn't, we need to reconsider the relationship.

But what's at stake here is much more than the level of tidiness in Mona and Dan's apartment, should they share one. The real issue is how they can talk about their differences, how well they can hear each other, and how committed they are to finding a solution they both can live with. The worst-case scenario is that they'll each dig in their heels and get stuck in an endless cycle of fighting, complaining, and blaming. The best-case scenario is that they'll both be flexible, creative, fair, and sincere in their attempts to consider each other's feelings and hear each other's voices. If they limber up their brains, they'll find a way to resolve the problem—unless it runs much deeper than the issue at hand.

What would I do in Mona's situation? I wouldn't break off a relationship because my boyfriend was a slob. But I would end it if I felt that the other person didn't consider my feelings, refused to change behavior that was obviously painful to me, and pleaded helplessness ("I can't change") in response to reasonable and fair expectations. I'd also take a good hard look at how my own communication (like nagging or being critical) might be contributing to the problem. I wouldn't pick up after him unless I could do it quickly and without resentment, say, sweeping through the house and dumping all his stuff on his one big armchair. Maybe I wouldn't clean as often or as thoroughly as I used to. I'd also be happy to make a deal. For example, I'd do double duty on cleanup, and he'd do a double shift of shopping and cooking. Couples do best when they can lighten up and accommodate each other.

Mona is smart to be struggling with this particular issue sooner rather than later. Marriage (a subject we'll get to later) tends to make it more difficult for two people to really hear each other and negotiate their differences. Gloria Steinem once urged an audience to do one outrageous act a day, and she suggested as a start that women say to the man they live with, "Pick it up yourself." Someone in the audience agreed that was a fine idea, but how do you make him do it? A small, elderly lady in the back of the large hall caught Steinem's attention and spoke out. "I nail his underwear to the floor," she said. "Nail as long as you need to!" advised a second woman, "and then get the floor done over." Of course, our voice is arguably a preferable tool to a hammer for driving a point home, but some people take drastic measures when they don't feel heard.

-§-

The challenge of intimacy tends not to evoke our most mature selves.

-§-

For some of us this particular issue ("I'm neat, he's a slob") would be a minor one, along the lines of "I like vanilla ice cream, and he likes strawberry sorbet." But for Mona, it was right up there with the big ones—he wants children and I don't, or I love sex but he's not interested. For this reason, Mona should take all the time she needs to see if she and Dan can find a solution they both can live with comfortably. She shouldn't give up her own living space until she's clear about where Dan stands and what's acceptable to her.

-§-
Couples do best when they can lighten up and accommodate each other.
-§-

Maybe Dan will decide to neaten up, at least to some extent, although clearly he'll never meet Mona's standards. Or, alternatively, Mona may decide that she's going to find a way to live with Dan's messiness, because Dan is flexible and fair on other important matters. They may try living together to see how it goes, or they may decide to marry and keep separate places. But if Dan is clear—whether through his words or his behavior—that this aspect of his behavior won't change, Mona should clarify to herself, and then with Dan, what she can and can't accommodate. She should not decide to marry him and then complain about it.

We need to know what we're looking for in a partner, and we should never believe that our love (or nagging) has the power to create something that wasn't there to begin with. Nor should we ever marry for love alone. We need to examine our core values and beliefs (what really matters to us in a partner), so that we know where we can compromise and where we can't.

How we each compromise is a deeply personal matter. No one else can know whether you should disqualify a potential partner because he or she lacks something important to you: money, good looks, reliability, humor, personal hygiene, an erotic imagination, warmth, a love for the outdoors, or tidy personal habits. Such decisions ("Is she the one?" "Am I compromising too much?") can be excruciatingly difficult to make, but no one else can do this work for us. The clarity of our voice rests on the clarity of our self-awareness regarding what we want and feel entitled to, and what we are willing to settle for. It can take time, patience, conversation, and silent meditation or reflection to sort this out.

What Are You Looking For?

Most of us think we're clear about what we want in a mate. While individual tastes vary, we want a partner who is mature and intelligent, loyal and trustworthy, loving and attentive, sensitive and open, kind and nurturing, competent and responsible. I've yet to meet a woman who says, "Well, to be honest, I'm hoping to find an irresponsible, distant, ill-tempered sort of guy who sulks a lot and won't pick

up after himself." Or, "Hey, can you fix me up with that cute friend of yours—you know, the one who is totally self-absorbed and conversationally impaired."

And yet few of us really evaluate a prospective partner with the same objectivity and clarity that we might use to select a major purchase. We wouldn't buy a used car off the lot just because it looked great and felt really comfortable to drive. We'd check out its history and ask for the facts, with our radar out to detect dishonesty or hype. We might consult with a clear-thinking, car-savvy neighbor. And we'd enter the negotiation with a few criteria of our own that were deal-breakers—maybe air conditioning, good mileage, or safety features such as antilock brakes.

We need to be at least this careful in matters of the heart. In the name of love, we may lower our standards, silence our questions and concerns, and even abandon our friends for someone we probably shouldn't trust to water our plants when we leave town. We may keep sleeping with someone whose behavior is equivalent to waving a big red flag in our face.

Of course, in picking an intimate partner, we don't compile a list of key criteria and then proceed with the selection process in a totally intellectual fashion. But it's not a bad idea to consider this approach. Some women have found it helpful to jot down the top five traits, qualities, and behaviors that are important to them in a life partner ("financially stable, reliable and responsible, talks about problems, shares household responsibilities, likes my kid") and then to refer to their list in evaluating the relationship in question.

-§-
We should never believe that our love (or nagging) has the power to create something that wasn't there to begin with.
-§-

We need to keep reaching for the facts through conversation and observation. It's data if your boyfriend won't visit your family or if he tells you that all his previous girlfriends and ex-wives were big losers. It's data if you stop voicing your wants, expectations, and questions because you're afraid to put him to the test. No one fact or combination of facts should make us reject someone if we have a really good feeling about that person and what's happening between us. But we need to keep moving in the direction of becoming more real ourselves and more objective about our partner.

The Voice of the Body

Words aren't the only ways we get information about each other. Talking is essential, along with observing whether the other person's talk is backed up by responsible action. But we also learn a lot about another person through the full range of our senses. Choosing an intimate partner is not a purely intellectual matter but also a task of the heart, which goes beyond language to involve feelings, desire, chemistry, and intuition.

-§-
Few of us really evaluate a prospective partner with the same objectivity and clarity that we might use to select a major purchase.
-§-

In truth, we come to truly know the other not only through words but through an intuitive understanding or "reading" that comes through the body. We know, through our bodies, whether a particular interaction leaves us feeling energized, uplifted, and inspired—or the opposite. We know, through our bodies, whom to trust, or believe, or avoid. What we call intuition and "gut reactions" is shorthand for the extraordinary human capacity to process information about another person that is beyond words.

Recently I sat for twenty minutes at a bus terminal in Providence, Rhode Island, and watched a small group of young men and women communicating in American Sign Language. I found one of these guys so appealing that I wanted to kidnap him and take him home to Kansas to be my friend. Okay, maybe he was a bigot who was telling his friends how upset he was at the prospect of the government banning his assault rifles, but I doubt it. Nor was I responding to anything as obvious as body language, good looks, poise, or grace. We are constantly taking in nonverbal information about people that we sense automatically and effortlessly.

If a person's words tell me one thing ("I'm feeling close to you") but my automatic knowing intuits something different (I sense distance, disconnection, a "not-thereness"), I put more trust in what I feel than in the words I hear. I know when another person is distracted, even when that person claims to be paying attention. I make automatic judgments about who is kind, trustworthy, and forthcoming and who is not. Of course, we all make mistakes (we think the other person is standoffish when actually she's shy), but it's interesting to think about how automatically we can get a sense of the other person that doesn't rely on the content of what is said. To read other people with some accuracy we need to feel comfortable, safe, and relaxed in their presence—and to trust our gut when we don't.

The most important voice we need to trust in a relationship is our own. We need to trust ourselves to perceive and process important information. We need to use a clear, strong voice to bring our knowledge of the relationship into sharper focus and test out what's possible, rather than comfort ourselves with fantasies about how our partner might change in the future. We need to speak up and insist on fair treatment and respect.

If we can't do all these things, it's difficult to fully trust the other person or the future of the relationship. If we do trust ourselves, we'll know in our gut that there are some behaviors we just won't tolerate and some places we just won't go—even if we do make an initial poor choice.

The challenge in all intimate relationships is to preserve both the "I" and the "we" without losing either when the going gets tough. If we're faced with a choice, we need to choose speech over silence, keep our behavior in line with our stated values and beliefs—and save ourselves first.

-§-
We need to keep reaching for the facts through conversation and observation.
-§-

I should add that we learn a great deal about a partner by observing him among both our friends and family and his. In contrast, you won't know him or her well, no matter how much you talk, if you insulate your relationship from other key relationships. So you need to do a lot of talking (and listening, observing, and thinking) in varied settings and situations to refine the process of knowing the other person and being known.

The Honeymoon Is Over

Marriage—or living under the same roof—often solves the problem of the Velcro stage—denying, excusing, or sentimentalizing differences. The next stage of the relationship finds two people angrily polarized around the differences they failed to notice or initially found appealing. They may dig in their heels with little flexibility to openly consider the other person's point of view and honor a reasonable request for a behavioral change, confusing angry exchanges with "being real" and having an authentic voice.

Whether you've been part of a couple for four—or forty—years, you will still have to face the challenge of differences. Long-term relationships suffer when we don't face differences with tolerance, humor, and respect. They also suffer if we become so tolerant of differences that we expect too little from the other person, or settle for unfair and compromising arrangements that erode our sense of self.

Judith Orloff: Dreaming Light into Black Emotions

13

You're never given more than you can handle. It may not seem that way at the time. But I believe it is true. Our higher power asks a lot of us. It used to get me mad. Some situations seemed too terrible to face. I'd protest, "I can't do it. I don't have it in me." But I did—and I had to see that. So must you. What your mind says and what your inner guidance relates may conflict. For that reason, look beyond the mirage of walls and detours. Don't be hoodwinked by how daunting they seem. My spiritual teacher says, "Heaven is not a dead-end road." I promise, there's always a path there. With intuition you will find it.

Listen to Your Dreams

I'm nine years old. My mother and I are sitting on the bench of our baby grand piano in the living room. A fire is blazing. She's teaching me to play Beethoven's "Moonlight Sonata." I follow her steady fingers, one by one, memorizing each note and chord. I'm entranced by how she smells, how she concentrates so intently. But somehow the music, in its wistful beauty, is taking her from me. I feel and see my mother—yet I have the horrible sense I'm losing her. As I play, as she listens to me, an icy panic wells up in my chest. I fight back tears, determined to complete the piece.

Judith Orloff, M.D., is a board-certified psychiatrist and assistant professor of psychiatry at UCLA. She is transforming the face of psychiatry with her assertion that we are keepers of an innate intuitive intelligence so perceptive that it can tell us how to heal, and prevent, illness. She has spoken at medical schools, hospitals, the American Psychiatric Association, Fortune Magazine's Most Powerful Women Summit, and alternative and traditional health forums. Her books include *Second Sight* (Warner Books, 1997), *Dr. Judith Orloff's Guide to Intuitive Healing* (Three Rivers Press, 2001), and *Positive Energy* (Harmony Books, 2004). Learn more at www.drjudithorloff.com.

For months after my mother died of cancer, I had this recurring dream, a mix of grief and childhood memory. I resisted writing the dream down or even thinking about it. I didn't want to remember those days when after school just the two of us would spend hours together at our piano. I didn't want to remember the way her eyes lit up as she taught me the music that so transported her. Especially our favorite, the "Moonlight Sonata." After my mother's death I could barely stand to hear it, afraid of loving her so much I might explode. Those first weeks I longed not to feel anything—and still this dream came. And came. The truth of it kept calling out. Finally, I let my guard down, allowed it to touch me. My dream was helping me understand that the music my mother and I shared (our relationship) continued beyond life into death. I felt she was urging me to let my guard down, allow feelings of loss to touch me—yet not intuitively lose touch with her. The dream, in its wisdom, burst open my sorrow so I could begin to heal.

Dreams are your path out of darkness, a built-in survival guide to life. From preventive premonitions to instructions on how to get through everything from depression to stress, dream messages are liberating. Not just because of their intuitive foresight or their uncanny capacity to cut to the bottom line, but because of their unerring, compassionate, personalized intent. In dreams you're in the spotlight. Paramount is your happiness, your healing, your peace of mind. When you are floundering or in the pits and a dream comes—as mine did—make the most of it. Or before you go to sleep, pose a question; invite dreams in. Unbeatable problem solvers, they can both warn of emotional tumult and lead you through rocky phases if they arrive.

-§-
Dreams are your path out of darkness, a built-in survival guide to life.
-§-

How can dreams convey trouble before the fact? The trick is to stay alert for your predictive symbols, which may be unique to you. I train my patients to look out for them. You can too. Watch what I mean. Jill, a workaholic architect, is prone to fits of rage that scare others. Before such a fit, Jill typically dreams she has forgotten to stock up on canned food for her sweet bulldog, Max, who ends up neglected and ravenously hungry. Translation: Jill is being told she's been ignoring her own needs for tenderness and self-care, which must be fed. If she listens, she often can avert the episode. If not, it comes in full force.

I'd like you to pin down your intuitive alarm signals. Be aware of recurring dream symbols that foresee distress—especially regression to an unsettling phase of life, being out of control, or abrupt loss of financial, emotional, or spiritual support. Here are some common themes:

- You're trapped in a house where you used to live with no way out.
- You lose your wallet and are stranded without credit cards or cash in a dangerous neighborhood.
- Your car is careening down a steep hill. You wildly pump your brakes, but they've given out.
- You ask for your familiar dream guides, but they don't come. You feel alone, lost.

We are creatures of habit: symbols foreshadowing difficulty tend to repeat themselves. Like clockwork, when problems loom, there they are. For example, every time my patient, Jack, a recovering heroin addict, has a "slip" dream in which he mainlines the drug, he tells me. In the past he didn't; he'd go out and use. Many recovering addicts and alcoholics have slip dreams, in which they see themselves using drugs or drinking again. These dreams are typically upsetting—always reminders of the tenaciousness of addiction and possible indications of relapse. They need to be analyzed and understood. Realizing the significance of a slip dream, Jack and I could work together to safeguard his sobriety.

The language of dream-intuition can save you. Stay aware. Know your vocabulary. Act quickly on messages you receive. Doing so buys you time. Get to the crux of what's off kilter before it has a chance to manifest. Whether adversity is better prepared for or entirely averted, you'll come out ahead.

What's marvelous about dreams is that you don't have to be on an even keel to query them. Your clarity while awake and your clarity while asleep can be radically different. No matter how down you feel in ordinary reality, in the dream realm all is well. It may be useful to think of human life with its turmoil as of the earth and dreams as of heaven. The good news is that information is constantly being channeled to us. Spiritual guidance for the material world. This is all the more reason to turn to dreams when we're at a low. Sometimes the process may feel like blind man's bluff—your eyes are masked, you have no idea of direction—yet invisible forces carry you. Indeed, some dreams can point to a positive outcome long before it seems possible. They give assurance in face of current troubles that specific solutions will be found. Our minds or emotions may be kerflooey, but our intuition, the stuff of which dreams are made, will save the day.

-§-
Pin down your intuitive alarm signals.
-§-

When in doubt you can always ask a dream, "How can I feel better?" That's a simple beginning. As usual, the posture is to put out your request, then await the response. Being sincere is the most you can "do." Attempts to force or actively visualize results will stymie intuitive flow. Try not to worry about whether an answer will come. Just go to sleep; see what happens. The next day write your dream down. Try this for a week. Whether you get a one-word answer or an elaborate rehabilitation plan, welcome what you're given and go with it.

My patient, Lois, had chronic depression. She wasn't much interested in anything. She'd get a little better, then she'd get a little worse. In therapy we didn't seem to sustain progress. Then I said, "Maybe your dreams know more than we do. Why don't you see what they have to add?" Lois was as half-hearted about dreaming as she was about everything else. But she did her best and consulted her dreams. The results surprised even me. One day she came into my office weeping. "In my dream I saw the face of a child," she reported. "She was lost. I know that girl. I know who she is." Then more tears—a breakthrough for some one so cut off. Puzzled, I asked, "Who is it?" "My daughter!" Lois exclaimed. "Daughter?" I wondered. Lois was single, nearly a recluse.

-§-
At times dreams are able to heal more than medical science can.
-§-

Here's where dream magic entered. Lois told me, "In 1962, at sixteen, I got pregnant. I felt so ashamed. My parents sent me away to have the baby; we put her up for adoption." A painful chapter closed, or so she thought. In Lois's dream it resurfaced like gangbusters, starting her on an amazing journey to locate her daughter. Through a combination of detective work and good luck, they reunited five years ago. Mother and daughter: that union anchored the axis of Lois's life. For so long there had been only depression, a vague, numbing fog. During a lifetime birth can happen more than once. Lois's dream had been the midwife for such change.

At times dreams are able to heal more than medical science can. They offer fresh air and open space. Whether your dream says, "Take a break from your girlfriend," or "Meditate an hour a day," or predicts, "Don't worry. Your depression will lift soon," I'd take the message seriously. It could be that you just wake up "knowing" you must nurture yourself more. Or that it's high time you deal with your anxiety. Accept this input at face value. The loveliness of dreams is that your relationship with them is continuing. They are a resource that forever grows.

Healing into wholeness is taking full advantage of approaches that best fit your needs. It requires a measure of logic and intuition, setting blinders and prejudices aside. If you're hurting and come to the situation intuitively open to the possibilities of what can help, healing will flow organically. If, however, you have a mind-set fixed in stone, never pausing to tune in to your intuition, you'll deprive yourself of the creative instincts nature has given you to surmount crises.

On this note I recently received an all-too-true e-mail from a friend that made me smile. I want to share it with you. Aptly, it is entitled "A Brief History of Medicine" (author unknown).

2000 BCE: Here, eat this root.

1000 CE: That root is heathen. Here, say this prayer.

1850 CE: That prayer is superstition. Here, drink this potion.

1940 CE: That potion is snake oil. Here, swallow this pill.

1985 CE: That pill is ineffective. Here, take this antibiotic.

2000 CE: That antibiotic is artificial. Here, eat this root.

Healing has come full circle over the centuries. What's in one year is out the next—then it's back again. Our task is to reconcile extremes, recognize every method with merit, treat the whole person. To understand your emotions, explore all that will contribute to your growth. There is no one way. Talking therapy, medication, meditation, herbs, homeopathy, energy healing, spirituality, dreams—a rich tapestry of alternatives that can elegantly interact. What matters is which one moves you. There is spirit to any path you choose. Remember to align with it.

Emotional wholeness has many variations. One scenario is that your depression or anxiety completely lifts. Another may entail living with some imperfections. This is a matter of courage; it doesn't represent defeat. A schizophrenic man at one of my workshops told me, "I still hear occasional voices, but they're more distant. I have a strong spiritual practice, meditate every day. It's allowed me to really reduce my medication." How incredible! This man doesn't sit home all day and worry about his voices. He gets out in life and lives it. The fact is that, despite your efforts, some discomfort may remain. You then have a choice. You can focus on the 90 percent of you that's better or the 10 percent that's off. If, for now, you can't get rid of every symptom, try amicably coexisting, a strategy different from just learning to "live with it." Your meditation then becomes harmonizing with your discomfort, no resistance, continually refocusing on your strength within.

-§-

Living with some imperfections doesn't represent defeat.

-§-

Some of us carry a deep-seated sorrow that is often misread as a deficit. I've had it as far back as I can remember, whether I'm happy or down, whether my life is going well or not. What I've come to understand about this sorrow is that it's neither depression nor what's commonly perceived as grief. In fact, it's a soul-quality—a form of empathy that allows us to penetrate people, attune to a collective sadness that longs to be quelled. Some sorrow, like fresh rain, purifies, expands the soul. Appreciating the positive qualities of what once seemed to me a negative emotion, I now trust it, believe it lends integrity to the intuitive process. If you identify, try to view such sorrow as a mystical linkup with the world, not as a trait to fear or eliminate. Many seers—including my own best teachers—have described a similar feeling. Allow it to teach you compassion and be of service to those in need.

A blessing of emerging from the dark is using what you've gained to help people. The schizophrenic man I mentioned earlier shows others with schizophrenia how to meditate, a pivotal aspect of his recovery he wants to share. Who could better address the spiritual nature of their experience than he? I also have a friend, a recovering alcoholic, who teaches meditation to men at a homeless shelter, many struggling with alcoholism. Every Wednesday at 6:00 A.M., in a rickety trailer in a parking lot, a group of men gather to tune in to themselves. Sacred time. Guidance involves both receiving and giving back. To think of it this way keeps the cycle of healing renewed.

Learning about darkness and light is our challenge as humans. The dynamic of this pairing is stunningly mirrored in the night sky. During workshops I have participants meditate on the interplay of starlight, the moon, and the vast backdrop of blackness. Why? To see how radiant it all is. Last summer, on a remote island in western Canada, conditions were ideal. In the midst of the spectacular Perseid meteor showers, I sent sixty-five people out in silence to experience them. My only instructions: "Take it in, all of it. And remember to make wishes, as many as you want." So there they went, some swimming in the bay, others snuggled in sleeping bags in the pine forest, watching shooting stars galore. Bursts of white light arcing across the sky. The next morning people said, "There were so many I used all my wishes up!" Can you imagine? No wishes left, everything in the heart spoken for! Don't forget—wishes in the dark have power. In trying periods remember to make them. Angels are dancing all around. You will be heard. In *The Inferno,* when the dark time is gone, the poet Dante writes of light as the ultimate victor:

E quindi uscimmo a rivider le stelle.

And so we came forth, and once again beheld the stars.

Adam Lehman:

Imperfect Perfection

Many of us do not love ourselves—not really. In our culture, self-love is confused with self-indulgence, with fulfilling the ego's desires, thus making "love thyself" taboo. Our lack of self-love has resulted in an epidemic of low self-esteem. Furthermore, without an established love of self, our ability to love others is based on a weak foundation. Consequently, rather than loving from a pure heart space, our pursuit of intimate and social relationships is rooted in avoidance—wanting not to fulfill our fear of being alone.

The pattern of low self-esteem, with a deep-seated fear of aloneness, is one I often see in clients, present in innumerable ways. A person might come to my office with symptoms ranging from back pain to serious disease states, digestive disorders to depression, or even non-symptomatic pursuit of personal growth. Yet during the assessment process, as we investigate what is blocking his or her innate healing ability, a lack of self-love and fear of being alone often show up as major causal issues.

The process of healing takes time and energy. As a result, healing takes a back seat when something requiring more urgent attention arises. Survival overrides healing, neurologically and energetically. *After all,* the body says, *what good is healing if you're dead?* Healing can be returned to when the threat has passed.

Adam Lehman is the co-founder and director of the Institute of Bioenergetic Arts and Sciences in Sonoma, California. As well as maintaining a private practice, Adam teaches programs and presents at conferences throughout the U.S. and internationally for people interested in becoming practitioners of Energy Kinesiology as a means of helping others heal and reach their full potential. He is the founder and president of the Energy Kinesiology Awareness Council (www.healthybodyenergy.com), dedicated to raising awareness of the benefits of muscle monitoring. His own website is www.kinesiohealth.com, and he can be contacted by e-mail at adam@kinesiohealth.com.

The main vehicle of the survival system is fear. When triggered, our subconscious response automatically gives that fear precedence, and other, "unnecessary" systems are shut down. The problem is, as social beings, our fear of aloneness—whether real or perceived—represents a constant threat to survival. The resulting continuous shutdown of non-survival systems leads to a broad range of chronic physical, emotional, and/or behavioral symptoms, disrupting both our health and relationships. The metaphysical body must adapt as well, as the chakras and other energy systems work to maintain a connection with the physical being, while still functioning as a conduit to the universal source.

The question becomes, *what drives our fear of aloneness when we live in community with so many others?* The answer is separation. This is largely a cultural problem. There are countless examples of indigenous, what we often refer to as "primitive," cultures that have a solid foundation of community, avoiding the self-esteem issues we find ourselves facing. However, in our culture, separation became a common message and has continued to be amplified in recent generations. A whole swath of baby boomers were subject to "modern" birthing practices—forceps being among the most invasive—then whisked away to a sterile room and allowed only minimal contact with the mother's warm body.

Even with a proper bonding experience, other social challenges reinforce the message of separation: dual-career parents depending on day care, racial and religious biases, abusive home environments, and so on. These relatively recent developments are contrary to the more natural, tribal instinct of nurturing. Now, overwhelmed by cultural "advances" and parabolic population growth, our loving/nurturing instinct has been replaced by the immediate perception of the need to survive, generated by often-unnecessary separation.

-§-
"Love Thy Neighbor As Thyself"
— Matthew 19:19
-§-

With separation beginning at birth or shortly thereafter, and reinforced throughout early life and beyond, we immediately face pain and grief at a time when our resources to deal with them are entirely undeveloped. With nowhere to turn and no means of seeing the big picture, we subconsciously blame ourselves for neglect and abuse. "I must not be worthy of love. If I'm not worthy of love, I must be a bad person." This self-judgmental lack of love ends up supporting our fear of eventually being alone.

To survive, we push down and suppress the pain of our wounds, and then compensate in order to function from day to day. In doing so, we avoid feeling what's inside and instead develop "outside" strategies. Perhaps we become "the pleaser" as a means of attracting love and attention, being the "good boy" (or girl) as a means of filling the void. Or maybe we become the angry, rebellious child as a reactive expression to our pain—hoping someone will notice, but often driving further wedges between our loved ones and us.

-§-
Energy Kinesiology integrates the entire realm of the healing arts and allows the practitioner to utilize those portions of any modality that are specific to the client's needs.
-§-

Later, our path to becoming "functional" adults requires that we become "independent," and thus we break further away from an already fractured family structure. Our focus is now on individual survival. But, as a result of the suppression and avoidance that gets us to this point, there is still a child within each of us who is yearning for love and attention. When our ongoing need for love is denied, the stage is set for even more pain. This leads to further separation—from ourselves and our own ability to receive and express love; from those we desire love from; and from our higher self, whose "soul" desire is to nurture and guide the physically manifested being in a cradle of all-encompassing love. Separation has become the status quo.

From here, we're supposed to find partners, fall in love, and start a family? With the model we have to work from?

The challenge, now, is to become consciously aware of our outwardly focused, reactive survival mechanisms, and choose, instead, to look within—to heal the pain and grief of separation, open the door to loving ourselves, and build a solid foundation from which to grow our individual relationships, our community, and our planet. To do this, we must heal the wounds of the child self, bring the child and adult together as a mutually supportive team, and bond them with the loving nurturance of the higher self via energy balancing of the chakras and other metaphysical systems.

When Grace first came to my office, it was to find relief from eczema—a painful skin condition that had been plaguing her for years. She suffered from chronic swelling, dry redness, itching, and soreness located around the backs of her knees and legs, all of which are typical of this problem. She had been to many doctors, and used a variety of cortisone creams and moisturizing lotions, but experienced no lasting relief.

As an Energy Kinesiologist, I use muscle monitoring (commonly known as muscle "testing") as a primary assessment tool. This gentle, hands-on method acts as "the voice of the subconscious," and provides a critical advantage by allowing me to get information directly

from "the source." Information accessed with this method is directly related to the presenting problem, even though the client is not aware of it. Muscle monitoring not only assists in identifying the cause of the issue, and what is preventing healing, it also allows the body to communicate what is necessary to remove the blocks and facilitate a return to health. In doing so, Energy Kinesiology integrates the entire realm of the healing arts and allows the practitioner to utilize only what is necessary—specific to the client's needs—from a broad range of modalities. This means a truly holistic approach that combines physical, biochemical, emotional, and/or energetic balancing tools, all in one efficient session. Combined with the client's conscious knowledge and awareness, muscle monitoring gives us a complete picture to work with in the healing process.

-§-
Awareness initiates a healing response in the body.
-§-

With Grace on the table, we "activated" the eczema by scratching it and having her look at it, and used a technique to hold it in her body's neurological circuitry. Doing this created the context her body would use to provide relevant information. To activate her conscious awareness, I asked Grace, "What's the problem with having the eczema? What bothers you most about it?"

While I expected the answer to be about the physical discomfort, Grace instead responded, "I'm embarrassed to wear shorts or bathing suits. I can't enjoy the warm weather like everyone else, or hang out at the pool or the beach. My legs are disgusting!"

To make matters worse, Grace strictly wore pants—which held in the heat, causing more irritation. But she would rather suffer this than have her legs exposed.

"What would happen if others saw your legs?" I asked.

"I don't know. It would draw attention. People would think I'm ugly."

Following this further, Grace conceded that attention drawn to her legs would lead to being judged, to not being perfect.

"And what happens if Grace is not perfect?" I asked.

A moment of thought was followed by, "I'm not worthy."

"Not worthy of what?"

"Ummm… I guess of being loved."

"And what happens if Grace isn't loved?"

Tears begin to run out of the corners of her eyes. "She…she ends up alo…alone."

All of this information and emotional content was added into the neurological circuit we had established with the eczema.

The irony of this pattern was two-fold. Wearing pants during the hot weather still drew attention, as people wondered why Grace wasn't wearing more comfortable clothing. If asked, she would come up with an excuse, a little white lie. Not feeling good about this, she often avoided social situations that might expose her. So she either attracted unwanted attention, or ended up alone. Grace's fear was, as fears often become, a self-fulfilling prophecy.

With the underlying fear now established, we pursued this fear's origin. We were quickly led to her family environment.

Grace had grown up in a household where her mother was critical and abusive. At an early age, Grace watched as her older sister, Joan, was verbally railed at, then slapped or spanked if she stood up for herself. The father, passive to the equal extreme, would do nothing to stop the abuse or provide protection. And while these were Grace's conscious memories, it was likely that she had had even earlier experiences that created insecurity in her environment. Bringing up these memories activated the neurological circuits related to them, allowing us to capture these pathways in our circuit.

With this emotional content now added, muscle monitoring was employed to explore the energetic aspect. When stress showed in the kidney meridian, it was clear why. Emotionally, this meridian represents fear or anxiety, usually internalized. It is interesting to note that the skin is often referred to as the third kidney, becoming an outlet for toxicity when the kidney organ is compromised in doing its job. Offering this observation to Grace, a conscious connection resulted in an "ahhhhhhh..." of recognition.

"You mean my eczema is related to my fear of my mom, and wanting to be invisible in my family?"

This awareness alone initiated a healing response in the body, as the defensive posture of fear started to relax. Through muscle monitoring, Grace's body indicated that it would benefit from acupressure and the use of a flower essence to defuse emotional stress. When these were completed, the kidney meridian came into balance—not just in general, but in specific reference to the circuit we'd created. I asked Grace to think about some of the stressful events we had been discussing, naming them, and to tell me how it felt to think about them now. She looked at me matter-of-factly, and said, "It's okay —I don't feel as charged as before." There were no tears. She also offered that her legs felt "cooler" where the eczema was.

Over the course of a few more sessions, we continued to explore issues brought up by the eczema. They followed in the same theme, unwinding the story in the order the body needed. This is another advantage of using muscle monitoring, as it allows the body to go through its healing process at its own pace. This avoids the discomfort of a "healing crisis," when the body is forced to release more than it is capable of handling at one time.

In one session, Grace spoke of having been shy at school, and not having a lot of friends. One year she had established a close connection with one of her teachers, someone she could trust. But the teacher had gotten married in the middle of the year and moved away. Her closest friend had been the boy next door, who she had grown up playing with. But, when his father got a new job, they had moved across the country. Going back even further, to a time identified as relevant through muscle monitoring, Grace spoke of her birth as having been quite difficult. True to the times, she had been denied a natural bonding experience with her mother, and was fed formula rather than breastfeeding. While she had felt this pattern of abandonment, she had never put all of it together in a way she understood. And she certainly never thought that any of this was related to her eczema.

Fast forward to present circumstances: Grace's career, a job she held for a long time, was unsatisfying. She was never recognized for the work she did, but was afraid to pursue anything else. Even though she hated her work, it provided security and paid the bills.

Grace had been through many relationships, even married once, but all were short term. In most cases, she had been the one who'd left. She told a variety of elaborate stories about why this was the case, with her partners' behaviors always having been unacceptable in one form or another. Through the course of these relationships, each with its own "unique" circumstances, Grace's pattern played out again and again. Suddenly, she realized she was 42 years old and hadn't had a relationship that lasted more than a year.

Needless to say, Grace's self-esteem was very low. She was disconnected from her dreams, her ideals—in fact, she didn't even know what they were. Grace had been putting all her energy into mere survival, and had nothing left over for anything else.

In one session, I asked Grace, "Do you love yourself?" She began to laugh and could not regain her composure for several long minutes. She couldn't even understand the concept, and we spent a good part of the session simply identifying what loving herself might mean. That became a major theme, and barometer, for the work we did going forward. The pain and grief of Grace's childhood traumas had been suppressed and avoided in her day-to-day life. And, yet, little Grace was screaming to be recognized, nurtured, and allowed to express herself. Her vehicle for getting this recognition was through the eczema. It just needed adult Grace to pay attention.

In another session, I guided Grace through a visualization process, one of several necessary steps to "rewrite the tapes" of perception that had kept Grace stuck for so many years. While I held specific reflex points on her forehead to activate brain centers critical to problem solving and choice, I asked: "What is it that little Grace wants?"

"I don't know."

"Does she know?"

"I…I guess so."

"Well, ask her... 'Grace, what do you want?'… What does she say?"

"She wants to feel safe. She wants to be loved."

"And what does little Grace need to feel safe and loved?"

"I don't know. It's not something she's often experienced. Certainly not from Mom and Dad."

"Is there something you can offer little Grace that would help her feel safe and loved?"

"I could hold her…"

"OK, go ahead and do that. How does she feel now?"

The points on Grace's forehead, under my resting hands, started to pulse.

"She feels better. But she's a little wary of this."

"Is there anything you'd like to say to little Grace? What would she like to hear from you that might comfort her?"

"That I love her."

"OK. Go ahead and tell her that."

Grace went inward to speak to her child self. The tears started to flow.

"How does she feel now?"

"She's feeling better. She's smiling."

The pulses were now significantly stronger.

"Is there anything else you can offer to little Grace?"

"No. She just wants to keep being held."

"OK. Just keep holding her then." I paused. "Would it help little Grace to know that you, adult Grace, are there for her whenever she needs you?"

"Sure. She would like that!"

"Go ahead and let her know that... How does that feel?"

"She's relaxed now. She smiling and wants to play."

"Okay., have a little play time with her." Another pause. "Is there anything little Grace would like to say to you?"

"She says, 'Thank you.'" Grace paused, then smiled. "And she loves me, too."

The pulses were beating strongly, and were synchronized between the right and left sides. This often signals a completion.

"How does that feel to you, knowing that little Grace loves you, too, and is there for you?"

"It's wonderful. It's amazing to have that connection. I feel lighter."

"Great! Take a deep breath."

Once we completed the process of establishing the connection to her child self, muscle monitoring showed that Grace had imbalances in her root and solar plexus chakras. Another advantage of using Energy Kinesiology is its ability to get information about metaphysical energy systems even if you are a person who can't see or sense them. In Grace's case, the root chakra was extending too far out, striving for that sense of grounding, safety, and trust that had so long eluded her. The solar plexus chakra, conversely, was pulled in, an introversion for protecting the fragile self-esteem while holding back her expression of personal power. Because the emotional connection of the visualization had begun the process of re-writing the tapes of perceived aloneness, it was now much easier to bring these chakras into an alignment through simple balancing techniques. This alignment held, because the stress of the related subconscious and conscious references being held in the circuit had been defused. The triggers to the fight or flight survival response had been deactivated. This alignment created a mutually supportive environment in which Grace could discover new choices, experience new behavior, and attract more healthful situations in all areas of her life. These choices were now congruent with her conscious desires, her ideals, and inner knowing—her higher self.

Less than a month later, Grace found a new partner who was more available, more supportive, and more intimate with her than anyone had been before. Released from the bonds of co-dependency, she could experience freedom and closeness, established through trust—something that had not existed in any of her prior relationships. Meeting this new partner coincided with her choice to pursue a new career—one in alignment with her dreams—instead of working just to survive. Previously, Grace had been too afraid to make this move, not believing she deserved it, and feared what others might think if she failed. Her friends noticed the "new" Grace had "come into her power," brimming with self-confidence. This positive feedback supported Grace's transition, further dissolving the patterns and behaviors that had kept her stuck in negative thoughts and attitudes.

-§-
As fear is the vehicle of survival, compassion is the vehicle of love.
-§-

New neurology is now established; the energetic body is vibrating at a different rate. And the eczema is healing and almost completely gone. It's a whole new life.

Regardless of the symptoms and history of our illnesses, the process of healing the wounded child and metaphysical energy systems, and integrating them with the present time adult-self, is critical. Past experiences don't have to continue controlling our lives. As fear is the vehicle of survival, compassion is the vehicle of love. Directing this compassion toward ourselves, as well as toward those whom we consider to be the perpetrators of our pain, allows us to move beyond fear and survival mechanisms. Doing so means that we take responsibility for our lives, and that we are no longer prisoners of reactionary fear.

Establishing a deeper connection with ourselves, and generating new bonds through trust, we are in tune with and respond to our environment, rather than reacting to it. A new and harmonious flow is established with our higher self and all it represents. A balance now exists between the physical and energetic, past, present, and future, self and universe. Out of this process emerges a whole, vibrant being, at one with him- or herself. The dynamics of intra- and interpersonal relationships change dramatically, and these changes are both felt and observed. The entire being shifts to reflect the new attitudes and behaviors. Essence is present, thriving, glowing. True healing has begun. Martha Graham puts it this way:

> There is a vitality, a life force, an energy, a quickening, that is translated through into action. And because there is only one of you in all time, this expression is unique. And if you block it, it will never exist through any other medium and will be lost. The world will not have it. It is not your business to determine how good it is, nor how valuable, nor how it compares with other expressions. It is your business to keep it yours clearly and directly, to keep the channel open.

John Travis:

Why Men Leave—A Hidden Epidemic

Men leave their families in a multitude of ways. remain in the home, many fathers are often emotionally absent—through depression, workaholism, violence or abuse (physical or emotional), or a retreat into addiction to substances, media, consumer goods, sports, food, or sex.

Most men in the "developed" nations today never bonded (or very poorly bonded) with their mothers. Most people don't even notice how disconnected modern people are from each other, compared to cultures where the bond is still intact. Yes, we talk of alienation and notice how much people in Mediterranean cultures touch each other, but we make no connection between these phenomena and how our bonds among each other, with nature, and with the divine have been torn asunder. I maintain that this unnoticed, silent epidemic is the source of most societal ills. Fathers leaving their families is only the tip of an iceberg.

As infants, most men in our culture have been bottle-fed and subjected to other culturally-endorsed patterns of normative abuse, such as sleeping alone or being left alone to cry when their needs weren't met. Biologically, the male is the more fragile gender of our species and developmentally lags years behind females—well into adulthood. Instead of getting the extra nurturing needed to compensate for being the weaker sex, by age five, males in almost all cultures get far less nurturing than females. It's no surprise, then, that most of the

John W. Travis, M.D., is a co-author of the *Wellness Workbook* (Celestial Arts, 2004), and *Simply Well* (Ten Speed, 2001). He co-directs the Alliance for Transforming the Lives of Children, (www.aTLC.com), which champions a culture of compassionate individuals, families, and communities—who have fun with, learn from, and responsively and lovingly interact with children. He lectures on why men leave, and many other areas of wellness for both adults and children. His Wellness Inventory Online is available at www.thewellspring.com. John and his family divide their time between Australia and the United States. He welcomes feedback and comments at jack@atlc.org.

unbonded boys in our culture grow into men who spend a good deal of their lives unconsciously seeking a nurture-source to provide them with the nurturing they were denied as infants/children (fueled by advertising that prominently features the breasts they were denied). Part of their survival mechanism is to learn to deny their feelings and project their unmet needs for nurturing onto substitutes, such as women, and other externals, such as consumerism, workaholism, and other addictions.

We unbonded men may manage pretty well in our marriages for a while, but when our primary source of nurturance gives birth and suddenly turns her focus toward the newborn, we usually lose much of the nurturance we were getting from our partners. This is almost inevitable given the demands on parents trapped in with what I call the nuclear family disaster (NFD) experiment our culture is trying. Mothers, especially, cannot begin to get their normal adult needs for nurturance met unless they are one of the few living in a tribe, close-knit community, or extended family.

-§-

Even if they remain in the home, many fathers are often emotionally absent.

-§-

The Northern European cultures have, in the name of civilization and progress, gradually destroyed the tribe/village/extended family/community and replaced it with the nuclear family disaster. This, in turn, has melted down into the single parent trap (SPT). These spread rapidly throughout the world as the northern Europeans busily exported their experiment in isolation to every continent but Antarctica, first via missionaries and conquest, and now via the media and multinational corporations. The consequences are immense, leading to overwhelming pressures of isolation, particularly for women, who often end up bearing the total responsibility of their children.

At the same time, our sudden exposure to an infant who has not yet been fully "trained" in the denial of her own needs—for suckling at the breast, being lovingly held in arms, being constantly in the presence of her caregiver, and so on—and expresses them vocally in no minor manner, will usually stir up our suppressed memories of our denied needs as infants, plunging us into deep pain—conscious or unconscious.

With the resulting increase in pain levels, we usually step up our adopted/chosen means of defending against our feelings—be it via medication, having affairs, rage, depression, addiction, or violence (physical or emotional). This is the first level at which men leave. When or if the defense mechanism fails, because the real need is not addressed, many of us think the only thing we can do is to depart from the stimulus and leave our homes.

Girls in our culture also get far less nurturing than required and suffer a similar experience of failed bonding. They have the opportunity, however, of recreating the experience of a secure bond through their unique ability to have a biological bond with a fetus in pregnancy (and the concurrent hormones). If they are able to preserve that bond by resisting our cultural norms and raise a securely attached child, they are often able to heal much of their own unbondedness, but witnessing this may simultaneously exacerbate the father's restimulation of his own primal wounds, trigger his defenses, and increase the likeliness of his leaving.

Since depression was my defense mechanism of choice, I understand that coping mechanism better than the others, but I believe my theory explains equally well why the other defense mechanisms, such as addictions and violence, similarly lead to broken bonds and the passing on of our trauma to another generation.

Sourcing the Pain

I was born in the farmlands of western Ohio in 1943. Like most babies born in those days, I was dragged out of the womb, drugged (via my mother's general anesthetic, which took weeks to wear off), with cold, metal forceps, grasped by sticky rubber gloves, and plunged into bright lights—instead of being gently greeted with warm hands in subdued light. I was doubtless held upside down to drain my lungs (I'm not sure if I was slapped or not, but that was the norm of the day). Stinging silver nitrate was put in my eyes. I was wrapped in cold, scratchy fabrics instead of being allowed to mold my skin against the warm skin of the person with whom I'd been intimately connected for nine months. A little while later, I was taken to the nursery where I was placed in a plastic box beside Carol D., born earlier that day. I spent my next 10 days there (the norm for the early 1940s). Arlene and Marlene soon joined me, twins born a few days later. I was given a cold, rubber nipple with a bottle of a fatty, antigenic substance instead of the miracle food that three million years of evolution had prepared for me.

-§-
The Northern European cultures have, in the name of civilization and progress, gradually destroyed the tribe/village/extended family/community and replaced it with the nuclear family disaster.
-§-

Then, a day or so later, I was immobilized on a board and, without painkillers, the majority of the most sensitive nerve endings of my penis were amputated. Then followed the standard "normative abuse" parenting practices of the 1940s:

1. artificial baby milk—probably Carnation or Pet Evaporated Milk
2. a four-hour bottle schedule. I got hungry every three hours and cried that last hour, until I learned it was no use and made a decision about the world that is so basic to my brain's neural organization that it still impacts almost everything I do—"Asking for what you want doesn't work."
3. restraint in a crib or playpen,
4. deprivation of the continual movement of being carried in-arms
5. sleeping alone in a separate room.

Most of these "improvements" in child rearing were devised by men citing untested "scientific" ideas, all of which have since been proven to be destructive to human bonding. I don't blame my or other parents of that age; they naturally followed the cultural winds, and the promise of science and technology to cure the world's ills was, in 1943, still an untarnished vision.

I used depression as my primary defense from the start. While my primary defense appears outwardly as depression, it's just one of a standard set that unbonded children/adults cling to in their attempts to escape the pain of the early needs deprivation that still eats away at them. The others are addiction, violence, chronic illness, and ecocide (destruction of the environment)—symptoms of what James Prescott named Somato-Sensory Affectional Deprivation Syndrome (SSADS) in his early bonding research.

-§-
It may take a village to raise a child, but it takes a community to keep the parents sane.
—Sobonfu Somé
-§-

I created a "safe" world of my own in my head that allowed a sense of control (since I had no control over being fed, touched, or moved). The fact that I was disconnected from the matrix of my life by being isolated from others limited my ability to express my needs and get them met—hence the periodic depressions. No one recognized my depressions, including me, until I was in college—people just thought I was "quiet."

My condition is not atypical of most men alive today who were raised by "modern" cultural standards. One friend, though raised in California, was fortunate in that his mother was from South America. He was breast-fed well past age two and has always seemed happier than any other person I know.

My Stroke Supply

Having never experienced a nurturing mother, I've subsequently spent most of my life looking for a replacement.

I thought getting married and becoming a doctor would somehow fulfill me, so at age five I blindly set on a course of twenty-two years of school that would handle the latter, and assumed somehow the right "girl" would magically appear about the time I became a doctor. Although I had few social skills, I wasn't deterred in my belief that she would appear.

-§-
Having never experienced a nurturing mother, I've subsequently spent most of my life looking for a replacement.
-§-

Much to my surprise, marriage midway through medical school didn't suddenly make my life better, just more complicated. My feelings of emptiness got worse as my depressions deepened. After three years of marriage and several crises, my wife said we had to have a baby or split. I thought I had to comply, since divorce wasn't an option in my family. Reluctantly, in 1972, I became a father.

It was great at first, the excitement of a new being, but then the reality hit—I was a lot lower on my wife's attention list. I began to get more and more depressed, leading eventually to our getting into therapy. There I learned I actually had feelings, and could express them, though with great difficulty even to this day. We began learning about the unconscious patterns we'd been playing out in our symbiotic marriage, but seemed relatively powerless to change them. However, my experience with this reparenting therapy group became the basis for my pioneering work in wellness and, later, my observation that failed bonding/attachment leads to the need for remedial work as adults.

Despite learning a great deal about my inner workings, I still was depressed most of the time. When our daughter was two and a half, the pain became so great that I realized I had to leave in order to keep my own sanity, as I was sometimes close to being suicidal. I abandoned my first daughter, with whom I had never really bonded—clearly out of my own inexperience with this phenomenon.

The cycle began again with another intense, three-year relationship. I was still unconsciously seeking the mommy I never had, and, while I reveled in the attention she gave me, it wasn't enough, and she felt drained by my neediness. It was around this time that I first heard of the book *Magical Child* and author Joseph Chilton Pearce's efforts to reframe children's legitimate nurturing needs, but I didn't think it had any applicability to me and subconsciously, I didn't want to stir up my painful childhood recollections. I tried to learn to love myself and follow the tenets of self-responsibility I was helping to promote at the

time, all the while struggling with my chronic depression. I was only marginally successful. Deep down, something always felt wrong.

A year later I met and fell in love with an Australian, Meryn Callander. As our love blossomed, we were often challenged in our new-forming relationship, but we managed, and a year later, married. Meryn and I also began to work together professionally, first with authoring books, and then creating authentic community, especially for helping professionals who are often lonely and unable to connect with peers on an emotional level. It was through Meryn's studies of feminist spirituality that I became aware of the estrangement rampant throughout Western culture leading to the authoritarian institutions that surround us, like medicine, law, and the educational system. I had been struggling with aspects of this phenomenon in my work with our Wellness Resource Center the previous seven years, but had no understanding of the bigger picture.

I thought I was gradually overcoming my depressions through continued work on myself in growth-oriented seminars I both led and participated in. Friends who had known me a long time could see a difference—years of hard work on painful issues were paying off.

One of the things that fed me the most was lying in bed at night in Meryn's arms, usually watching TV, and having my head, chest, or tummy stroked. We spent an hour several nights a week, doing that before going sleep, and 15 minutes or so in the morning, alternating who would cradle whom. Unlike the common male stereotype of always thinking about sex and wanting more, what I mainly wanted was nurturing attention from a mother figure, though I was only dimly aware of this. I would sometimes think something must be wrong with me for not being more sexually interested. Being held and stroked was the lifeline that kept me going, though I didn't fully get how desperate this need was until I lost most of it.

Taking the Plunge Again

Like most of our friends at the time, Meryn and I assumed we would not have children together, but after ten years, in her late thirties, Meryn's biological alarm went off. I couldn't imagine reopening the painful experience of being a father again. At the urging of a friend, I read Jean Liedloff's *The Continuum Concept*. I suddenly saw the estrangement that we'd been studying was not innate to "the human condition," but a direct result of how we isolate babies and young children. Personally, I could also see how the old wounds I thought I had handled in therapy were still there. I also thought I might make up for my greatest failure in life (being a father) and get it "right" this time with a new approach.

Until then, I had lived a pressured life of deadlines (self-imposed) using adrenalin to make myself accomplish things, always feeling like some unknown but dreaded thing was gaining on me if I didn't have something concrete to show myself at the end of each day. I gave lip service to focusing on love and relationships as my highest values, but I was driven by the need to do something to earn my keep. This is still far more true than I would like.

-§-
I had no idea of the depth of pain and envy that would be opened up from constantly being with someone who knew what her needs were, expressed these needs, and got the nurturing every infant needs and thrives on.
-§-

For four years, early in our relationship, Meryn and I had lived a life of voluntary simplicity in the mountains of Costa Rica. We both longed to return to that simpler life. Along with our decision to have a child, we sold our big house, cut back on the seminars that we'd been facilitating, and bought forty acres in a remote part of Mendocino County, California, seven miles past the end of the power lines.

We became homesteaders. I set about turning an unfinished cabin into a solar-powered home. We read and wrote intensely on attachment parenting. We prepared to give birth to our daughter at home with a midwife, complete with a warm water pool provided by a friend.

The birth went well, and while I thought I was now better prepared for becoming a father, I had no idea of the depth of pain and envy that would be opened up from constantly being with someone who knew what her needs were, expressed these needs, and got the nurturing every infant needs and thrives on.

And, as I should have expected, Siena's arrival supplanted much of my nurturance, but I kept busy dealing with water and electrical systems. We quickly came to the realization that the "in-arms" attachment parenting we were attempting was designed for an extended family, not for our nuclear one. Bringing Meryn's mum over from Australia to live with us helped, but it often seemed, given our commitment to Siena being constantly "in arms" until she, of her own volition, moved on, we still had an arms shortage.

While we provided her with a degree of physical nurturance unknown to most children in the West today, and she blossomed from it, our relationship got more and more strained. I went deeper into depressions, alternating with periods of hyperactivity to keep us

afloat financially and make up for the downtime of my crashes. It was unsustainable.

I tried to meet my own needs on a number of fronts: building, therapy, men's groups, and spending time in nature; all to no avail.

It was only after a year of soul-searching, moving across the country to Virginia in 1996, and finding an intentional community that appeared to fulfill many of the ideals for which I'd searched during the previous twenty years, that I found some peace with my process and began to write about it.

Despite half of a lifetime of therapy and personal growth work, I still struggle with my barely suppressed rage, which usually shows up as depression, a chronic clenching of my jaw, and a knot in my stomach.

But even now, nearly eleven years after my second daughter's arrival, I am struck by the contrast between witnessing her needs being expressed and fully met, and how most of us were treated. I spent over a thousand nights lying in the bed near her while she nursed. This gave me a new awareness of my own subjugated oral needs around which I've spent my whole life and career trying to compensate. While being with my daughter still sometimes activates deep and painful places in me, I see her as a spiritual teacher, challenging me to continually deal with the years of walled-in pain that keep me disconnected from the family/tribe/planet that is my birthright.

-§-
If you have not found the gift in your own wounding, please keep looking.
-§-

The Road to Healing

My personal journey reveals just one of the many ways that failed bonding can show up in a family dynamic. Fortunately, it's within our wounds that our gifts are revealed. Certainly my work in wellness has been strongly influenced by my pain, and without seeing it in the larger perspective of a personal journey, I think I'd have just gotten lost in the suffering. If you have not found the gift in your own wounding, please keep looking.

A word of caution: After observing myself and others who have worked with these issues for over half of our adult lives, I am no longer certain that the childhood wounds of not having a secure bond with anyone—or the popularized euphemism for this condition "low self-esteem" (Liedloff describes bonding as feeling worthy and welcome)—can be healed beyond short-term breakthroughs and temporary remissions. But I do think we can learn to better manage our pain and be less controlled by it.

Depression is one of the largest public health problems in our culture, along with addiction, violence, and chronic disease—all symptoms of SSAD. The reactivation of this pain in our attempts to create a family of our own is a serious condition to reflect on before the birth of a child. I had, and continue to have, a difficult time with it, so I don't think it's easy for young people who naively enter into parenthood unaware of their own wounding.

To prevent perpetuating failed bonding among our young, further exacerbated by dysfunctional nuclear families—themselves an artifact of the authoritarian cultures—we need to recognize what a secure bond looks and feels like and begin challenging the normative abuse of detachment parenting we see everywhere.

We see and hear these myriad symptoms of alienation and failed bonding every day in the news, but we never hear about the real cause—how we treat our babies and children. If we look closely, we can see these symptoms in our own lives, understand the real cause, and begin to get our own needs met with the support of self-awareness books and classes, support groups, therapy, and open, honest communication with our family and friends, rather than being blind to and driven by our unmet childhood needs. We then have a better chance of meeting our children's needs through applying the wisdom found in the Alliance for Transforming the Lives of Children's Blueprint of Principles and Actions.

-§-
We need to recognize what a secure bond looks and feels like and begin challenging the normative abuse of detachment parenting we see everywhere.
-§-

As more men become aware of the dynamics between their own unmet needs and seeing their children's attempts to get theirs met, the widespread denial of this problem will come out in the open and men will be better able to cope with their issues instead of denying, hiding, inflicting them on others, or medicating them.

Men will then be able to help society understand and own the wounds of unbondedness that have not only reached epidemic proportions in recent generations, but are also perpetuated by cultural and economic agendas. By re-creating communities, extended families of choice, and other as-yet-not-discovered ways of supporting each other in providing the nurturing we never got, we can break the cycle of abandonment and separation inflicted on children in the form of medicalized births, bottle feeding, circumcision, early day care, and the like.

When we face and accept our own wounding and when we can open our hearts to tend our own needs, we will unleash the compassion that gives us the strength to remain with our families and create a world that nurtures everyone.

THICH NHAT HANH:

Embracing Negative Energies

Sometimes we are overwhelmed by the energy of hate, of anger, of despair. We forget that in us there are other kinds of energy that can manifest also. If we know how to practice, we can bring back the energy of insight, of love, and of hope in order to embrace the energy of fear, of despair, and of anger. Our ancestors are capable of negating the unwholesome energies, or what Christians might call the evil spirit within us, by bringing back the Holy Spirit in order for us to heal and to be healthy and joyful and alive again.

In Buddhism, we also talk about these kinds of energies, the negative energies and the positive energies. There is a little difference though. In the case of Buddhism, we don't have to chase the evil spirit away; in fact we embrace the evil spirit, the energy of anger, the energy of despair, the energy of hate, the negative energies. Embraced by the energy of mindfulness, they are transformed. They don't need to be chased away.

What do you do in order to embrace and transform them? You have to call in to yourself, you have to help manifest the energy of love, of understanding, and of peace in order to embrace these kinds of negative energies. Listening to the bell, for instance, is one of the wonderful ways to generate the energy of peace, to generate the energy of mindfulness. These energies will help to take care of the negative energies. For instance, when you are angry you can always practice like this:

Thich Nhat Hanh has been a Buddhist monk and a peace activist since the age of sixteen. He is the master of one of the most prominent temples in Vietnam, and his lineage is traceable directly to the Buddha himself. He has survived three wars, persecution, and more than thirty years of exile. He has written more than one hundred books of poetry, fiction, and philosophy, including *No Death, No Fear* (Riverhead, 2002) and *Going Home: Jesus and Buddha As Brothers* (Riverhead, 1999). He was nominated for the Nobel Peace Prize by Martin Luther King Jr. He makes his home in France and in America in the state of Vermont. Photo by Plum Village Practice Center, France.

Breathing in, I know the energy of anger is in me.

Breathing out, I embrace my anger.

It is a wonderful practice. You just practice breathing in and out to be aware that anger is in you. You know that when you are angry it is not good to say anything. It is not good to react or do anything. "Breathing in, breathing out, I recognize there is anger in me" is the best thing to do. If you know how to do it, the energy of anger will not be able to harm you or the people around you.

During this practice, the energy of mindfulness is in you, alive, because you continue the practice of mindful breathing in and mindful breathing out. Mindful breathing helps the energy of mindfulness to be alive, and this enables you to embrace the energy of anger, to recognize it as existing. You are put in a very safe situation. You don't have to chase anger out of you. You allow it to be in you, you embrace it tenderly, and then anger will subside, and the danger is overcome. During the practice you have helped anger, and it will be transformed slowly. This practice enables you to acknowledge your anger with a smile. While you practice breathing in and out, acknowledging your anger and smiling toward it, the energy of the Buddha is in you. The Buddha is in you, the Buddha as an ancestor is protecting you. You know that the Buddha is not an idea. The Buddha is true energy. The energy of the Buddha is the energy of mindfulness, the energy of peace, the energy of concentration and wisdom.

-§-
When the Bodhisattva of Compassion comes down to hell, hell stops being hell because the Bodhisattva brings love to it.
-§-

If you are a Christian, your practice should be similar. When the evil spirit is within you, the spirit of despair, anger, violence, and hatred, you have to be aware that it is in you. You ask Jesus to come and be manifest within you in order for you to be able to recognize the negative in yourself and to embrace it. With prayer and contemplation, with the reading of the Bible, you put yourself in a safe situation. You are able to contain, to control, to transform the negative energy in you. For those of us who practice mindfulness, we believe that the energy of mindfulness (which is the energy of the Buddha) is the equivalent of what our friends call the Holy Spirit.

The Holy Spirit is the kind of energy that is capable of being there, of understanding, of accepting, of loving, and of healing. If you agree that the Holy Spirit has the power to be present, to understand, to heal, to love, if you agree about this, then you have to say it is the same thing as the energy of mindfulness. Where mindfulness is, there is true presence. Where mindfulness is, there is the capacity to understand. You have the capacity to accept, to become compassionate, to love, and therefore to touch the energy of mindfulness so that it may become manifest in you. The Buddha as a spiritual ancestor is manifest in you. You are able to allow the Holy Spirit to be in you, to guide you, to shine on you like a lamp. Jesus is then alive in you that very moment.

It is possible to know the Buddha and at the same time know Jesus. There are people who have roots within both the Buddhist tradition and the Christian tradition. In my hermitage, I put a lot of Buddha statues on my altar, about ten or fifteen very small Buddhas one centimeter high and larger ones too. I also have a statue of Jesus as my ancestor. I have adopted Jesus Christ as one of my spiritual ancestors.

During the Vietnam War I worked very hard in order to stop the killing. When I was in Europe and in North America I met with a number of Christians who really embodied the spirit of love, of understanding, of peace, of Jesus. Thanks to these people I have deeply touched Jesus as a spiritual teacher, a spiritual ancestor.

Just imagine a kingdom where there is no suffering at all; it is very distressing. The joy to be alive can be there only when you know what dying is. The joy of being healthy, of being able to walk and run and breathe, will not be possible without your experience of death and sickness. Our hope, our desire, and our aspiration for a kingdom or a place where suffering does not exist should be re-examined.

The people who live in that Kingdom are not supposed to suffer at all. It seems that they should experience only happiness in their daily lives. This is something absurd and impossible. A pure land, a Buddhaland, or paradise, is not a place where suffering doesn't exist. My definition of paradise is the place where love exists, where compassion exists. When the Bodhisattva of Compassion comes down to hell, hell stops being hell because the Bodhisattva brings love to it.

-§-

It is possible to know the Buddha and at the same time know Jesus.

-§-

Yet love cannot exist without suffering. In fact, suffering is the ground on which love is born. If you have not suffered, if you don't see the suffering of people or other living beings, you would not have love in you nor would you understand what it is to love. Without suffering, compassion, loving-kindness, tolerance, and understanding would not arise. Do you want to live in a place where there is no suffering? If you live in such a place, you will not be able to know what is love. Love is born from suffering.

You know what suffering is. You don't want to suffer, you don't want to make other people suffer, and therefore your love is born. You

want to be happy and you want to bring happiness to others. That is love. When suffering is there, it helps give birth to compassion. We need to touch suffering in order for our compassion to be born and to be nourished. That is why suffering plays such an important role even down here in paradise. We are already here in some sort of paradise surrounded by love, but there is still jealousy, hatred, anger, and suffering around us and inside of us.

-§-
We need to touch suffering in order for our compassion to be born and to be nourished.
-§-

It is because we are struggling to free ourselves from the grip of suffering and affliction that we learn how to love and how to take care of ourselves and of others, not to inflict on others more suffering and misunderstanding. Love is a practice and unless you know what suffering is, you are not motivated to practice compassion, love, and understanding.

I would not be willing to go to a place where there is no suffering because I know that living in such a place I would not experience love. Because I suffer, I need love. Because you suffer, you need love. Because we suffer, we know that we have to offer each other love, and love becomes a practice.

The Buddha of love, Maitreya, will never be born in a world where there is no suffering. This is the right place for the Buddha of love to be born, because suffering is the element from which we can create love. Let us not be naïve and abandon this world of suffering, and hope for a place—whether we call it nirvana or the Kingdom of God or the Pure Land. You know that the element with which you can create love is our own suffering, and the suffering we experience every day around us.

Part Four

Passion: Crucible or Chrysalis

from the inside molting our human skins
born out of their arduous longing for this other, the beloved,
the ache of it all endured,
a weaving maturing of souls verging into oneness,
circling auguring ever-deeper into the Source of incarnation itself,
everything quickening the hopes and fears
of each lover there ever was or will be.
~Stuart Sovatsky, *Your Perfect Lips*

John Gray:

Relationship Mind-Fields

I have worked with many people who have had the same type of partner or relationship over and over. There is an old saying that when one door closes, a new one opens. But if the old door doesn't close fully, then it's the same door opening again and again. To truly close a door, we must become self-aware and find forgiveness.

We really don't know how to be happy. Before you can find a fulfilling partnership, you have to learn to be happy without a partner. It's a cliché, but it really is true. That doesn't mean it's easy, though. If you want to go in a new direction, you first have to acknowledge that the things you have seemed to be attracted to are not good for you.

It takes time to figure out how to tell whether someone will make a good partner. When we are young, we explore and learn as we go through the minefields of life. As we get a bit older, we learn to recognize and interpret the signs of a healthy individual.

Some signs and signals you need to be very clear about and walk away from. If someone hits you, that is a sign that they are not ready for an intimate relationship. Violence is a sign that that person lacks any sense of maturity. You need to spare yourself from being a victim—and spare them from becoming more violent—by leaving.

But there are other signs that just need to be correctly interpreted, since the behaviors that lead to a dysfunctional relationship can be the same as those that lead to a healthy one. For example, a partner might

John Gray, Ph.D., is the author of fifteen best-selling books, including *Men Are from Mars, Women Are from Venus* (HarperCollins, 1992), the number one best selling book of the last decade. In the past ten years, over thirty million Mars and Venus books have been sold in over forty languages throughout the world. He has appeared on *Oprah, The Today Show, CBS Morning Show, Good Morning America, Larry King,* and many other shows. He has been profiled in *Newsweek, Time, Forbes, USA Today, TV Guide,* and *People*. John Gray is a certified family therapist, and is the premier Better Life relationship coach on AOL. More at www.MarsVenus.com.

pull away and withdraw. This is a normal occurrence in a relationship. You just need to give that person some room, have a little patience, and support them when they open up again. However, when someone is violent in a relationship, they often shut down before the violence occurs. If you were involved with a violent person in the past, then when a present partner shuts down you might mistakenly assume that they are going to be violent, too, and become afraid or upset. But they are not about to hit you, they're just shutting down.

Feelings of jealousy also require careful interpretation. The trouble is that people generally don't own jealousy as their own problem. In order to break through a detrimental pattern of this kind, it is important to be able to identify the difference between jealous feelings that are appropriate, and those that are inappropriate.

If you are in a committed relationship and your partner is spending all his or her time with somebody else, the feeling of jealousy is appropriate. However, if your partner is simply making a few calls here and there and you are jealous, the feeling is not appropriate. When communicating about these feelings with your partner, first recognize whether the problem is a result of his or her actual behavior, or if it is your own. Ask yourself whether it is important to bring this message of feeling jealous to your partner. Maybe it would be better to talk about your feelings from the perspective of "I miss you and would like to spend more time with you."

-§-
Before you can find a fulfilling partnership, you have to learn to be happy without a partner.
-§-

Another pattern to be aware of is being attracted to partners who are not available. It is very common for people to fall in love with someone who is already taken, or who does not have the maturity to be in a relationship. Why is it that we want something we can't have? Why is it that the things we can have we don't want? How about passionately desiring what we can have? How about wanting and needing that? Part of the human neurosis is that we seem to dismiss that which comes easily and seek after the things that don't. This is a symptom of unresolved issues within ourselves.

When we are in a negative pattern we tend to feel like victims, not acknowledging that we contribute to the problem by staying in that relationship. Even when there truly is a villain, most victims, when they explore the situation, will see that they have allowed that person to continue to victimize them. They will see that there were many signs along the way, but they chose not to see them or take action.

Often a person in a victim pattern feels uncomfortable saying no. This can be because he or she is afraid of hurting someone, doesn't feel worthy of better treatment, or is taking too much responsibility for making everything "right." The fear of leaving feels greater than the other kinds of pain involved.

The lesson that must be learned, especially when this is a repeating pattern, is to fully resolve the emotional upset that is being felt. This means getting in touch with feelings of hurt, anger, and disappointment or guilt. The person will need to explore the fear they are feeling, both in the relationship and in terms of leaving. And they will have to learn how to let that partner go and find forgiveness.

When all those feelings have been explored, they will be able to find a sense of understanding. That is the essence of forgiveness—letting go and moving on, recognizing that the two of you just didn't fit well together. You weren't just a victim; you also allowed the situation to continue. Staying in this kind of relationship will always bring out the worst in someone who is victimizing you. This is the only level of accountability that can be found in this kind of situation, but it is necessary to find it.

In a healthier relationship, without a victim or a villain, the solution to negative patterns will always come when you ask yourself how you are contributing, and what you can do. Then, you can talk with your partner about how to work together. The same kinds of problems emerge in both healthy and dysfunctional relationships. The difference is that, in a healthy relationship, you are able to talk things through and come to a resolution together.

In a relationship in which you can't talk it through or find resolution, you are like a square peg in a round hole: you cannot make it work. Staying in such a relationship and expecting your partner to make it work with you will actually make things worse. You are either just too different, or else your partner is unavailable and unready for a relationship. It is unloving and unsupportive of you to try to get more from them, because in doing so you are trying to change that person; and trying to change someone will always bring out the very worst in them.

-§-
The same kinds of problems emerge in both healthy and dysfunctional relationships.
-§-

When you are not feeling good about yourself, and your self-esteem is low, the results will show clearly in your life. Harmful relationship patterns are a sign that you are not coming from a place of real self-love. But what does it mean to love yourself? In *What You Feel You Can Heal,* I explain how we can learn not to depend on someone else to feel good, love ourselves more, or increase our self-esteem.

Often, when people marry young, they don't give themselves the chance to explore who they are, what makes them happy, or what

makes them unhappy. They don't really know what they like or don't like, what they want or don't want, or how to react to things. They also don't have a sense of knowing their true selves—the loving human beings who have particular needs, deserve to have those needs met, and understand that other people have the same rights as well.

Women are more vulnerable in this regard than men, because they tend to easily lose themselves to relationship at a time in life when they are just learning who they are. This happens when they try to nurture somebody else too much, without nurturing themselves.

I look at the twenties as a time when individuals need to be much more selfish, so that they can prepare for their thirties, when they can begin to grow into unconditional love. The twenties need to be a time when we learn to love ourselves. This is not to say that people in their twenties cannot or should not be in relationships; they just need to be careful not to make sacrifices during that time.

-§-
Unless you know who you are, you can't make a sacrifice without giving yourself up.
-§-

I am a big believer in meaningful sacrifice as you get older—but unless you know who you are, you can't make a sacrifice without giving yourself up. It takes a while to become anchored into who you are, so that you can give unconditionally to someone without feeling like you are giving yourself away. If you know who you are and you love yourself, you will tend to be naturally drawn to the people who are available and well suited to you.

Scott Peck:

Smart Selfishness vs. Stupid Selfishness

18

Part of the complexity of life is that at one and the same time we are individuals, members of family and work organizations, and members of society. Indeed, it is almost arbitrary to separate these categories. But it is sometimes necessary to make such arbitrary distinctions in order to talk about anything in detail and depth. Therefore, let me focus first upon what I believe to be the most critical of the many choices that we make as individuals in our hearts and minds.

As always, consciousness precedes choice; without it, there is no choice. Thus, the single most important personal choice that we can make in our lives is the choice for ever-increasing consciousness. Consciousness, however, does not make choices easy. To the contrary, it multiplies the options.

To give an example of the complexity of choices, consider how we might deal with our anger. In the midbrain, there are collections of nerve cells or centers that not only govern but actually produce our powerful emotions. One of these is an anger center. In *Further Along the Road Less Traveled,* I wrote that the anger center in humans works in exactly the same way as it does in other creatures. It is basically a territorial mechanism, firing off when any other creature impinges upon our territory. We are no different from a dog fighting another dog that wanders into its territory, except that for human beings definitions of territory—or boundaries—are so complex and multifaceted.

M. Scott Peck, M.D., was a nationally recognized authority on the relationship between religion and science. He authored the epoch-making book, *The Road Less Traveled* (Simon & Schuster, 1978), as well as *The Different Drum: Community Making and Peace* (Simon &Schuster, 1987), *Meditations from the Road* (Simon & Schuster, 1993), *Denial of the Soul* (Harmony Books, 1997), and many others. As a result of his pioneering community work, Peck received the 1994 Temple International Peace Prize, and the 1996 Learning, Faith, and Freedom Medal from Georgetown University. He died at his home in Connecticut in September, 2005.

Not only do we have a geographical territory and become angry when someone comes uninvited onto our property and starts picking our flowers, but we also have a psychological territory, and we become angry whenever anyone criticizes us. We also have a theological or an ideological territory, and we tend to become angry whenever anyone casts aspersions on our belief systems, even when the critic is a stranger to us and speaking into a microphone thousands of miles away.

Since our anger center is firing much of the time, and often very inappropriately—sometimes on the basis of perceived, rather than actual, infringements—we need to be flexible in dealing with situations that easily provoke our wrath. We must learn a whole complex set of ways of dealing with anger. Sometimes we need to think, "My anger is silly and immature. It's my fault." Or sometimes we should conclude, "This person did impinge upon my territory, but it was an accident and there's no reason to get angry about it." Or, "Well, he did violate my territory a little bit, but it's no big deal. It's not worth blowing up about." But every once in a while, after we think about it for a couple of days, we may discern that someone really did seriously violate our territory. Then it may be necessary to go to that person and say, "Listen, I've got a real bone to pick with you." And sometimes it might even be necessary to get angry immediately and blast that person right on the spot.

-§-
There are at least five different ways to respond when we're angry.
-§-

So there are at least five different ways to respond when we're angry. And not only do we need to know them, we also have to learn which response is appropriate in any given situation. This requires extraordinary consciousness of what is going on both inside and outside of ourselves. It is no wonder that very few people learn how to deal well with their anger before they are into their thirties or forties, and many never learn to do so constructively.

In fact, it is the ability to learn how to deal with all the problems and challenges of life in a constructive manner that defines psychospiritual progress. Conversely, that which refuses progress is in opposition to our growth and ultimately self-destructive.

The Path of Smart Selfishness Versus the Path of Stupid Selfishness

To grow, we must learn to discern between that which is self-destructive and that which is self-constructive. When I was in practice, I would no longer allow any of my patients to use the word "unselfish" after about five sessions. I would tell them that I was a totally selfish human being who had never done anything for anyone or anything else. When I watered my flowers, I did not say to them, "Oh, look, flowers, what I'm doing for you. You ought to be grateful to me." I was doing it because I liked pretty flowers. Similarly, when I extended myself for one of my children it was because I liked to have an image of myself in my mind as a reasonably decent father and a reasonably honest man. In order to maintain those two images side by side with any integrity, every so often I had to extend myself beyond what I might normally feel like doing. Besides, I also like pretty children.

The truth is that we rarely do anything without some gain or benefit to ourselves, however small or subtle. Making a donation to charity helps me feel good. Someone who claims to be "sacrificing" a well-paying job right out of undergraduate school in order to go on to law school so she can "better serve society" is also better serving herself. A woman who "sacrifices" by staying at home to raise her children rather than going out to work may do so because she "believes in family," but she also personally benefits from this decision. We can look at monks and nuns and think, "God, how unselfish they are. Look at all that they have sacrificed: sex, family life, personal property ownership, and, in some ways, even autonomy over their own lives." But they are in it for the same selfish reason as anyone else. They have decided that for them that is the best path toward joy.

So selfishness isn't always a simple matter. What I would do was ask of my patients that they distinguish between the path of smart selfishness and the path of stupid selfishness. The path of stupid selfishness is trying to avoid all pain. The path of smart selfishness is trying to discern which pain or suffering, particularly emotional suffering, is constructive and which is unconstructive. Because I write a great deal about pain and suffering and discipline, a lot of people think I am some kind of pain freak. I am not a pain freak, I am a joy freak. I see no value whatsoever in unconstructive suffering. If I have an ordinary headache the very first thing I am going to do is get myself two super-strength uncapsulized acetaminophens. There is no virtue inherent in that headache, either per se or to me. I see absolutely no value in such unconstructive suffering. On the other hand, there are types of suffering in this life from which we have many constructive things to learn.

-§-
There are types of suffering in this life from which we have many constructive things to learn.
-§-

My preferred words for "constructive" and "unconstructive" are, respectively, "existential" and "neurotic." Existential suffering is an

inherent part of existence and cannot be legitimately avoided—for example, the suffering involved in growing up and learning to be independent; the suffering involved in learning how to become interdependent and even dependent again; the suffering that is associated with loss and giving up; the suffering of old age and dying. From all these kinds of suffering we have a great deal to learn. Neurotic suffering, on the other hand, is that emotional suffering which is not an inherent part of existence. It is unconstructive and unnecessary, and rather than enhancing our existence impedes it. What we need to do with neurotic suffering is get rid of it just as quickly as possible because it is like carrying ninety-eight golf clubs around the course when all you need is ten or twelve to play a perfectly good game. It is just so much excess baggage.

-§-
One of the basic choices we make in life is whether to follow the path of smart selfishness or try to avoid all problems and take the path of stupid selfishness.
§-

Fifty years ago, when Freud's theories first filtered down to the intelligentsia (and were misinterpreted, as so often happens), there were a large number of avant-garde parents who, having learned that guilt feelings could have something to do with neuroses, resolved that they were going to raise guilt-free children. What an awful thing to do to a child. Our jails are filled with people who are there precisely because they do not have any guilt, or do not have enough of it. We need a certain amount of guilt in order to exist in society, and that's what I call existential guilt. I hasten to stress, however, that too much guilt, rather than enhancing our existence, hinders it. Neurotic guilt is unnecessary and depletes our lives of joy and serenity.

Take another painful feeling: anxiety. Although it may be painful, we need a certain amount of anxiety to function well. For instance, if I had to give a speech in New York City, I might be anxious about how to get there, and my anxiety would propel me to look at a map. If I had no anxiety, I might just take off and end up in Quebec. Meanwhile, there are a thousand people waiting to hear me give a talk in New York City. So we need a certain amount of anxiety in order to exist well—the kind of existential anxiety that propels us to consult maps.

But once again, there can be an amount of anxiety above and beyond that, which, rather than enhancing our existence, impedes it. So I could think to myself, "Supposing I had a flat tire or got into an accident. They drive awfully fast on the roads near New York City. And even if I do manage to get to the place I was supposed to lecture, I probably won't be able to find a parking place. I'm sorry, people in New York, but it's beyond me." This kind of phobic anxiety, rather than enhancing my existence, limits it and is clearly neurotic.

We are naturally pain-avoiding creatures. But just as it would be stupid to welcome all suffering, so it is stupid to try to avoid all suffering. One of the basic choices we make in life is whether to follow the path of smart selfishness or try to avoid all problems and take the path of stupid selfishness. To do so, we must learn how to make this distinction between neurotic and existential suffering.

As I wrote in *The Road Less Traveled,* life is difficult because it is a series of problems, and the process of confronting and solving problems is a painful one. Problems, depending on their nature, evoke in us many uncomfortable feelings: frustration, grief, sadness, loneliness, guilt, regret, anger, fear, anxiety, anguish, or despair. These feelings are often as painful as any kind of physical suffering. Indeed, it is *because* of the pain that events or conflicts engender in us that we call them problems. Yet it is in this whole process of meeting and solving problems that life finds its meaning. Problems call forth our courage and wisdom; indeed, they create our courage and our wisdom. Problems are the cutting edge that distinguishes between success and failure. It is only because of problems that we grow mentally and spiritually.

The alternative—not to meet the demands of life on life's terms—means we will end up losing more often than not. Most people attempt to skirt problems rather than meet them head-on. We attempt to get out of them rather than suffer through them. Indeed, the tendency to avoid problems and the emotional suffering inherent in them is the primary basis of all psychological illness. And since most of us have this tendency to a greater or lesser degree, most of us lack complete mental health. Those who are most healthy learn not to dread but actually to welcome problems. Although triumph isn't guaranteed each time we face a problem in life, those who are wise are aware that it is only through the pain of confronting and resolving problems that we learn and grow.

-§-
Problems call forth our courage and wisdom; indeed, they create our courage and our wisdom.
-§-

Choices of Responsibility

Most people who come to see a psychotherapist are suffering from either a neurosis or what is called a character disorder. As indicated in *The Road Less Traveled,* these conditions are at root disorders of responsibility: the neurotic assumes too much responsibility and the person with a character disorder not enough. As such, they are opposite styles of relating to the world and its problems. When neurotics are in conflict with the world, they automatically assume that

they are at fault. When those with character disorders are in conflict with the world, they automatically assume that the world is at fault.

Even the speech patterns of neurotics and of those with character disorders are different. The speech of the neurotic is notable for such expressions as "I ought to," "I should," and "I shouldn't," indicating, to some extent, a self-image of an inferior person who believes he or she is always falling short of the mark, always making the wrong choices. The speech of a person with a character disorder, however, relies heavily on "I can't," "I couldn't," "I have to," and "I had to," demonstrating a self-image of a being who believes he or she has no power of choice, and whose behavior is completely directed by external forces totally beyond his or her control.

Before 1950, the term "character disorder" didn't exist as a separate diagnosis or category. Most psychiatric disorders were called neuroses, and neuroses were generally divided into two categories: ego-alien and ego-syntonic. An ego-alien neurosis was one in which the person's ego fought against a problematic condition. Since the individual didn't want to have the condition, he was willing to work toward alleviating it. An ego-syntonic neurosis, on the other hand, involves a condition a person's ego doesn't even want to identify, much less see as problematic in his life.

While I was an Army psychiatrist on the island of Okinawa, I met two women, both of whom had strong fears of snakes. Many people have a fear of snakes, so this wasn't unusual in itself. What made their fear problematic—and phobic—was the degree of incapacitation caused by it. To say the least, when daily routines are interrupted or neglected because of fear, it creates difficulties in many aspects of the person's life.

Okinawa was a natural place to see such phobias because of the dreaded habu, a snake unique to the island. It's poisonous, and its size falls somewhere between that of a large rattler and a small python. It also sleeps only during the day, which means that it does its roaming at night. There were about 100,000 Americans at Okinawa at the time; only about once in two years was one bitten by a habu, and half of those bitten had been walking out in the jungle at night, not around the Army housing sections. Adequate information was dispensed. All Americans were told about the snake, and all the hospitals had the necessary antitoxins to treat bites. Overall, not one American had actually been killed by a snake for years.

The first woman, who was in her early thirties, came to see me at my office. "I've got this fear of snakes and I know it's ridiculous," she said. "But I won't go out at night. I can't take my children out to the movies at night and I won't go to a club with my husband at night. It's really silly of me, because I know that hardly anyone gets bitten. I feel so stupid." As her language suggested, her phobia was ego-alien: it didn't fit with her self-image and was therefore conflictual to her. Although she was housebound most of the time and especially fearful of going out at night, she was willing to acknowledge that this was a problem in her life, and she wanted to find ways to lessen her fear so that it would not interfere with all her activities.

Freud first pointed out that phobias are often displacements from a real fear. What we found in therapy was that this woman had never faced up to existential issues involving her fear of death and fear of evil. Once she started dealing with such issues, although she still remained timid, she was able to go out at night with her husband and children. Thanks to treatment, by the time she was preparing to leave Okinawa, she was on the path of growth.

I learned about the second woman's fear of snakes only when I began talking to her toward the end of a dinner party she hosted. She was in her forties and the wife of an executive. In talking with her, I learned that she had become a recluse. She mentioned with enthusiasm how much she looked forward to going back to the United States, since she was housebound in Okinawa. "I can't go out because of those horrible snakes," she said. She knew that other people managed to go out at night, but said, "If they want to be stupid, that's their problem." Moreover, she blamed the American government and the island for her problem because "they should be doing more about those horrible snakes." As is typical of those with phobias that are ego-syntonic, she didn't see the fear as being her problem. She never sought out treatment even though the crippling consequences of her fear were evident. She had allowed her phobia to totally get in the way of living a fuller life. She refused to attend any social gatherings away from home—even those that were important to her husband's job—and she didn't seem to consider how this might jeopardize his career.

As these two cases demonstrate, neurotics are relatively easy to work with in psychotherapy because they assume responsibility for their difficulties and therefore see themselves as having problems. Those with character disorders are much more difficult to work with, because they don't see themselves as the source of their problems; they see the world rather than themselves as being in need of change, and therefore fail to recognize the necessity for self-examination.

Thus, a significant part of the existential suffering of life is the suffering involved in constantly discerning—or choosing—what we are responsible for and what we are not responsible for and maintain-

ing a healthy balance. Obviously, the character-disordered person avoids that existential suffering. What may not be so obvious is that the neurotic also does. By simply assuming that everything is her responsibility, she will ultimately suffer more through neurotic suffering—even though she does avoid the existential suffering of having to make choices, the kind of suffering that may be involved in saying to people, "No! I'm drawing a line."

The problem of distinguishing what we are and are not responsible for in this life is one of the continuing challenges of human existence. It is never completely resolved for all time. We must continually assess and reassess where our responsibilities lie in the ever-changing course of events that shape our lives. There is no formula for how to do it. Each situation is new and we must discern all over again the choice of what we are and are not responsible for. It is one that we must make thousands upon thousands of times, almost up until the very day we die.

Donna Eden & David Feinstein:

The Energies of Love

A relationship begins with the meeting of two very different energies. These energies come together and merge into a new energy field that has, literally, never before existed on the planet. You are then left to your own devices to figure out how to make it all work. Meanwhile, this union of energies determines the way you communicate, the way you fight, the way you love, and the way you want to be loved.

It is more than likely that you will be drawn to a partner who is energetically very different from yourself. You will also have much in common, things like shared values and passions; but on a more fundamental, energetic level, we tend to attract partners who are of a very different cloth. This can be exciting, especially at the beginnings of relationships, when the world is being opened up in new ways through the unique perspective of our beloved. In the good times, we enjoy the growth and intimacy that seem to occur spontaneously, as our partner's energy complements and rounds out our own. But in the tough times, these differences become enormous obstacles, triggering a deep stress response when we feel threatened, rejected, or unable to connect.

A key to experiencing relationship as an opportunity, a challenge to grow together, rather than as a battle or power struggle, lies in

Donna Eden, a pioneer in the field of holistic healing, is among the world's most sought-after, most joyous, and most authoritative spokespersons for energy medicine. She has taught some fifty thousand people how to understand the body as an energy system. Her best-selling book, *Energy Medicine* (Tarcher, 1999), has been translated into ten languages, and is a classic in its field.

David Feinstein, Ph.D., a clinical psychologist, is the author of seven books and more than fifty professional papers. He has taught at The Johns Hopkins University School of Medicine and Antioch College. He coauthored *The Promise of Energy Psychology* (Tarcher, 2005), and *The Mythic Path* (Elite, 2006). You can find out about their work at www.InnerSource.net.

understanding that you don't only have different ideas, behaviors, or feelings—you have entirely different energetic profiles. You are as different from your partner energetically as you are physically! When you want to improve your relationship, certainly psychology is important. But if you can understand the *energy* of relationships, this understanding will help you in ways that are more fundamental and more immediate.

We often joke—or half-joke—that if *we* can make it, any couple can make it. While our basic values, mercifully, complement one another's effortlessly, our personalities and temperaments are about as different as those of any two people we know. But we have been together for twenty-nine years, and have used these differences as a springboard for a still-growing body of personal and professional work.

Early in our relationship, David invited Donna to be a guest in a hypnosis class he was teaching. The evening's session focused on the various ways people code experience, based on Richard Bandler and John Grinder's work in Neurolinguistic Programming. There are four distinct types, which trace back to basic modes of processing information: seeing, hearing, feeling, and thinking. A good hypnotist will work one way with individuals who organize their inner world in a manner that corresponds with how they *see,* and another way with those who organize their inner world in a manner that corresponds with how they *feel.* David was presenting this information as a conceptual system to be used within the context of psychotherapeutic practice.

-§-
You are as different from your partner energetically as you are physically.
-§-

At the break, he stole a private moment with Donna, hoping to hear how impressed his new sweetie was with everything he had to say to this group of older, more seasoned, professional psychotherapists. Instead, she said, "Well, it was interesting to learn the characteristics of each of the four types, but I can see a way to determine a person's style using a simple physical test. After all, each of the types carries a different kind of energy."

Besides the little ego twinge he felt because she had not been dazzled enough to even comment on his teaching prowess, David was incredulous. How could a *physical* test pick up on these *psychological* differences? This was preposterous, and he was happy to share that revelation with her. Undaunted, Donna immediately turned her idea into an experiment, using the class members as subjects. Sure enough, those who he had identified as visuals tested differently from those who had been identified as kinesthetics, tonals, or digitals. By the time the class reconvened, this had become the buzz and was the only thing people wanted to talk about. So Donna wound up taking the rest of the evening, teaching a technique she calls energy testing and showing how it can be applied for determining people's representational styles. It was an exciting evening for all involved, though the remainder of David's planned agenda had to be put on the shelf. If he could have heard his guardian angels at that early point in the relationship, they would have been saying, "Get used to it, David!"

As it turns out, although Donna's idea seemed preposterous to David, it has proven itself in our work with hundreds of couples as a valid way for understanding how the partners process information during relationship stress. Just as each of us is born with a completely unique physical structure, we are also born with a completely unique "energy structure." The human brain has some one hundred billion neurons that each connect *electro*chemically with up to ten thousand other neurons. The brain's electrical impulses constitute an incomprehensibly complex energy system that maintains your habits of perceiving, thinking, and responding to your world.

Just as your brain is an energy system with complex electromagnetic pathways, so is your heart. And the signals generated by your heart are even stronger than those emitted by your brain—much stronger in fact. The electromagnetic field produced by your heart can be detected anywhere on the surface of your body using an electrocardiogram. It also extends a number of feet away from your body, radiating in all directions, where it can be detected by an instrument called a SQUID-based magnetometer.

So, when we say that there are four distinct energetic profiles, we are talking neither about abstract concepts nor something spiritual or otherworldly—we are talking about energy that is measurable, palpable, and *accessible,* which you can learn to work with consciously. Change the energies that travel through your nervous system and you can change your mood, your mind, and your life. Learn to make sense of the way your energetic disposition colors your experience of the world, and the way your partner's colors his or hers, and you will be able to work together to create an even stronger relationship based on deepened intimacy and understanding.

-§-
Change the energies that travel through your nervous system and you can change your mood, your mind, and your life.
-§-

You are wired to treat a threat to your closest relationships as a survival issue. This means that when stress is caused by difficulties with your partner, your perceptions narrow, your capacity for logic diminishes, and your readiness to fight or flee is heightened. In fact, the closer a person is to you, the harder it is to keep that person in perspective when you are feeling stress about the relationship. And

the way you blur and distort the one you love has everything to do with your primary sensory or "representational" mode, which itself grows out of your particular energetic style.

Your primary sensory mode is not the actual *act* of seeing, hearing, or feeling. Rather, you *organize your inner world* most closely according to the *principles* of seeing, hearing, feeling, or abstract logic. Human thought is extraordinarily flexible, and each of us normally combines all four modes. But we instinctually tend to put more emphasis on one or two of them; and when we are under stress, particularly relationship stress, all but our primary mode fades into the background. We distort the one we love according to the principles of the sensory mode we trust the most. The other three modes simply shut down. It is not a choice but a physiological, energetic response. And when this occurs, we cannot help but distort and act inappropriately. It's the natural thing to do.

-§-
We distort the one we love according to the principles of the sensory mode we trust the most.
-§-

Your primary representational style or channel is far more than a mere psychological difference between you and others. *It is built into your physical energy* structure, and our impression is that it is built into your genes. When Donna (who sees energy in a clairvoyant-like manner) carefully watches a couple in a stressful situation, she will see one of four distinct energetic modes emerge in each partner. This energy corresponds with a way of experiencing the situation that is patterned after seeing, hearing, feeling, or thinking (the visual, tonal, kinesthetic, and digital "representational channels"). See if you recognize yourself and your partner in the next four paragraphs. Understanding your partner's representational mode, and your own, is one of the most important steps you can take for strengthening the bridges that connect you.

If a person's primary representational channel is *visual,* the energies of the body concentrate in the head and the upper chest during times of relationship stress. The energies then move outward through the eyes, head, and chest, appearing to tunnel toward the other person who, incidentally, experiences the visual as having tunnel vision. Without the other modes to round out the picture, the visual style loses perspective, normally its greatest strength. With the energy radiating outward, attention moves to the other, with a focus on how the other is the cause of the problem. The visual's "helpful" analysis is experienced by the other as judgment and blame.

If the primary mode is *kinesthetic,* the energies move inward, rather than outward, during interpersonal stress. Whatever energies the partner is emanating are absorbed by the kinesthetic's body. They blend with the crisis that has already been triggered into a muddle of internal energies that seem to implode upon themselves. The distinction between oneself and the other is long gone. The energy concentrates in the center of the heart, radiates out to the trunk of the body, and becomes slow and heavy, like sludge. Thinking is not supported, as the most vital energies have left the brain. Grounding and stability are also compromised as the energies in the hips, legs, and feet become weak. Thick, painful energy also accumulates in the heart and chest of kinesthetics, until they feel like they are about to burst or to drown. From this constellation, kinesthetics are required to make the choices that will shape their relationships.

For a *digital* under stress, it is almost the opposite. Most of the energy accumulates in the forebrain. The body is so cut off energetically that the heart and the gut have little influence on the person's experience and, in fact, the language of the heart is muted. Meanwhile, a rich choreography of energy is unfolding within the brain. Energy from the back brain rushes to the cerebral cortex, the front brain, with a primal force. The verbal reasoning and logic of the front brain overshadow the primitive needs of the back brain, giving them the appearance of clarity and calmness. This seems to the digital to be the paragon of rational, civilized thought. The system is closed and encapsulated. Not only do the energies of the heart and gut have no pathways to consciousness, the energy of the partner bounces off like rubber bands shot at a granite wall. The partner's logic, feelings, and desperate pleas do not upset the digital, who is not *consciously* trying to dismiss the other. The other's concerns are just not relevant and will be put to rest when the partner grasps the logic of the digital's superior understanding.

The style of someone who is *tonal* can resemble a blend of the other three. The energy concentrates in two locations: 1) the solar plexus, and 2) the area between and including the ears. The vibratory rate of the outside world is sensitively registered by the tonal and then reverberates in the organs that govern intense emotion, such as the stomach, liver, gall bladder, kidneys, spleen, pancreas, and adrenals.[1] Under stress, the partner's comments may activate a torrent of inner emotion that is not particularly related to the actual words or intended meaning. The tonal's acute sensitivity, which under peaceful conditions lends itself to exquisite aesthetic sensibilities, leads to a cacophony of painful and contradictory emotions under stress. Everything seems to scream at the tonal under stress, sound becomes extraordinarily personal, and the distinction between the sounds generated by the partner and

-§-
Energy dynamics can become a source of strength, rather than a source of division.
-§-

those generated by the internal organs is lost. A rich drama of incompatible emotions may be enacted until the tonal has little choice but to escape from the bombardment.

Things get really complex when two different energy types enter into a relationship, and they begin to trip all over one another's ingrained tendencies. Recently, at a seminar in Seattle, a couple in the audience volunteered to let us discuss their likely communication and conflict patterns, based upon our reading of their sensory energetic types. The interactions (transcribed here from a videotape) began with Donna energy testing them each to determine their primary sensory mode. Then we made a few "lucky" guesses.

-§-

"High-banding" is a habit that can be cultivated.

-§-

Donna: Dan's style is tonal. Annette's style is visual. Visuals can see very well what you're doing wrong [*laughter, first from Dan and Annette, then from the entire group*]. And it may feel at times that she's blaming you, but for her, it's just so disappointing that you aren't seeing it in the obvious way. [*more laughter*]

Dan: Were you in the back seat of our car? [*laughter*]

Donna: I knew she was visual as soon as I looked into her eyes. There's a power that comes out of a visual's eyes. You *know* it when you're being looked at by a visual. Annette, your secondary mode is kinesthetic, so you've also got a lot of feeling. But when the distress is really bad, you go into visual, where you desperately want him to see things as you see them.

David: So more and more, you see what he is doing wrong, and you are really wanting to persuade him to do it *right.* Seems perfectly reasonable, doesn't it! Meanwhile, for Dan, as a tonal he is able to hear between the lines. And that can be great. The best therapists are tonal or have a fair amount of tonal. They can hear what is meant even when it is not being said. The trouble, when you go into stress, is that sometimes what you hear doesn't have too much to do with what is actually going on.

Dan: You really were in the back seat of the car! [*much laughter*]

David: But it's comforting to know that it's not just that your partner is totally hopeless [*more audience laughter*]. The dynamics at work here are so basic that once you understand how they play out in your relationship, they can become a source of strength, rather than a source of division. But for most couples, the differences in their representational styles are under-appreciated and misunderstood. Annette, it must be exasperating when you find yourself in the middle of an argument for having said things you never said. Next, you're watching him go into a major retreat.

Donna: Tonals can check out totally. They can be looking right at you and not taking in a thing [*Annette's expression affirms this so strongly that the audience roars*]. The whole dialogue can be in their heads, so you are not heard at all. On the other hand [*turning to Dan*], you're dealing with a visual, so all the bad things you think she is saying may be exactly what she means. [*much laughter*]

David: So part of the trick is to realize that sometimes what you think you're hearing between the lines, really is what she is saying, but sometimes it isn't. So there you have it.

This is just one of the possible combinations, but chances are that you may be starting to see yourself or your partner reflected in one of these types. The only quick, dependable test we know for determining your primary energetic sensory profile is the one Donna invented all those years ago—but to perform it you need detailed instruction in energy testing. You can see this demonstrated in our *Energies of Love* DVD program.[2] The technique itself is quite simple, and instruction in energy testing is widely available.[3]

By creating a workable map of your own sensory energetic system, and by understanding your partner's natural sensory energetic tendencies, you give yourself a tool that is reliable and useful for building intimacy. In the heat of conflict, when it feels as if your partner is against you—or even downright crazy—you can turn to this understanding and step back from your own instinctive reactions. A working knowledge of the sensory systems makes it easier for you to give your partner the benefit of the doubt, and to put his or her behavior into the highest possible understanding and light; we call this the high band.

-§-

Make a pact with your partner to *stop, look,* and *listen* when conflict arises.

-§-

Much of the misinterpretation that causes you to direct hurtful, negative, and harmful motivations toward your partner stems directly from a lack of understanding that your partner is a different energy, responding to the same situation as you are, but in a very different way. The great news here is that this means high-banding, giving your partner the benefit of the doubt and thereby shifting the energy, is a habit that can be cultivated. Even if you may lose it in the most intense moments, with practice, the high band can become more of the default position—the place you come back to.

But, while grasping these concepts intellectually may help you peg deeper dimensions of your struggles, understanding alone is not

likely to shift the patterns. In order to get to the point of being able to "high-band" a situation in the first place, you have to be able to interrupt your own energetic sensory crisis, the fight-or-flight response to relational stress, and return to a place of relative composure.

If two people are within conversational distance, fluctuations in the heart signal of one correspond with fluctuations in the brain waves of the other. This means that when one partner experiences meltdown, the changes in his or her electrical system occur in his or her brain and heart, as well; this, in response, triggers measurable electrical changes in his or her partner's brain and heart. This electrical dissonance makes it extremely difficult to stop the ride, and we realized early on in our work that this needed to be our first focus in improving intimacy and communication. Not empathy, not analysis, not insight. Conscious intention in working with the four energetic profiles can bring about incredible shifts in chronically dysfunctional relational responses. But in acute situations, when one or both partners are already triggered and understanding has flown out the window, you need concrete techniques to bring the energy back into balance.

-§-
Changing the energy becomes a shared achievement.
-§-

It is much easier to create a crisis plan when you're not *in the middle* of a crisis. This is why we recommend that you and your partner make a rock-solid pact, when you are feeling a strong connection, to *stop, look,* and *listen* when conflict arises. We explain this process in detail in our *Energies of Love* DVD, and in an upcoming book of the same title, but the basic principles are simple—though not necessarily easy. Even if your partner refuses to work with you, you can use these techniques on your own to effect real energetic change.

Before reactive, stress-triggered energy patterns can be reined in, the very first thing you must do is to literally stop what you are doing, thinking, and saying. This is harder than it sounds. Every fiber of your being is engaged in a rapidly escalating conflict. You've just been insulted, dismissed, or weathered an accusation that no person with any self-respect would leave unanswered. And you are supposed to *stop?* Impossible! When fight-or-flight hormones are surging through your body and you are caught in your primary sensory mode, a momentum takes over that has its own life. It may feel dreadful, but it is compelling. Stopping at such a moment is the hardest part of this formula. But if you don't stop, the biochemistry of fight-or-flight reflexively takes you over. If, on the other hand, you can honor your pact with one another and shift the agenda from pursuing the conflict to *changing the energy,* you can break the spell and move into the biochemistry of tend and befriend. And changing the energy itself becomes a shared achievement.

One very simple, physical technique for grounding your energy is called the Three Thumps. Certain points on your body, when tapped with your fingers, will affect your energy field in predictable ways, sending electrochemical impulses to specific regions of your brain and releasing neurotransmitters. By tapping three specific sets of points, you can activate a series of internal responses that will restore you when you are tired or stressed. You can also tap these points at any time during your day that you need a boost. The Three Thumps include: the "K-27" points (the 27th acupuncture points on the kidney meridian), which are located in the tender hollows just beneath your clavicle; the thymus, which is located at the sternum (where gorillas thump); and the spleen "neurolymphatic" points on either side of the ribcage, about four inches beneath your underarms. Among other things, tapping on these points helps your system to metabolize the stress energy that you experience during conflict, so that you can come back into your own center and approach the situation with more calm and compassion. Do not be overly concerned about finding the precise location of each point. If you use several fingers to tap in the vicinity described, you will hit the right spot. Tap hard enough that you hear the tap, but never so hard as to risk bruising yourself.

While the Three Thumps technique is done alone (though, preferably, in unison with your partner), another excellent energy balancing exercise, the Spinal Flush, is done by one of you for the other. It is a gift you can give to one another. It not only feels good, it also releases toxins that are generated by the fight-or-flight response back into the lymph system, where they can be eliminated. The Spinal Flush tends to balance each of the meridians, the body's energy pathways. And, it is a kind act you can do for your partner before you are *feeling* kind or able to say kind things.

1. Have your partner lie face down, or stand, three or four feet from a wall and lean into it with both hands. This positions the body to remain stable while you apply pressure to your partner's back.
2. Massage the points down both sides of your partner's spine (but not directly on the spine), using the thumbs or middle fingers and applying body weight to get strong pressure. While most people can tolerate and will enjoy considerable pressure on these points, check to be sure you are not pressing harder than your partner wants. You will be massaging from the bottom of the neck all the way down to the bottom of the sacrum.

3. Go down the notches along the vertebrae and deeply massage each point. Staying on the point for at least three seconds, move the skin up and down or in a circular motion, with strong pressure.

   Upon reaching the sacrum, you can repeat the massage. When completed, "sweep" the energies down your partner's body from the shoulders, and with open hands, drag it all the way down the legs and off the feet. Repeat the sweep two or three times.

   Once you have stopped and redirected the energy flow, you and your partner can move into the next stage of the process by looking at the situation in a manner that *respects* your partner's primary mode and *expands* you beyond your own.

Your automatic, primal response to stress shapes your relationships. It is during the tense times, *at least* as much as during tender ones, that the foundation of a relationship is set. Keeping your energy balanced and in harmony with your partner's will allow you to move with more integrity through the difficult moments.

Energy techniques are powerful tools for reducing the heat of a conflict. Meanwhile, an emotionally-focused understanding of your fundamental energy type, and of your partner's, gives you a map of the differences in how you perceive, communicate, argue, love, and want to be loved. The combination of these techniques with this understanding has given couple after couple an inlet to deeper intimacy, and a greater ability to find one another during the inevitable stormy times.

---

1 This formulation is derived from the time-honored and strikingly sophisticated "five element theory" of traditional Chinese medicine. See, for instance, "The Meridians and The Emotions" in David Feinstein's *Energy Psychology Interactive* (Ashland: Innersource, 2004), pp 234–240.

2 Donna Eden and David Feinstein, "The Energies of Love" DVD, available from www.innersource.net.

3 See, for instance, Chapter 2 of Donna Eden's *Energy Medicine* (New York: Tarcher/Penguin, 1998).

Stephanie DeRosier: The Thousand Archetypes of Love

Love is not linear. Sex is not rational. Emotions won't cooperate with the mind's methodical attempts to analyze lust's sticky substance. The brain will not sit idly by and watch while the heart, lungs, groin, and guts break from convention and dive headlong into the sensual experience. And the spirit can never thrive when deprivation exists in any part of our being. This is the crux of the matter: All ends must meet, must join together in some semblance of harmony and participation, if ever a fully engaging and satisfying experience of sexuality is to be had.

But where do we get permission to be alive in every way—to take the risk of opening our eyes when we kiss, to touch every part of ourselves as well as another without fear of reproach? Somewhere deep inside lies a memory of such freedom and bravery. It must surface if we are to be women who love. We must grant the permission today that was not granted to us as children, young girls, or teenagers. We must, with the love and support of others, liberate ourselves from the prison of our minds, the minefield of our hearts, and the dragon's lair of our sex. We must brave the fire of honesty that strips away deceit and illusions of security—stand naked in front of the mirror to face every curve, wrinkle, follicle, dimple, and pimple until the inherent beauty and sensuality pours out into the room for our eyes to see. We must look forward to imagine the possibilities and back to face the

Stephanie DeRosier is a Licensed Massage Therapist with a B.A. in Philosophy. Stephanie manifests her dream for the world through her company, The Love Project, where she uses creativity and the chakra system to clear the blocks that prevent people from being what we naturally are: clear channels for divine creativity and love. Through The Love Project, she writes, teaches classes, gives consultations, and does hands-on healing work. Born in Helena, Montana, Stephanie now lives in Ojai, California with her partner, Rob, their gentle black lab, Coda, and Maizy, an independent outdoor feline. Photo by Rob Clement.

source of the fear, anger, hurt, and pain that shuts us down, leaves us believing there is only room for one part of us at a time in life.

We must be willing to face ourselves, and the roads we've traveled, in the archetypal journey through lust, love, passion, and pain... without judgment.

Penthouse magazine used to have a comic strip featuring a beautiful, big-breasted dominatrix who loved to be tied up by strange, sadistic, mad scientist-looking men in dungeons—on her way to conquering the world or slaying bad guys. Or something like that. I read them in my spare time as a child. Sensuous, adult magazines taught me how to be sexual. How to be a sexual object. I was a sensitive, impressionable young child. I was four.

-§-
To an already conflicted youth, society offers the gallant mixed message of "don't have sex" and "just do it."
-§-

I remember my first crush. He was taller than me, and a few years older, but he never seemed to mind my watching him, his hair dancing in the sun, skin golden like honey, swirling down the corkscrew slide and running under the big kid swings on the playground. I was five.

By the lamplight of my little blue bedroom, piles of stuffed animals all around, I reached my first orgasm. I was seven.

It's shameful. In a culture of so much sexual currency we do not protect the innocent sensuality of youth. The Maiden's budding breasts and glowing skin are inherently attractive; and, without healthy instruction and support from elders, can often invite experiences both dangerous and unexpected.

While the other fifth-grade girls were padding their white, lacy training-bras in hopes of catching the sixth graders' eyes, I was wiping my clammy little hands against my dusty corduroys, praying none of my guy friends would notice my already-too-small tan trainer. They noticed. Though other girls might've envied me, I was devastated as the letters on my bras increased from trainer to DD in three years' time. Drunken men made passes at me as I waited on bar stools for grown-ups to take me home. I had unwittingly become the woman in the pictures. I was in eighth grade.

"Let me rub your back," he said as the TV rattled on across the little musty living room.

"Nah, I'm okay. Really, I'm fine."

"Here, it will feel good."

He moved the wooden massage roller over my back. Under my shirt. Closer to my side. Around near my breasts. My mind went blank, aching legs, silent scream. *Help me.*

"I have to go to the bathroom."

"Wait."

"No! I really have to go!" He released me. I ran, hid, pressed my small frame against the door. Begged empty space for someone to save me. *Mommy. Call Mommy.* The phone seemed a hundred miles away from the door. Would he stop me? No, he's a coward. I'm just a little girl.

"Mommy?"

"Honey? What's wrong?" Tears welled up in my eyes, lips quivered in fear and anxiety.

"Mom, I want to come home." I was twelve.

To an already conflicted youth, strangled by hormones and loneliness, society offers the gallant mixed message of "don't have sex" and "just do it." As teenagers, we are full of desire, but for what? We are full of angst, but over what? Before long, it doesn't matter what the real answers may be. We let desire and curiosity guide our ship, drawn by an unnamable feeling that what we long for is "out there" somewhere. The archetypal journey begins unfolding through the flesh. And we grasp one another, aching for the world to meet us in the places we feel most alone. Mythic characters of Heroes and Rebels find their places in our beds—looking, perhaps, for their own counterparts, seeking the shadows they themselves have yet to embody.

-§-
Sex was the best—or fastest—way to feel "good enough," at least for right now.
-§-

Two sentences comprised the sum of my sexual guidance. "You come from a very sexual family," and, "Make sure it's with someone you love." At fifteen, these defined the parameters of my new goal: losing my virginity. Somewhere inside, I suspected I wasn't emotionally prepared—that I was selling my innocence for a ticket to nowhere. But boys were intoxicating. The taste of their lips, the texture of their tongues, and the musky, delicate scent of their skin filled my body's yearning. Desire won the round. So, I waited until the first sign of having "fallen in love," and let the young gentleman know with stunted, nonverbal cues that I was ready. As much as one can expect an eighteen-year-old boy to be, he was present, thoughtful, and kind.

Like an animal let out of a cage, my hunger led to a long chain of sexual partners and innocence-defiling, lust-filled encounters. Perhaps I took the easy way out, choosing sexuality over chastity, excess over restraint. But it was just too hard to say no—to my curiosity, my desire, my unending need for approval, and the particular kind of attention found in the arms of a teenaged boy. If I was a slut, there were bigger ones. If I was a prude, then there is no such thing.

My eyes fluttered open to the slow, deliberate notes from U2's "With or Without You" as it flowed from the soft glow of the alarm clock. The wrestler awoke and moved closer…touched me in the darkness…made love with me again. I was fifteen.

High school came and passed. Two among the many had a hold on me for years to come—one haunted, the other broke my heart. The Artist loved me so honestly and openly that I couldn't help but love him back. He officially broke my heart at the end of my junior year. It was a death of faith from which I felt sure to never recover.

-§-
Somewhere inside, most of us believe that if we could just meet that perfect someone, then love wouldn't be so hard.
-§-

The other, the quiet Rebel, shook my heart and trembled my soul. Like a ghost, he moved through my world, leaving sighs and cravings behind. I couldn't tell him the truth. I could never be that honest—or that vulnerable. Together, they reflected my innermost experience of love: a toggle between the safe, levelheaded life and a fiercely passionate, but volatile one. The Artist and the Rebel mirrored my own duality—an immense power I struggled to escape and embrace.

A wounded animal will chew off its own leg to break free from a snare. Friends and grocery tellers often suffer the venom of a widow's grieving tones. And young girls cut themselves to release their inner agony. Our pain, unaddressed, takes us for a ride. This is the "value" of intoxicants—to numb the blinding pain of an untreated wound. Sex became my drug, the magic elixir that brought comfort and confidence to an insecure and lonely life. For me, it was the best—or fastest—way to feel "good enough," at least for right now.

"I didn't know you had sex with John."

"Um."

"He taped it. Did you know?"

"Oh God."

"I haven't heard it myself. I don't want to, even though we weren't together then; but his best friend told me about it. I was kind of embarrassed for you."

"Oh my God." I was sixteen.

Halloween. Acid. The end of a party. He kissed me, pressed me into the couch. I kissed back at first, then got scared. Blacked-out drunk. I didn't want this. He pulled me down onto the floor—his best friend passed out in a chair three feet away. *Don't make noise*...paralyzed. He pulled my pants down. Too big to push off of me.

"No. Please. No. Don't."

"Shhh, Steph. Be quiet."

"Don't. Don't." Then inside me. One tear, then another. I couldn't get away. I was seventeen.

Disappointment, shame, and fear of ridicule are terrific motivators for a wounded heart to pick one person and try to make it last. These dark feelings, however, often manifest the darkness in us. Our relationship paths often spiral downward, toward further abandonment of self for the illusion of security found in another.

After high school, I attempted the seemingly stable realm of serial mini-monogamy. One boyfriend led to another; lovers would come and go. With so many passing connections and no clear boundaries of my own, I soon felt awash with the Wounded Prostitute; trading seconds of security for pieces of flesh and soul. I was emotionally homeless in a dangerous, lonely world.

Eventually, I sought refuge in the company of a young man who had the makings of a Great Protector. And he was. The Loner shielded me from everyone—except himself. Our chemistry was fierce, the sex intoxicating, and the relationship quickly became violent. The first bite to my face shook me, but when I yelped out in pain, he said he couldn't help himself, he wanted me so much—magic. Our world soon dwindled to the two of us, leaving no one to see my bruises or to watch me wasting away.

Pinned to the waterbed. Hands going numb. Wrists held tight above my head. His weight heavy on me.

"Get...off of me." *Fight back the tears. Don't let him see your fear.*

"I will when you LISTEN TO ME!" I was twenty.

The morning he was taken to jail I heard a tiny, frightened voice inside, pleading "Run, run for your life." And, I did.

Bitterness descended upon my heart: years of longing for connection, miles of flesh only to find myself alone in agony, with nothing to show for the time but bruises and disappointment. I had opportunity to seek sexual solace among a group of bisexual women. But I knew I would fail there just as I had with men, that the mess and the pattern

would be the same. I could not abide that and turned my eyes to the floor. The damage to my heart, body, and mind seemed irreparable. And I buried this awareness deep in the caverns of my soul, hoping no one would ever know how broken I was—not even me.

-§-
The Place of Unraveling gives us a chance to live from faith—if we are willing to let things fall apart.
-§-

Somewhere inside, most of us believe that if we could just meet that perfect someone, then love wouldn't be so hard: we'd feel good about ourselves, relationship would be a safe place, and good sex would never end. The search for the perfect partner, the answer to our prayers, drives us repeatedly to an emotional pivot point, where we choose to keep trying, or bag the relationship idea and go it alone. Even in surrendering to solitude, the notion often persists. For many, this remains the most nagging, puzzling facet of the human heart.

I fumbled for the phone, half-awake. It was my gynecologist… genital herpes. I buried my tear-stained face in the pillow, disgusted and afraid. *No one would ever love me now.* I was twenty-one.

But along came the Hero: alone at the cafe, sipping espresso, with his long hair, leather jacket and motorcycle helmet by his side. In his presence, my heart felt like the calm blue of the Caribbean. He offered soulful stability, free from the reckless world of drugs and alcohol I'd known all my life. I let my world melt into his and put the weight of my life in his hands. It was too much. It always is.

There we were—The Hero and the Butterfly Princess, with dragons to slay, castles to clean, and the glamour of perfection to maintain so the world would not see us dying inside.

"When are you gonna start having babies?"

"You would have such beautiful children."

"You know your mother's dying to be a grandmother."

"You're going to make a wonderful mother, Stephanie." I was twenty-five.

A lifetime of perfectionism set me up for a devastating fall from grace when I had two miscarriages instead the beautiful child everyone was hoping for. It's impossible to be a "good mother" if you can't even get them into the world. I blamed the Hero and God, but mostly myself, drowning in pain. Some women get back on the proverbial horse and try again. I shut down.

Often, on our sexual path, we come to a Place of Unraveling, where we no longer find refuge in the story we've been telling. We address the mirror to find a woman we don't recognize, along with closets of "clothes" that don't fit us. The makeup smears and we get a glimpse of the real woman underneath all life's contracts and conventions. We have a choice then, to reclaim who we are. It's a matter of willingness...to go to any length. When we are willing to grab our own hand and go forward, a Great Power fills us. The Place of Unraveling gives us a chance to live from faith—if we are willing to let things fall apart.

For years I'd tried to control my marriage: crying, complaining, pacing the floor at night waiting for him to come home. He loved me, he heard me, but nothing changed...until I shut down. Then the castle crumbled. We entered therapy after several sexless months, and I began the slow, terrifying journey toward wellness—facing the sexual abuse of my childhood and the effects of an early entry into the delicate and dangerous adult world of sexuality. These rites of passage ripped a hole for my soul to shine through. With the constant, compassionate support of my therapist, I removed the first layers of armor that had prevented me from loving or trusting myself. And, with the gift of great spiritual direction, we came to the end of our marriage in a state of love and relative peace.

-§-
The One is not human. It is an archetypal force whose traits manifest in each of us.
-§-

My personal work had brought me to a point of...well...wanting it all. I had seen how each of my relationships had lacked connection on one level, if not many. I was done accepting less! I was seeking someone with whom I could share all of myself—spirit, mind, voice, heart, guts, sex, and roots. And I wanted him right now...

After two stumbled, embarrassing attempts to convince old friends to fall in love with me, I met the One. I thrust myself into love, gorging on the passion I'd denied myself through the coldness of my marriage. And he received me with great enthusiasm, until one day he went away. Suddenly, without warning, my intensity went unrequited once again. Though my pattern of cold and hot was now horribly clear, I still wanted someone to love me back. My heart broke again as I began to understand that he was not the One...*because there is no One.*

For, the One is not human. It is—as with all the others—an archetypal force whose traits manifest in each of us, to one degree or another. The One has the power to make all the pain go away, to cast aside all doubt, to build confidence in another, to forge a bond of safety with another, to promise all will be well and deliver on that promise for all time. These are the qualities of God, not a human being, no matter how wonderful one may be. With this awareness comes the solemn

understanding that the highest hope to have for a loved one is the freedom to be human, and that we need the same for ourselves.

And so it is with me: I am not the Butterfly Princess, though her magic and mischief shine in my eyes. I am Steph. Just me.

And, as Steph, I have been searching all my life for Him, the one wonderful Him to make my life complete and give me the love I so deeply desire. Every time I think I've found Him, the world seems lighter and more beautiful, and perhaps for a time it is. Because love, however naïve its origins, does bring hope and wonder to our lives and should never be minimized or trivialized. Without love, life simply is not worth the breath or the work. Still, the true source of love comes from one's own heart; if we continue to look outside ourselves, we will never find it.

-§-
As I take the time to love myself directly, others gain permission to love me in their own way.
-§-

5 A.M. We stood facing each other in the dim light of the empty parking lot. Holding hands, we gazed into one another's eyes for a full fifteen minutes. He did not look away. This was the most intimate moment of my life. I was thirty.

Finally, the Other snuck up and kicked my spiritual travel into overdrive with his honesty and persistent nudging toward self-actualization. I was still impulsive, intense, and willing to immerse myself in another's world. His patient, structured, quiet, and methodical nature blessed me with a clear picture of my own Shadow. We struggled as our mirror journeys to the same place led us in opposite directions. I tried so hard to hold the connection that, when the cord finally snapped, I landed squarely in own my lap—face-to-face with a lifetime of unmet grief. Somehow, as the hailstorm of loss poured from my chest, I stayed present. I took care of myself, let other women support me and, above all, did not seek solace in another man. With that change in behavior, something fundamental began to shift with my experience of love. I grew more patient and tolerant of the grieving process.

One day I found myself placing pictures of the Other, the One, and the Hero on my shelf, all blended together. Their faces, smiling back at me or kissing my cheek, sent me reeling. I understood then: the changes in our relationships came about because we needed room to grow, *not because I was unlovable.* I could feel them all loving me. They'd loved me all along! My only error had been in expecting love to look and feel a certain way before I could accept it. As I take the time to love myself directly, others gain permission to love me in their own way. Their loving becomes an expression of their being instead of a statement about me.

I move forward today knowing that the love that I want is from myself. When I love myself truly, through every crappy mood and judgment I carry, I can trust myself. Then, I can go into the world and learn to trust others. Every archetypal energy carried by a lover resides, as well, in me. I am all these: Maiden, Artist, Rebel, Prostitute, Loner, Hero, One, and many others. The souls who carried these energies for me were and are my teachers.

I also move forward, having encountered some difficult truths about the world. We don't protect our children. We send mixed sexual messages to our teenagers, who could use our support instead of our own displaced fears and desires further mixing them up. And, we habitually look outside ourselves for the core of love. Yet, the love or resentment we might feel for another is often nothing more than our own energy bouncing back at us to help our soul grow. Our Guides wear cloaks of many colors. And, though I may bless them with kisses or curse them in anger, I try to love them in the same way I try to love myself.

I've not yet come to where I'm going. That feels clear. But, having regained my own love along the way, I feel as if a lost friend has finally made it home. That just feels good.

The street of intimacy has a million stop lights and intersections—innumerable storefronts with tantalizing images of magic-made-real inside. The road is often lonely, even with the best of companions. Still, we continue our work. Why? So that sexuality can be a respected part of ourselves, not something to be controlled by or ashamed of; so we may feel safe in loving someone, without needing to be by one another's sides at all times; even just to look in the mirror with love and know we are enough. And we are. By the sheer fact of being here, we've earned a seat at the table of life—one of respect, compassion, and consideration. Because love is the fabric of our existence.

Stan Hall:

From Righteous to Curious

Nearly every game we humans play has, as its goal, beating the opponent. Winners are perceived as better and celebrated. Losers are condescendingly patted on the back and consoled with the words, "What matters most is how you played the game." Nice try, but the subconscious mind—the part of us that largely runs the show—is not so easily fooled.

According to cell biologist Dr. Bruce Lipton (www.brucelipton.com), we live in a type of hypnotic state until somewhere in the neighborhood of six years old. Very little conscious discernment of right and wrong is available until that time; it simply has not yet developed. A child's mind is designed to discover which behaviors get his or her needs met and which do not, and to instinctively absorb strategies that maximize happiness and success. If undiscerning consciousness has a choice between feeling celebrated for winning, or placated for losing, which do you think it will choose?

Behaviors that garner approval are largely based on either being right or doing it right. The resulting kudos form the foundation of our self-esteem. Most of us operate from the axiom, *In order to be a valuable person, I must be right and I must win.* We learn to showcase our brilliance from the time we are tots. This often morphs into a "know-it-all" persona of various stripes. By the time we are teens, we have

Stan Hall, MBA, is a dedicated Certified Advanced Instructor for a remarkable process for healing subconscious beliefs called PSYCH-K. He has a valuable combination of fifteen years of corporate service along with a simultaneous self-study of consciousness, spiritual development, and alternate realities. His extensive study and practice includes three years of training with the Foundation for Spiritual Development in San Rafael, California; Brainwave Neurofeedback training at the Biocybernaut Institute in San Jose, California; Avatar; DNA Manifestation; Crystal Healing Dimensions; and academically, an MBA through California Lutheran University in Thousand Oaks, California. For more about Stan, visit www.LifeMuse.org.

crafted a sense of self that serves to bolster our ego when needed, and protect us from rejection at all costs.

By the time we reach puberty and begin to have our first romantic feelings, subconscious approval-seeking behaviors are solidly in place. We piece ourselves together in hopes of attracting love, only to find that our "winning formula" has created a Frankenstein-like distortion of our true self. As we wander farther and farther away from our true nature, we eventually hit a wall and our unmet needs surface—often with a vengeance. That's when the "know-it-all" wakes up to a sobering realization: *I don't even know myself.*

Above All, Be Right

"Not me," you say? We like to think that we have escaped this trap, but the need to be right runs most of us more than we realize. Here is a quick reality check: Ask yourself, *Have I ever been in an argument?* If the answer if yes, the need to be right affects you, at least to some extent.

-§-

"The most important things to learn are the things you learn after you already know it all."
—Source unknown

-§-

Arguments are strategies to prove we're right, and we pay a dear price for them, especially in our intimate relationships. The subconscious fear of being wrong or imperfect creates quite a chasm between partners. If left unadressed, these fears can completely block the path to growth and learning that is vital to any joyful relationship.

The need to be right stems from an inability to self-validate. We grow up receiving an immense amount of external validation from parents, teachers, babysitters, and the like, until our nervous system is programmed for performance: *Do this or that, and you will get a treat!* We learn that happiness is in the reward, and fall into the trap of looking outside for praise and verification of our essential worth. In the process, we learn to hide the parts of us we presume to be imperfect.

Likewise, we develop a wide array of skills to help us work through difficult, unfamiliar, or uncomfortable interactions. We learn to manipulate others in the service of fulfilling our agendas, whatever they may be. Watch how parents treat a misbehaving child, and the source of these patterns becomes obvious. In the intensity of the moment, a parent will attempt to control the child through physical or psychological means, to serve his or her own need for convenience or relief from frustration. In so doing, the parent's in-the-moment need overshadows the child's long term need to be nurtured through wisdom. Such experiences can scramble a child's sense of right and wrong. Strategies to avoid penalty or manipulation displace the natural desire to serve life. It is as though we learn to back our way into relationships with other humans, instead of going head on. No wonder relationships are so complicated!

This type of learned behavior is neither bad nor wrong. However, by noticing how, when, and where the patterns play out, we can begin to see the limitaitons and decide whether or not they really work. If not, break out of it and begin to develop the skill to express your wants and needs in a way that feels authentic and actually engenders an authentic response. When we venture out of the patterned norm and explore beyond the game, we get to trade in what is comfortable for something wonderful.

Letting go of the need to be right creates a fresh approach to relationships. Instead of being colored by defensiveness, insecurity, and even contempt, our relationships blossom when self-responsibility, curiosity, and appreciation fill the air around two people. Then, a remarkable synthesis can emerge, wherein each partner becomes both teacher and student to the other.

Managing Impressions

Impression management, a term coined by Dr. James Hardt of the Biocybernaut Institute, refers to our tendency to mask undesirable or destructive tendencies. We present a good impression with outward behaviors that get us what we want. Having discovered that some of our automatic reactions are unwelcome, we learn to manage these behaviors. Often, these overrides become new subconscious reactions, and we lose touch with what is happening.

Unraveling these overrides is like peeling the proverbial onion, a necessary exercise if we want the true self to be free. In my own life, freedom only began to dawn when I unraveled the overrides that concealed my dark side.

As a child, I took great pleasure in torturing cats as an expression of my misunderstood cruelty. The hearty thwack I received on the backside of my head each time I was caught led me to a clear understanding that this was unacceptable behavior. In turn, I devised an effective, covert substitute. The cats were happier, but others in my life began to pay the price. I began throwing tantrums, destroying things, and lashing out at others—both physically and verbally. I even considered suicide, not because I wanted to die, but simply out of spite. I was the kid who would flare at bullies when they picked on

-§-
We don't have to know the origin of our habits to make a change.
-§-

the weak kids. I put myself in harm's way time and again. My rage was so strong, it didn't matter how big or tough the bully.

Later, when this strategy created more problems than it was worth, I turned my rage toward women. Physical abuse was never my thing; emotional abuse worked perfectly well. My modus operandi was to get a woman to fall in love with me, then sabotage the relationship and break both our hearts. This cycle continued for more than thirty years before I gained conscious awareness of it, through an intense brainwave feedback process that included very insightful counseling. I have no idea where the behaviors came from; cruelty is not a theme I recognize in my family. Fortunately, we don't have to know the origin of our habits to make a change.

Impression Management in Bed

Most of what I learned about sex in college was "how to get laid." Prior to that, the shame and guilt instilled by my parents kept my pants on. As a young adult, peer influence and normal curiosity took over. To gain the esteem of my new moral arbiters, my buddies, I subscribed to the Get the Notches on Your Headboard philosophy.

Within a couple years, I had perfected my strategy and had my choice of almost any girl on campus. Everything I did was designed to attract sex. I masterfully created the illusion that I was available, while covertly looking for some imperfection and excuse to bolt. In a heartbeat, I could conjure up "why things won't work" and move on to the next target. I had a very strong need to be liked, however, so I wove in a strategy to ensure this as well. After the fact, most of my conquests acted like old friends when we crossed paths on campus or at parties.

Over the years, I co-created a lot of painful experiences with a lot of women. To know sex as a function of love was impossible for me. In fact, the only way I could relate sex to love was to fool myself into believing that sex was *a path* to love: *If I get her to sleep with me, she will fall in love, and then I will fall in love with her.*

Moving from the "big fish in a little pond" situation of a small college campus in South Dakota to the anonymity of the Los Angeles area forced a change in strategy. For men, being "sensitive" was just coming into vogue. Women were less attracted to the macho type and wanted the subtly powerful, sensitive type. *Okay,* I said to myself, *I can play that game.* It took a few years to get it down, but a wonderful woman eventally showed up. A few months into the relationship, I realized that nothing—not even this wonderful woman—was making me happy. Six months of talk therapy left me mostly unchanged and the relationship ended. I couldn't stand being with myself, so I couldn't stand being with her. She was too clearly reflecting my own internal strife. Of course, I didn't know this at the time and twisted the facts to make it look like *she* was responsible for the failure of the relationship.

I went on a mission, reading book after book in hope of becoming the "perfect" partner. After a few more years of intense study, another angel flew into my life. With great finesse, I played the role of the perfect partner and my angel "fell in love." My impression management scheme could have won me an Academy Award. Steadfast and true in my conviction to maintain a committed relationship, I handled every challenge with certitude, ensuring my mate that everything would work out. She took longer than I expected to fall for the ruse, but finally did. As soon as I had her, the shift happened.

-§-
In embracing true love—including self-love—compromise becomes obsolete.
-§-

Within days of her turn of heart—when she finally opened up to me and embraced our relationship—I blew my own cover. My scheme fell apart almost overnight. It was not fun—for either of us. I was no longer honest and forthright and basically stopped caring. My true colors came out for the first time. Launching a smokescreen defense, I claimed she could not possibly understand me. How could she? I didn't understand me either.

Shortly after, we broke things off. Letting go was extremely difficult, and I behaved so badly that reconciliation was out of the question. My complete inability to be genuine and honest made the break-up excruciatingly painful for both of us.

That pain marked a turning point. It brought my attention to the importance of being authentic, even transparent, and of letting go of my impression management schemes. It was the last time a break-up involved such intense pain and sense of failure.

In hindsight, much of my reading on the subject of dating and relationships, which seemed to provide amazing insights at the time, did little more than show me how to adjust my behavior and devise a new strategy to elicit a preferred response from another. The underlying social conditioning of men and women may well make it seem like the two genders are from different planets. However, if we do not grasp the fact that men and women live within an interwoven noosphere that demands nothing short of total truth and integrity, the genders will remain lost in love—and lost in space.

In the words of Jiddu Krishnamurti, *"It is no measure of health to be well adjusted in a profoundly sick society."* Our biggest challenge is

to move beyond the idea of "rules" in dating or any kind of game in relationships. Recreate yourself and your relationships in alignment with your internal, innate wisdom, and you will embark on an incredible evolution.

The Nature of Love

Nearly everything we do is a strategy to meet one or more needs. Coupling may meet our needs for sex, caring, intimacy, companionship, partnership, and spiritual communion. What many people call falling in love is often just falling *for* need. Love is, by nature, unconditional. Love does not put another off balance, or cause a loss of identity, or anything else that involves a fall. Love is unconditionally supportive, life enhancing, uplifting, and limitless. If one is truly in love, one rises, expands, and unifies.

-§-
Recreate yourself and your relationship in alignment with your internal, innate wisdom, and you will embark on an incredible evolution.
-§-

Compromises are often deemed necessary in relationships to keep the love going. In reality, compromises are only necessary when one or the other is unwilling to embrace the internal change presented by any given situation. In embracing development, growth, actualization, and true love—including self-love—compromise becomes obsolete.

Effecting Lasting Change

As stated earlier, most of our beliefs and perceptions were programmed into the subconscious mind before the age of six. The subconscious controls everything that does not require conscious attention, from biologicial functions to emotional reactions and perception of memories. The quality of all experience is a direct function of how we perceive our environment. Change your perceptions and your experience will change. Making change at the subconscious level is essential, and requires special intervention. Conscious insight does not change our subconscious beliefs. Affirmations do not change our subconscious beliefs. Behavioral interventions may work for a time, but in the long run, the subconscious will reassert its programming without constant reinforcement from outside. Special tools are required to get down into the subconscious and rearrange the matrix of our precognitive mind. The tools I rely on most in my own work come from a process called PSYCH-K. This process is equipped with specially designed protocols that ensure permission, commitment, clarity, and participation at all levels of the mind.

And They Lived Happily Ever After

Imagine if each of us embarked upon a relationship with the curiosity and optimism of a great warrior, as defined by Angeles Arrien in *The Four-Fold Way:*

> The principle that guides the warrior is *"showing up and choosing to be present."* The developed warrior shows honor and respect for all things, employs judicious communication, sets limits and boundaries, is responsible and disciplined. The warrior demonstrates right use of power and understands the three universal powers of Presence, Communication, and Position.

We do not have to be perfectly disciplined and have our "game" on at all times. We just have to show up and be real. Here are some specific suggestions for joining this evolution:

1. **Stop justifying:** Allow yourself to stop searching for justification for what you feel or do. This is nothing more than the conscious mind making excuses for an obsolete subconscious reaction to a situation. The more you justify, the less opportunity you have to recreate life as you truly desire and deserve.

2. **Start acknowledging:** Openly acknowledge what you feel or do. The moment you objectively acknowledge what has happened, a space is automatically created for self-reflection and self-consideration. This space provides a break in the drama and an opportunity to ask yourself, "Is this what I really intended?" or "Is this what I want to continue doing?" Acknowledgment is significantly different than blaming or pointing fingers.

3. **Deactivate judgment:** Suspend all judgment of what you feel or do. When caught in a moral dilemma of right vs. wrong, you become disconnected from the internal wisdom that allows loving redirection. Blame is a function of judgment is a function of fear. When in fear, we have two main options: fight or flight—neither of which offers a path to positive change. Letting go of judgment disengages you from blame and creates a space for true response-ability. In a state of fear, you have no ability to respond, only the capacity to react.

-§-
We do not have to be perfectly disciplined at all times. We just have to show up and be real.
-§-

4. **Activate curiosity:** Allow yourself to observe your feelings and behaviors with objective curiosity. This is where the fun begins. Questions bubble to the surface, allowing you to detach from ideas adopted before discernment was available. This is empowering. Redesign your life as you intend.

If we choose to perceive each other, particularly those with whom we are physically intimate, as angels holding up our mirrors through any pain or discomfort we experience… If we choose to suspend our need to be right… If we choose to consider that *how we are* is more important than *what we do*… We will experience a huge break from the impulse to be perfect and begin the internal adventure of self-discovery. Most importantly, we will engage in the evolution of self-creation through conscious intention.

Carlos Castaneda writes of an inscription in stone at the head of the Bunny Flat Trail in Mt. Shasta, Californa. It is the perfect summary for a relationship: "All paths lead nowhere... choose one with heart."

Part Five

Healing the Heart of Relationship

to know the mirror in all its faces
is to see beauty in everything
in these masks of bones and skin
we are no different
we are one with history, the light passage that unlocks
the air, soil, water, fire of becoming.
we understand beyond the insistence of an alphabet
waves of you enter me like the sun
~Blake More

Lou Montgomery:

Theater of the Erotic

The human psyche is inherently dramatic and dialogic. Think about it. We are always in dialogue—we dream, actively imagine, inwardly argue with dead parents and rejecting lovers, and talk to different parts of ourselves constantly. Our inner dramas are just as potent as our outward expression. When we dream we are the scene, the prompter, the player, the producer, the audience, and the critic. Likewise, in our imaginations we are, as Jean Houston calls it, *polyphrenic*—embracing conflicting tensions and hosting a variety of images.

In *Healing Fiction,* James Hillman writes: "Poetic, dramatic fictions are what actually people our psychic life. Our life in soul is a life in imagination." Rather than seek centeredness and integration, as is the goal of a monotheistic psychology, we might find more stability in learning to be patient, flexible, courteous, and even loving toward our multifarious selves—respecting each in their autonomy and hearing their unique messages. Rather than reducing the characters, creatures, and landscapes that visit our imagination, we can respectfully listen and discover what they need from us, not what we want from them. When we become attentive and hospitable to our inner characters, each one has a chance to act itself out and tell us what it is doing. Creating a welcoming, sensuous environment for our own "innertainment" in itself is an erotic gesture that ensures pleasure, reciproc-

Lou Montgomery, Ph.D., is the author and performer of five original plays including *Family Baggage* and *Escaping the Matrix.* Dedicated to merging the fields of performance art and higher consciousness, she holds two Masters degrees: in Theater, and Applied Psychology. For sixteen years, Lou taught expressive arts psychotherapy in the Masters Counseling Program at Southwestern College in Santa Fe, New Mexico, while conducting experiential workshops internationally. She received her doctorate in depth psychology from Pacifica Graduate Institute. Lou has also written and produced a documentary film entitled *Dragonquest,* and is working on a new book, entitled *Acting Out.*

ity, and even passionate conflict. Our soul is endless, as are its images. Our interior life is a show!

Among the first bits of jargon I learned as a psychotherapist was the pejorative "acting out." In general, the term connotes behavior that is unconscious, narcissistic, reckless, and often downright asinine. We all know a friend or colleague who left a good twenty-year marriage to take off with the vapid, skinny secretary. We have all sighed, rolled our eyes, and said, "I know where this is heading," while shaking our heads as the desperate puer acts out his midlife crisis. Teen-age runaways, bored housewives, wealthy kleptomaniacs, premenstrual dish breakers, and clumsy failed suicides share a common, unconscious "acting out" designed "to get attention." On the national level, as political scandals pile up like thirty-car collisions and the revelations of our military operations abroad bespeak a regression to a barbarity we can hardly comprehend, we lament that America is acting out the neighborhood bully. You can't make up theatre this bad.

Framed differently however, acting out, as in *acting our way out* with conscious intent, can shine a spotlight into the darkest corners of our history, thaw frozen tundras of psyche, and liberate parts of self held hostage by paralyzing beliefs. It can also help us concretize new dreams and visions and, as Star Trek's Captain Picard says, "Make it so." Unconscious acting out tends to take us down the spiral into more rigidity and contraction, whereas conscious acting out takes us up the spiral into higher frequencies of energy and expanded options.

-§-

"All the world's a stage, and all the men and women merely players."
—William Shakespeare, from *As You Like It*

-§-

Most depression, anxiety, and crises stem from having had our spontaneity shut down. Truncated or starved of spontaneous self-expression, we begin to take ourselves far too seriously. We over-identify with our petty dramas and small local story, and remain blind to the fact that we exist within a vast, interconnected web—the big cosmic story. The primary dysfunction inherent in our stories often lies in the fact that they are simply not big enough to embrace our larger selves.

Jacob Moreno, the founder of psychodrama, called it being "role locked." Any situation, seen through a lens which has one locked in a role—say that of the jilted lover or the unappreciated and martyred mother—is not only one-dimensional, it can only be seen in black and white, like grainy 1950s TV. When we are stuck in a locked role, our primary relationships become arid and humorless. Having had the erotic juice that drew us to our lover in the first place squeezed out of us, we become brittle. Injecting a dose of irreverent clowning or spontaneous role-play is not only spicy and sexy; it can restore the trusting, lighthearted innocence that ignites truly erotic love play.

Indicators that one is role locked include shallow breathing, feeling brittle and hard, hearing voices that sound shrill or that are competing with white noise, a flat-line affect that seems like driving across West Texas, an intolerance of others that spreads and irritates like poison oak, or a sense of being painted into a corner that rims the canyon. "It's my way or the highway." Most of us have been there—in a lockdown cell of our own fabrication, wherein we police our every move and confiscate any contraband that might cheer or enlighten us. When role locked, we are insulted by the idea of fun but envious of anyone else's good times. Some of the more obvious tip offs to being role locked consist of taking ourselves ultra-seriously, convincing ourselves that nobody else "gets" it, producing reams of evidence to validate our positions, and taking up residence on top of our soap boxes. If only we could stop believing the headlines of our own and others' frantic tabloids and clenched realities.

-§-
Conscious acting out takes us up the spiral into higher frequencies of energy and expanded options.
-§-

Another byproduct of role lock is that "the story" tends to get written in stone. When we look back at the past through the windowpane of the present, things change as fast as the landscape whizzing by a speeding locomotive. We make it all up as we go. So how can these stories we freeze-frame to tell ourselves "what happened" have any validity? Well, our stories are tenacious critters, and so we must give them the respect they deserve. Like being caught in steel bear traps, there are times when you have to sacrifice a limb to get free.

Fortunately, we don't have to believe in our story any more than we do the Tooth Fairy. Our stories are just the way we love (i.e. become adrenalin-addicted to), scare, torture, numb, and distract ourselves—or, on the positive side, entertain ourselves at beddy-bye. Our identification with the story's "realness" becomes a negative feedback loop, and we are off to the races of misery and victimhood. Our story takes on cinematic certainty, and Central Casting readily supplies actors and Greek choruses to fill in all the necessary supporting roles.

Through play and spontaneity, however, new options magically surface like dolphin pods. Over and over, I have both facilitated and witnessed an instant shape-shifting from Munch's *Scream* to dancing prisms. It can shift in a nanosecond. Acting out is quantum mechanics. Veritable repertory companies of possibilities are accessed. We all have Tarot decks inside, not photo IDs!

More than inspiring spontaneity (a noble, if carnivalesque, vocation), acting out my performance art is my way of making love to the totality of the universe. Several things constitute this ecstatic exchange —the nature of humor itself, the ability to truly role-reverse, the way acting out relativizes and humbles the ego, the willingness to act out of the wound, and in all of this—the eros of gifting.

Self-disclosing parody is a most liberating practice. Comedy is the lubricant of the soul. It's about being a survivor and taking the path of the Fool. It's the cheapest and safest medicine we can get, over or under the counter. Humor is the best digestive enzyme known to man- and womankind—it can metabolize the lumpiest of woes. When we take ourselves too seriously, we inflate our problems like zeppelins. Laughter blows the blimps away. Laughter has been proven to have all sorts of curative medicinal effects, including: alleviating depression, promoting relaxation, increasing oxygen levels in the blood, reducing stress, lowering blood pressure, and increasing endorphin levels and, thus, our whole sense of well being. It keeps us socially attractive and binds us to those we laugh with. Laughter is perhaps the most loving medicine. As lover to my audience, I try to write comedy that will incite laughter to erupt and splash over the cultural demarcation line. As a love-struck comic, I am in a committed, long-term relationship with my audience. As Frances Miriam Berry wrote in the 1840s, "It is a very serious thing to be a funny woman."

The art of role reversal, or deep immersion in another role, is sacred erotic play. Ibn 'Arabi wrote, "Prayer is a dialogue in which the two parties continually exchange roles." I willingly walk in your shoes, see through your eyes, feel through your heart, leave the chair of my position and come sit in yours. What could be more intimate? The act of dramatic role reversal is *the* most potent practice I know of to engender true compassion—not just as a wannabe mental exercise, but as embodied reality where real shifts can take place.

-§-
Humor is the best digestive enzyme—it can metabolize the lumpiest of woes.
-§-

In terms of my inner romance, from which all other erotic connection develops, I keep things juicy by always experimenting, expanding my role repertoire, and training for new roles. As I act out what I stubbornly resist, rejected sub-personalities are integrated and the scar tissue of psyche is healed. The shadow demon lover is transformed to intimate Beloved. My erotic inner connection to Self matures, deepens, and gains wisdom.

Acting out serves as a way of making sense of things when former identities are radically shattered, or outdated worldviews need to be drastically dismantled. Acting out is the way we "act into" empowerment, freedom, and inspiration. Theatrical art has allowed me to *dis*-identify with my life drama and relativize my bruised ego. Getting enough distance from myself has constellated objectivity and psychological coherence, while penetrating to the core of my experience. Acting out is like a depth charge—the mini submarine in which I have initiated myself and taken others down into the deeps.

As long as there is still identification with the story, however, we are subject to the effects of its endless twists and turns. We are stuck in a cycle of always readjusting and regaining balance and equilibrium, or as Ram Dass puts it, still rearranging the furniture within the prison cell. Why would we be remotely interested in ending the drama if we revel in it so? Could it be that our ignorance constitutes a type of self-absorbed bliss?

When we peel back the melodramatic layers of narcissistic self-involvement, our core essence is available and shines forth as pure energy and radiant life force. Once the ego's inflated perspective is brought into appropriate scale, new doorways in consciousness open. Stepping out of the drama through exaggerating the personal drama, like tying a dead chicken around the neck of a poultry-killing hound and letting it rot, encompasses discovery of the soul's purpose and rekindles passion. One of the most important insights gleaned from ending the drama is learning the difference between life's inevitable pain and unnecessary suffering. Suffering is what we *add* to the basic suchness of life, which always includes pain. Through judgment, interpretation, and a kind of demand against life, we insist that it be other than it is. What ending the drama entails is simply *stepping outside* of the whole box we call our biography or personality or situation, and witnessing it from the perspective of the Self, rather than the ego. We need distance to see ourselves. From a detached vantage point, no one is "doing" anything to anyone else. The *lila,* or divine erotic play, is just playing out, and we can see life as the dream that is dreaming us, and take it all lightly!

-§-
"It takes two to know one."
—Gregory Bateson
-§-

When we consciously enact our dramas in a safely facilitated group container, we discover fresh ways to navigate through life. Often we have to see ourselves played back by others in order to recognize the joyless, strict limitations with which we straight-jacket ourselves. Being seen and heard in the moment, where insight is not only witnessed but reflected back in a group, amplifies the new role in every sensorial mode. Spontaneity can suddenly dance and eros can announce a surprising, scintillating, and mercurial entrance.

A couple whose marriage has become stale, brittle, and erotically challenged decides to enact their impasse. The wife feels trapped in the role of a homebound mother—deprived of creativity and affection. "I'm totally stuck here while he runs all over the place! He never wants to be here, and even when he *is*, he's not present."

The overworked husband feels oppressed by constant criticism and lack of appreciation. "No matter what I do or how hard I try, I can't do anything right. All she does is bitch and complain. I dread coming home." Both feel dry, misunderstood, and hopelessly raw and exhausted. Through psychodramatic enactment, the hidden story within the story emerges. The legacy of their respective unavailable and narcissistic parents has created inappropriate and toxic parental bonds, and has tainted the lenses through which each views the other. Both are role locked in outdated and unconsciously inherited scripts, and neither feels empowered to write a new one. The husband has gradually "disappeared," like his passive aggressive father, and the wife has unintentionally morphed into her mother's role of the perpetually dissatisfied, nagging harpy. As a starting point, dramatically exaggerating "what is so"—each playing both themselves and the other—loosens up role rigidity and allows humor to begin applying its magic salve.

Through the subsequent action of the drama, the toxic parental bonds of guilt and unworthiness are identified and released. The grossly distorted lenses through which the husband and wife have been seeing each other are named and removed. A series of ever-deepening and truthful role reversals allows each to contact the other's reality. Taking on his role, the wife feels true empathy for her husband's stressed and thankless efforts. Conversely, from within the perspective of his wife's role, the husband contacts the palpable grief and frustration from being starved for juicy affection and social stimulation. Both are shocked and humbled by the revelation of the other's felt experience. Emotions surface, lubricating their dry and heretofore abrasive connection. Witnessing their relationship objectively rather than defensively, new options appear. Recriminations spontaneously give way to authentic forgiveness as knee-jerk reactions subside, letting hearts, rather than broken records, speak. The group's tender empathy, containment and mirroring nourish the longing in both partners to be understood and appreciated. Everyone is held and instructed in the erotic meta-space of compassion. Room opens up for affectionate humor and mutual acknowledgement. Eros once again takes up residence, sparkling in the eyes of all the drama's participants.

Truthful acting out oftentimes demands concrete embodiment of that which we find most abject, embarrassing, or terrifying. It can consist of a direct confrontation with shadow sides of ourselves we would rather forget—like dirty underwear buried at the back of the closet. Oftentimes, the entry point is through the body itself—its pains, secrets, and humiliations. But like the mythic treasure that lies in the depths of the dragon's lair, pure gold emerges from digging in the dirt. It has been my experience that, after taking on the most taboo subjects and embodying the most repulsive characters, I have felt as liberated as a convict let out of a dungeon, squinting into the light of day. Our wounds serve as gateways and openings to the numinous. They call out to us, wanting to be heard, remembered, and loved back into wholeness. Tending wounds is a deep, sacred function of art and eros.

Well-crafted dramatization is an embodiment of eros. It includes and celebrates the Other. Like the god Eros, erotically infused enactment is inclusive, open, celebratory, courageous, energizing, compassionate, fresh, youthful, and innocent. In its highest form, dramatic expression is not only a sensual exchange between players, but a sacred sacrament between player and the universal life force. As African spiritual teacher Onye Onyemaechi says, "Praise takes all of you. Give it all away. Hold nothing back."

Like performance art itself, *acting our way out* is erotic commerce. The spirit of any gift is kept alive by its constant donation. Our gifts need to constantly move, be consumed, used up, and perish. I think of my performances as Tibetan Buddhist sand paintings—intricately and lovingly wrought, and then scooped up and thrown to the winds. The gift that is freely exchanged moves in a circular fashion throughout one's community to the world at large, and has both momentum and fertility. It cannot be manipulated but, rather, circles into mystery, lightening as it moves. As the gift is given away, it feeds us again and again. As eros, erotic exchange, its libido increases with giving. Like Dionysian wine, as it freely pours itself out, the gift only becomes a rarer and finer vintage as it passes along. The more the gift is used up, the more it is worth. The gift we give binds many souls and gathers generosity, always tending toward community. When we are in the gifted state, we are in an erotic state. As both performer and facilitator, it is my great joy to expend myself copiously and excessively. It is my desire to gift my works to the world precisely in the measure with which they have been wrought—in love.

-§-
Well-crafted dramatization is an embodiment of eros.
-§-

Caroline Myss: Leaving the Wounded Relationship Tribe

In order to better understand the complexity of human relationships, it is helpful to understand the workings of the tribal mind. All of us are born into a "tribal mentality" of various forms. These include our family unit, religious background, country of origin, ethnicity, etc. The tribal mentality involves our spirit in specific thought forms held by the group; it effectively marinates an individual in the tribe's beliefs, ensuring that all believe the same. The structure of reality—what is and is not possible for the members of the group—is thus agreed upon and maintained. While the tribal mentality has definite benefits in terms of establishing common ground and ensuring group survival, it is not a conscious agreement. At a certain stage in our evolution, both personally and collectively, the tribal mentality must be challenged.

As a species, we have become incredibly dishonorable. We don't think twice about breaking vows or promises. We can't even keep our word to ourselves anymore. I'm hoping that people will begin to recognize the need for a personal honor code independent of the tribe. We need to learn how to treat everyone—regardless of tribal affiliation—with absolute honor.

Every one of us is plugged into the tribal mind. We finance the belief patterns of the tribe by directing a percentage of our life force into maintaining our affiliation with the tribe. What that means from an energetic point of view is that our individual energetic circuits go

Caroline Myss, Ph.D., is dedicated to creating educational programs in the field of human consciousness, spirituality and mysticism, health, energy medicine, and advancing the science of medical intuition. She has an international reputation as a renowned medical intuitive, and with C. Norman Shealy, M.D., Ph.D., co-founded the American Board of Scientific Medical Intuition, which offers professional accreditation in this emerging field. Her book *Anatomy of the Spirit* (Three Rivers, 1997), was a *New York Times* best seller; her sixth book is *Invisible Acts of Power* (Free Press, 2004). Her personal passion is the mystical history of America. Full information is at www.Myss.com.

into prolonging the life force of the tribe to which we belong. This involves an implicit agreement to think like the tribe thinks, to evaluate situations and people the way the tribe does, and to believe in right and wrong according to tribal values and tribal ambitions. As long as the tribal mentality remains unexamined and transparent to awareness, we unwittingly subject others to our tribal laws.

When we are plugged into tribal thought forms, we can easily believe in nonsensical prejudices held by the tribe. Examples of this in our world are obvious. Tribal mentality allows us to hold a position or attitude about an entire group of people: "All fat people are lazy," or, "All Irish are drunks," for example. A tribal thought form may have no truth to it whatsoever, but individuals hold to such beliefs because that perspective is what the tribe has agreed to believe. Innocent children, born into the hatred and prejudice of their parents and ancestors, grow up inside a tribal mentality that sponsors the endless march toward war. People grow up hating other people—people they have never seen—based on group affiliation. This is the shadow side of the tribe.

Inevitably, some among us come to a point where we want to break out of the tribal mentality. This is inevitable because the nature of consciousness pushes us to evolve. At some point, the individual wants to explore, develop, and manage his or her own consciousness without the limitations of the tribal mind. It is easy to spot these mavericks when they start to question and unplug from tribal mentality—they hang out on the periphery looking bored and restless, or whimsical and dreamy. Others will act out the agitated hothead as they challenge tribal ways.

-§-
We can't even keep our word to ourselves anymore.
-§-

What often triggers the dark night of the soul for an individual is just this tribal revolution. We get to the point where we think, *I want to make decisions on my own. I want to manage my own perceptions, my own emotions, and my own choices.* But the assumption of the tribal mind is that everybody loves being part of the tribe. And in many ways, we do. Knowing where and to whom we "belong" is crucial to our self-concept and sense of safety in the world. When we begin the real deep journey of questioning, *What do I believe?* and start to individuate from the tribe, we often enter a dark night of the soul. It is, by necessity, a passage we take alone.

It's one thing to reject what we don't want to believe anymore. But that doesn't necessarily mean we automatically and always know what we do believe. All we know as we enter the dark night is that we can't go back—even when the tribe is the only world we've ever known. At this inevitable point in our development, the tribe doesn't feel right anymore. It no longer offers us comfort, and that previously comforting feeling of familiarity begins to feel like a trap.

This dark night passage pushes us to look at our false gods—the belief patterns we've become invested in and to which we have given our spirit and life force. For example, think about all of the superstitions or attitudes held within the thought forms of society at large that find us trembling and afraid of God. The whole notion that "God will punish you if you misbehave" can be seen as a widespread tribal thought form. Most of our notions about God, including the idea that God is a biological figure who looks like us, are patterns of belief that come into question as we pass through the dark night.

-§-

This dark night passage pushes us to look at our false gods—the belief patterns to which we have given our spirit and life force.

-§-

In the tribe, we evolve by growing within the context of group perceptions at the group's speed. We adopt and outgrow many mythologies until we finally take a stand and say, "God, I want you not through a group; I want direct contact. I don't want a diluted, toilet-water version of you in which I've agreed to experience you through the evolution and slow motion of a family, the slow motion of my job, and the slow motion of church once a week. As a tribal member, I've kept you at bay and I've agreed to let my life evolve at a certain speed."

If you want more direct contact, a more direct line to God, ask for it. God will say, "Okay fine, you'll get that. But here's the thing—we're going to change the world you came from and you'll have to leave that world behind." That is the dark night of the soul. It begins with a decent into what I call "necessary madness."

It happened to me in the spring of 1982 while I was living in Chicago. At that point in my life, I very much wanted a husband and children and to live that sort of ordinary life. I had started a successful newsletter and thought for sure my dream was about to come true. Working from home and writing about human consciousness, I thought I'd hit pay dirt. I had everything I wanted. I remember walking down the street with a dear friend, and saying, "I never thought I could be this happy."

Then, in the blink of an eye, my life disintegrated. The same dear friend died of a heart attack. I lost a cousin. My magazine went belly up. Although incredibly difficult, the dark night helped me develop a relationship with life that is characterized by spiritual endurance.

By August that year, I was in serious trouble. I would spend days at a time literally lying in bed all day long, thinking, *Exactly why do I get up? If I get up, what'll I do?* Finally, I'd force myself to get out of bed.

Then I would find myself sitting on the floor, going through stacks of paper and moving them from one side of the room to the other, as if some solution to the madness could be found in those papers.

At last, it dawned on me that I had to make choices. Complaining about this situation didn't change anything. I had to go into action. An opportunity arose to start a book publishing company with two new friends, but that required moving to New Hampshire. I remember thinking, *New Hampshire? Is that a state? Where is it?* This is how removed my European tribe mentality was from New England. Realizing I had to do something, I left Chicago and started my life anew.

Once I relocated, I started doing intuitive readings for people. By 1984, I had become well-known in the area as a medical intuitive. Then I met Norm Shealy, a respected brain surgeon who had trained at Harvard. Norm put my intuitive abilities through a rigorous test over the next several years. From 1984 until 1992, we did intuitive readings in a medical setting much like a residency.

-§-
As long as a person is part of the tribal mind, he or she will heal at the tribal speed.
-§-

Medical intuitive training should include a residency program like the one Norm Shealy put me through. I feel very strongly that we will have this in the future because this is such an essential skill. We have to have people who can read energy. Machines can't pick up a memory pattern. Professional medical intuitives, skilled at reading the human energy system, will be a great asset to the medical team of the future. But energetic medicine is not for people who hold deeply to tribal fears.

As long as a person is part of the tribal mind, he or she will heal at the tribal speed. If the tribe decides cancer cannot be healed and he is plugged into that perception—he has agreed to experience the illness and its outcome along the lines of the tribal view. If the tribe says, "Very few people heal," then he is plugged into the perception that says, "Healing is not the norm. Healing is very rare." If this man is plugged into a tribal belief system and decides to try energetic medicine, he won't get help. His energetic body is connected to a tribal belief pattern that says, "You need chemical medicine, and maybe you'll make it, but most people don't." As long as he remains plugged into that perception, he will need all the chemical and medical help he can get.

We each have three versions of reality to choose from. We can choose what I call the "toiletwater" version in the first column; this version relates to the first three chakras—survival, sexuality, and power—and largely relates to the tribal mind. Or we can choose the "cologne version" in column two, which relates to chakras four through seven—the heart, the center of communication, the third eye, and the crown center—all of which relate to individuation. Finally, we can choose the "perfume version" in column three, involving chakras eight through ten. These have to do with unity consciousness and the evolution of awareness into higher forms of thought. Whichever version we choose, it comes down to the question: which version of truth do you want? In the toilet-water version, we agree to experience God and everything at the toilet-water level, consistent with tribal mentality at a predetermined speed.

-§-
For a large segment of the population, the language of wounds has become the first language of intimacy.
-§-

The twisting of truth and small lies that occurs in the tribal mind is no small matter. It is the societal mechanism by which the individual loses real power. People are accustomed to thinking about how they lose energy when they are hurt, but not about how we lose our energy through dishonorable acts, through telling and living lies, and distorting facts.

One of the ways I see this playing out is in the phenomenon I call "woundology."

For a large segment of the population, the language of wounds has become the first language of intimacy. Prior to the current therapeutic age—which is only about forty years old—the first language of intimacy involved the sharing of personal and family data. Where our family came from, what our family values, any family secrets we keep—a mad aunt or uncle—these were the details that comprised intimate sharing. Divorce and financial information was also considered very intimate. A person never talked about their inner life and emotions, only about the details of what was going on in their external lives. People didn't show or share feelings because they didn't have individual feelings as such; the heart was a tribal instrument. The journey involved mourning if the tribe was in grief, or celebration if the tribe had a piece of good news. The tribe determined the content of a person's heart and its pulsation.

The therapeutic age has brought about a very different situation. Now, we not only share our feelings openly and willingly, we have begun to define ourselves by our wounds. Let me give an example of how the woundology phenomenon plays itself out.

I was in an Indian restaurant in Scotland talking with two male-friends when the female friend I was to meet for dinner walked up and greeted the three of us. After I had introduced her, another man

walked over and asked if she was free on June 8 as he thought she might like to attend a lecture on that date. All he wanted to know was if she might be free June 8th, a question that required little more than a "yes" or a "no" answer. Instead she began an elaborate discussion about June 8. "Did you say June 8th? No, no. Any other day would be fine, but not June 8th. That's the day my incest survivor group meets and I have to be there because we never let each other down." She went on and on for at least a full minute.

Later I asked her, "Do you realize that in a brief introduction, you told two men whom you have never met before that 1) you had experienced incest, 2) you were still in therapy about it, 3) you were angry about it, 4) you were angry at men, and 5) you needed to determine the course of the conversation—all within less than a minute?"

She replied, "Well, I am a victim of incest."

To which I replied, "I know that. Why did you have to let them know that?"

From here, her woundology and tribal mentality took over. I had asked her a conscious question from what I have called the "cologne water" column involving her feelings, communication, intuition, and higher mind. But she was operating from a tribal mentality. The group mind within the incest survivor community has a belief about how to heal this particular wound. The tribe says, "You need a group." The tribe says, "You have a right to be angry." People get together in support group tribes and function much like ethnic, national, or family tribes. Tribal mentality would not allow her to reflect and say, "You're absolutely right. I've been processing this for eighteen years and I think that's long enough." Or, "I'm going to take a look at what this taught me, and move on to a whole new life."

-§-
The tendency toward tribalism keeps us stuck in negative cycles in our intimate relationships, and can really play havoc when a relationship is ripe for transition or has come to an end.
-§-

Instead, she did what the tribal mind dictates, refusing to be challenged in the way "we" think and the way "we" have decided the incest wound gets healed. As the one who offered the challenge, I was excluded from the tribe. That was the first time it struck me that I could not be sure people wanted to heal. Sometimes belonging to a group is more important than striking out alone in the direction of healing.

The tendency toward tribalism keeps us stuck in negative cycles in our intimate relationships, and can really play havoc when a relationship is ripe for transition or has come to an end. Long before we discover the freedom that comes with letting go and forgiveness, we learn the tribal mentality that would have us do vengeance. Tribal mentality teaches a righteous stance: an eye for an eye, and a tooth for a tooth. When we feel violated, the first thought is vengeance, rather than forgiveness. Tribal mentality has gender-specific undercurrents—women do vengeance differently than men. Either way, the tribal mentality that holds "breaking up is painful" or "betrayal warrants retaliation" rules the day. Any mediator who oversees divorce and child custody proceedings could site the hundred thousand ways this thought form plays itself out.

And yet, we have hope because tribal mentality is currently going through a vast transformation as consciousness expands. We have now cracked a code that proves we are designed for enlightenment, both spiritually and biologically. There are seven levels of evolution through perceptions of power that all human beings are designed to pass through. I have spoken of this in depth in my book, *Anatomy of the Spirit.*

As a medical intuitive, I interpret energetic information. The human body transmits energy that forms an energetic system around the body. This energy contains data, including a complete biographical profile. By reading the energetic biography, we can see how a person has invested his or her energy—into what thought forms, into what relationships, and into what memories. Each of these energy investments pays a dividend. That dividend, whether positive or negative, plays a role in the development of cell tissue. What I have done as a medical intuitive is map out what investments result in what diseases; I am able to help people by reading where they are losing their energy. Then I teach them how to evaluate and monitor their own energy field.

Although each case presents unique factors, getting your energy back requires making different choices than the ones that caused the loss of energy. This is just as true for challenges to our physical health as it is for challenges in relationship. Either way, healing revolves around this crucial question: *Do you want to make different choices?* And the answer to that, quite often, is *No.* What I have realized is that being healthy isn't as appealing to people as I first imagined. Quite frankly, in many cases, it's not appealing at all. What is appealing is being out of pain. And often, old patterns are difficult to relinquish because—in the short run—they do relieve the pain. Change is terrifying because short-term pain relief must be given up, but healing requires learning to tolerate the pain that comes with change. Fortunately, the edgy pain that comes with new behavior—with making the choices that will change your life—is often short-lived.

Thought alone, or action without thought, doesn't heal. We need the chemistry of conscious thought and direct action combined. I

introduce people to the fact that they have circuits of energy coming into the top of their head and that this energy equals their life force. Every thought or attitude we have—whether consciously chosen or unconsciously adopted through the tribal mind—does in fact, invest our vital life-force circuits into that thought or attitude. This is true whether the thought form is one of betrayal and vengeance, or understanding and forgiveness.

The tribe operates by first, second, and third chakra vocabulary. Betrayal is a second chakra issue. The first, second, and third chakras record the actual physical event we consider a betrayal. Chakras four through seven record our interpretation of that event and its impact. Chakras eight through ten record the meaning of that event. So what we have are three distinct versions of the same event. The first involves human reasoning, human law and order, human logic, and human facts that we can see, hear, taste, smell, or feel. There aren't any energetic facts at this level. The second level expands to include a fuller spectrum of who we are—embracing emotion, heart, and intuition—but it means we have to give up reasoning from our five senses. What has to fail us at the second level is the tribal experience. Human justice, human reasoning has to fail. This involves a Judas experience, some form of betrayal of this system.

-§-
A betrayal experience is necessary in order to let go of the tribal mind and individuate.
-§-

At the third level, everything is interpreted symbolically. From this level, we see that a betrayal experience is necessary in order to let go of the tribal mind and individuate. What betrays us is this form of tribal consciousness. It's not about any one person betraying another. From this perspective, the people in our lives chose their roles and their relationship to us before we're born. One signs up to be a betrayer; another to be a lover; another to be a friend. All are only players who have agreed to play a certain role in our life. What becomes important at the symbolic level is the theme of the play, the theme being that, in order to let go of the tribal mind, we must have a betrayal experience. From that point of view, it matters little who betrays us. From the perspective of higher consciousness—not the body, nor the personality, but the higher self—it doesn't matter what form the betrayal takes.

The Judas experience teaches us that all is fair. Even though an event may not register as human fair—it's divine fair. This is how we learn to go higher, we learn to trust God's divine plan. A major event often triggers this betrayal experience. It could be the loss of all our money, or the failure of a marriage. I had my company stolen from me. I consider that a big experience, a form of rape. It took me years to get over that betrayal. But I'm over it. I figure I would rather leave this planet loving that person again. Today, we can actually talk, and we've agreed to meet in New York and laugh our heads off because we made it through a very rough journey and have come full circle.

What form betrayal takes does not matter. What matters is that a whole system of consciousness—the tribal mentality around vengeance—no longer holds us enthralled. We no longer have faith in those patterns of thought. Through this transformation we learn a whole new level of trust. We break the habit of telling tribal lies, we become worthy of trust and honor. Honor plays a vital role in a strong and healthy person. The positive side of the tribal mentality is that the tribe also has a higher-order honor code that teaches how to respect the earth, the land, and other people's rights.

When we start to see the events of our lives symbolically instead of literally, the illusion of the physical facts gives way to a larger truth. The journey is an incredible solo flight through the middle path, through our interior. Herein lies the secret of energetic healing.

Gay Hendricks:

The Chemistry of Blame

There is a great fundamental issue that overrides many of the things we can do to heal ourselves and the world: the human tendency to step into feeling like a victim and blaming others, instead of taking personal responsibility.

It's not just a habit; it's an addiction, just like a chemical addiction.

When you step into the victim position by pointing the finger of blame, you short the circuitry in yourself that allows you to feel the natural organic ecstasy of fully standing in a co-creative position with the Universe itself. That's the fundamental developmental task we face at this stage of our evolution: opening up the wiring that allows us to feel organic ecstasy for longer and longer periods of time.

At present, most people can't sustain the feelings that arise with this opening, so they slip into a dangerous addiction to blame with its corresponding feeling of a gleeful *gotcha!* Once we're accustomed to a certain internal chemical state, we feel comfortable with that state even if it's attached to really dysfunctional behavior like that glee that arises from apportioning blame. When we try new behavior and our neurochemistry changes, it feels uncomfortable at first. Moving to a new emotional and biochemical state may feel foreign. Even though it may be a healthier one, it is unfamiliar.

Gay Hendricks, Ph.D., is the author and co-author of twenty-five books in conscious relationship, conscious business, and body-mind transformation. Included are such enduring bestsellers as *Conscious Loving* (Bantam, 1992), *Conscious Breathing* (Bantam, 1995), and *Conscious Living* (HarperSanFrancisco, 2001). Before founding his own institute, he was Professor of Counseling at the University of Colorado. Over the twenty-four years of their relationship, he and his wife Kathlyn have raised two children, accumulated a million frequent flyer miles and appeared on more than 500 radio and television programs. You can see him on the web at www.hendricks.com.

Usually in couples therapy, the first issue to be addressed is: Are you willing to make a commitment to solving the problem? One of the most typical responses is, "Well, I'd be committed if she were." It takes about an hour and a half of discussion to work through that objection, until at some point in the process, both people bond and turn on the leader. I tell my students that those are the only moments during which you're earning your keep as a therapist. Both members of the couple turn to you and say, "Hey, what the hell are you suggesting here? Are you suggesting that it's not his fault?" That's always a sweaty moment, but it's the instant when transformation can come. Once you're through that issue, the possibility of getting out of the field of blame and actually taking responsibility opens up.

-§-
When we try new behavior and our neurochemistry changes, it feels uncomfortable at first.
-§-

"Are you willing to stay completely away from blaming anyone, and instead make a sincere commitment to resolving all the issues we confront?" I've asked that question of thousands of people, many of whom had traveled great distances to visit me, or were paying me very large sums of money. Even with stakes that high, ninety-nine times out of a hundred, the person goes into the default position of blame immediately. Weaning people from that automatic behavior takes a great deal of patience and repetition, and a nimble set of therapeutic interventions.

The tendency to default to blame is the huge issue confronting couples and societies today. Wherever you see it appear, that's the area where healing is needed. There's only one solution, and that's to take one hundred percent impeccable responsibility—and create a space for the other person to take one hundred percent impeccable responsibility as well. Responsibility has a contagious effect. The initial level of responsibility is going from blame to being willing to consider what you're getting out of—or contributing to—the problem. Senior level responsibility is being so impeccably clear that you become a space into which it's possible for other people to step.

You then have to confront a person's despair that the problem is not solvable, which is always accompanied by about fifteen levels of justification. But when both people have made a commitment to resolving the issue, ninety percent of the work is done. Both people have then stepped into a co-creative role with not only the other, but with the Universe itself.

A particular couple comes to mind. They came to work with my wife and me on their relationship. Both partners were Ph.D.s who had written brilliant scholarly papers, but when either of them encountered anything they perceived as a threat, their academic, intellectual understanding flew out the window, and they immediately became convinced that they knew that the other person was wrong.

The first thing that we did was to repeatedly ask them if they would be willing to take responsibility for healing, and to make a commitment to solving the issues. When confronted with the question, they would spin out and become more entrenched in the position that it was the other person's fault. They had endless justifications for this certainty, and thus continually dosed themselves with this highly addictive drug.

It took all of the first day and well into the night to produce a shift, but in the middle of the night, the husband couldn't sleep. His anxiety got worse and worse. In a state of desperation, he said, "Okay, I'm willing to commit to solving this problem." That created a space for the wife to commit to the same thing. The next morning, they came in willing to solve the problem.

In a nutshell, the problem was that she had had a sexual affair and he couldn't forgive her. They'd gone 'round and 'round with it for the better part of a year. On the second day of therapy, the reason he couldn't get over it became really clear.

One of the questions that I commonly ask people is, "Has anything like this ever happened to you or anyone you know?" At first the husband said, "No," but then, as we got deeper into the question, it turned out not only was the real answer, "Yes," but his entire early life had been shaped by his mother running off with another man and leaving his dad with four little boys to raise. It was inevitable that his wife's infidelity, or something like it, was bound to happen to him, because he had it so thoroughly sealed off this early experience. When we seal something off from our consciousness inside, it has to be brought to our attention in some way by the outside world.

-§-

The tendency to default to blame is the huge issue confronting couples and societies today.

-§-

Suddenly, he realized that his wife was illuminating this old experience, and he said to her, "Oh, you played this role in my life for me." At the end of the second day they were in each other's arms. She said, "This was inevitable. I had to play this role for you." And he responded, "Yes, this was my bad dream you wandered into." He asked her, "Can you forgive me, for getting you involved in this nutty scheme of my unconscious?" That couple represented one of the best examples I've ever seen of what's possible when both people take responsibility.

There are a lot of programmed-in and even biologically-based characteristics that make human males and females different. I'm

interested in what's underneath that. The deeper you go inside, the more human beings look alike. The further you go toward the surface, the more different we look. The fear a woman feels when she's upset about the guy not picking up his socks corresponds to the fear the man feels when he's upset that she's on his case. The superficial differences point to some underlying unity.

To deal with these situations, we voice our fears, then look underneath them. As a therapist, I point out repeatedly, "Okay, having said that your husband is a worthless piece of shit, tune inside. Do you feel happier?" The person begins to recognize that although they feel that "glee-gotcha" feeling that comes from assigning blame, they don't feel happier. So I help people make choices about whether something can make them feel happy, rather than just gleeful, by inviting them to make tiny choices that are actually huge choices. I say, "Do you choose being right or being happy?" I've had people come back months later and say, "I hated you for asking me that question—but it changed my life."

And here's the great advantage of asking this question: we each only have to make the choice once. That choice changes the whole playing field. Afterwards, it's simply a matter of practice. It's similar to getting on a bicycle for the first time. You travel ten feet, then wobble and fall over. You get back on and you master going twenty feet. The first time was the moment in which everything changed. It's the same with mastering personal responsibility. Once a person shifts out of glee and experiences the real joy of claiming responsibility, everything is changed. They're launched into the process of learning. How do they remember that they're in that process and trigger that experience on a regular basis in everyday life? By discovering how great they feel when they do it, and how miserable they feel when they don't.

-§-
Do you choose being right or being happy?
-§-

Twenty-five years ago Kathlyn and I knew we wanted to create something different with our marriage. We looked around to find other couples to model our behavior on, but we found nobody whose relationship we would have traded for our own. We had to make up our path ourselves. It took a long time, but now it's been the better part of a decade since my wife or I have said one critical thing to each other. It's years since I've experienced blame, since I've had that chemistry in my body. I am past the point where I ever want that drug, because I feel good and I don't want to bring myself down. We are living in that clear space of impeccable responsibility that offers the possibility for other people to step into it. We choose to be happy. It's easy now.

Francine Ward:

Healthy Self-Talk

Loving others starts with self-love. For many people, the idea of self-love generates negative thoughts and feelings about narcissistic, ego-driven people. We think of those who care little about others unless they can further their personal or professional goals. On the contrary, if you genuinely love yourself, you engage in behavior that includes both honest and continual self-care, and kind and generous treatment of others.

There's an age-old theory that you can't love someone else until you truly yourself. This point has been debated by countless experts and the popular answer is, indeed, you cannot love someone else until you truly love yourself. And I agree. How can you care for, honor, or cherish another person if you don't honor or cherish yourself? How can you give away something you don't have? How do you even know what it looks like or feels like if you've never really experienced it? There's a wonderful old saying that is applicable here: Charity begins at home. First love yourself, and then you can love someone else, without judgment and attachment.

For so many of us, men and women alike, our self-esteem is dependent on something outside ourselves, such as our spouse or the man or woman we are dating, the neighborhood or house we live in, the job or career we've chosen, or the amount of money in our bank account or stock portfolio. Without those things, we perceive our-

Francine Ward is a life coach, inspiring author, and powerful motivator with a proven track record of achievement. From high school dropout, drug-addicted, alcoholic prostitute to Georgetown-educated lawyer, successful entrepreneur, and twice-published author, her message is simple—take courageous, life-affirming action and the results will follow. Her mission: To encourage and support people in walking through their fear, so they can live amazing lives! She is the author of *Esteemable Acts: 10 Actions for Building Real Self-Esteem* (Broadway, 2003) and *52 Weeks of Esteemable Acts: A Guide to Right Living* (Hazelden, 2005). Visit Francine at www.esteemableacts.net.

selves as nothing, unless we're taught otherwise or have role models who show us a different example of how to see ourselves.

Make no mistake about it, we are taught how to view ourselves. We learn to value or devalue ourselves as men and women by the examples we see in the movies, on television, in magazines, and at home. And the music we readily listen to reinforces the message of self-care or self-loathing. Sometimes the message is subtle and sometimes it's flagrant. It's always our choice what we do with it.

For years I accepted my role, as was told to me, of being the pretty trophy on the arm of a man. I was the woman with no opinion, particularly if it differed from that of my companion. As a result, the men in my life defined who I was. I behaved in a way that was pleasing and non-threatening to men. I dressed in a way that was attractive to men. I walked in a way that was sexy to men. And if they weren't impressed, I was devastated, often changing clothes several times before I found something I thought they would like. I was a chameleon, able to change into whatever was expected of me. I believed my role models on television and in the movies who said that my purpose in life was to find and satisfy a man—at whatever the cost. I paid a high price for "at whatever the cost." Not surprisingly, that behavior transcended my relationships with men. I was also that way with everyone I came in contact with—bosses, girlfriends, and family. Over time, the greatest gift I've ever given to myself was learning to become my own best friend.

-§-
Make no mistake about it, we are taught how to view ourselves.
-§-

Learning how to love myself has been a lifetime process and one that will continue. The job is never done. Self-esteem is contingent on what you are willing to do to nurture it. How are you demonstrating self-love in your life? What esteemable acts are you doing today? In your Esteemable Acts Journal write your answers.

Actions Speak Louder Than Words

If love is an action, how do you express self-love? Some people believe that standing in front of a mirror saying "I love you" is an expression of self-love. Others think if you wear beautiful and expensive clothes, that's an expression of self-love. But self-love starts with having the courage to be who you are, regardless of what others might think. It is about having the courage to live your dreams, to do what makes you happy in life, so that one day you won't wake up saying, "I wish I had." Self-love is about self-care, making your health a priority. Self-love is revealed in your willingness to stay focused on the things you say are important. It's about having the courage to set boundaries and protect them. When you love yourself, you're willing to make agreements with yourself—and keep them. Self-love is demonstrated in the daily choices you make, in the relationships you have, in your willingness to see yourself clearly, and in how you manage your money. Indeed, self-love is very much about the things you do more than the things you say.

Self-esteem comes from doing esteemable acts. Here are some additional actions you can take that will move you closer to real and lasting self-love.

Eliminate Negative Self-Talk

Negative self-talk is one of the most destructive behaviors we engage in, because after a while, we start to believe that's who we are. It becomes as much a part of our culture as sex and violence on television, and equally harmful. The injurious process starts with calling yourself derogatory names, such as stupid, idiot, dummy, or whore. Then, before you know it, these words become such a working part of your vocabulary that you're desensitized to their self-negating effect. Because you call yourself names, you consciously or unconsciously give others permission to do the same. It's an esteemable act not to call yourself derogatory names.

-§-
Self-love starts with having the courage to be who you are, regardless of what others might think.
-§-

In your Esteemable Acts Journal make a list of the negative words you call yourself or have ever called yourself. Be as honest as you can; no one will see this but you. Remember, the more honest you are in seeing yourself clearly, the better you'll be able to change. Now, next to each word, discuss why you label yourself that way. Then replace each word with a more positive description of yourself. The way to really change that old pattern is to practice using the new words whenever you can and behaving in a way that is aligned with those new words.

Walk Away From Unhealthy Jobs and Relationships

When we don't like ourselves, we settle for seconds in jobs and relationships. Outwardly we say "I matter, I'm important," yet when we look at our lives we see ourselves stuck in jobs we hate and relationships that are abusive. And abuse is not just physical. Often it's easy to become accustomed to emotional and mental abuse, because we don't see the lingering physical scars, but the effects of emotional and mental abuse are just as damaging in the long run. Mental, emotional, and physical abuse eats away at your self-esteem. And if you're living a lie, not only is there abuse, but there is guilt and shame, too. Allowing people to speak to you in a way that is inappropriate (whether in public or at home), turning the other cheek when your spouse or companion has an affair, or allowing someone to take advantage of you in business because you're afraid to speak up are all forms of abuse. How can you love yourself when you tolerate such behavior? There are always excuses for staying in unhealthy relationships and jobs, but after a while the excuses stop working and you're challenged to take action on your own behalf. It's an esteemable act to walk away from unhealthy jobs and relationships.

-§-
Troubles are resolved when there is a diversity of thinking, and sometimes that means having the courage to be the one to speak up.
-§-

In your Esteemable Acts Journal make a list of the jobs you've had over the last five years. What did you like about each one? What did you not like? What about your present job? Do you enjoy what you do? Why? If not, why not? Why do you stay in a job you hate, what's the payoff? How does staying in a job you don't like move you further away from self-love?

Now, turn your attention to your relationships and make a list of the most important ones in your life today—for instance, your list might include your spouse, mother, father, teacher, manager, and sibling. Answer the following questions: Describe the kind of relationship you have with each of them. What do you like most about them? What annoys you the most? How does each relationship make you feel good about yourself? How does each relationship make you feel bad about yourself?

Speak Up in the Moment

Speaking up in the moment is another positive step toward real and lasting self-love. It keeps us from holding on to grudges that eventually eat away at us, because our anger at others eventually turns into anger at ourselves for not taking better care of us. Sometimes were afraid to speak up because we don't think we have anything important to say. Sometimes were afraid no one will want to hear what we have to say. Sometimes were afraid of being judged, and sometimes we're afraid of the conflict that is sure to arise when we say what we feel. But if you don't speak up when you have something of value to contribute, you do yourself and the problem-solving process a disservice. Troubles are resolved when there is a diversity of thinking, and sometimes that means having the courage to be the one to speak up with a new or different idea. It's an esteemable act to speak up in the moment.

One thing to remember about speaking up: The way you say something is as important as what you say. Most often people will respond positively to thoughtful words rather than words that irritate. So choose your words carefully. It can make the difference between someone hearing and understanding what you're trying to say and someone disregarding you.

In your Esteemable Acts Journal write down five things you wish you had said in the moment over the last three weeks. As you go through this day, make a note of the times you didn't say something you really wanted to say. While you can't go back and change the past, you can make an effort to take better care of yourself in the future by speaking up in the moment.

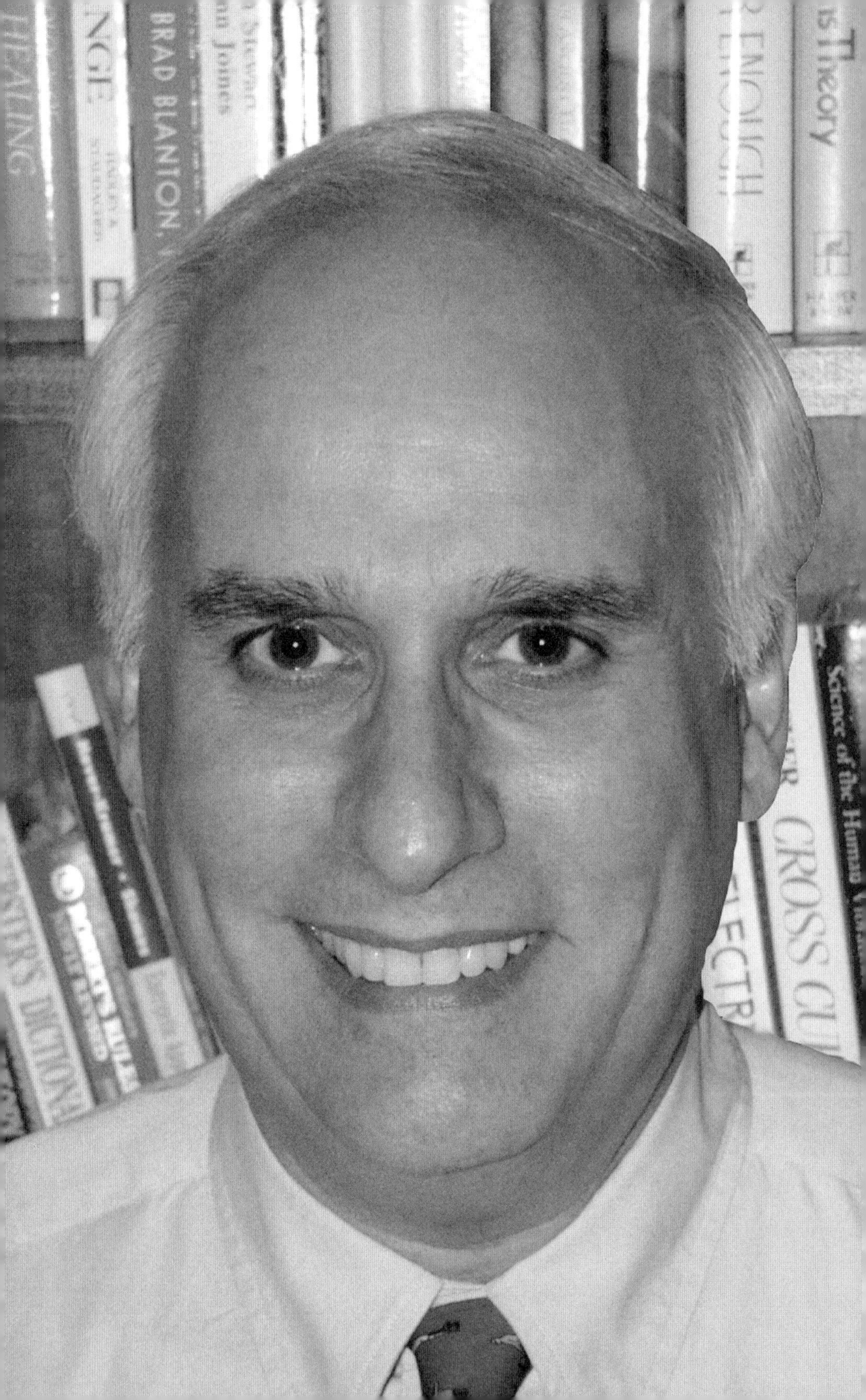
BRAD BLANTON
Science of the Human

Fred Gallo:

Catch Your Triggers Before You Fire

In the beginning of a couple's relationship, romance and passion flourish. The couple is excited, fascinated, enthralled, obsessed, and charmed out of their minds! In short, they are romantically *in love.* However, as time passes, too often the romance and passion fade and die. While some couples part after romantic love is gone, others remain together due to the fact that they really do love each other. And others remain together for various reasons: marriage, the children, finances, religion, and fear—fear of failure, fear of being alone, fear of the unknown, and fear of not being able to find true love.

There is also a general consensus that, if a couple has true love, the romantic love inevitably passes over to a deeper love. Move over *eros,* center stage *agape,* a love that is portrayed as spiritual, not sexual, not physical. But why should this be? Not that the spiritual side of love isn't a good thing; it would be heresy to denigrate the spirit and Platonic love. But why not have both? You know, have your cake and eat it too! There's really no reason why eros can't survive just as eternally as the spiritual side of love. Surely, eros adds spice to life and to that deeper love. Oh, yes, passionate love is physical *and* psychical, with all that wonderful emotion that gives lovers' lives meaning and significance and makes them want to contribute to the happiness of the beloved. Romantic love is healing. That sounds pretty good to me,

Fred P. Gallo, Ph.D., is a clinical psychologist. He is the author of six books, including *Energy Psychology: Explorations at the Interface of Energy, Cognition, Behavior, and Health.* (CRC, 2004) and has also published numerous articles and book chapters. After practicing many approaches to psychotherapy and energy therapies, he introduced the term "Energy Psychology" and has been offering training internationally in these approaches since 1993. Dr. Gallo is associated with the University of Pittsburgh Medical Center (UPMC). He is a member of the American Psychological Association, the Pennsylvania Psychological Association, and the Association for Comprehensive Energy Psychology.

even quite spiritual. After all, aren't *meaning, significance, contribution to,* and *connection with another person* also spiritual?

So what's been happening to eros? Why all the bad press? I'm convinced that it is the result of a far-reaching *limiting belief* about romance and passion. And this belief comes in many guises:

- Romantic love doesn't last.
- Romantic love inevitably fades.
- Romance is not real love.
- Romance is self-absorption.
- Romance is a sign of weakness.
- Romance is silly.
- I'm not a romantic person.

In short, this limiting belief maintains that passion and romance cannot be sustained—and some would even say that it shouldn't be sustained, since it distracts from the more important things of life. You know—working, knitting, miniature golf, taking out the garbage, and such.

Let's look at that word, *sustain.* To sustain means to uphold, support, and "to supply with *sustenance."* Related words include *food, fuel, nutrition,* and *nourishment.* If passion and romance die, then surely they did not get enough nourishment, resulting in frailty and eventual starvation. They've been starved for affection, attention, meaning, and significance! So, to carry the metaphor to its logical conclusion, isn't the solution to *feed* the passion and romance in order to allow them to regain strength and vitality? Of course, if the passion and romance are truly dead, it might take a monumental effort to resurrect the poor souls. Yet the effort is certainly worth it, unless you have reached that proverbial point of no return and are repulsed at the idea of reviving passion with this person. Assuming that you haven't reached that point, or, at the very least, that you intend for a future relationship to flourish with passion, please read on.

-§-
Romantic love is healing.
-§-

Reviving Romance

Romance fades when lovers are neglectful or do damaging things to each other. To reverse this pattern, here are some important questions to consider. Take out a pencil and some paper now and write down your answers.

1. On a scale of 0 to 10, how would you rate your Subjective Units of Relationship (SUR), with 10 indicating ultimate

passion and romance, and 0 indicating a big fat zero? If your SUR is 8 to 10, you're hopelessly in love. Scores below this range can benefit from some additional attention. Please read on.

2. If you didn't have a loss or significant reduction of passion and romance, what specifically would be different? Go into detail.
3. If something were to magically transform your relationship into a supremely passionate and romantic one, how would you know that this had happened? How would your behavior be different than it has been lately?
4. What would a friend who knows you really well observe and feel about your new behavior?
5. Recall some moments and events when you and your lover felt really passionate and romantic about each other. How would you rate the SUR during those moments and events, 0 to 10? Describe them in detail.

Contrast this with what you have been doing, thinking, saying, and feeling lately. Again, think back to when passion was alive and thriving. Recall those times in detail.

- What were you doing then?
- What persistent thoughts did you have about your lover?
- What was different about the way you talked to each other?
- How did you play with each other?
- Can you remember all the fun?
- What was different about the way you touched and kissed?
- How did you hug and hold each other?
- What was it like to look into each other's eyes?
- Were your tone of voice and choice of words different then?
- What about the way you moved and smiled?
- How did you feel about the way your lover smelled and tasted?
- Remember the gestures and facial expressions that were so endearing?
- What was different about your behavior then?

Remember when you were enthralled with learning everything you could about your lover? There's always more to learn, and it's time to resume the adventure of discovery!

It is important to understand that thoughts, behaviors, and feelings are intimately connected. If you have negative thoughts about someone, it is understandable that your feelings will be congruently negative. Resentful thoughts elicit resentful feelings; angry thoughts result in angry feelings; hopeful and loving thoughts produce hopeful and loving feelings.

Try this experiment. Vividly imagine a lemon. Look at it up close. If it's not already sliced, slice it and look at the insides. See the rind, all those sections, the seeds, and little packets of lemon juice. Can you smell the lemon fragrance? Now bite into your imaginary lemon and notice the sensation in your mouth. What happens? Most people experience their mouths watering, along with a sour and bitter sensation. So what accounts for this? Where is the lemon? Obviously, there is not a real lemon, just an imaginary one. The lemon is simply in your mind. The thought of a lemon sends energetic messages through your body, like electricity through a wire, and you experience specific sensations. Mind and body are intricately joined. You get to experience your thoughts as though they are real.

-§-
If you consciously practice the loving behaviors for two to four weeks, you will find that they become increasingly easy and natural.
-§-

Ok, so you thought about it, imagined, recalled, got in touch with what it was like when the passion and romance were thriving. Excellent! Yet that's not enough; now you need to do something with those thoughts and feelings. We all know that words pale in comparison to vivid images. *A picture is worth a thousand words.* Well, there is something even more powerful than a thousand pictures, and that's action.

If you consciously practice loving behaviors for two to four weeks, you will find that they become increasingly easy and natural; your feelings and thoughts will also change. It won't be long before you *realize* that this is the way you *really* think and feel about your lover, deep within the very core of your being. Your chosen behaviors will start to become automatic, even unconscious in many ways. But stay conscious, too! This is just the beginning. Persistence pays big dividends. You can't just *wish* or *hope* for things to be better; you've got to really *want* it, and you've got to give the *want* reality by persistently and consistently putting it into action. In this way you elevate the *want* to an even higher level; it becomes a *must.* And if both you and your lover act from *must,* the benefits will exponentially increase.

Shifting Out of Reverse

Now that all sounds easy enough, doesn't it? Well, at least on paper! However, consider this analogy: It doesn't matter how much you intend to drive forward; if your car or truck is in reverse, it isn't going to happen. And it doesn't matter how hard you step on the gas. You still won't get to your intended destination any faster if you're driving in reverse. Obviously, you have to shift out of reverse and into forward gears if you are going to move forward. The same holds true with actualizing passion and romance in your relationship. Even if you know what to do to create the love that you want, if your actions are incongruent with your expressed intention, it isn't going to happen. And if your actions are incongruent with your expressed intention, something is interfering with the *must.* What is it?

-§-
Psychological reversal is a misalignment of intention and action, such that the actions tied to the intention prevent its fulfillment.
-§-

In Energy Psychology we have the concept of *psychological reversal* or, simply, *reversal.* This is a self-sabotaging tendency to treat what's healthy as if it is unhealthy, and what's unhealthy as if it is healthy—thus the term *reversal.* Psychological reversal is a misalignment of intention and action, such that the actions tied to the intention prevent its fulfillment. When you are reversed, you behave incongruently. Your intention and actions are not on the same page and you repeatedly shoot yourself in the foot.

What causes this state of affairs? Actually, we all become reversed at times. It's part of the human condition, spoken of in many spiritual traditions. Paul, of the New Testament, speaks of this in his letter to the Romans, Chapter 7, verses 12-16:

> I cannot understand my own behavior. I fail to carry out the things I want to do, and I find myself doing the very things I hate. When I act against my own will, that means I have a self that acknowledges that the Law is good, and so the thing behaving in that way is not my self but sin living in me.

Psychological reversal does not necessarily involve sin, but it does go against your stated values and intentions. The causes occur at many levels. It can be seen as a conflict between the conscious and the unconscious mind, between the right and left cerebral hemispheres, or between higher cortical areas of the brain and areas of the more primitive limbic system, which is constantly scouting for danger. Reversal may also be a disruption of energy flow through acupuncture meridians and the nervous system. At one level you want one thing, and at another level you want something else—or feel that, if you follow your conscious intention, you'll lose something. In this sense, there is a conflict of intentions. And guess which intention is winning the battle? For example, you might want to lose weight, but eating certain foods gives you immediate comfort and joy. You don't want to lose these resources along with the weight. The comfort and joy of eating certain foods *outweighs* your intention to weigh less.

With romantic love, the reversal might involve a feeling of resentment, vulnerability, or some other fear. Passion and romance are avoided, since they are associated with fear. However, it is also possible that the reversal of energy is fundamental, while the cognitive considerations are really secondary or tertiary. That is, perhaps a person behaves as though he or she doesn't want passion in his or her life simply because the energy is reversed, not because he or she doesn't really want the passion. As Paul said, "I fail to carry out the things *I want to do,* and I find myself *doing* the very *things I hate."*

-§-
The best way to change is not through self-rejection, but through self-acceptance.
-§-

The causes of reversal are many, and sometimes there may be underlying considerations. And, while it can be useful to understand the underlying motives, psychological reversal is often a simple matter to correct. Physically tapping at specific acupuncture meridian locations on your body while stating an affirmation can help to disengage reversal and help you to realign with your intentions of creating passion and romance in your relationship. Here's one way to accomplish this:

1. Bring the lack of passion and romance to mind.
2. Alternate tapping on the little finger side of either hand (karate chop point) and under your nose.
3. While tapping, think or verbalize several times, "Even though I have this passion and romance problem, I deeply love and accept myself."
4. Do this often, and observe the ways that passion and romance are jump-started in your relationship.

Correcting reversal is a function of two factors: alleviating energetic blocks, and accepting yourself with the problem that you are experiencing at the time. The best way to change is not through self-rejection, but through self-acceptance. An affirmation, when combined with tapping on the side of the hand (the third acupoint on the small intestine meridian) and under your nose (the twenty-sixth acupoint on the governing vessel), balances energy and consciousness in the direction of health and highest good. Of course, you still have to do things to activate passion and romance. This method simply helps to disengage the reversal that prevents you from doing what you know how to do.

Resentments and Other Negative Emotions

When you harbor anger, resentment, and hurt feelings, these emotions and surrounding events need to be resolved before the relationship can move in a positive direction. It is difficult, if not impossible, to get to passion when negativity blocks the pathway. While there is a lot to be said for a *change of heart*—making a decision to let go of the past and move on—a simple Energy Psychology technique can often facilitate and speed up the process.

Let's say that your lover did something that hurt you deeply, or that you had an argument and terrible, hurtful words were exchanged. These actions or words have a way of replaying in your mind along with the hurt and scared feelings. In the broad sense of the term, this is a *trauma.* Maybe at the time you also made a decision to quit feeling so deeply about him or her. You backed off on your feelings so that you wouldn't get hurt again, and maybe to give your lover a bitter taste of his or her own medicine. Maybe you concluded that the two of you are incompatible, that your "lover" isn't good enough, or that you are unlovable. Or maybe you're actually trying to help your lover in some way by letting go, sensing that he or she can't handle the passion. Regardless of the belief you installed, you gave the axe to love and now passion and romance are greatly diminished or gone.

When you're stuck with a trauma and the associated belief, there are several Energy Psychology techniques that can help to rapidly dissolve the trauma so that you can move on in a better way. Here's how you do it:

1. Think about the painful event and rate your current feelings using Subjective Units of Distress (SUD) from 0 to 10, with 0 representing no emotional distress and 10 being ultimate distress. This is the SUD level now, as you think about the event, not the way you felt at the time the event occurred.
2. Treat any possible reversal by alternately tapping on the little finger side of either hand and under your nose, while stating several times, "Even though I am still upset about what happened, I deeply love and accept myself."
3. While making statements related to the event such as "the argument," "what she said," "what he didn't do," "I'll never love again,"or any statement that accurately references the

event, tap five to ten times at each of the following locations: between your eyebrows on the forehead (the third eye point, or midway between the twenty-fourth and twenty-fifth acupoints on the governing vessel); under the nose (the twenty-sixth acupoint on the governing vessel); under the bottom lip (twenty-fourth acupoint on the central vessel); and on the upper section of the sternum or chest bone (over the thymus gland or at the twentieth acupoint on the central vessel).

4. Check the SUD level again, measuring how intense it feels on a scale of 0 to 10. Has it decreased? Usually it does.
5. Even if the SUD hasn't decreased, repeat the tapping sequence several times, since sometimes it takes a few rounds before the negative emotion starts to dissipate or completely resolve. If the SUD level has decreased by several points, go to step number nine.
6. If this tapping sequence doesn't work adequately, use the following alternative sequence: beginning of the eyebrows near the bridge of the nose (second acupoint on the bladder meridian); directly under the eyes (second acupoint on the stomach meridian); six inches below the armpits (twenty-first acupoint on the spleen meridian); under the collarbones next to the chest bone (twenty-seventh acupoint on the kidney meridian); on the inside tip of a little fingernail (ninth acupoint on the heart meridian); and again under the collarbones (twenty-seventh acupoint on the kidney meridian).
7. Check your SUD level again. Has it decreased?
8. If the emotional pain hasn't decreased, or has not decreased significantly, repeat the tapping sequence several times. Sometimes it takes a few rounds before the emotion starts to dissipate, or is completely resolved.
9. Assuming that the SUD has significantly decreased after one or a few rounds of one of these tapping sequences, add the following *brain balancing procedure.* While tapping on the back of either hand, between the little finger and ring finger (third acupoint on the triple warmer meridian), do the following: close eyes; open eyes; rotate eyes clockwise several times slowly, in a complete circle, while alternating humming a tune and counting; rotate eyes counterclockwise several times slowly, in a complete circle, while alternating humming a tune and counting.
10. Check your SUD level again. Has it decreased?

11. If the SUD has decreased somewhat, repeat the tapping sequence that worked best for you.
12. Keep alternating an effective tapping sequence and the brain balancing procedure until the SUD gets to 1 or 0.
13. If progress stalls at any time, repeating the psychological reversal correction will often help.

A Significant Shift

Once you are no longer experiencing distress about the event, reevaluate what happened. Was your lover in an insecure state at the time of the event? When we are in low moods, we often say or do things that we would not do otherwise. Was your lover psychologically reversed at the time? Are you able to let it go now? Is it appropriate to let it go now? Are you now able to reaffirm your love? Or are there other events that need to be neutralized first? Often, treating one event elicits others that need attention. If so, use the process described here to resolve any and all issues that get in the way of your having the love that you want and deserve.

Most people report that, once a trauma has been relieved in this way, their thoughts about the event significantly change. The event is more distant and they feel more tranquil, serene, and at peace. If before they felt damaged or wounded, after doing the Energy Psychology technique they experience themselves in a healthier way. If you notice a shift of this sort, you can strengthen and reinforce it by doing the following:

1. Rate the level of positive belief and emotion on a scale of 0 to 10, with 10 now representing the positive end of the continuum. This is referred to as the Positive Belief Score (PBS).
2. Now tap on the back of either hand, between the little finger and ring finger (third acupoint on the triple warmer meridian), while attuning to the now more positive belief and feeling. Your intention is to increase the strength of this new understanding by visualizing or thinking about it in other ways, while tapping.
3. Observe as the PBS increases. As a goal, the strength of the emotion and belief should be within the 8-to-10 point range. Usually this will result in a significant shift within a few minutes, at most.
4. If the progress stalls at any point, treat for psychological reversal in this way: While tapping under your nose, say,

three times, "Even if my positive feelings and belief don't get stronger, I deeply love and accept myself."

5. Then resume tapping between the little finger and ring finger.

I'm assuming that any altercations between you and your lover were not physical abuse, or any other highly destructive behavior. Resolving a trauma is a good thing to do, since it is in your best interest; but what you choose to do afterwards is another issue. The processes described here are not intended to enable you to remain in a destructively unhealthy relationship. The purpose of these exercises is to help you to reclaim passion and romance in an otherwise healthy relationship.

There is much more to consider than has been covered here. There are degrees of being in love, and degrees of wanting to rekindle romance. The more you *truly want* to have a romantic relationship, the better, in terms of being able to make it happen. No technique, no matter how elegant and powerful, can ever replace the power of intention and the willingness to make something happen. What we have covered in this chapter is merely an adjunct to assisting *you,* in whom the true powers lie.

Wayne Dyer:

Four Pathways to Mastery

The ancient Kahunas of Hawaii used the metaphor of the flow of a running stream to represent the divine force because they recognized that the universal intelligence we call God is always moving and flowing. Reconnecting with the flow of that Source is essential in order to attract whatever seems to be missing in your life. You have much more power to manifest what you desire than you might think. This is the essential message of my work and many of my books.

All of us have the capacity to attract what we want, whether that is a relationship, a promotion, or some other form of abundance. Let's talk about this in the context of someone who wants a loving relationship but has not been able to manifest one.

The place to begin, as always, is within. First and foremost, we must honor our worthiness to receive what we want. Men and women in our society have been conditioned to believe themselves not worthy. This belief holds that it is selfish to want good things in our lives. We've been conditioned at a very basic level to feel that we shouldn't want more and should be satisfied with what we have. This stems from the belief that we don't deserve to have what we would like because we have been bad and, therefore, are not worthy. Until we release this false belief, our very feelings of unworthiness put a huge obstacle in the way of manifesting the relationship we want.

Wayne Dyer, Ph.D., called the "father of motivation" by his fans, is one of the most widely known authors in the field of self-empowerment. Despite a childhood spent in orphanages and foster homes, Dr. Dyer has overcome many obstacles to make his dreams come true, including getting a doctorate in counseling psychotherapy from Wayne State University and the University of Michigan. Dr. Dyer has written many books, including *The Power of Intention* (Hay House, 2005), and *Inspiration: Your Ultimate Calling* (Hay House, 2006). He has appeared on over five thousand programs, including *Oprah* and *The Today Show*.

The universal intelligence we call God, Spirit, or Consciousness, is everywhere and in all things. There is no place it is not. The infinite flow of this stream feeds all. When you put a great, big obstacle—your feeling of unworthiness—in front of a running stream, it will not stop the flow of the divine force. The divine force will just go around your unworthiness and flow someplace else. That's exactly what happens when you decide you really would like to manifest a loving relationship, but simultaneously say to yourself, "I'm really not worth it," "I'm not good enough," "I've been bad," or "I'm a sinner." If you are saying this to yourself, the force will not work with you. It doesn't work with that which doesn't believe it *deserves.* This, then, is the place to begin—we have to overcome the societal conditioning that says we are unworthy.

-§-
You have much more power to manifest what you desire than you might think.
-§-

Almost all of our conditioning tells us that we can't manifest. We believe we can't attract to ourselves what we want, because we think we are separate from God. From this point of view, our ability to manifest anything depends on whether God wants it for us or not. Seeing ourselves as connected to God, rather than separate, puts us in the flow of the infinite stream and revives our capacity to attract what we want into our lives.

We are not in the business of creating, but of attracting. Everything that is created in the universe is here already. We are not creators so much as "re-combiners" of that which has already been created. We have to let go of the idea that we are going to create something out of nothing, and instead attract to ourselves what is already here. We can elaborate on this concept using the metaphor of a plum tree. When you look at a plum tree, notice that it has roots, bark, a trunk, branches, leaves, blossoms, buds, and eventually, plums. Now ask yourself, "What part of this is not plum essence?" The answer is, "It's all plum essence." When we see a plum we don't think, *Well this round purple fruit just showed up from the invisible spirit world of 'plumness' and manifested in our physical world. Somehow the fruit just appeared.* The truth is that the tree is meant to plum and it produces plums. The plum tree grows out of this world, and we are the same.

We divide ourselves up into spirit and human, but essentially we are all a part of the same world. We grow out of this world, and we are connected to everything in this world. In order for us to have what we want in our lives, we have to overcome the idea that somehow it's coming from another place and see ourselves as attracting and recombining the elements we would like to have in our lives.

The problem is that we have allowed our egos—the part of us that believes we are separate from God and separate from each other—to dominate our lives. Most people think of God in terms of a monarchy, where God is the king and we are the subjects. As subjects, we are inferior to this invisible king. According to this viewpoint, not only are we inferior, we are also stained by sin and, therefore, untrustworthy. As long as you subscribe to the notion of God as separate, you will always be lost.

If you take a glass of water and separate it from its source—the ocean—and ask the glass of water to sustain life, what happens? The glass of water begins to evaporate. It can't sustain life on its own and flitters away. That's a powerful metaphor for what happens when we believe that we are separate from our source. God is like the ocean, and we're like that glass of water. We try to sustain life and do all that we are capable of doing, but if we do it alone, we wither away instead.

Another problem with seeing ourselves as separate is that God becomes something like a giant vending machine in the sky. We put in our requests in the form of prayers, and then the vending machine dispenses the answer to our prayers based upon how well we've followed the rules. Of course, someone told us the rules at a time when we were not able to question what we were being told. In many ways, we are still operating from this perspective, even though we now have a critical faculty and a far more developed sense of the rules. A broader perspective will give us another way to look at this, wherein we are not separate from God, but, rather connected—"pieces of God," if you will.

In order to manifest the relationship we want, we need to align our intention with the divine intelligence. Simply put, when Spirit begins to rule in our lives instead of ego, we can literally manifest or attract to us everything we perceive to be missing. That's really the essence of it. We manifest from Spirit; we are connected at the invisible level of the life force to everything in the universe. Everything that is observed in the physical world has as its source that which is invisible. This means we must surrender to the Spirit and to the invisible part of ourselves. Learning to manifest is really nothing more than learning to manifest another aspect of our selves.

-§-

We are not in the business of creating, but of attracting.

-§-

In the process of manifesting, it's also important to remember that great things have no fear of time. We've got to let go of the idea that what we want to manifest has to be done on our schedule. *A Course In Miracles* says, "Infinite patience produces immediate results." When

you know that you want something and you have infinite patience, you know your desire is going to manifest. The immediate result you get when you know something is going to manifest is peace.

What is important is the essence of what you want to manifest, rather than the thing itself. For example, you want to find a relationship, but the essence of what you want is to love another. What you really want is to fulfill your need to love, and that will be fulfilled. Once you know that—and are absolutely certain of it—the details will get handled. Know that the end is secure, and let the "how" take care of itself. Your job is to not say *how;* your job is to say, *Yes!* Get all the obstacles and the nos out of the way, and what you want will show up. It will be so simple that you will wonder why you made it such a struggle.

-§-

Learning to manifest is really nothing more than learning to manifest another aspect of our selves.

-§-

Before something wonderful happens, we often experience some kind of fall. In other words, even your struggle is purposeful. This comes from the Kabbalah, and I have found it to be very true. Ultimately, to get to a higher level in our lives, we have to generate the energy to do so. A fall of one kind or another almost always precedes a spiritual advance, because the fall itself helps us generate the energy we need for the next leg of our journey.

There are four pathways to mastery: Discipline, Wisdom, Unconditional Love, and Surrender. The Pathway of Discipline is what we send kids to school for—to learn something, to work hard, and practice, practice, practice. Whether you want to learn to play tennis, do math, write, or dance the Macarena, you must work and practice to discipline the body and the mind. But you have to show up and do the work.

The Pathway of Wisdom opens when you apply intellect to your discipline. You begin to question: "How do I do this?" "What form should this take?" "When is the best time to do this?" "Who should I consult?" This is what we think of as higher education, but we make a mistake if we assume we're educated once we have information and knowledge. Information and knowledge are not equivalent to mastery. When they are applied to a disciplined study, they lead to wisdom—and that is where mastery is achieved.

The Pathway of Unconditional Love is open to those who love what they do and do what they love. If you watch the great masters, or anybody who is really terrific at what they do, you will see that they exude a special kind of love. Watch Barbra Streisand, or Rudolf

Nureyev, or Tiger Woods. They each love what they do and, when they're in it, they are in the flow and have *become* what they do.

When we are really inspired like this, we don't think about how we feel or how much money we have. When we're inspired, everything seems to work. This is when we seem to reach our highest level of creativity. To be inspired means that you have really transcended your body. For example, when Picasso was asked about his paintings, he said, "When I enter the studio, I leave my body at the door the way the Moslems leave their shoes when they enter the mosque. I only allow my spirit to go in there and paint." You've got to trust in Spirit, because it is the source of manifestation.

The ultimate pathway, however, is the Pathway of Surrender. This is where you surrender the "little mind" to the "big mind." After you've done the discipline, applied the wisdom, and fallen in love with what you've done—you surrender. You must understand that it's not you, the puny, little, skin-encapsulated ego, that is doing this thing. You are in this world, but you are not of this world.

There are 483,364 words in *A Course In Miracles,* and the word "beware" only appears once: "Beware of the temptation to see yourself as unfairly treated." You have to really watch out for the idea that other people's successes mean that you haven't been fairly treated. Resist the temptation to compare yourself to others. This is crucial in order to be able to manifest whatever you want.

I grew up in the east side of Detroit, in an area where there was a lot of scarcity, poverty, and hunger. Even growing up in an orphanage, I never woke up saying, "I'm an orphan again today, isn't this terrible? Poor me." I never felt that I was unfairly treated. There were a couple of very affluent neighborhoods nearby, but I never thought for one second that those people had more than I had. It just seemed that they got what they were entitled to, and if I really wanted those things, then I would have them, too. Using these principles, which I discuss at length in my books, I have manifested everything I want. I have a beautiful family and enough abundance to take care of them. Now I put my attention on manifesting for other people, helping those who are less fortunate. For example, I manifested the time to write a book called, *A Promise Is A Promise,* about a woman whose daughter has been in a coma for twenty-seven years. This woman has cared for her daughter every two hours, twenty-four hours a day, for over a quarter of a century. I also manifested a publisher for the book and have donated all of the proceeds to help this woman get out of debt.

-§-

"Infinite patience produces immediate results."

—*A Course In Miracle*

-§-

Give thanks for all that shows up in your life, including the stuff that you perceive to be negative, the things you wish hadn't happened. Don't take anything for granted. And understand that what you want to manifest is not for your personal ego, but rather to help you be an instrument of peace. I encourage people to do morning and evening meditations on gratitude, to give thanks for whatever they *do* have, rather than focusing on the feeling of lack or despair for what they don't have.

The highest pathway that we can get to—the Pathway of Surrender—is also called the Pathway of the Spirit. Jung talked about the archetypes of the Warrior, the Athlete, the Statesman, and, ultimately, the Spirit. When you're asking about finding your purpose, you're in the Athlete or Warrior stages. You're asking the question, "What am I here for?" based upon what you are supposed to do with your body and your talents. But when you get past that, you realize that this isn't who you are—you are not your body. Then you realize that the only thing you can do with your body, and with your life, is to give it away. Start your relationship from that place, and your desire to love will reach its greatest fulfillment.

-§-
Give thanks for all that shows up in your life, including the stuff that you perceive to be negative.
-§-

As Dan Millman writes, in *The Way of the Peaceful Warrior,* it is helpful to remember that, "There are no ordinary moments." Every moment is an eternity in itself. Bliss is the present moment, and we do well to understand this. When we meditate, we are really trying to go beyond the mind. What I have found is that, if I can get totally and completely into the moment, the mind disappears. As the mind disappears, God appears.

You have to surrender the little mind to the big mind, and turn what you want over to God. You can do this in any moment in your life. There is no moment that isn't equivalent in value to any other moment. Then you must trust, and know that what you want to manifest will happen. If you follow these principles, you'll see your dreams manifest—just like that!

Part Six

Wonder in the Flesh

When I became God's Lover,
the fire and earth of this form became consorts;
air met water and they began to swoon.
Masculine took feminine into his heart
as he took her hand and all were raised on a current of bliss
to the purple vein of rapture.

When I became God's Lover, I knew that I was wonder in the flesh.
My mouth became as wide as the sky drinking dark sweet secrets beneath a
boiling burst of moon. Eyes in the forest watched. And laughed.

When I became God's Lover, the essence of "yes" that secret touch at the
tip of the tongue that comes with surrender filled the whole of my clawing
hunger. All that is left of me now is a taste for nectar.

~Geralyn Gendreau, *When I Became God's Lover*

Gloria Jean:

Portals to the Infinite

I am sitting cross legged on the floor in Tetitla, one of my favorite places in Teotihuacán, Mexico, gazing into the eyes of the Eagle that was painted there thousands of years before. Suddenly, the Eagle flies from the wall, grabs my heart with its beak, and tears it from my chest. I gasp and nearly topple over. The Eagle, hovering in front of me with my heart in his beak, seems to be waiting for something. I have no idea what is happening, and the urge to take back my heart is strong; but I find a place of trust within me, where I have no need for protection or control. I step into the unknown as I say, "Take my heart. It is yours. I give it to you freely."

With a blinding flash of light, I am inside the Eagle, soaring over Teotihuacán, looking at "Teo" with the Eagle's eyes and perspective. The view is so vivid and beautiful that it takes my breath away. We glide over the Temple of Quetzalcoatl and then above The Avenue of the Dead, where I see the perfection of the plazas that lead from "hell" to "heaven," and I recall the personal hell I had been in when I began my journey here several years before. I feel so much gratitude to this sacred place that has facilitated my transformation, and to myself for returning here again and again to leap into the mouth of the two-headed snake to die to fear and be reborn as love.

The Eagle slowly circles over the Pyramid of the Moon, and I am acutely aware of how Teotihuacán, "the place where men become gods," always reflects to me how I'm creating my life. It mirrors for me both my self-limiting illusions and my own magnificence and perfection. We soar over the

Gloria Jean is an inspirational teacher who loves witnessing the miracles that happen when people shed limitations of past conditioning and open to their pure creative potential. She has the ability to make esoteric teachings easy to understand and to integrate into everyday life. Gloria is a nagual woman and Toltec master trained by don Miguel Ruiz, author of *The Four Agreements* (Amber-Allen, 1997). She teaches from the wisdom of the heart as she guides groups on transformational journeys to sacred sites, facilitates workshops, and mentors apprentices. For full details of her work, see her web site at www.WomanReborn.com.

Pyramid of the Sun, and I remember the many times my teacher, don Miguel Ruiz, took me to the top of the pyramid and had me connect with my personal ray of light from the sun and merge with my Self beyond limitations. I thank the Eagle for this miraculous experience and he tells me that, from this day forward, I will live in his heart and see through his eyes. With that, I am back on the floor of Tetitla – both in my physical body and expanded to Infinity. I'm being supported by two of my fellow journeyers, and all I can do is weep with joy.

-§-
"Knowing others is intelligence; knowing yourself is true wisdom. Mastering others is strength; mastering yourself is true power."
—Lao-tzu
-§-

Over the course of eleven years and more than twenty journeys to the ancient home of the Toltecs, I have received many lessons of the heart. Teo's gift to me is different each time, but it is always exactly what I am ready to receive and always pushes me to expand. That day in Tetitla, the Eagle taught me about love without fear. He claimed my heart with unconditional love, as if he were saying, "I want your heart and I'm taking it…and you are free to say yes or no." I said yes because I *wanted* to be taken by that kind of fearless love, and I understood that I needed to meet him with the same kind of love. There could be no uncertainty, no holding back. I saw clearly that withholding my love from anyone was withholding my love from myself, denying myself the experience of love coming out of me. I saw that fearless love did not depend on being loved in return. It is its own gift to itself.

About two months before my experience with the Eagle in Tetitla, I was assisting on a power journey to Greece, where I met a man from the Netherlands who was to become my spiritual partner. Two weeks after Tetitla, he came to visit me at my home in California. The first morning that I awoke in his arms, I saw him as the Eagle and gave him my heart without hesitation, without conditions. Today, our practice in spiritual partnership is to keep our hearts open by removing any and every obstacle to the free flow of our love.

Our group has been granted special permission to spend time in the cave under the Pyramid of the Sun after the site has closed for the day. The sun is a bright orange, pulsating orb sitting low on the horizon as ten of us enter the pyramid and follow two guides down the steep, ladder-like staircase with only small flashlights to illuminate the way. The air becomes danker and more humid as we descend deeper into the pyramid and, finally, into the four-part, cloverleaf cave that has been called the Heart of the Universe. I spread my poncho on the ground, sit with my back against the side of the cave, and prepare to dream into the energy of this place. The guards turn off their lights and we are in absolute darkness for the next hour.

For me, Teotihuacán is a sacred place, a portal where the channel of communication between divine and human is wide open. Many such portals exist on the planet, and in my experience, one does not need mind-altering chemicals or plant medicines to access them. I offer a silent prayer, "Reveal what needs to be revealed, and heal what needs to be healed," and go deep inside my heart. Soon I begin to sweat and wish there was some fresh air to breathe. My discomfort increases, the long hour looming ahead of me as palpable claustrophobia begins to take over. I fight the feeling down, but the more I fight it, the stronger it becomes, until I can't bear it any longer and say into the darkness, "I'm in trouble."

From across the cave our group leader says, "What's the trouble?"

"I feel claustrophobic and think I'd better leave. I don't want to disturb anyone."

Voices from around me reply, "You're not disturbing us."

"Anything else?" our leader asks.

"There's not enough air to breathe," I say.

"There's plenty of air to breathe," she replies.

The moment expands and I see the choice clearly: There's not enough air/There's plenty of air. Past experience tells me what will happen if I keep telling myself there's not enough air to breathe. The others believe there's plenty of air. What will happen if I choose that belief?

"Okay," I sigh, "I'll stay and see how it goes."

The only thing I can do is sit with my fear and be willing to feel it. Each time I say yes to being with the fear, it grows a little stronger. I keep saying yes, and it keeps building. I'm having an interaction with an entity of my own creation. Energetically, it is like pushing through a giant marshmallow. I am deep within the "marshmallow" and have no idea how big it is or how to get out the other side, so I just keep saying yes moment by moment. Time has stopped and all that exists is this experience, my communion with fear.

After what seems like hours, I am aware that I am willing to be with this fear forever, if that is what is needed. With that thought, I move out the other side of the "marshmallow" and into the most profound peace I've ever experienced...peace vast, deep, and embracing. I do not ever want to leave this place. I am peace itself. Fear has released its grip on my heart, and love is radiating out of me like the rays of the sun. I hear a voice saying, "You will feel fear again, but you will never let it stop you because of this experience." Then I remember my prayer, "Reveal that which needs to be revealed and heal that which needs to be healed." I have created this experience for myself with my intent.

The cave has become a womb. Silently, I say, "Oh, I see...You are the Heart of the Mother."

I hear, "No, you *are the Heart of the Mother." I don't know what that means, but it touches me deeply.*

"It's time to go," the guard says, switching on his lantern.

I hear a silent voice, "Pick up a stone and take it with you."

I resist, "Oh, no, I really don't want to take anything from this sacred place."

"Pick up a stone and take it with you."

I bend down in the shadows, pick up the first stone my fingers touch, and slip it into my pocket. Later, during the evening meeting, I remember the stone, take it out of my pocket, and see it for the first time. It is in the shape of a heart.

My experience in the Heart of the Universe transformed my intellectual grasp of concepts into visceral understanding. Let me explain. Previously, I had understood the teaching that "our story controls our emotions." I had grasped the fact that, from infancy—some say even while we're in the womb—our emotions arise from pure perception because we haven't yet developed the ability to evaluate and interpret what we perceive. Gradually, we take on the beliefs and opinions of those around us, and those beliefs and opinions become the lens through which we interpret and experience our lives. Eventually, the story, and not the perception, causes our response. That day in the cave, not only did I see how the story I told myself generated my emotional response, I also felt it so deeply that every cell in my body registered the recognition—and I was thus physically changed.

-§-
We are evolving faster than we think.
-§-

Some time later, an incident from my everyday life reinforced this understanding. As I was walking out of the local coffee shop one day, I passed a young man sitting alone at an outdoor table.

"Hi," he called out.

I smiled and nodded, thinking, *How nice of him to say hello. This is such a friendly town.* I felt happy.

As I walked toward my car, he said, "So, how ya doin'?"

That's odd, I thought, *why is he still talking to me? Is he making a pass at me?* I felt a little flush of indignation.

As I unlocked my car, he said, "Why don't we make plans to get together?"

I thought, *This guy's a little strange. Maybe there's something wrong with him.* I felt a stirring of anxiety as I climbed into the car. As I backed out, I looked over my shoulder at the young man and saw that he was wearing a cell phone gadget on his ear. He was talking to somebody else! In less than a minute, three different "stories" in my head caused three different emotional responses in my body...and not one of the stories was true. I had a good laugh all the way home.

Another understanding that was deepened in the cave was that I have the power to change my story to one that gives me a response that I like. Many people don't realize that they can *choose* their point of view. Do you know people who seem to be eternal optimists? What kind of stories do they tell? And the pessimists...? Story increases its hold on you the more often you repeat it to yourself or share it with others. Your story is your creation. Create with awareness and tell stories that open your heart and make you feel good. As don Miguel writes, "If you can see yourself as an artist, and you can see that your life is your own creation, then why not create the most beautiful story for yourself?"

-§-
No evolution occurs without movement from the known into the unknown.
-§-

Fear came to me that day—not just as an emotion, but also as a presence sitting with me in the cave beneath the Pyramid of the Sun. It helped me see clearly how the ego-mind uses fear in an attempt to keep us "safe" within the parameters of the known. Yet no evolution occurs without movement from the known into the unknown. You can allow fear to imprison your heart and keep you from feeling and expressing your love, or you can move through it and find out what is on the other side.

I am about to lead a group of women to the top of the Pyramid of the Sun. It is our final day together...the culmination of a journey filled with miracles. The pyramid, pulsating with purple and white light, looks more like dancing molecules than a solid structure. I connect with the top, and what is usually a strenuous climb becomes easy, almost effortless. At each level, we walk around the pyramid in a counter-clockwise direction, stopping at the four corners to offer a prayer. I ask this repository of ancient wisdom to open us to the experience of Self beyond form. I reach the top and sit on the center point. With my intent, I connect to the base of the pyramid and into the black light at the center of the Earth. I connect with my personal ray of light from the sun in the manner taught to me by don Miguel Ruiz. I perceive a column of purple light emanating from the top of the pyramid. I ascend into that light and gaze down on Teotihuacán and the Earth below as they become smaller and smaller, until they disappear into the dark.

Another lesson of the heart reveals itself to me. I see that there is a point along the ray of light between formlessness – Source, God, the Unknowable – and human form. As I pass through it, I understand that point to correspond with the heart or essence of the human. I experience myself as the Infinite itself. I move back and forth through the point until I realize it's a portal! – a doorway that is always open – and that I, as a human, have the capacity to experience both selves, human and divine, simultaneously. I hear the words, "The human heart is the portal to Source. Remove the barriers to free passage." I am pulled through a vortex and find myself again atop the pyramid. I open my eyes, witness many beautiful humans enraptured by the experience of the Infinite, and realize that we, as a species, are evolving faster than we think.

We have the wisdom to identify the barriers to the experience of our divine Self, and the power to remove them. The grace I received atop the Pyramid of the Sun led me to use my heart as a guide, a perfect feedback mechanism for where I am in relationship to divine Self. The more I focus my attention on what my heart shows me, the stronger and clearer its signals become.

The silent voice of the "heart" can be felt as sensation in the trunk of the body. Many people feel it in the chest, but some feel it more in the solar plexus or lower abdomen. You can learn to read the particular voice of your heart. It may speak to you as tightening, pressure, density, or contraction, for example, when you need to see how you are creating an obstacle. You may feel sensations of loosening, warmth, tingling, lightness, expansion, etc. when your heart is opening. When you first begin listening, the sensations may be very subtle, but the more you focus your attention, the clearer they will become. Your heart will show you where you have created obstacles to your authentic self, and you can then make choices that will remove them.

-§-

"It is only with the heart that one can see rightly; what is essential is invisible to the eye."
—Antoine de Saint-Exupéry, *The Little Prince*

-§-

Your authentic self expresses as love. In every moment, you are either emanating love—with words, thoughts, actions, or more primarily, with the energy of your being—or you are interfering with that emanation. Another way of saying this is that you are either in your integrity or you are not. To live in your integrity is to move beyond the illusion of separation, to be able to freely pass through the portal between form and formless until you live every moment as divinity in human form. This is the essence of the Toltec mystery school, which facilitates the removal of obstacles to the full experience of your Unknowable Self, freeing you to create Heaven on Earth. This is the opportunity offered by the sacred city of Teotihuacán, the place where the human awakens and becomes God.

Leonard Shlain: How Women's Sexuality Shaped Human Evolution

When I was a second year medical student, I began to wonder why human females menstruate. My interest was piqued one day while on teaching rounds in a large ward. Shifting from bedside to bedside, our knot of students listened intently as our professor explained the purpose for three basic laboratory tests ordered on every in-patient: a chemistry panel, a urinalysis, and a complete blood count.

What caught my eye that morning was the column of "normals" listed on the lab slips parallel to the patient's test results. Of the chem panel's twenty-six numbers, none exhibited any differences between the values of a man and a woman. And why should there be? Sex has nothing to do with the way a lung or a stomach goes about its business. The same held true for the urinalysis. The CBC, however, was different. The red cell, hemoglobin, and hematocrit values for men and women were surprisingly askew. I thought that was very strange.

A red cell's chief function is to transport oxygen. Deprive any complex creature of this most precious element and it will rapidly die of asphyxiation. Yet, a man normally has a fifteen percent higher concentration of circulating red cells than a healthy woman. Mystified over this discrepancy—even after taking into account that, generally, a woman is smaller in stature and has less muscle mass than a man—I

Leonard Shlain, M.D., is a surgeon who has authored three critically acclaimed, best-selling, award-winning books: *Art & Physics* (Harper, 1993), *The Alphabet Versus The Goddess* (Penguin, 1999), and *Sex, Time, and Power: How Women's Sexuality Shaped Human Evolution* (Penguin, 2004), which recently won the Quality Paperback Book Club Award for Non-Fiction. A professor of surgery at the University of California, San Francisco, Dr. Shlain holds several patents for innovative surgical devices. His remarkable books and insights have changed the way many readers view themselves and the evolutionary process that brought us to where we are today. See www.SexTimeAndPower.com.

posed the question that eventually prompted me to write *Sex, Time and Power:* Why would a woman need less blood than a man?

I raised my hand and asked the professor to explain the reason for this disparity. He gave me a withering look, implying that the answer was obvious, and retorted, "Women bleed and men don't." I reddened.

I remember thinking at the time that his curt answer could not be the whole story. Years later, I wondered why a species would evolve whose females—but not males—operated routinely on less than a full complement of tankers to ferry a fuel as crucial as oxygen? One could argue that the female has a normal amount and the male has a fifteen per cent excess capacity. Either way, the inequality begs for an explanation.

-§-
The key factor shaping human sexual relations was our ancestor's fateful decision to stand up and begin walking on two feet.
-§-

Like nested Babushka dolls, at the heart of the red cell is hemoglobin's spark plug—the iron atom. Iron and oxygen, due to the salutary arrangement of their outer electron shells, eagerly seek out each other's embrace. Once merged, the two form a molecule called iron oxide. Everyone is familiar with this substance—we call it rust.

Rust has a signature red color. Iron oxide in rock lends to the Grand Canyon its spectacular chromatic array. It colors the fields in Kenya, the plantations of Hawaii, and rust's distinctive hue made the earth of Scarlet O'Hara's beloved plantation, Tara, red. The hemoglobin molecule, with its precious complement of iron atoms, makes blood red and white skin pink, and it tints medium-rare steaks with a distinctive ruby sheen.

Hemoglobin transforms iron's strong affinity for oxygen into a delicate "grasp and release" maneuver, allowing oxygen to be easily acquired in the lungs and readily relinquished further down the line to the cells. The felicitous combination of iron, oxygen, and hemoglobin is central to the process that facilitates the neurons in your brain to extract meaning from the sequentially aligned squiggles you are reading on this page.

Among the 4,000 species of mammals, only a few females menstruate—and those that do experience minimal iron loss, or menstruate very infrequently. Phyla other than mammals do not experience cyclical blood loss. The human female loses the most blood the most often. When added to the fetal iron transfer, blood loss from the most traumatic delivery of all mammals, failure to consume the placenta (as most other mammal females do), and iron deficits during lactation, menses can be viewed a potential threat to a woman's health.

Why would natural selection saddle a species with what appears at first blush to be an extremely deleterious adaptation? Why wasn't it culled from our genome long ago? No reproductive physiologist has identified the incontestable plus menses confers upon the human female that could offset its negative consequences for a Pleistocene ancestral woman. Constant teetering on the edge of an iron deficiency anemia and exposed to increased pregnancy risks do not balance the monthly flushing of "bad humors"—the explanation proposed by Hippocrates and Galen 2,000 years ago, and universally accepted until only recently.

Because I chose to become a surgeon, blood became a central concern of mine. Throughout my career, on occasions too numerous to count, I have glanced up from a particularly vexing operative field to anxiously monitor a forest of IV poles with their precious transfusions hanging like ripe fruit. I have had many years during which to contemplate the nature, importance, and vitality of the red liquid. These musings have convinced me that significant differences in iron levels between the sexes were the initial driving force behind many uniquely human cultural innovations.

-§-
The female evolved cognitively faster than the male in the area of sexual relations.
-§-

The key factor shaping human sexual relations was our ancestor's fateful decision to stand up and begin walking on two feet instead of four paws. Aligning our vertebral column perpendicular to the earth, instead of horizontally, positioned a mass of intestines that towered over the bipedal hominid's anus. Consequently, the bony hole in the pelvis narrowed—otherwise the unfortunate individual might be turned inside out when out for a stroll after a particularly heavy lunch. While the pelvic inlet's circumference was constricting, the brain of this two-legged creature underwent a remarkable hyperinflation, resulting in a one-third increase in volume in a comparatively short planetary time period.

An evolutionary crisis occurred with the advent of Homo sapiens, approximately 150,000 years ago. The fetal brain had ballooned so that it now threatened the continuation of the species. No other female of any other species routinely summons help to deliver, and no other species has as much difficulty bearing her young. Paradoxically, the single greatest cause of death among archaic human females was giving birth.

This precipitated a most unusual evolutionary event. Ancestral women experienced an extreme environmental stress originating from within their bodies that did not similarly affect men. The female needed to evolve cognitively faster than the male in the area of sexual relations. And then, she *got it!* The female made the crucial connection between sex and pregnancy.

Realizing that death was a possibility as a result of engaging in sex, she acquired a power no female of any other species has ever wielded: She became the first female among three million sexually reproducing species to be able to consistently refuse sex when she ovulated. Philosophers call this Free Will.

-§-
The human female's reproductive cycle has taught us to maneuver within the dimension of time
-§-

Her ability to choose a course of action different from the insistent commands of her potent hormones and instincts resulted from genetic mutations. The impetus for Original Choice's installation in her genome was natural selection's imperative to grant women veto power over impregnation. She evolved on a cognitive level more quickly than he did because the Sword of Damocles hung over her sex, not his.

To acquire the resolve necessary to refuse sex when she was ovulating, this one breakaway female primate not only underwent a major overhaul in the design of her brain (as did the male), she experienced a gear-grinding resetting of the major timers within her reproductive system. A perplexed *Homo sapiens* discovered to his dismay that he had to respond to the challenge she posed or lose the opportunity to pass on his genes.

Simultaneous changes in his genome compounded his problem, particularly when his eagerness to have sex with a woman, any woman, increased. Other males of other species express interest in females only when the females enter their period of heightened sexual receptivity, called variously, "estrus," "heat," or "rut." The rest of the time their attitude toward females can best be characterized as apathy. The human male became the first male of the multitude that desired sex—with any female—all the time.

The psychosexual emergency precipitated by this dissonance of desire between the sexes set the stage for a battle, the tocsin sounds of which have reverberated down through all the generations ever since "Mitochondial African Eve" proudly held up her firstborn for all the other members of her pressed band to behold. It also forced early males to concentrate their emerging mental powers to formulate the question that lies at the heart of male/female relations: "What does a woman want?" Stripped to its essence, the real question behind his plaintive query is: "What must I do to convince her to let me have sex with her?"

From their observable behavior, there is little to suggest that, among the vast, heaving, rutting biomass of sexually reproducing species, there are any individuals who have the faintest idea about the purpose of all this thrusting. For a woman to make the connection between sex and the first signs of pregnancy, she would have first had to recognize a time period longer than a month.

Can it be a mere coincidence that the average length of the human menstrual cycle is 29.5 days, which exactly corresponds to the length of a lunar cycle? Examining the estrual/menstrual cycles of our closest primate relatives reveals that a bonobo chimp averages 42 days, chimpanzees 37 days. The few other menstruating primates wander all over the scale. None but a human has entrained with a distant celestial event. Unlike sea creatures, whose sexual cycles are set by the lunar tides, Homo sapiens are land animals. Why, on earth do females have this improbably close connection to the moon's periodicity?

Virtually all other animals are incapable of long range planning. Foresight has proven to be a human's most formidable weapon, propelling us up the predatory ladder until we occupy the top rung unopposed. Perhaps the dramatic changes that occurred to the human female's reproductive life cycle served primarily to teach our species the invaluable secret of how to maneuver within the dimension of time. This insight allowed humans to escape from the thin slice of the ever-present Now occupied by other creatures, roam the canyons of the past, and explore the misty plains of the future.

Julie Gerland:

The Winged Dragon

I experienced my first passionate love relationships as a teenager growing up in the materialistic society of Hong Kong. Like the tropical climate in the land where I was born, my love life was full of hot, humid days and sweet, sensual fruit, followed by thunder and lightning, gale-force winds, and turbulent seas. I learned at a young age that the amazing passion I was endowed with was not only a source of great pleasure, but also could induce cruelty, violence, disease—even death. Burning in the "dragon's fire" of my own instinctive desires, I was unaware that I was destined to "tame the beast"—to fly on its back into unknown realms and harness the dragon's true creative power.

At the age of fourteen, while I was in a discotheque with my boyfriend, a Chinese man came up to me and proclaimed that I was *his.* An obvious member of a notorious gang, he was determined to prove his claim. My boyfriend, a trained martial artist, stood his ground in the face of the challenge, and a fight broke out between the two men. When they moved to the street, knives came out. A group of friends jumped to our defense and held off what had rapidly grown into a crowd of attackers, while my boyfriend and I escaped into the night on his powerful Norton 750 motorbike. Cut, bruised, and trembling, we feared for our lives should the man try to claim me a second time.

Julie Gerland has, for more than thirty years, inspired and helped countless numbers of people to heal and transform their lives from soul to cell. She is co-founder of Association Suryoma and director of The Holistic Parenting Programme: Preconception to Birth & Beyond, which empowers parents and training professionals to participate in the regeneration of humanity. Julie and her husband, François, are co-founders of Providence, a holistic community in the French Pyrenees, where they live and receive people from around the world for individual stays, sessions, workshops, and professional trainings. She travels and teaches internationally. Visit www.suryoma.com.

The power my sexuality had over men had been a great and sometimes overwhelming mystery from the time I entered puberty. Dramatic events like the nightclub incident were on the increase. I wanted to give love and happiness to my partners, but my magnetism consistently provoked the fire of jealousy, possessiveness, anger, and frustration. I feared that this would lead to a serious tragedy. With no guidance, I began to feel more and more helpless. Eventually, I fell into a state of emotional chaos. In a peak of uncontrollable despair one day, I did the unthinkable. I swallowed all the sleeping pills I could find in my parents' bathroom cabinet, washed them down with vodka, and promptly passed out. My cry for help went unheard—or so I thought.

This Fire Within

Thrilling sensations can carry quite a heavy price tag, as our thirst for pleasure is never quenched, and the resulting frustration and cruelty can be limitless. Did God make a mistake in creating the sexual force? Did He give it to us to make us suffer?

Relationships are the basis of life. But so often, our stories are full of tragedy. Many of those who are in a marriage want out, and many of those who are not in a marriage want in. Women have been brainwashed by the pervasive image that equates sexy glamour with success. We lack role models who express the deeper truth of the human soul—men and women who drink the eternal elixir, that powerful cocktail of love and wisdom, and show us that love can not only last, it can be an exquisite dance.

The dragon, that fabulous beast of mythology, is symbolic of our instinctive forces. But the fire-breathing monster with the serpent's tail also has wings. The forces embodied in the mythical dragon possess a spiritual dimension and higher destination.

-§-
The dragon is symbolic of our instinctive forces. But the fire-breathing monster also has wings.
-§-

From a spiritual perspective, all energy comes from a divine source and is destined to return to the divine abode. Hermes Trismegistus, the thrice great mage of ancient Egypt, says of the sexual force in his Emerald Tablet: "From earth it rises and from heaven it falls, it receives power both from the higher forces and from the lower forces... it is the most forceful of all forces."

When I was fifteen, my family moved back to my parents' native England because of my father's financial situation. After all the excitement and hustle-bustle of Hong Kong, we suffered withdrawal in the quiet monotony of the English countryside. But this was the place Spirit had chosen to answer my cry for help and give my life new meaning.

One night, after going to bed as usual, I felt a strange presence entering my room. My heart began to race as my body filled with adrenaline. In the middle of the room, a point of light appeared and began to shine. *That is no ordinary light,* I thought. As the light spread, it grew so bright I could no longer see anything in the room. Then the light consumed me completely. In a moment of mystical ecstasy, I experienced the intense power of transcendent love. The quality of the light was immensely powerful, yet gentle and healing. I felt completely known, loved, protected, guided, and safe. The innate intelligence and unconditional love that lay hidden and masked by the incessant turmoil of passions and desires had revealed itself to me in an intimate way.

When the Student is Ready...

When I woke at dawn, my consciousness had radically changed. A feeling of knowing and being connected I had never felt before filled me. I somehow "knew" that my father would get a job back in Hong Kong and that I was to stay in the UK. Destiny had called me, and I had to follow its call.. Although I was only sixteen, now feeling the timelessness of my soul, I consecrated my life to this Light, to God.

Over the next five years, my colorful life swung like a pendulum. I spent periods of time offering my love energy to God as a celibate mystic and experiencing the ecstasy of that union. Then I would share my love in relationships as a passionate lover. Both felt incomplete. For me, God and man were still separate. Lasting fulfillment still eluded me.

-§-
The very force that has caused so much havoc and degeneration is now being harnessed in service of a positive future for humankind.
-§-

Then, in 1980, I attended a program that delved into Western mystery traditions at Findhorn. During my time there, I was given a photo of a man with long white hair and a matching beard, dressed all in white, and carrying a staff-like cane crowned with a crystal. Tears of joy rolled down my cheeks when my gaze fixed, trance-like, for the first time on the photograph I clutched in my hands. I had just discovered the Bulgarian spiritual master Omraam Mikhaël Aîvanhov, who—despite his eternal archetypal appearance—was born in 1900. Filled with an intense wave of déja-vu, I knew that this was not our first meeting.

I took my place amongst the neophyte initiates of Omraam's esoteric school and, over the following seven years before his maha samadhi— Hindi word for a realized yogi's conscious departure from the physical body at death—had the privilege of spending many months with him at his centers in France and Switzerland. Each moment in the presence of this fully enlightened being is written in gold on my soul.

Taming the Dragon

We have entered the era of reconciliation between man and woman. A peaceful revolution has started in the world to overthrow the current regime wherein mutual domination for self-gratification is the rule. The dragon that makes us cry out with the pain of separation and victimization is now being tamed by those who have learned to return this instinctive force to its divine source. The very force that has caused so much havoc and degeneration is now being harnessed in service of a positive future for humankind.

-§-
In the crucible of his or her own being, an initiate on the destiny path will go through an often grueling process of transformation.
-§-

Initiations that once took place in temples and sarcophaguses are now given in "ordinary life." With my hand firmly in the hand of my guide, I was eager to continue the amazing initiatory journey my life had become. Once-guarded secrets were being revealed in a language that even a child could understand.

"The real tragedy of mankind," Omraam said, "is that they have not understood that this energy of love is not merely for pleasure, but will permit them to do spiritual work of the greatest importance, work which will allow them to become conductors of this mighty force to transform the world. This force can change cinders and lead into gold, precious stones, and diamonds. This transformation can only be made by the power of love, not by any other means. From now on, search for the attitude, the thoughts, feelings, and plans which allow this divine energy to be controlled and guided."

Omraam gave many talks on the role of men and women. He described, in great detail and with gorgeous, moving poetry, our destiny as benefactors of humanity through the wise use of the sexual force. He explained that we would learn to circulate our energies in a different way and that the very dragon that had enslaved human nature would become a winged dragon. On the back of that dragon, he promised, we would travel through space to the infinite and penetrate the "holy of holies."

"Sexual energy can be compared to petrol," he said. "If you are ignorant and careless, you will get burned by it; your very quintessence will be destroyed and consumed. Initiates are those whose knowledge permits them to use this force to soar above the universe."

In the crucible of his or her own being, an initiate on this destiny path will go through an often quite grueling process of transformation. In the quest for the philosopher's stone, he or she will harness the lower instinctive passions, the untamed dragon nature. Then, like the dull, fuzzy caterpillar who changes into a gorgeous butterfly, that man or woman will emerge from the chrysalis to manifest unforeseen creativity, beauty, and power. The light of Spirit and the vast, unconditional love of the divine Mother will then begin to both guide and flood day-to-day life.

When the Woman is Ready...

After my time with Omraam, I returned to Hong Kong. The effect of my magnetism had now changed, and I began to attract a growing number of people who sought me out for guidance and help. But I had neglected my own health and eventually found that I could not be of help to anyone without attending to my own needs. The time had come for me to return to the chrysalis and go even deeper. Years of chaotic emotions and contraceptive pills had affected my health. Time spent in the clutches of the dragon's claws had exacted their toll, and my body was crying out for repair. Forced by ovarian cancer to learn life's laws and live in harmony with them, I began a new leg of my journey: to visit and tend to my neglected cells. Over time, my health returned—but more than that, I developed a conscious relationship with my body. And that prepared me for the next step.

-§-
Just as man can fertilize woman physically, she can fertilize him in the emotional realm.
-§-

During my time in France, I had become friends with a fellow disciple who was also an airline pilot. When François came to visit me in Hong Kong, we enjoyed a deep platonic friendship. He invited me to stay with him in Paris were I to return to France. When I left my residence in Hong Kong, I took François up on his offer. One day, as we were sitting facing each other over tea, I suddenly began to feel an intense sensation throughout my body. "I want to manifest in Man," the still, small voice of Spirit said within me. From the look on François' face, I knew that he, too, was experiencing something quite remarkable. All at once, our energies began to take an upward path with great, and yet gentle, intensity. I was loving God in man. This was not attraction; it was an amazing state of being. I felt as if my whole body was having an orgasm of unknown amplitude and quality—and it did not stop! Riding a wave of pure intention, I merged with the divine masculine principle.

Loving God in Man

Simultaneously, François' pure love and deep prayer for my well-being impregnated his life force; it seemed to flow like a river of subtle etheric energy down his spine and out through his second chakra, where a man is emissive. I received these scintillating etheric particles, which then rose like a warm flame, opening and softening all the cells and organs of my body. When this energy reached my heart, my consciousness merged with the vast ocean of oneness. Like a virgin, François' heart was likewise open—eager to be penetrated and known by this mysterious feminine force which began filling the well of his being. "Please don't hurt me," I heard him say in my mind.

I experienced the ecstasy of loving God in man and all my being remaining intact. I was filled with the Light I loved and experiencing union with all. We spoke creative words of blessings and prayers for each other and the world. The light shone intensely, like suns, in our heads.

"When man opens his heart in trust to his deepest love," says François, "and only wants to give, bless his beloved, and unite with his divine Mother, he feels an exhilarating sensation. It is as if the fragrance of a rose fills the chalice of his solar plexus and heart. He feels full, complete, and fertilized. Everything seems possible. He feels radiant, strong, and generous like the sun. When the light penetrates his higher mind, his whole perception changes. Life and the world feel beautiful and attractive. His beloved and the universe become one and unveil inner realities, producing incredible sensations."

-§-
Achieving a constant flow of bliss is not possible until we transform our hidden shadows.
-§-

He continues: "During these moments of bliss I realized that my mind had to be kept in check. Like the serpent in the Garden of Eden, mind wanted to control this state and reproduce it at will. No intellect can control Spirit! Its job is to humbly serve Spirit to facilitate the marriage of spirit and matter in the three-dimensional world."

François and I began our life together soaring on the wings of the dragon. Day after day we consciously expressed love through creative words, glances, blessings, hugs, and moments of union. Our exchanges went from the depths of our subconscious to the illumined heights of the superconscious. Filled with love, we were now "making light." When it takes an upward direction, the sexual force brings an experience of bliss. We feel loved, and we allow this love to flow out of our heart sending blessings to our beloved, our families, and the world. We feel connected with all. Consecrated to the Kingdom of God on Earth, we like to "donate" our love energy to a particular "charity"—a specific place or person we feel inspired to send a blessing.

The interlaced polarity between man and woman is also symbolized by the caduceus: just as man can fertilize woman physically, she can fertilize him in the emotional realm. At the mental level, man is again emissive and woman receptive. Seeing that his intellect is at the service of Spirit, she is inspired to penetrate and fertilize his higher philosophical mind. Like the mythic Isis, a woman can unveil the structure of the universe for herself and her man. Bliss is the child of this complete union. Contemplating this awe-inspiring beauty, like the God in Genesis, he then "sees that it is Good."

Fall from Grace

After years spent preparing our bodies, minds, and spirits, François and I were living in joy beyond our greatest dreams. But our experience confirmed that achieving a constant flow of bliss is not possible until we transform our hidden shadows. Little did we know that our exquisite landing in the "Garden of Eden" would activate a descent. We now had to anchor this volatile bliss state and build it an abode in the dense matter of our bodies.

-§-
It is time to rescue our imprisoned inner children and rewrite the programming.
-§-

When the powerful light created by the union of our sexual force and Spirit penetrated deep into the dark ocean of our subconscious and unconscious, it revealed repressed emotional, mental, and physical suffering. A torch had begun to shine on what felt like sea monsters lurking in the darkness. We had discovered the metaphorical "lead" of the alchemists that is to be transformed into the "gold" of inner qualities and self-realization. The reactivation of these wounds was an open invitation to heal the past and change our core beliefs about ourselves and the multi-dimensional world in which we live.

Hermes referred to this work when he said: "Thou shalt separate the subtle from the dense with the greatest industry." We often know the cause of our superficial suffering, but much of this "lead" stems from our unconscious. We are influenced by everything we live from the moment of our conception through our time in the womb and during birth. All that our mother lives during this period has an impact, as no barrier exists between her powerful emotions and the forming baby. During infancy and childhood, we are totally vulnerable, and we download emotions and core beliefs directly into our neurology. Often limiting and painful, this programming lies hidden in our unconscious until we begin the process of transformation.

François and I had not been programmed to live in paradise—to bathe in a sunrise cocktail of love hormones where feeling safe, wanted, unconditionally loved, and consciously connected to our divine source is the norm. Like many "ordinary" earthlings, we had been prepared for a life of struggle, ruled by stress hormones. It was time to rescue our imprisoned inner children and rewrite the programming.

"Unless you become like little children you will not enter the Kingdom of God," Jesus said. The innocent child we once were is still alive within us. This part of us needs to receive love and understanding. When difficult and painful memories surfaced, we validated them and infused them with our new vision of life.

But something wasn't right. A persistent voice in François kept saying, "This is too easy; you don't deserve this." Listening to it was enough to cause him to fall out of our shared state of grace and into despair.

"You are not doing enough; you must work more, serve more; you must sacrifice yourself for the sake of your partner," said his deeply ingrained core belief. "Love has to be earned." Becoming a rescuer, he used every drop of energy to serve and help, often giving until he fell into a state of complete exhaustion. None of the gratitude he received in return could ever satisfy this part of him. As he grew increasingly tired and dissatisfied, he fell into the role of the victim—feeling used and unappreciated by an ungrateful world. In desperate frustration, he would then get angry and turn into the persecutor. The resulting guilt and shame would make him sacrifice even harder in the hope of repairing the damage and restoring the flow of love. For a time, this cycle eclipsed any hope of regaining our lost paradise.

-§-
Peace and fulfillment are born from a sacred way of loving.
-§-

We began to wonder if we would ever heal this "unmerry-go-round" that was keeping us out of paradise. With increasing compassion, I watched François battle with the winds of his mind and emotions rather than float in the ocean of love. Slowly, over time and with great tenderness and care, we managed to de-hypnotize ourselves and transform our destructive core beliefs into peaceful certitude that ours is a loving universe. Having gained this priceless gift of experience, we are now able to help others turn their rescuer energy inward and take care of their own needs—physical, emotional, and spiritual. The persecutor is given the mission to keep the rescuer in check, doing his right job. Finally, no longer the victim, the inner child blossoms in the unconditional love of the divine Mother.

Then, we entered the immensity of the causal dimension of our being, where we began to take full personal responsibility for everything that happens to us.

And Yet Another Dawn

This is true freedom. This is the dimension where one can actually sense and feel and see that for every action there is an equal reaction. Indeed, what we do to others comes back to us. By accepting the responsibility for our actions in previous lives, we can resolve our karmic debts. Atonement and self-forgiveness then open the prison door of the mind. We walk humbly through the narrow door, ready to fly at the speed of light on the winged dragon. The past, present, and future lie open before us and merge into one eternal *Now.* We experience and identify with an ocean of unconditional love and compassion. Everyone and everything is but a reflection of the Self. Liberated from time and space, we stand as free cosmic beings able to conduct the creative Light that participates fully in the evolution of humankind and planet Earth.

Another day has begun in the Pyrenees. As the darkness of night is dispelled and the brilliant sun rises over the horizon, men and women gather to greet and commune with this potent source of life. After a sunrise meditation, François and I slowly walk back to the heart of our retreat center. The birds in the majestic old oaks sing sweet hymns of praise, while animals play and flowers embalm the warming air. On this sacred ground overlooking the majestic mountains, my sense of awe is continually inspired—my inner paradise is now reflected in this magnificent symphony of Spirit, Nature, and Man.

Peace and fulfillment are born from this sacred way of loving. Many people believe that peace is a boring state. It is not! It is a state of intense sensation. Leaving behind fear, protection, and adrenaline addiction, we embrace love and allow the cup of our union to overflow with divine nectar—powerful bliss hormones like oxytocin and others science has yet to discover.

As our master once said, "Humans are used to suffering. They must now prepare their nervous systems for the incredible intensity of the joy that awaits them."

Miracle thinking is strengthened by faith. If your faith is strong, does this mean that your desired miracle will happen every time? It won't if the result you've chosen is not in your highest and best interest, and for the highest and best interest for all. However, cultivating a Miracle mindset will move you closer to receiving the highest good that is intended for you, which may or may not bring you the specific outcome you desire. The trick is to maintain your Miracle Mindset and stay the course, regardless.

We've got this little space called "life"...and it happens between birth and death. It's just this little space with our name on it, for however long we have it, so make the best of it. Apply some of these Miracle thinking tips and come up with more of your own. The more you develop your Miracle thinking mindset, the more miracles will flow to you to heal yourself and the heart of the world.

Leo Buscaglia:

Couple Rituals and Traditions

There are peoples and cultures in the world rich in tradition. They are the first to attest to the fact that their traditions have been mainly responsible for keeping them together, maintaining for them a sense of self as well as togetherness and offering them the dignity and strength to face tomorrow.

It has become popular these days to devalue tradition as romantic, ritualistic nonsense having little or no value to the present. We have discontinued wakes, Sunday family dinners, holiday get-togethers, the very human happenings which in the past bound us together in memory. In so doing, we have lost our sense of history. "Do you remember the day when________?" Is that not cause enough for celebration? The old song revived. The note scratched on the back of a postcard, reread. The cake commemorating another year of life. The public renewal of marriage vows. Families who assemble at the graveside of dead members on their birthdays and assure each other that none of them will be forgotten, that love remembered is a part of each of them which makes them eternal.

My family celebrated everything: birthdays, holidays, Saint's days, sad times, happy times, anything which would bring the family together. My mother kept a calendar from which you could select almost any day as one for celebration! Every day, after all, is someone's birthday! We had traditional foods on designated days: risotto on Sundays, polenta on Fridays. There was the soup pot con-

Leo Buscaglia, Ph.D., renowned lecturer and University of Southern California professor, authored many books, including *The Fall of Freddie the Leaf: A Story of Life for All Ages* (Holt & Co., 1983), *Living, Loving and Learning* (Ballantine, 1985), *Loving Each Other* (Ballantine, 1986), and *Born for Love* (Ballantine, 1994). In 1984 he founded the Felice Foundation to recognize and aid those who have dedicated themselves to human betterment through the dynamics of helping one another. Untold numbers have been touched by his insights into how we seek happiness and create loving relationships. More at www.buscaglia.com.

tinually cooking on the stove, setting the air alive with a savory aroma changing according to leftovers which were added—pasta one day, peas and carrots the next, some chicken or beef the next. Whether the soup was thick or thin was determined upon Papa's income that week, Mama's shopping, and the degree of leftovers. The time was always right for our warm bowl of soup. I can taste it still!

Was there a greater ritual than bagna calda? Here, gathered over a steaming pot of olive oil, garlic, herbs and sardines, we communally dunked crisp vegetables, catching the delectable drippings on crisp Italian bread and laughed and talked and stuffed our faces.

-§-
There is a joy in the planning, even if the dream is unrealized.
-§-

A ritual is defined as an established form of ceremony. A tradition is defined as the handing down of information, beliefs, and customs by word of mouth or by example from one generation to another. These are things which bind and bond us; they are valued bonds that make working toward and facing tomorrow meaningful. As they are passed along from one generation to another, they always remain something certain in a world of uncertainty. They offer an easily understood meaning to what might otherwise seem senseless.

Share Your Hopes and Dreams

Dreams elevate us beyond the mundane. They enrich our future with possibility. To dream together adds an element of wonder to our relationships and gives us something to look forward to. We dream of tomorrow's successes, of the children we desire, of the recognition we need, the travel we plan, of monetary security we hope for. We dream of peace, of pleasure, of joy. We must be careful, though, that we do not become so attached to these dreams that when they fail to materialize they shatter our belief in life. As long as the trip to Hawaii or Switzerland or Bangkok or Tokyo can always be put off, without trauma, the sustained idea may one day make these trips a reality. There is a joy in the planning, even if the dream is unrealized.

I recall that one of my dreams since childhood was to hear a crystal clear temple bell in a mountain monastery in Nepal. I was a product of mystical Lost Horizons and idyllic Shangri-las. Many thought that for a boy from East Los Angeles, this was truly a "pipe dream." Yet, there was something in me that knew that it would happen. I had only to concentrate and believe in the dream. It took years for the appropriate time but the sound of the bell was nonetheless clear and magical for having been dreamed about for so many years!

We all have hopes. Some of us see these as impossible and keep them to ourselves. We are certain that people will laugh or call us mad if we express them. How surprised we are that when we do share our hopes with others they eagerly tell of equally anticipated dream. A dream is a private place, and there is something special about sharing private places with those we love. It is one more way of allowing ourselves to be known.

You Will Need Courage

There can be no relationship in weakness. Timidity, uncertainty, fear of risk prevent us from coming together.

Relationships require us to be bold, to assert, to commit. Problems in human interaction are inevitable. There is no such thing as a perfect relationship which is utterly secure, happy, and binding. By the very nature of a relationship, this cannot be. How can we expect that others will desire to be always with us? How do we expect to find someone who always will find happiness in the same things in which we find happiness, care about the same people, have the same interests, or want to be doing the same activities at the same time? We can only realize this with robots, and they make cold bedfellows. By the very nature that relationships require two or more, there will always be differences. When we form a relationship we must give up the desire of the perfect resolution. Disagreements and frustrations are inevitable. Some we will solve. Others will seem unsolvable at the moment, but we will overcome them in time. Others may, indeed, be insurmountable. "The problem is not that there are problems," says Dr. Theodore Rubin in *One to One,* "the problem is expecting otherwise and thinking that having problems is a problem."

We need courage to meet what comes and know that whatever it is, it will not last forever. Nothing lasts forever. Not pain, not joy, not even life. We need to accept the fact that the only way anything will ever be accomplished exactly as we want it, is if we do it. So if we choose to delegate, then it is natural that the results will vary in some way from what we intended and we must learn to accept it. If we have enough strength to take full responsibility for our failures as well as our successes, then our self-respect is nurtured and grows. When we join others for mutual strength and support we will have to develop the courage of coexistence. "The important thing is to be able at any moment to sacrifice what we are for what we could become," said Charles Dubois.

It's up to us to give our relationships a chance. There is nothing greater in life than loving another and being loved in return, for loving is the ultimate of experiences.

Francesca Gentille:

With My Body I Thee Worship

It's early Saturday afternoon. We have finished the morning chores and savored a delectable brunch of goat cheese, prosciutto, and sun dried tomato frittata, along with a pot of blackberry sage tea. *Voodoo Roux,* my favorite world beat CD, is playing in the background. White lotus incense gently scents the house.

I look across the table with playful eyes and reach out my hand. My beloved smiles knowingly as I half drag, half guide him to our bedroom. We drop his Indonesian lounging pants and my Balinese sarong on the carpet along the way. With tender reverence, I lay my lover down and look into his eyes. We both quiet our minds and begin to deepen and lengthen our breathing.

As we breathe and slow down, we will leave linear time aside along with the cares and concerns of day-to-day life. For the next several hours we will be "between the worlds." We will leave mundane reality behind and enter the realm of infinite possibility. All "have tos," "shoulds," and schedules are put out of mind.

We will enter into the oldest magical act of the divine within creation—the weaving of masculine and feminine energy through hormonal arousal and intercourse. In this sacred space that is our very own, we will call one another by name and by the names of the gods. We will recall that I am Field and Fruit, and he is Seed and Plow. We will focus our thoughts on love and on healing. This is our ritual.

Francesca Gentille is an outrageous media personality, relationship coach, and intercultural minister. A catalyst in the use of transformational compassion to reclaim the sacred in life, love, feelings, boundaries, and sexuality, she is the founder of the LifeDance Center for Sacred Living, and a distinguished board member for the Celebrations Of Love Institute. She is a radiant example of authentically empowered aging, becoming an acclaimed teacher of Tantric flirting at the age of forty, discovering the power of compassionate boundaries at forty-three, and evolving the ability to be a genuine soul mate at forty-five. Contact her at www.LifeDanceCenter.com.

Original Blessing

Imagine: It is 10,000 years ago on the eve of solstice. Depending on whether you are above or below the equator, it is either the longest night or longest day of the year. Let your mind's eye travel north and south, east and west. Everywhere you go the people are gathered. They are drumming, chanting, singing, and dancing. Their movements are rhythmic. Their hips sway and thrust. Men leap. Women undulate. Their bodies shine with sweat. Their breath is long and deep. Their eyes are bright. They are all participating in a celebration that honors the turning of the seasons, and the cycle of life. Their dance is a prayer, an invocation, and an enticement to fertility itself.

Fertility, and the sexuality that fuels it, are the sacred forces that bring life to the world. All the people know that without the sun and the moon, the seed and the earth, the man and the woman, The God and the Goddess, we would have no new life, no food to eat, no children to carry on the future of the people. The most special, sacred, and beautiful woman is filled with new life. She is pregnant. She is the female microcosm of the Divine Feminine macrocosm, giving forth new life. Children born nine months after the festival take the last name of the gods. These children of the solstice belong to the gods as well as to the community. Names like Godfrey, Godkin, and Godley celebrate this ceremonial origin.

-§-
Fertility and sexuality are the sacred forces that bring life to the world.
-§-

As the evening continues, people of childbearing years will pair off and mate. Their sex acts will inspire the earth and its animals to be fruitful, and give more precious children to the community. In the ensuing 5,000 to 7,000 years the healing forces of sexuality will be studied throughout the world by healers, teachers, priests, priestesses, shamans, and magi. A wealth of knowledge about sexuality's healing properties will form the foundation of Chinese Medicine and the Tao. Sexuality will be used to balance the body's energy, hormones, and emotions. The healing dimension of sex will become integral to Hindu and Buddhist Tantra, Native American Quidoshka, and will be celebrated in the temples of love throughout the Middle East and Europe.

For over 10,000 years sex was the Original Blessing that sanctified every aspect of life.

Sacred Sex on the Most Wanted List

Depending on where in the world you live today, sexuality became public enemy number one some 200 to 5,000 years ago. The driving, unstoppable power of sacred sexuality—with its healing properties, its veneration of women as divine, and its potential to give direct and personal access to the divine—was demonized. Hierarchical warrior tribes, and their sky gods, overran earlier cooperative cultures and a dominator social structure emerged. Sex became a sin, the road to perdition, the loss of our souls and a pathway to hell. In her book *When the Drummers Were Women,* Layne Redmond chronicles the rise and fall of women's divinity and musical creativity. She writes:

-§-
For over 10,000 years sex was the Original Blessing that sanctified every aspect of life.
-§-

> This male god is asexual in essence. Because the goddess (and the fertilizing god) is denied there can be no sacred marriage rite. There can be no sexuality. In fact, sexuality, because it is excluded from the nature of deity, is considered wrong. The power to arouse a man sexually is no longer divine. It becomes original sin. Eve's body became not the means to sacred communion with the divine, but the source of evil released into the world. The underworld, shadowy cave and sacred womb of holy initiation, becomes hell.

Not only did women lose the sacred dimension of their sexuality with this massive cultural shift, men did as well. Emotional knowledge was now devalued. The legacy we are left with is the "battle of the sexes"—virgins and whores, wimps and bastards.

Raised as a conservative Christian in the Midwest, I had my own inner battle to reclaim my sexuality. As a young woman, I dressed and undressed in the dark. I was ashamed to look at my body. I wore briefs under my pantyhose whether I was in a dress or slacks. I was nervous about the smells, smears, and secretions of my body. I didn't look at men below the waist. The only sexual training I recall receiving from my mother was, "Men will try to lift your dress. Don't let them. Don't let men touch you." As I write this, I still feel sad at the loss of all those years when I was out of touch with my body's innate wisdom and cut off from my genital soul.

The Genital Soul–The Body Soul

What do I mean by my *genital soul?*

Through experience and research, I discovered that—just as I have a synaptically wired Bodymind, I also have a spiritually woven Bodysoul. God/Goddess didn't make a mistake when our bodies were created with instincts, desires, secretions, and emotions. Our body is not separate from our soul. Our body is our soul.

When we dive down deep and listen to the slower paced inner wisdom of the heart, gut, and genitals, we receive crucial information for our healing. This knowledge of the Bodysoul that includes the genitals pervades many cultures, as Angeles Arrien sensitively explains in her book, *The Second Half of Life: Opening the Eight Gates of Wisdom:*

> At any age, the body can teach us to honor our limitations, trust our instincts, express our love, and sustain our health. It is our primary instrument for expressing our love and creativity, and making our contribution to the world. Many traditional societies believe that the body is the perfect architecture for supporting our life dreams and our journey; otherwise we would not be here. According to the Polynesians and most Island peoples, the body must be respected, because it is both of the Earth and of the Mystery.

Deeply spiritual, I often prayed and meditated by quieting my mind and reaching up and out to receive divine guidance. After being filled with a sense of peacefulness in praying, I would sadly return to my body. I would feel almost numb from the waist down. Periodically during the year, a passionate nature would arise and act out in sudden erotic flings and entanglements that I felt were bad or anti-spiritual.

Reaching out for insight was normal. One day, I sat in quiet meditation and reversed the direction of focus, reaching inward and down. Instead of beating myself up for another bad girl episode, I asked my genitalia what she had to say. What she shared sent a shudder through every part of me: *I am sacred, listen to my divine truth and give birth to your sexual wisdom.*

What would happen if you asked your genitals' soul what they have to say? "Thanks for checking in… I was wondering when you'd bother to listen…" If you listen further, they might talk to you like mine did, "I'm more than just your thrust and squeeze, your slap and tickle… I am divine. I am the creative and generative life force. I long to be adored. I have the power to heal the world. I am a team player. To love me, love the rest of my body and soul."

The pain, anger, suffering, and beauty you get in your answers may come as a surprise.

Kernels of Our Erotic Awakening

Human beings are down out about our "down under" far too often. When our needs for touch, sexual expression, and intimacy are unmet we can feel rage, confusion, longing, and deep sorrow. Denied the sanctity of our desires and a loving relationship with our genitals, we can unconsciously manipulate, complain, criticize, control, demand, and use power—over one another in order to connect. Pushing to get what we want, we become the unconscious predator and tyrant. Giving in to the push of others results in depression and resentment. We become the unconscious victim.

Swirling around inside our heads are the painful arrows of expressions like: *Don't touch yourself; Don't let men touch you; Go out and "get some" to prove you're a man; Do it but don't talk about it; Like it but not too much; Pervert; Bitch; Slut; Bastard; Bad Boy; Stud; Sex Goddess; Macho Man; Hard Body.* Our language is flooded with conflicting messages about our genitals, our bodies, and our sexual passions. For many of us, the origin of the battle between the sexes begins with the self-hatred we feel about "down there."

To turn around the topsy-turvy indoctrination we've received, we look at the core of the matter. Our matter—our body—*matters.* In essence and actuality, we are connected to the universal force of life. This power lies in our genitals. In the male, it is the catalyzing seed of life. In the female, it is the embracing egg of life. What is more godlike and magical than the ability to create life? And what could be more foundational and connective than sharing the desire to participate in the ecstasy of the erotic act?

The language we choose, and the intentional artistry with which we use it, are a rich palette for our erotic awakening. Exploring and experimenting with modern and ancient meanings of words can empower our sense of sexual wholeness. When we release the labels of sexuality that limit and denigrate, we can begin to celebrate the earthy, aromatic pits of our body. Ancient shards of sacred sexuality can still be found in the world today in the poems of Rumi and Hafiz, in the Song of Songs in the Bible, in the British wedding ceremony, and in everyday language.

-§-
Our matter—our body—matters.
-§-

The words "With my body, I thee worship," are included in the traditional marriage vows commonly used in Great Britain. They harken back to pre-Christian times when we knew that our bodies mirror the divine. They remind us to worship, to adore, to revere, to venerate, to cherish, and to honor one another with our bodies.

Until about ten years ago, I had more complaints about men than I had compliments for them. I was angry and resentful. I felt used and underappreciated. No lover was ever truly good enough after the first blush of being "in-love." I would fall in or out of love and I didn't know why. I was out of control with longing; I had never been adored. I was convinced that men were intentionally withholding the "goodies" of love.

But the real problem was my thinking that *men* were the problem. I was unaware that I was unable to receive. Body worship was not in my repertoire—I did not know how to give or receive it. Yes, I was a good lover, and I knew how to get a guy to "do me," but invariably, I felt empty afterward. The high was short-lived, the downside too long. One depressing "morning after," I vowed to take back the power of my own ability to love and get aroused. I became committed to finding a way to bring the sacred back into sexuality.

-§-
Venus was no one-dimensional, bodacious babe.
-§-

Precious sexual mystery teachings are found in fields as diverse as biochemistry, brain chemistry, anthropology, modern psychology, and quantum physics. Even the dictionary holds amazing secrets. Embedded in the historical meanings of words like *venerate* are seeds of sensual empowerment. If you look up venerate in *Webster's Unabridged Encyclopedia Dictionary* you will encounter definitions that include: awe; respect; honoring a sacred personage, originally referring to Venus and to desire. Venus was no one-dimensional, bodacious babe. True to the paradoxical expansiveness of Deity, she was Goddess of Love and Beauty *while* being a Warrior and Wanton. Her son, Eros, wielded the arrows of transformation that could not be denied.

Venus inspired not only awe, but fear. To claim the power of Venus was to train as a conscious wielder of transformation and magic. The erotic arts and the magical arts have always been entwined. To engage in conscious loving is to engage in sex magic.

Sex magic and sacred sexuality are our birthrights. The life force of sexuality is woven into our blood, breath, and bones. It is primed and programmed into our most fundamental mating instincts. In states of arousal, our hearts beat faster, we take in more oxygen, and our bodily systems are flooded with euphoria-producing chemicals like phenylethylalamine, oxytocin, and endorphins. When sexuality is combined with joy, love, pleasure, and laughter, it substantially enhances our immune system function.

The magical dance of sexual energy begins long before penis meets vagina. As any jealous sweetheart can tell you, sex takes place anytime we engage in thoughts, touch, or the exchange of energy with the intent to raise feelings of sexual arousal. When we consciously use our thoughts and intentionally combine them with sex, the exchange of energy creates a powerful force that can be applied to healing, creating vision, enhancing intuition, and deepening intimacy. This practice can be done alone, with a friend, or with a beloved.

-§-
The magical dance of sexual energy begins long before penis meets vagina.
-§-

When we consciously engage in sexuality, we become holy lovers and sexual shamans. We become divine union. We transform the "War Between the Sexes Over Sexuality" to the "Harmony Between the Sexes With Sexuality."

Four Keys to Erotic Empowerment

Ordinary sex is simply energy—hormones and instincts expressed through behaviors. When sex is paired with healing, and open-hearted intention, its energy evolves and becomes divine. Sacred Sex is sim-ple but not easy. It is a lifelong path of spiritual growth and enlightenment.

Before making love, I like to think of the Four Keys to Erotic Empowerment:

Intention

What is the highest and best intention I can hold for my lover and myself right now?

Invocation

What spiritual practice can I combine with my sexuality to invite the Divine into my heart, body, mind, and genitals?

Intuition

Am I checking in with the wisdom of my body soul, genital soul, and heart?

Immersion

Am I releasing: have to, should, deadlines, timelines, performance, goals, and agendas?

Am I fully present in this moment with my beloved?

The keys remind me that I am accountable for bringing the sacred to the relationship.

It is now the end of the afternoon. The deeply golden sun is casting an amber light across the rumpled bed. My beloved and I have just woken up from a precious, post-coital nap and cuddle. Our skin glows. Colors in the room appear to shimmer with life. The world holds a sense of peace. We notice the roses in the garden, the sensuous breeze, and the scent of our bodies.

We feel centered, energized, connected, and refreshed. The intimacy and healing we have shared will last for days. Life will still be challenging at times, but from this place of renewal, we will have the courage and patience to practice compassion more effectively. Our relationship can now be a sacred container for love. Full and vital, we can contribute blessing not only to one another and our children, but also to peace on the planet.

LINDA O'KEEFE:

33

Dream All Over Each Other

My eyes opened to the rising sun and immediately filled with tears. The only one who had ever truly loved me was gone, and another night had passed. Would this be the day when I could finally bring myself to end it all? Although I certainly had enough willpower and self-hatred, I hadn't been able to go through with it. My morning ritual—pondering, wondering, *How can I possibly go on with this excruciating pain?*—kept me partially paralyzed in the bed that had become my only home.

One desperate midnight, I reached out to a friend, and that conversation marked a turning point. The next day, I picked up a book she had recommended. Back home in my bed, with little expectation and even less hope, I opened to the first page and read: "God is the part of us that wants to live, when everything else in us wants to die." For the first time in two years, I took in a full breath. *If that is true,* I thought, *I must have a lot of God in me!*

Inspiration can touch us at the most desperate moments. A glimpse of inspiration can carry us to safety through a dark night of the soul. Imagine, then, the tremendous potential of learning to harness inspiration and consciously call it up every day of our lives.

Fifteen years ago, hope came to me in my bed and helped me hang on to this dear life. I followed that thread of hope for the next two years. When I was able to finally, fully surrender, that thread led

Linda O'Keefe, CISW, is a life coach, the founder of Options For Growth (www.OptionsForGrowth.com), and co-founder of Core Creatives, LLC. Options For Growth began as a fledging private practice in the south suburbs of Chicago, Illinois, and grew to offer the services of numerous therapists and body workers—as well as classes on spirituality, creativity, and soul healing. With her husband Lance, Linda went on to found Core Creatives, LLC, a three-month course that reignites participants' creativity, life purpose, and spirituality. Linda today writes and speaks about the power of inspiration, while dividing her time between Tucson, Arizona, and San Diego, California.

me out of the paralyzing web of my unfulfilled dreams and helped me weave a whole new life when I met my twin soul.

Lance came in the guise of a business associate. Two years later, on a perfect Sunday in 1995, we married on the basis of vows drawn from *A Course in Miracles*. The declarations we made on our wedding day were and are grounded in the understanding that a "holy relationship" is the highest form of honor to our spiritual growth.

-§-

A glimpse of inspiration can carry us to safety through a dark night of the soul.

-§-

The word *holy* is derived from the same Latin root as the word *whole*. By its very definition, then, a holy relationship requires that *all* of who we are as human beings be present and accepted within the sacred boundaries of the relationship. The *Course* promises that, as long as we are committed to hiding none of ourselves, the energy of God is conspicuously present. It is almost as though a third entity, the Divine Relationship, has been created. That entity thrives on the individual choice for inspiration.

No pain-free option exists when it comes to human life. Loss, betrayal, degradation, prejudice, fear, and death, among others, are required courses at Human U. All we have to do is turn on the daily news to be reminded of that reality. Reporters practically scream about just how many horrible things are happening all around us. On commercial breaks, we are sold shiny images of how we should look, smell, and feel, what we should own, and who we should want to be. What is the God in us to do with this input? Since it's part of the human experience, ignoring it isn't really an option. But if we tried to spiritually survive on this banquet, we'd starve in record time.

I would never be described as a Pollyanna, but I am a sucker for seeing the glass half full. Though the wounds of humanity are paraded through my office on a day-to-day basis, I have an unshakable faith in the human spirit. But it takes ongoing effort: I have to make a clear and conscious choice again and again. The same is true of relationships. If we want to support and create the energy of inspiration in our relationships, we must begin with a choice that will be followed with action. If we become complacent about what we allow into our lives and our relationships, we will be burdened with a heavy load of that tabloid baggage the wounded world brings to the front page every day.

One way Lance and I have tended to the life of our relationship is by renewing our vows every five years. The months leading up to the ceremony become an exercise in inspiration, moving both of us to tears many times before the moment actually arrives. In preparation, we re-read the copy of our original ceremony, reliving the beauty and blessing of that day. We talk about the shifting sands as well as the solid ground in our relationship. We ask others to offer their support and talents to the ceremony, acknowledging that it takes a community to nurture and inspire a relationship. From this place of intention, the invitation to help plan and attend the ceremony is actually a "thank you" card, as bringing loved ones together to celebrate with us honors their invaluable gifts.

On the evening of our ten-year ceremony, our patio was stunning in its black, lavender, and gold dressing. Dangling rope lights sparkled within the frame of the Catalina Mountains, just miles behind our home, as our honored guests arrived with the descending sun. At twilight, our friend Kathleen welcomed all, and the ceremony began. Our friends presented poems and songs about the grit and glory of love, offering encouragement and inspiration. When my twelve-year-old nephew told everyone how happy he always felt around us, we looked at each other, then at the happy tears in many eyes. A delightful, electric sensation of pure joy ran through my body. Here was a perfect way to bring inspiration home.

Creating It Yourself

If we want to create the energy of inspiration—and sustain it—in the everyday life of relationship, we must begin with choice, and be willing to follow that choice with action.

Take a moment and reflect on the last time you felt truly inspired in your relationship. Go back to that experience in your mind. What were you doing? See if you can remember the sounds and smells, what you saw, what sensations moved through your body. Really breathe that in for a moment, and be with the whole gestalt. Be with it a moment longer. This deep concentration will ground it in your body.

-§-
It's just as inspiring to support each other's passions as to share in them.
-§-

Would you choose to feel this way frequently? Not only is it within your power to do so, but this kind of choice can open the door to a magical realm where relationship becomes a remarkable, self-renewing resource. And making such a choice, as a couple, takes you into territory you could not have imagined before.

Take the time to really pay attention to what inspires you and what doesn't. The contrast between the two becomes pretty apparent once you've called forth a felt sense of "inspired" and grounded it in your bones. Now bring this awareness into practical focus by mak-

ing a list of what lifts you up and what drags on your energy. Pay attention day to day, for a few weeks. Let the list emerge from your experience.

Be sure to bump to the top of the list anything that inspires both you and your partner. Set a recurring date for these choices, whether walking in nature or going to a foreign film. Remember that it's just as inspiring to support each other's passions as to share in them. If he loves sailing and you get sea sick, it makes more sense to help him find a friend who would love to go out for a sail than to buy a box of Dramamine. While he is on the bay, you can enjoy some precious time alone or take in a great girlfriend film. In the evening, you will both be refreshed—or tired, as the case may be—and excited to share your solo discoveries with the other.

Dream Together

Remember when your relationship was brand new and you couldn't find enough time in the world to spend together? Chances are that one of the earliest, dearest conversations you had was about your dreams. Holding each other in the night, you spoke the words you had saved for this special moment and dreamed all over each other. Have you always wanted a family? How many children? A house on the lake, to invent a new source of sustainable energy, to create a committed relationship that feeds your very soul? Did you have a sense that this incredible person lying next to you was the only one who could ever grasp and understand these dreams? Did you encourage each other, knowing that you could accomplish anything, side by side?

As the days of work and children, carpools, and house payments pass, these conversations can fade to distant memory. This happens in part because we are living some of the dreams we shared in the beginning, but the truth is that new dreams are always presenting themselves—if we pay attention. If I asked you right now what dreams you have for your relationship, how would you respond?

One fantastic way to bring magic back into a relationship is to make regular "dream dates." Instead of the age-old dinner and a movie, set aside specific and special time dedicated to dream conversation. It's important to structure this time so that you have no responsibilities or interruptions, no computers or phones. Set the stage with uplifting props—maybe candles, soft music, a favorite food, or drinks. Create a nurturing atmosphere, then let your imaginations soar. Share one at a time, and keep the conversation focused on passion and possibilities. Be outrageous. Let yourself play with what it would be like to realize the dream. How might it look, feel, smell, and taste?

If you begin to stray off into the "hows" or reasons why it might not be possible, redirect the conversation. You can look at the pros and cons, explore the possible risks, and plan the next steps another time. For now, your assignment is to revel in the dreams and the sweet feelings they bring.

If you both decide one dream is ripe to pursue in the present, schedule another time to have a planning session. Stay in the bliss of your dreams for as long as you have the energy!

Create Together

Creativity is the Divine expressing itself through us. After all, we were created in God's image. We each have within us the power of creation. That means we are capable of bringing something into the world that is uniquely our own, whether it is a work of art or a new way of getting through to our spouse. We seem to forget that creativity is not reserved for famous artists, and that even the little things in life can benefit from our unique individual "tweak"—that perspective or sensibility only we can bring to the table.

We create our relationships every day. Each day, each hour, and each moment bring opportunities to play with new concepts, conversations, or lifestyle choices. We create solutions to challenges that arise, routines that support our desires, systems for navigating our busy lives. We create moods, ambience, clarity, and, sometimes, discord. Most of us slip into habits and re-create familiar conversations, conflicts, patterns—the "same old, same old." But even the most tired old pattern presents an opportunity, each time we enact it, to suddenly wake up, break the spell of unconscious reactions, and create something new. A new focus of the conversation, a new perspective on the conflict, shaking out an old pattern—we never know when our insides will finally say enough is enough and forge a whole new path. Paying attention and making a conscious effort brings us closer to that critical moment when the high road of infinite ingenuity suddenly pulls us out of a rut.

-§-
Creativity is the Divine expressing itself through us.
-§-

Remember Intent

A love relationship has one major foundation: the original intent upon which it was co-created. Yet, this intent can often be overshadowed by the daily grind of life together. When this happens, we tend

to spend more time massaging our differences than reinforcing the common values and intentions that brought us together.

During the marriage ceremony, we state our intent to our beloved in the form of vows. The traditional vows are to love, honor, and cherish, but many couples now write their own, clarifying what they value most about relating to one another. These vows can be the thread that runs through a life together, a commitment to acting from the best parts of us during the course of the sacred relationship.

It's easy to create reminders of our original relationship intent. Create a display or a piece of art you will see everyday: vows typed over one of your wedding photos, a collage of pictures and key words from your vows, or a framed poem or song lyrics that embody your intent. Anyone can do this, even without having had an official ceremony, or many years after the wedding day. In addition to clarifying the best of who you are, your reminder will show how you intend to live that best in your everyday lives.

Acknowledge Beingness

Our spirituality is defined by our *beingness* and does not rely on what we have accomplished, how much money we make, or what, at any level, we are doing. We each have intrinsic value, simply because we exist. When we allow ourselves to rest in the space of that value, our consciousness lifts above the common concerns of life. When we experience that silent "in the zone" space, we can lose track of time while doing something we love. Sometimes "being" taps us on the back in the middle of a scenic drive to work, or in the middle of a noisy family dinner. Sometimes we make the effort to create it through meditation or a walk in nature. Whatever way this being-sense is created or shows up in our lives, it reminds us of our spirituality.

-§-
Our spirituality is defined by our *beingness* and does not rely on accomplishments.
-§-

A list of ways to nurture beingness in your relationship can include anything from daily meditation or yoga to a ritual after-dinner walk. Let your imaginations lead you to even more personal and creative ways that hinge on what is most meaningful to you both.

The Magic Ratio

For a relationship to thrive, it is vital that you verbalize what you see and sense in the moment that lifts you up: "You seem to be glowing this morning, and I love that," or, "I sense you're feeling a little nervous about that meeting today, and I want you to know I'm behind you," or "I can see that you are excited about that idea, and I get a kick out of that." This act of acknowledging what you perceive and appreciate in the moment, rather than fixating on what you want to change or make go away, is essential.

Simple but effective, focusing on appreciation makes relationships thrive. John Gottman, author of *The Seven Principles for Making Marriage Work*, writes: "Amazingly, we have found that it all comes down to a simple mathematical formula. No matter what style your marriage follows, you must have at least five times as many positive as negative moments together if your marriage is to be stable. The magic ratio is five to one."

Being with what is, and noticing and sharing what it touches in you, adds sparkle to your life together. This ongoing acknowledgment of the "little things" keeps us engaged, attentive, and connected with our loved one. And it is equally powerful when used to create inspiration with children, aging parents, siblings, friends, and even co-workers. Just imagine introducing a conversation at the lunch table about what dreams your co-workers have for their lives!

As C. S. Lewis said: "Aim at Heaven and you will get Earth thrown in. Aim at Earth and you get neither." Inspiration is the doorway to your own private heaven. The challenges and heartaches of life are often the very stepping-stones that lead to that door. Choice is the usher, and linking arms with conscious choice can bring you to the threshold of an inspired life. Inspiration—the God in you—is never lost. Even in the darkest rooms of your private hell, the inner light is unafraid. Make the choice and lean in. Your dream life awaits—inspiration is your true home.

Part Seven

Daring Love's Risk

The searching over, finally,
that empty space filled or, rather,
swells into an escalating hunger
a home to root blossoms forth
on earth (in the body) as it is in heaven (in the heart-mind).
Do you love this awakening in us?
I already know the answer.
~ Stuart Sovatsky, *Your Perfect Lips*

John Welwood:

On the Razor's Edge

While most of us enter relationships somewhat unconsciously—without understanding what we're getting ourselves in for—the challenges of forging an authentic connection with another person inevitably spur us to become more conscious, to examine ourselves more deeply, and to develop greater intention, courage, and awareness in the way we live. Hermann Hesse wrote a beautiful story about this—in which a man's attraction to his beloved completely transforms him, by compelling him to set out in search of himself and his true aim in life.

The story begins with Anselm as a young boy who is captivated by the irises in his mother's garden, and ends with his life-altering attraction as an adult to a woman named Iris. Both attractions—to the flower and to the woman—serve as pathways into his own soul. But like most of us, Anselm does not recognize that his romantic attraction contains this deeper impulse—to connect with what is most real inside himself.

As a child, Anselm experiences the magic of being alive most vividly when he is in the garden, communing with butterflies and pebbles, making friends with beetles and lizards, and taking special delight in the iris:

> When he stared into her chalice and allowed his thoughts to follow that bright path toward the twilight interior of the

John Welwood, Ph.D., is a clinical psychologist who has been a practicing student of Tibetan Buddhism and Eastern contemplative psychologies for thirty-five years. The former Director of the East-West psychology program at the California Institute of Integral Studies in San Francisco, he is currently Associate Editor of the *Journal of Transpersonal Psychology*. He has published more than fifty articles on relationship, psychotherapy, consciousness, and personal change, as well as eight books, including *Journey of the Heart: The Path of Conscious Love,* (Harper, 1996), and *Perfect Love, Imperfect Relationships: Healing the Wound of the Heart* (Trumpeter, 2005).

flower, his soul looked through the gate of a heavenly palace, and with him glided gently the whole world drawn by magic into the lovely abyss, inward and downward, where every wish found fulfillment and every intimation came true.

Through contemplating the secret recesses of the iris, Anselm is unwittingly connecting with the depth of his soul, an inner movement described by Mirra Alfassa, a close associate of the Indian sage Aurobindo:

> *To find the soul one must step back from the surface, [go] deep within, and enter, enter... and then there is something warm, tranquil, rich, very still, and very full, like a sweetness—this is the soul.*

This kind of movement from surface to depth reveals the source of all fulfillment in life—the essential aliveness and presence at the core of our nature, whose great beauty and abundance are described in certain spiritual traditions as a "wish-fulfilling gem" or "jewel beyond all price."

Like Anselm, we all enter this world possessing an intrinsic radiance that shines forth from our inner core. We are born into a vast palace of powers and possibilities; our being contains boundless potential. From deep within us we can bring forth a wide range of resources, such as strength, wisdom, compassion, tenderness, joy, humor, and generosity. This is our divine birthright. As children, most of us have some intimation—if only for a few brief, shining moments—that we arrive here "trailing clouds of glory as we come."

-§-
We are born into a vast palace of powers and possibilities; our being contains boundless potential.
-§-

In the Hesse story, the time comes when Anselm starts to construct a false self to shield himself from the pain of his own loss of being. Adopting a bold and worldly air, he turns away from the magical garden of his youth where he once contemplated the peace and joy within his soul. He starts to live in his mind, eventually becoming a scholar and professor of great renown. Yet once he achieves this status, he also realizes that his life has become flat, stale, joyless.

This is what happens when we lose touch with our soul. To make up for our loss of being, we try to establish our value through having and doing: "I have, therefore I am. I do, therefore I am." This leaves us with a tremendous sense of emptiness and frustration; no matter how much we have or do, we still sense that something is missing. Eventually we imagine that finding someone to love will fill up our emptiness and set everything right.

Thus Anselm finds himself becoming fascinated by a delicate, beautiful woman by the name of Iris. Something about her seems strangely familiar, and she evokes feelings in him he is unable to name. Although drawn to her, he also has his doubts. She doesn't fit in with his professional life and worldly designs. And he senses that a relationship with her could wreak enormous changes in him—a prospect that both frightens and intrigues him.

When we start to fall in love, such mixed feelings are not unusual. The prospect of new possibilities, new beginnings, new worlds opening up causes our soul to expand. The doors of our one-room flat swing open and we feel excited about the possibility of reinhabiting the larger palace of our being. Yet something stops us at the threshold. There are no lights on in the neglected rooms and corridors of the palace. There are cobwebs in the corners and who knows what else? As we expand in love, we start to encounter closed-off parts of ourselves, with which we are not on friendly terms. This feels dangerous and threatening.

If I have shunned and denied my need for love, for instance, then when this need arises in a relationship, I won't know what to do with it—how to feel it, how to express it, how to handle it. It seems like a black hole that could engulf me and swallow me alive. What will happen to me if I acknowledge this need? Will I lose all my strength? Who will I be? My very survival appears to be at stake.

Standing on the threshold of this long-neglected part of myself, I feel raw and shaky. I'm not an expert here. As my conscious identity—my façade of self-sufficiency—is undermined, a deeper unconscious identity threatens to emerge. I fear that I will become like a dependent, needy child, at other people's mercy. Demons appear, trying to discourage me from crossing this threshold. "Get back!" they say. "You closed off that room for good reason. Do you really think you can handle what's in it? Watch out! You might really lose it if you go there!"

It's true: I might really "lose it." But that's what makes love so intriguing: Losing it—letting go of old, confining identities—is totally exciting and totally frightening. This makes for a most interesting situation. I am pulled in opposite directions: expanding and contracting, wanting to go forward and wanting to maintain my defenses at the same time.

This is why intimate relationship can be such a potent vehicle for wisdom and awakening. It allows us to experience both sides of our nature—the call of our larger being and the fear and insecurity of our false self—at once, right next to each other. On this threshold, where

part of us wants to expand and part of us wants to pull back, we stand on a razor's edge—the boundary of the unknown, and the frontier of a whole new way of being.

Thomas Moore:

Shadow of the Soul

The heart has its own reasons. When we try to understand why relationships come into being and fall apart, why some families are nurturing and others devastating, why some friendships endure long absences and bitter arguments while others fade, we come face to face with the unknown core of the human heart. Of course, we spend a great deal of time coming up with all kinds of explanations for unexpected turns in emotion and feeling, but these "reasons" are more rationalizations and simplifications than understanding. We are left with Plato's solution, that relationship is based on a form of madness, erotic madness. Rather than finding solutions for understanding and controlling this heart, we may have no recourse but to honor its mysteries.

The heart is a mystery—not a puzzle that can't be solved, but a mystery in the religious sense: unfathomable, beyond manipulation, showing traces of the finger of God at work. Like the resurrection of Jesus or the mission of Moses, the angelic visitation to Mohammed or the enlightenment of the Buddha, the heart has its own mysteries every bit as profound as the mysteries we encounter in the religions of the world. Everything associated with the heart—relationship, emotion, passion—can only be grasped and appreciated with the tools of religion and poetry.

Thomas Moore, Ph.D., is a leading figure in the field of contemporary depth theology, whose work focuses on the soul and emerging ideas about spirituality. He taught at Southern Methodist University, The Dallas Institute for Humanities and Culture, and Lesley College before authoring the *New York Times* bestseller, *Care of the Soul* (HarperCollins, 1992). Since that time, he has published many books, tapes, CDs, and videos, including *Soul Mates* (HarperCollins, 1994), *The Re-Enchantment of Everyday Life* (HarperCollins, 1996), *The Soul of Sex* (HarperCollins, 1998), and *Dark Nights of the Soul* (Gotham Books, 2004). For more information, visit www.careofthesoul.net.

Yet, in our time we have tried to apply to the heart the same kind of mechanical and structural thinking that has made an astounding technological world. We regard marriages and families and speak of systems, we analyze whole societies according to grids and charts, and we try to help people "relate" to each other by organizing groups and developing exercises for communication and intimacy.

When we focus our attention on the soul of relationship, instead of on its interpersonal mechanics, a different set of values comes to the foreground. We are now interested in fantasy and imagination. We begin to see relationship as the place where soul works out its destiny. We are not so concerned with how to make relationship "work," because the soul point of view isn't ambitious in that way. It doesn't make love a life project. Instead, it recognizes the truth in a line from John Donne, that great poet of soul and relationship: "Love's mysteries in soules doe grow."

Concerned about the soul, we don't ask why something has happened in a relationship, or how to make it better. Rather, we wonder about the soul's own purposes: "What is happening in the soul when we fall madly in love? What is the soul wanting in its fantasies of separation? What is this longing for deeper love, and why does it never seem to be satisfied?" With our focus on the soul, we won't feel the impossible burden of "doing" relationship right, as though we had full control over the intimacies that develop between people, and so we need not become so discouraged as we make our way through our emotional dilemmas. Instead, we may live through the mystery of endings, crises, and turning points in love, marriage, friendship, and family, and submit to the life that is always germinating in them.

-§-

Relationship is based on a form of madness, erotic madness.

-§-

In the modern world we also tend to see everything as if it were a machine, including our most precious relationships. Notice how quickly the metaphors of computer language have infiltrated everyday speech, how nonchalantly people say they are "programmed" to act the way they do. As a result of this kind of mechanization in our thinking, we've lost an appreciation for the mysterious factors that bring people together and force them apart. In the face of difficulties that have profound roots, we bring to relationship a fix-it attitude, assuming that all failures need to be corrected. When our focus is on the surfaces of life, we seek out mechanical causes and solutions to problems, but if our attention were on the soul, we would explore instead its dreams and fantasies, its own unpredictable intentions.

Jung pointed out that even though we experience the soul intimately, still it has an objective quality. We can look at soul without identifying with it. If I ask, "What is wrong with me that I can't have a long-lasting relationship?" the question borders on narcissism—the focus is on "me." To get to the soul, we might direct our questions more outward: "What does fate want in its demands on me? What is the meaning of this continuing failure to find love? What am I made of that my heart moves in directions different from my intentions?" This shift from self-reflexive, narcissistic questions to a more open, objective point of view is in itself a fundamental move toward soul.

The soul is a wide, spacious area in which fate plays a great role, and in which family, society, and history—personal and cultural—are major influences. Much of this material is beyond an individual's power either to invent or to control. As the Greek mystical philosopher Heraditus taught, "The soul is its own source of unfolding." It has its own reasons, which may be only dimly apparent to consciousness. If we want to see the soul in a relationship, we have to look beyond our intentions and expectations.

Another advantage of regarding relationships from the soul's viewpoint is that it offers us a more tolerant attitude toward the down side, the shadows and gaps that will inevitably present themselves at times. Ordinarily we assume that a relationship should be smooth and complete, and when trouble arrives, we think the relationship itself is open to doubt. But matters of soul lie beyond simple judgments of good and bad, or smooth and rough. In initiation rites around the world, the neophyte is profoundly stirred by some kind of pain, perhaps from ritual incisions or sleeplessness and fasting, and out of that experience a new level of awareness dawns. Religion recognizes pain and failure as important in the soul's deepening and sophistication. We can apply this insight to relationships as well: pain and difficulty can sometimes serve as the pathway to a new level of involvement. They do not necessarily mean that there is something inherently wrong with the relationship; on the contrary, relationship troubles may be a challenging initiation into intimacy.

-§-
We begin to see relationship as the place where soul works out its destiny.
-§-

When we look at the soul of relationship, we may find positive value in failures, endings, complexities, doubts; distancing, the desire for separation and freedom, and other troubling aspects. We can see these as initiatory opportunities rather than simply as threats. Soul often hides in the darkest corners, in the very places we would rather avoid, and in the very problems that tempt us into disillusionment, and so, we have to be intrepid when we look for it in our lives.

Yet another special quality of soul is the way that it expresses itself in enigmatic images. The soul lives in the realm of imagination,

and influences the direction and quality of life through a kind of poetics, a language of image and symbol. When a couple comes to me for therapy, I usually ask one to sit quietly and listen as the other talks to us about her memories, her dreams, her fantasies and images of her life, and of marriage and intimacy, sex and closeness. In this way we glimpse the soul, which is really the deep seat of relationship, and which would be ignored if we emphasized instead only the mechanics of communication and interaction.

Although I always recommend that we take time simply to observe, to look at relationship with tolerance and a quiet mind until we begin to see the deeper layers of soul, this does not mean that we should not "work on" our relationships. There is a place for such work, especially if we understand work alchemically rather than heroically. Just as the alchemist watches the processes of nature so that he or she can play an artful role in them, so we can enter the deep processes of a relationship by closely observing its chemistries. This kind of work, however, is ninety percent observation and ten percent action. As we watch the soul without heroic interventions, our attitudes may change, allowing alchemical transformations to take place on their own accord—changes in the coloring of our moods, the weight of our thoughts, and the textures of our feelings.

-§-
If we want to see the soul in a relationship, we have to look beyond our intentions and expectations.
-§-

Soul-centered effort on behalf of relationship has yet another quality that makes it different from more familiar modern schools of love and intimacy: the soul is not dedicated to perfection. Work with the soul is not at all aimed at achieving an unblemished, unruffled relationship; on the contrary, it has an appreciation for human limitation and folly. The alchemical view of the soul's progress makes room for the putrefaction of decay, and melanosis, or blackening—shadow aspects highly valued in traditional alchemy. Relationships have a way of rubbing our noses in the slime of life—an experience we would rather forego, but one that offers an important exposure to our own depth.

Kay Richardson:

Declarations of Peace

We turned the corner at the end of the forest trail and felt the cool spray of Silver Falls as it crashed into the river rocks below. Lush, green ferns and evergreens surrounded the falls in the billowing mist; the light of the sun created sparkling jewels of light all around. It was a perfect place to make a fresh start.

My partner, Eric, and I had hiked to this very spot in Mount Rainier National Park two months before. On that day, a tangle of intense emotions had brought us to a heated crossroads in our relationship. Neither of us understood the other. We were each in our own universe, caught up in feelings and reactions that stood in stark, painful contrast to the peace and grandeur of Silver Falls.

Today was different. We revisited this road from a higher emotional vantage point—discussing our past argument from a comfortable distance and with an ear for understanding. By really listening to each other, we created a bridge of intimacy between our vast inner worlds.

On the way back to our campground, I followed a strong intuition to ask Eric if he felt open to setting an intention for a stable and lasting peace between us. This was a new idea for him, but we were feeling so connected in the moment that he was willing to go with it.

Kay Richardson, MFT, is a life coach and healing artist whose gentle spirituality and collaborative style invite clients to step into their true selves and create their highest dreams, bringing head and heart together in purposeful, compassionate action. Since completing her post-graduate training in Postmodern Systems Therapy, Kay has worked with clients across the U.S. Her workshops integrate body, mind, and spirit, and include energy work and spiritual life coaching. Kay also invites healing as a performing artist, creating transcendent exchange through heartfelt expression. She studied acting at Freehold Studio in Seattle and recently recorded an album, entitled *Peace on Earth Now.* Find her at www.kayrichardson.com.

We stepped off the trail into the canopy of green, held hands, took a deep breath, and said, "We connect with Spirit and our higher selves. We co-create with the Universe a stable peace between us, and give thanks for support in doing this." It was both simple and momentous, as if in that silent wood a resonant gong had sounded as the Universe responded, "So be it!"

-§-
There's no "one right way" to set intentions together. What's important is that your unique relationship, creativity, and spirituality are reflected.
-§-

In that moment, we ended a cycle of breaking up. After several years of ongoing clearing work within and between us, we now have a stable, sustainable peace that allows room for conflict while keeping us connected in a fundamental way. Our intention has served as a touchstone—a commitment to ourselves, to each other, and to Spirit—and a beacon to guide us through all the healing needed to make a stable peace possible.

Paving the Way for Intimacy

Setting intentions with your partner can be a powerful way to align you spiritually and pave the way for real intimacy. Have you wondered how to touch your partner to really turn him or her on? First, touch her soul. Touch his soul. Find out what's really important to your partner and connect spiritually by setting intentions to make those dreams come true.

"Setting intentions together is great foreplay!" said my friend, Paulette. Her husband, Stephen, often asks her where and how she wants him to touch her to "get her going." "It's not mechanical," Paulette responds, "I just need to connect with you."

"I'm not sure it's the same for Stephen," she told me. "He's physically attracted to me all the time. I'm the one who needs to feel a deep, intimate connection in order to want to have sex. When we take the time to set intentions, and are really open and honest, *that's* when I feel the most intimate. And, our sex is *way* better. For both of us. I'm way more into it, which makes him way more into it—it kind of spirals. Those are the times when our sexual experiences feel spiritual."

What a beautiful synergy! Paulette's story illustrates how setting intentions can open the door to real intimacy on all levels.

Creating Clear Mutual Intentions

There's no "one right way" to set intentions together. What's important is that your unique relationship, creativity, and spirituality are reflected. To inspire your process, I've found the following to be essential elements of a clear intention.

• **Staying Connected**

First, take the time to connect, even in a simple way like holding hands and taking a deep breath. Paulette and Stephen put their heads together, literally, holding hands and touching foreheads when they set intentions. See what fits for you, so you both feel you're in this together.

Then, open your awareness to Spirit and your true Self. What words really resonate for you? Spirit, the Universe, God or Goddess, a Higher Power, Consciousness...? There are as many ways to connect with the spiritual realm as there are unique human beings on the planet. When setting mutual intentions, find the language that rings true for both of you.

This can be a wonderful discussion, bringing you closer as you share beliefs and experiences that make up your worldview. If you have different ways to connect spiritually, honor them both in your process. Setting intentions together can create a mutual connection with Spirit, while also acknowledging your individual spiritual paths.

-§-
Our desires are potent, and our words are potent reflections of our desires.
-§-

• **Staying Active**

Part of the power of setting intentions together is in taking active responsibility for our lives, while partnering with the Divine and each other. An active intention can be created by finishing the phrase: "We co-create with the Universe..." In this way, we acknowledge our choice about what we focus on and attract into our lives. Free will is a powerful thing. Using language that reflects this power of choice is key.

• **Staying Positive**

Focus on what you want, rather than what you don't want. If, instead of focusing on peace, Eric and I had set the intention to stop creating such extreme arguments or to stop breaking up, we would have directed our energy toward arguing and breakups. It's a subtle shift that makes a big difference. Our desires are potent, and our words are potent reflections of our desires. We actually attract our experiences with our language and focus. So stating intentions in a clear, explicit, positive way makes a positive difference!

• **Staying in the Present**

By stating our intentions in the present, we step into them, right now. If we had said, *"We want* a stable peace," we would have put our intention out into the future, where it would have remained, rather than experiencing it directly in the present. Our experience would have been the "wanting," rather than the "having." There's power in claiming your intention now; even if you're not experiencing your desired outcome yet, you will attract it as a result.

• **Putting It in Your Knowing**

When you claim what you are co-creating in the present and then embrace a sense of really *knowing* that it's already happening, you demonstrate faith that you've been heard and that your intention matters. You experience what it feels like to already have what you are asking for.

-§-
When creating your intention, focus primarily on its essence, and then let specific forms arise from moment to moment.
-§-

Paulette shared this great example. "Two weeks before Stephen's Optimist Club dinner, we set the intention to win the $10,000 'draw-down' jackpot. Touching foreheads and holding hands, we said, 'We set the intention to win the Golden Grand Jackpot.' We thought of our intention almost every night, visualizing not having to worry about money during the months when I'm not teaching.

"Then, four days before, I got a peaceful feeling, like we had already won. And the night of the event, I still felt really calm. Toward the end of the dinner our ticket was in the top 10, and I knew we were going to win. And sure enough, we did.

"The money was great—don't get me wrong—but more than the money, it was such a lesson because it was so undeniable. It really hit us that this process is powerful!"

Paulette went on to say that this experience brought them closer, making them feel more like partners in co-creating—not only with the divine but with each other. Because she had really put this intention in her knowing, she was completely calm when they won!

• **Focusing on the Essence**

When you get down to the essence of any particular form, you reach the heart of what you really want to experience. This frees you up to receive, and the Universe to respond, in numerous unexpected ways.

Freedom from financial stress was the essence Paulette and Stephen envisioned in their intentioning. "A stable peace between us" is the essence Eric and I have attracted in many forms. Sometimes it means remembering the other person is on our side, even when we're bogged down in conflict and they've just said something that really hit a nerve. Sometimes it means feeling safe to be completely real and vulnerable. Or it shows up when we take some time and space on our own, rather than "dumping" a bad mood on the other and making it about the relationship.

Over time, we've created a strong foundation of peace that keeps us connected, even when we're processing our own perspectives. If we had focused too narrowly on just one form of this, we would have limited the bigger essence of what we wanted to attract. So when creating your intention, focus primarily on its essence—such as peace, abundance, romance, playfulness—and then let specific forms arise from moment to moment.

• **Noticing in the Now**

When you directly experience the essence of what you want, pause to notice and really feel it. Express gratitude to Spirit and your partner. Recognizing the fulfillment of your intention attracts even *more* of it and brings you fully into the present as you realize you're living the life you've always wanted.

• **Making it Physical**

A fun way to take intentions a step further is to create a tangible expression with special meaning just for the two of you. Develop your own idea, or create a symbol and give it a place of honor in your home.

Symbols are powerful; they can bypass any lingering beliefs that might get in the way of manifesting your intention. One way to create a symbol together is to state your intention, close your eyes, and ask for a symbol to come to you. See what images or ideas naturally arise in your mind. Share your symbol with your partner and play with choosing the one that fits your intention best, or combining them. Draw a picture of the symbol, having fun with this co-creation.

-§-
When couples set intentions for their shared dreams, they develop a clear common focus and an even stronger connection.
-§-

Then, write your intention underneath it and meditate on this together. Imagine your symbol filling with light, beaming down on you both. Or visualize it filling with energy as you make love. Margot Anand creatively describes this idea in *The Art of Sexual Magic.*

If you have a place in your home for sacred things, such as an altar, this is the perfect place for your intention and symbol. Put copies in key places; keeping them in front of you can really add to the clarity and momentum of drawing your intention into your life.

Don't minimize the potency of directing a continual stream of desire and energy toward your intended goal. Stay connected, active, positive, and in the present as you set your intentions. Put them in

your knowing. Focus on their essence, notice them in the now, and bring them into the physical realm. As you make this process your own by discovering what fits your unique relationship and spiritual connection, you will find your dreams manifesting with an intensity and brilliance you never imagined!

Topics for Intentions

So, what kinds of things can couples set intentions for? Truly, there's no limit! The following categories may be useful as you generate your own list:

- **Intentions for the Relationship**

Any aspect of your relationship that you'd like to develop together, with the support of Spirit, can inspire intentions. For example, setting an intention for a great sexual relationship could be a powerful way to ask for help in this sometimes-challenging zone.

This can be a marvelously rich, creative process. It gives each of you a chance to voice your most intimate desires, opening up to a fuller knowledge of the other as you choose an intention for your sexual relationship that you can both embrace.

- **Intentions for Shared Dreams**

When couples define and set intentions for their shared dreams, they develop a clear common focus and an even stronger connection. Paulette and Stephen have set the intention for their shared dream of buying their own home.

-§-

"Intentions reside in the realm of imagination—the place where something new can be created together."

-§-

In addition to regularly focusing on their intention together, they've each taken responsibility for a part of the process. She's focused on the vision and the essence of space and joy they'll experience in having a comfortable place to live and host music gatherings. He's focused on making the money necessary to buy when the time is right. The intention serves as a clear reminder that they're in this together, actively attracting their common dream.

- **Intentions for Individual Dreams**

You can strengthen the bond between you by actively supporting your partner in attracting something they want. As in all areas of a relationship, it's important for the focus to flow back and forth—with the intentions of both partners receiving plenty of attention.

"My Five Dreams" is an inspiring exercise that provides plenty of room to create. I state mine daily, knowing that I'm putting energy into manifesting them all—even when, on any given day, my primary focus may be on just one dream or another.

I began this process by writing, "I co-create with the Universe..." and then listing five of my most significant life dreams. Once I felt a clear "Yes!" when I re-read each dream, I was ready to share them with Eric. Showing my sacred dreams to my mate, and asking for his support as I manifest them, feels both self-revealing *and* rewarding.

It can be powerful for couples to express individual intentions for their dreams side-by-side. You might each write down five dreams, or develop individual intentions in any way that feels right for you. Speaking about your highest dreams—and listening to your partner's—helps you to discover each other at a deeper level, both giving *and* receiving support for the new things you're attracting into your lives.

Clearing the Way for Manifesting Fully

Intentions need a clear space in which to grow. It took several years of healing before Eric and I fully experienced that stable peace between us.

Inspired by Wayne Dyer's book, *The Power of Intention,* Eric reflected on our clearing process: "We were coming at it from our heads for so long, from our fears about losing ourselves. That's part of our clearing—feeling solid in our own identities and excited about the new identity that comes with uniting...realizing that it doesn't jeopardize our own unique selves. We're not dissolving into one another, but creating a new thing. That new thing lives in the power of intentions, and intentions reside in the realm of imagination—the place where something new can be created together. The clearing is about really believing in the pure potential of things."

What are the things within your own life that need compassion, healing, or clearing? What about in your relationship? Are there any taboo subjects between you and your partner that you've buried? Are you "editing" what you say to avoid conflict? What helps the two of you clear the air in a productive way?

Going to couple's therapy can be a great resource and provide a safe space for effective clearing. You can also use the following tools on your own to open up your relationship, so that the intentions you set can manifest in surprising ways.

- **Forgiving Yourself and Your Partner**

You can forgive yourself for anything from the past you carry guilt about, and forgive your partner for any hurts they've caused that you're holding on to. Journaling is one way to get clear about lingering pain and regret. Then, from a spiritually connected space, you can simply say: "I forgive myself for..." Then, "I forgive you for ...." Forgiveness paves the way for deeper compassion, and for sharing in the lightness that comes from truly forgiving yourself or someone you love.

- **A Releasing/Embracing Ceremony**

A releasing/embracing ceremony is both a tool for clearing and another creative way to set intentions together. It starts with individual soul-searching, creating a list of things you want to release and embrace. Write until you get to the essence. A couple of items on my list were, "I release confusion and self-criticism. I embrace clarity and self-love." Include things affecting your individual life or relationship.

Listen with an open heart as you both share your lists and the stories behind them. Connect with each other, Spirit, and your higher selves, and speak out loud each of the things you're releasing and embracing. If you like, you can actually tear up or burn your "things-to-release" list to mark the moment in a powerful way.

Living the Relationship of Your Dreams

Setting intentions together can infuse your partnership with new energy and real intimacy. Sharing your intentions, and supporting one another in the ongoing process of focusing on what you *really* want to attract into your lives, can transform your relationship into the one you've always dreamed you could have.

It's exciting to find ways to set intentions that express your unique bond. I invite you to make these possibilities your own, clearing the way for the brilliant spark of your creativity. May your intentions build a strong bridge within your relationship, bringing together your inner worlds and connecting you as a couple to the spiritual realm—and may they open you up to a deeper intimacy, growth, and enduring love.

This is the promise of the art of blessing. In discovering how to bless, we add ourselves to the great work, which is, after all, simply the work of Life in pursuit of unfoldment, harmony, and the potentials of infinity.

37

Jane Vargas: The Art of Sexual Suggestion

Almost en masse during the sixties, women rejected their mothers' Leave-it-To-Beaver values and traditional marriages. They discarded Betty Crocker for Betty Friedan, and sweater sets for power suits. In the nearly fifty years since, women have claimed all the rights, if not yet true equality, of men politically, socially, and economically. No one can deny the obstacles overcome or stop the inexorable progress of women as they take their rightful place in society.

When it comes to matters of the heart, however, confusion and unhappiness govern many women's lives. Glass ceilings and other residues of discrimination hardly compare to the frustration women experience with respect to sexuality and dating. Disappointment in these private matters is reflected in books like *Why Men Marry Some Women and Not Others* and *How to Be a Babe.* If a woman is dating but dissatisfied—or clueless—she might seek guidance in a book written by a man, *He's Just Not That Into You.* Or, disgusted with the whole matter, she might wonder along with Maureen Dowd, *Are Men Necessary?*

In our sexually saturated culture, it's not difficult to find a sexual partner. The hard part is finding a life partner. Career success doesn't bring us our life mate; neither does casual sex, for the most part. Finding a satisfying relationship can be treacherous, and the perils of dating are ominous. Unsuccessful dating can slay self-esteem, pro-

Jane Vargas, Ph.D., has researched the art of sexual suggestion through the ages, examining this powerful, uniquely feminine expression of sexuality in paintings, movies, advertising, music, and dance. She believes that much of people's unhappiness in the search for the right partner is due to the direct approach we see in today's dating scene, and the resulting loss of play around the edges of sexuality. Dr. Vargas has also done in-depth research in the area of fetishism and writes a monthly advice column focused on this area. She lives in San Francisco with her husband and has two daughters in college.

duce heartache, and force women to adopt the common but erroneous view that "all the good ones are taken."

Perhaps it's time to go back and examine the roots of our discontent—and, by extension, men's—with the dating scene to see what went wrong. The current wave of discord between men and women happened gradually, starting in the sixties and seventies. In seeking freedoms overdue them, women lay claim to all the rights and privileges of men in every area of life, including sexuality. With respect to sex, women felt—at least initially—both liberated and powerful as they seized sexual liberty in a new world where value and worth was no longer seen primarily in terms of virtue. Suddenly, women had permission to have sex casually, the way men always had. And, because of the Pill, they could be intimate with virtual impunity, like men.

-§-

"Mae West could put more innuendo into the flicker of an eyelash than seemed possible."
—David Shipman

-§-

And that was the problem. Women took their newfound sexual freedoms and exercised them with similar abandon as men. Women rejected out of hand much of what their mothers had been: housewives, submitting to the patriarchy. Suddenly, women burned their bras and relegated their mothers' and grandmothers' quaint courtship behaviors to history, along with silk stockings and pin-up girls. Few took pause to consider that their moms might have wielded surprising power in this one area of their lives. They failed to look hard at how their mothers ended up with the men they married. On the face of things, it appeared that the man did the choosing, claiming whichever bobby-sox wearing, sweet young virgin he had set his sights on. But women were far more actively involved than we give them credit for in choosing their mates.

Subsequent generations of women judged and quickly rejected their forebears' standard of success—how well they married—for other goals. Perhaps if we slow down and tease apart the goal of marriage, which no longer defines women's success, and the means by which they got there, we will have a pleasant surprise. We needn't have the same goal our mothers had in order to appreciate the subtle talents with which that goal was achieved. But women are resistant to looking back or adopting behaviors from a regressive era. Nonetheless, it might very well behoove a woman to unbundle the public from the private realm of her life and cultivate talents that could be of benefit in the latter. Her forebears' "old-fashioned" behaviors may serve a progressive end, and help her achieve not just parity, but personal empowerment and more excitement in her private life.

To develop an appreciation for the mating skill set cultivated by women, we do well to examine a repertoire of behavior, demeanor, dress, and clever repartee that worked a particular magic on men—something rarely seen today. Maintaining sexual tension over time by alluding to the possibility of more, and thus piquing imagination even in chaste encounters, a woman kept the men in her orbit interested—until she decided which was the very best of the lot. The sexuality they expressed wasn't overt, but very quiet. She played with a suggestion of sexuality. The excitement a man felt kept him on edge with hope and longing, all the while proving his worth—his goodness, stability, wit, kindness, and resources—to a woman he hoped fancied him in return. Courtship was long-lived, and necessarily so, as it was a testing ground for both parties' future.

-§-

"Suspense is like a woman. The more left to the imagination, the more the excitement."
—Alfred Hitchcock

-§-

The woman reaped another benefit, too. Because much of the dance was on her terms, she received affirmation that she was desirable as a woman. The woman who valued the shared joy of sexual suggestion was partaking of a uniquely feminine behavior: a woman extends sexual suggestion and a man receives, not the other way around.

I am not suggesting that our place in society was better when we teased men from behind a fan. Mired in the patriarchy, clearly it was not. But when we lost the art of sexual suggestion, we also lost a unique and empowering step in the mating dance.

"But sexual suggestion is nothing more than manipulation!" some might object. "Control a man by stringing him along? Poppycock! If we've learned anything from feminism, it's to come together as equals, cards on the table, fact up and straight-forward."

This reasoning makes sense. The problem is that our brains are not wired solely for sensible reason and, as we all know, "the heart has its reasons whereby reason knows not." We often want what we cannot have. When something is scarce, it's more valuable to us. Evolutionary psychologist Helen Fisher says that to get beyond lust into the love and attachment phases of a relationship, we must, "play a few tricks on the brain." In other words, women need tools to keep men interested. Fisher writes, "The sense that one has a slippery grip on an elusive improbable treasure can trigger romantic passion." Perfect equality is the ideal, perhaps, but the straightforward approach doesn't always net the most thrilling romance or the highest quality mate.

Once upon a time—despite few freedoms elsewhere in society—women understood the power of a dropped hankie, wink of an eye, enigmatic smile, and clever repartee. Victorian England, for example, was an era so modest that piano legs had to be covered. Yet a Victorian woman knew how to tantalize a man she had her eye on with a mere peek of her forbidden ankle. She knew how memorable that peek would be, how it would rile his imagination later, how he would wonder what might be in store for him the next time they met. But for societal constraints, women might have been bolder with their intentions. Instead, they learned how to wield a fan or utter a double entendre to unleash the imagination.

In her dance with the opposite sex, yesterday's woman was as deft with a hankie as today's woman is with her cell phone. Today, women drop their drawers instead of a hankie. Young people don't even date, they "hook up," a term that conjures images of plumbing as readily as the desire to make love.

Today's woman rarely employs the ingenious use of her mind to dangle possibility and inflame the imagination of a man. Almost never does she string out a relationship and, as a happy consequence, keep the bloom on it. The few who do are often more successful than their girlfriends who believe they've "evolved" beyond such girly coyness.

The difficult part of dating is not getting sex, it's getting what we really want: relationship. With a new approach, travel to that destination will be slower—sometimes significantly—but this allows the journey itself to be the focus. What the fast track skips is swelling anticipation, a scenic side road that makes the ultimate destination all the more exciting and, in the long run, satisfying.

-§-
The power of sexual suggestion was the power of innocent sexiness. But it's a type of innocence that understands the effect she has."
—Pin-up art gallery owner
-§-

According to Charles Darwin's theory of sexual selection, we choose our mates not indiscriminately, but with purpose. Darwin developed the theory when he noticed that peacocks possessed brilliant and heavy plumage, neither trait conducive to escaping predators. Upon closer study, Darwin saw that the peahens were more attracted to peacocks with bright, abundant plumage and wanted to mate with the most embellished of the lot. As it relates to humans, Darwin wrote, "Women have more power [than men] in choosing, rejecting, and tempting their lovers."

Developed in 1871, sexual selection theory was resisted for over a hundred years, in part, says evolutionary psychologist David Buss, because it seemed to grant too much power to females, who were thought to be passive in the mating process. However, as the sexual selectors, women are also the gatekeepers of sexuality—that is, they determine whether a sexual encounter will occur, or not.

It may seem odd to view dating, love, and sex as strategic. But we never choose mates at random. A woman who presents herself with a warm smile, interesting conversation, and wearing high heels and red lipstick, draws men to her so that she may then look them over. And just as pheasant spurs and lion manes and peacock tails advertise themselves to the females of their species, a woman chooses her mate based on characteristics he possesses that she finds desirable.

One reason women are wired to be more cautious and require time to judge a man's worthiness before becoming physically intimate with him is because women are left with the evolutionary legacy of suffering a greater cost of having sex than men. Men replenish sperm at a rate of roughly 12 million per hour, while women produce a fixed lifetime supply of about 400 eggs. Besides having precious few eggs and relatively few pregnancies (whereas men can impregnate many, many women), women have a nine-month gestation period and then responsibilities once a baby is born. Men have none of this; it's an eggs-are-expensive, sperm-is-cheap argument. A man in evolutionary history could walk away from a casual sexual encounter having lost twenty minutes. A woman could walk away from it as well, but if she got pregnant as a result, she bore the costs of that decision for decades.

-§-

"Fire me up with your resistance; Put me in the mood."

—Bob Seger, *Till It Shines*

-§-

Modern urban singles look for partners in singles bars, at work, and through Internet dating sites, rather than out on the savanna at a tribal gathering. Because of such enormous environmental changes, many argue that evolutionary theory is not solely determined by genetics or biology, but by environment as well. For example, modern birth control has altered women's behavior concerning casual sex; they can have short-term dalliances with less fear of pregnancy. Geoffrey Miller, author of *The Mating Mind,* and Buss both conclude that human sexual psychology developed over millions of years trumps the past fifty. Buss argues that if environment had the same effect as ancestral dynamics, a man wouldn't care whether his wife, who takes birth control pills, was faithful. But he does. This constant, he says, demonstrates the importance of our evolved sexual psychology, designed to deal with cues from a world millions of years old that continue to function with tremendous force in today's modern world of mating.

By making sex not immediately available, women increase its value to men. They render it a scarce resource, and hence a valuable one. Also, sexual withholding in the early stages encourages men to evaluate a woman as a permanent partner rather than a temporary

mate. Buss's research shows that women eager to sleep with men right away even today are often perceived as too promiscuous and too sexually available, characteristics that men avoid in women with whom they seek long-term relationships.

The twin powers possessed by a woman who plays with sexual suggestion are her ability to incite a man's imagination and absolute knowledge of her own worth.

First, imagination: Ideally, a man and woman conduct a dance of shared pleasure that begins when a woman very subtly hints at erotic possibilities—through dress, demeanor, and words—and the man's imagination is tickled. When done well, a woman inspires without fanfare; her command is quiet: it's in the whisper he strains to hear; a snug suit worn with confidence; a perfume he is able to smell only when she passes by closely; a bon mot that can be taken two ways. All of these things are done in the context of life; they are not removed from life to a place where just sex occurs but are incorporated into a date, a chance encounter, or when dangling over tea after work with a male acquaintance.

-§-

"Sex is thought to be wholly dependent upon attracting attention and being attracted, of using flirtation to focus the attention of a specific member of the opposite sex. If our ancestors hadn't done it well enough, we wouldn't be around to discuss it."
—Joann Ellison Rodgers, *Sex: A Natural History*

-§-

The famous strip tease artist, Gypsy Rose Lee (who, in one performance, brought down the house by removing nothing more than a single glove), said that to create illusion, flesh must be "hinted at rather than hollered about." Cues from things we see, smell, hear, or feel represent a wealth of experiences on which our imagination thrives. Particularly within the realm of sexuality, a suggested gesture or image is capable of tapping into a person's entire encyclopedia of sexual experiences and desires, with which the imagination can run riot.

One reason the game of croquet was so popular in the 1860s was because men got to see the women players lift their skirts up over their petticoats revealing—gasp!—their ankles, and a little more besides. What must men have felt later, as they lingered over memories of having glimpsed forbidden treats?

Over time, inch by inch, it became acceptable for women to expose skin. Once the ankle became old hat, men hungered for a glimpse of calf. Then thigh. And so on, until *Playboy* disrobed her altogether in 1953. Of course, now a viewer of erotica, if he wishes, can see almost as much as the model's gynecologist.

When encountering most of today's sexual imagery, a man's mind is directed away from the mystery of what might be. Imagination is snuffed out and erotic tension deadened in the interest of directing our minds to a specific sexual act. A woman who poses nude with her legs apart and a "do me" look on her face triggers one response: doing her. There's no room for wonder.

And that's too bad because to experience wonder is to know magic. Witness a child examining the wrapped gifts beneath the Christmas tree. For weeks before the big day, he looks at, handles, and guesses at the contents of each tantalizing gift, his anticipation almost unbearably delicious. The same dynamic is at work when a woman stirs male desire, hinting at what's possible instead of just handing it over.

The second power, a woman's complete certainty that she has great worth, is reflected in her clothes, expressions, words, voice, and posture. She projects a kind of "knowing"; she is aware of the allure of her femininity. She appreciates the power of her vulnerability and all the ways she's not the same as, but different from, men.

"The signals of sexual interest are built into us," writes Joann Ellison Rodgers, author of *Sex: A Natural History*, and these signals transcend history and cultural boundaries. "A coy smile is a coy smile," Rodgers writes. Whether we're in twenty-first-century Australia or pre-modern Europe, we're built to broadcast and receive these signals. She adds, "All manner of coquettish behavior—long trivialized and even demonized as shallow, callow things—are gaining scientific respectability, as studies increasingly reveal these behaviors to have biological as well as psychological roots."

Courtesans—who may well have been around as far back as ancient Greece—made careers out of these dual powers. The mid-twentieth-century European courtesan, according to Simone de Beauvoir, enjoyed more power and independence than did any other woman in Europe. Her bread and butter, as well as the respect she was afforded, was based, in part, on her mastery of this lost art, which Alexander Dumas called "the power of the skirt."

Even though the courtesan earned her living by offering her favors to men, she was never "easy." Instead, she played a more interesting game. She enchanted magistrates and kings, men accustomed to controlling every aspect of their lives, including their wives. The courtesan's independence and mystery were a large part of her allure.

The sexually suggestive woman is enigmatic. She draws a man in slowly, with quiet reserve. Instead of being overt or assertive, she

simply holds a man's gaze while consciously touching a bit of her delicious décolletage, and making him wonder, would she allow me to move a little closer? He doesn't know, but waits with baited breath, his imagination working overtime. This creates powerful tension. Sophia Loren knows the game. It's she who said that a woman's appeal is fifty percent what you have and fifty percent what he thinks you have.

Are women the only winners in this paradigm? No! Men want to long for women. None of us wants what comes too easily. Satisfaction is greater when the prize is hard won.

Dressed in a white pleated halter dress, Marilyn Monroe—playing "the girl" in *Seven Year Itch*—has her neighbor's libido by the tail. She steps onto a subway grate to cool her ankles on a hot evening, and captures not only her neighbor's imagination, but that of men worldwide. And she still does, all these years later.

In *The Lady Eve,* Barbara Stanwyck blames Jimmy Stewart for ruining her shoes after she trips him, and then with humor and coyness lures him to her room. As nervous as a cat, he's attracted and aroused, and not at all sure what will happen next. She shows him her shoe collection and purrs a double entendre, "See anything you like?" She shoos him out of her room because she's "tired" and he leaves, flummoxed, but intrigued. Stanwyck's character has made the evening fun for both of them, and roused his interest while staying in the driver's seat of the relationship—where a woman belongs.

-§-
"A woman's most erogenous zone is her mind." —Raquel Welch.
-§-

These movie characters probably didn't know that suggesting sexuality instead of falling into bed with their leading man was all part of the elaborate plan of evolution. But they followed the design of sexual selection to the letter.

As old as time, these scenes from the movies reflect real life as it once played out between men and women. If women heed these lessons from long ago, they may reclaim this ancient power in love. For, contrary to what our mothers said, nice girls do chase boys—and they do it so cleverly that, when he sweeps her off her feet, he doesn't realize that he's the one who's been caught.

Spencer Sherman & Anne Watts:

Money: The Surprising Aphrodesiac

When my wife and I started dating, we shared our sex histories with one another on the first date. But we did not have a serious money conversation until we'd been together for almost three years—and then only when a specific concern made it absolutely necessary. The subject of money between us was taboo.

Bernhard Lietaer, author of *On Human Wealth: The Future of Money,* speaks to the money taboo: "If I asked you how much money you have and where it came from, it's actually more indiscrete today than asking with whom you slept last night." Further, he states, "Most people have about as much perspective on money as fish have on water." Fish are born in water, live, and die in water. They don't step out of it to look at what water is. Likewise, our beliefs about money are unexamined—until, that is, we look past the money taboo.

As my teaching partner, Anne Watts, points out:

> Beliefs about money fill all our heads. We all have them. They can be fed by major experiences or by simple messages we've picked up along the way. These translate into limiting beliefs like: *Money is the root of all evil; Don't trust people with money; Money equals safety; It takes money to make money.* The list goes on and on. These beliefs remain unexamined until

Spencer D. Sherman, MBA, CFP is CEO of Abacus Wealth Partners LLC (www.abacuswealth.com), and Kubera Portfolios LLC (www.kuberaportfolios.com). He is an expert in philanthropic and inter-generational planning and socially responsible investing. In 2005, Spencer was named one of the top 100 financial advisors in the U.S. by *Worth Magazine* and Bloomberg Wealth Manager.

Anne Watts is an insightful, compassionate counselor. She has been leading Love, Intimacy & Sexuality Workshops for the Human Awareness Institute since 1985, teaching on four continents, and works with individuals, couples, and families in her private practice. Anne is the daughter of Alan Watts, pioneer interpreter of Eastern religion and philosophy for the Western world. Photo by Michael Buchanan.

we are startled awake, often by our own discomfort, and we begin to see just what it is we are living in—those subconscious thought streams about money we swim around in all day.

It doesn't take an extreme circumstance to be startled awake. A little bit of discomfort can go a long way, as it did the day my wife and I first saw the house that we eventually purchased together. Glowing with excitement when she saw the backyard, Janine said, "Plenty of space to put in a garden." I could tell by her tone and the look in her eye that she was imagining a full-blown permaculture installation, complete with pond and multiple tiers. All I could see was a pile of invoices.

-§-

In most relationships, one partner controls the sex and the other controls the money.

-§-

I looked away, secretly hoping the garden idea would decompose. *Mustn't let on that we can afford it,* went my thinking, *she might insist on having it.*

At that stage in our relationship, all of our financial information was my secret. In my family of origin, the primary messages about money included: "Don't talk about it," and, "Money is the only thing that will give you security." In the absence of clear and conscious money talk, those undercurrents translated into thought patterns that held my own sense of prosperity in check. In essence, I believed that my job as the head of the household was to watch the purse strings and silently monitor my wife's spending to keep us secure.

Something about the juxtaposition of Janine's obvious pleasure at the idea of a garden and my obvious distress in the moment triggered a new awareness. Janine delighted at the thought of working the soil, picking out and planting seeds, watching those little cotyledons send the plant's first two tender green leaves up through the earth and then grow into broccoli, asparagus, collard greens, and beets. She wanted the pleasure of plucking our dinner salad straight out of the yard. She was giggling with delight at the thought, while I, on the other hand, looked and felt like quite the curmudgeon. What was that all about?

I began to examine my resistance and looked at what was behind the "mustn't let on" thought stream. Was it true that one shouldn't spend money on a garden? I felt into the feelings, and asked myself: Is this a new feeling, or a familiar old feeling?

I knew from the work I had done with Anne and the Human Awareness Institute—an organization dedicated to eradicating ignorance and fear in the areas of love, intimacy, and sexuality—as well as earlier training in meditation—that I could dive beneath the surface of my thoughts and gain valuable perspective if I paused for a few moments. This self-reflection and inquiry process is one of the skill sets Anne and I teach in our workshop, *Financial Intimacy and Freedom for Couples.*

I knew from experience that shifting my beliefs could radically alter my experience, and I wanted a radical new me to step in for the curmudgeon that particular afternoon. But I also knew that simply denying my feelings or sweeping them under the sod would not do. So I took a slow stroll around the side of the house and stayed with the feelings. *What does this feeling want me to know?* I scanned my body, relaxed my mind and allowed my awareness to do a full sweep. Almost immediately, a memory of my father came into my mind's eye and I watched him flinch when the eight-year-old me asked, "How much money do you make, Dad?" He flashed me a look of disdain that nipped that conversation in the bud—for good.

Once I connected the dots between these early experiences that told me to stay silent about finances and my difficult feelings, I was able to take a deep breath and relax. Immediately, a sense of spaciousness filled my mind. All of a sudden, I was much less attached to my original idea about the garden. From this place of openness I began to look into my present-moment thoughts and feelings. *A garden can increase the value of one's home,* came the first thought. That was predictable; my mind is ever watchful when it comes to the bottom line. Then, following on that, I realized that a garden could be quite a lovely sanctuary, a place of beauty, a place to enjoy the textures and smells of seasonal change, a source of high-quality fruits and vegetables for our family.

-§-
Money does not bring us happiness. Our happiness naturally arises when we release our attachments to money.
-§-

My thinking expanded further as I imagined throwing a party in our backyard, hosting community events, having a place to explore the natural world with my kids, and being able to appreciate the ordinary miracles of peach and almond blossoms. *It would be lovely to meditate out in the garden,* I thought. Walking back toward my wife, I said, "Actually, Janine, we can afford a garden." The garden has become all of the above and much, much more; it is the best investment I have ever made.

Whenever I tell this story, Anne likes to mention another important aspect of partnership and intimacy:

> This experience with the garden highlights the way in which two people's differing values can either create friction between them, or, if handled consciously, open new

possibilities for each while solidifying the couple's bond. Spencer grew up in the city where there were no gardens; they were simply not important to him. It had not occurred to him that a garden could add to the quality of his life. In relationships, distinct individual values such as gardening can become shared values for the couple, and thus expand each person's horizons.

In the workshop Anne and I teach together, we start by posing this question: What is the best way to deepen intimacy with your partner?

Most people, especially Californians, will answer: Talk about ecstatic lovemaking!

No, we assert. Talk about money.

Some say: Insane! Talk about money to increase intimacy?

Of course, we realize that what we are suggesting is counter-intuitive. After all, money is the number one identified cause of divorce in the U.S. And yet, from my experience as both a workshop leader and financial advisor, money-talk is the greatest aphrodisiac of all. Think about it. If you can be open, honest, and fully present with your lover while talking about such a taboo topic, what might you discover?

-§-
There are many parallels between a successful relationship and a successful investment strategy.
-§-

In most relationships, one partner controls the sex and the other controls the money. Anne writes:

> In other words, the man often controls the money because he has the higher earning capacity in most marriages—not in all cases, but the majority. Women often manipulate with their sexuality to get what they want financially. Same gender couples often display this same dynamic.
>
> It is interesting to note that both money and marriage only exist as an agreement. The paper stuff we know as money has no value outside an agreement as to its worth and value, and the same can be said of marriage. In both cases, what marriage and money mean to different people differs widely. You can think you are in agreement about something, and find out later that you weren't in agreement at all.

Money is associated with our deepest needs for security, nurturance, warmth, and, of course, pleasure. Money can also trigger shame, anxiety, worry, regret, resentment, and blame. It is also directly related to one of the darkest aspects of human nature—greed.

And greed has many disguises and layers, beneath which most of us have another major emotional tangle: Fear. Fear about money is fear for our survival. When we worry about money, we're really worrying about our ability to take care of ourselves and those we love. When survival is threatened in any way, even subconsciously, it becomes difficult to enter fully into a relationship, much less ecstatic lovemaking.

For couples, teasing all this apart so they can have clear and conscious agreements about money involves several steps: 1) exploring unexamined individual beliefs and pre-existing mind-sets, 2) looking to see what values are shared, 3) discovering what new values can be aligned with and focused on as a couple, and 4) releasing old ideas and ways of thinking. Exploring with a partner in these ways leads to the greatest vulnerability imaginable—great in the sense that this is where egos melt and two become one.

Let's start by examining some fairly common beliefs about money that stem from messages received since birth from family members, media, and the culture at large. These messages get distilled into attitudes and shape your life and world. Perhaps your family had less than other families when you were growing up, and you felt embarrassed by that. Or, on the opposite pole, your family was wealthy and your parents worried the neighbors would be envious, so you learned to hide money and lie about it. Perhaps you had money once but lost it all, and adopted the belief: *I am no good with money.* And then there is the all-too-common temptation to believe that *if only I had more money,* I would be happy. Your "if only" may find you dreaming of an inheritance, a winning lottery ticket, the profitable sale of your business, or a large salary increase. And yet many studies have shown that, unless you are living at or below the poverty line, more money will add very little to your life in terms of happiness and fulfillment.

-§-

They realized a freedom and joy independent of wealth.

-§-

Money does not bring us happiness. Our happiness naturally arises when we release our attachments to money. Limiting attitudes about money not only block financial success, they limit your ability to feel free and to experience abundance and peace around finances—no matter how much or how little you might have. This is the goal of our work with couples.

In my twenty years as a financial advisor, I have become convinced that transcending old beliefs about money is the surest way to reach a state of freedom, abundance, and increased intimacy. Anne writes:

Fear about money is like an infectious virus that lives within us and spreads its contagion to much of our thinking. When we are unconsciously protecting that fear, we end up building walls that act as barriers to intimacy.

It is common for couples to have different styles in dealing with money. These differing styles often lead to conflict. To avoid conflict, we start telling partial truths, withholding information, and telling small lies that grow bigger with time. For example, a woman I worked with was engaged to a man who had considerable resources. When they first met and became involved, she had a good job and was fully independent. Her partner loved this about her. When health problems caused her to lose her job, she became financially dependent on him. He accepted this, but a problem arose because she was accustomed to spending money on whatever she wanted, never conferring with someone else. She had a tendency to buy on impulse, driven by childhood experiences of deprivation. She grew up in a poor family, and always had to settle for secondhand or homemade clothes. As a working adult, she felt entitled to have whatever she wanted, even if it meant going into debt. When her fiancé began to question her choices, she became uncomfortable and rebellious. She began to make purchases on credit, becoming more secretive, more ashamed, and full of worry that he might find out.

He, in turn, feared taking on a bottomless debt through marriage. He postponed the wedding, and she began to fear that he didn't really love her. The situation escalated until the couple came close to breaking up. Finally, they began to share their stories. She mustered her courage to tell him the truth, and they worked out a plan whereby she could have her own account from which to spend as she chose, no questions asked. Today, she is no longer driven to buy on impulse. They discuss their finances with ease, and are happily married.

Without realizing it, we create huge erosions in our intimacy, which, in turn, have a chilling effect on passion. A relationship sprinkled with lies, omissions, and a lack of trust is in serious trouble and likely to die. The antidote involves uncovering our deepest truths by sharing and listening, thus building a foundation of compassion and trust.

There are many parallels between a successful relationship and a successful investment strategy. Don't overreact when the relationship gets rocky, and certainly don't leave on impulse. Similarly, don't respond to your fear at a low point in the market by selling. If I reacted to my wife the way many investors react to the market on a daily basis, I'd be divorced hundreds of times.

Every investment study confirms that buying low and selling high are the best strategies. Most investors, though, sell their stocks when the market decreases, like after 9/11, and buy when the market goes up, as they did during the tech boom in 1999. Likewise, when you're on the honeymoon enjoying that perfect moment on an island beach, it's easy to become attached to that experience and expect that the high will last forever. Being attached to that euphoria is unrealistic.

Markets and relationships go up and they go down. When a relationship gets rocky, like a low point in the market, this is the greatest opportunity for gain. Revel in this. Invest more of yourself in the relationship at those times, and you will receive the greatest payout. When I experience difficulties with Janine, I remember this and look to how I can grow personally and thus expand our range of intimacy. The most difficult moments in our relationships are really the most sacred ones.

One business owner—we'll call him Steve—complained during a meeting that, although quite successful, he felt trapped by his business. He and his wife could never agree on a spending plan and he worried about her shopping habits. He hated the lack of freedom that came with being tied to his business. I asked him, "What would give you a sense of freedom in your life?"

He replied, "If you can double my investment portfolio from $1 million to $2 million, all my financial worries would ease." A young financial advisor at the time, I loved the challenge and the potential reward of helping him find this freedom. Five years later, when his portfolio surpassed the two million dollar mark, I eagerly shared the news. But Steve wasn't nearly as happy as I was; his thinking had shifted. He now needed five million to feel secure. His money had doubled, but nothing had changed.

When I got home that evening, I felt devastated and worthless. I began to question my choice of profession. Did I get an MBA at Wharton and work sixty-plus hours per week for over ten years to see that financial success did not translate into happiness?

The next day brought a big revelation. I asked Steve, "What holds you back from feeling free and secure now?" He said, "Feeling free is for lazy people. A man is supposed to take care of others. If he's not working, he's being irresponsible. You can never have enough money."

Even the most superlative investment strategy would make no difference for Steve as long as he considered the solution to his prob-

lem *having more.* Doubling or even quadrupling his wealth would not lead to freedom. So I took a new tack, and worked with Steve until he could see that he had internalized a set of beliefs that kept him trapped. As he began to see this more clearly, he shared these insights with his wife. She felt included, and more connected to him. That led them into deeper intimacy, and she rallied to help him stay aware and release attachment to the old beliefs. The more Steve let go, the more abundant he felt. He began to live from a more empowered position about his finances: Freedom, work, and security are choices. They realized a freedom and joy independent of wealth. The more Steve let go of his attachment to his beliefs about work ethic, the less Helen needed to spend.

For many couples, confusion and worry about money is wasted energy. Reclaiming that energy with clear and conscious money talk allows a couple to reinvest their vitality, focus on intimacy, and dream the future as a team. Financial freedom for couples means revisiting both money and marriage agreements to form a coherent team comprised of two individuals whose talents and dreams complement and support one other.

All of the books, tapes, and courses that promise financial independence, as well as those that promise to improve our relationships, are mere distractions—unless we enter the dark caverns inside us and transcend our limiting beliefs about money, sex, and relationship. Accumulating more ideas, beliefs, and knowledge is not the way out. Instead, listen to the feelings and emotions in your body. Share these feelings and the stories connected to them with your partner. Tell your partner what you're feeling. This is where transformation happens—in the body. The body is the furnace that burns up old ideas, beliefs, and thinking habits that no longer serve us.

Here is an exercise we recommend to begin your discovery process:

Make a date with your partner. Set aside at least an hour, preferably two. Create a nurturing environment: lights low, candles, and soft music. Be sure all phones are turned off. Sit close and take turns sharing stories about money from your childhood. Notice how you feel as you share, and talk about this as well. While listening, stay open and curious. Be willing to learn something new about your partner. Repeat and reflect back what you heard as precisely as possible, without adding your thoughts or feelings at this point. Allow your partner to fill-in or correct what you may have missed or misunderstood. Then switch and repeat, so that each partner gets to be heard. Lastly, each share what feelings came up during the exercise, as well as any new insights.

Once you have warmed up and explored in this way, take time to tease apart the messages each of you received growing up and notice how they affect you today.

Next, take the limiting message, which has been forged into an unconscious belief, and turn it into an empowering message. For example, if your negative message was, "Money is scarce," you can change it to, "Money flows freely and I am responsible for getting my needs met."

A very important piece to the process comes next. Take turns gently, tenderly stroking each other, starting with the face. One strokes, the other receives, with no sexual agenda to the stroking. Your focus is on nurturing one another. Add loving words that include the empowering messages you have crafted and other messages like, "I love how good you are with money," or, "you are so precious to me," and so on. Do this for about ten or twenty minutes, and then switch. The power of this nurturing caress cannot be emphasized enough. Typically, we touch each other as a prelude to sexual intercourse. Touch can become loaded with all kinds of unspoken expectations, anxiety, and resentment. Tender caresses with the simple intent to nurture your lover are deeply healing and create a space of love in which healthy intimacy and truth-telling can occur.

We recommend setting time aside for this kind of touch on a regular basis. Anne thinks of this as "going all the way." The combination of deep, intimate sharing about money with tender touching is where the juice is. This is when money becomes an aphrodisiac.

The next time worrisome or difficult money thoughts come to greet you, just relax and remember that this thought is an invitation to intimacy with yourself and with your partner.

In his book, *The Seven Stages of Money Maturity,* my friend and colleague, George Kinder, writes, "letting go of thoughts and allowing feelings to be is key to opening our hearts around money." The disposition he recommends is one that also serves couples quite beautifully:

> Practicing...generosity and wisdom, we give without expectation of return, understanding that living is giving. We know both the limitations and the power of money, yet money no longer agitates us. We rest calm before it. In that calmness we can serve one another from the natural generosity that lies within and waits to be offered to the world.

Geralyn Gendreau:

Meet the Beloved

Nearly two decades ago, long before I discovered the sacred dimension of sex, the Beloved seduced me on the beach at Point Reyes. It was 1987, and the sphere of human thought was bubbling with excitement about the Mayan calendar and the prophesied end of time. The Harmonic Convergence was just around the corner, and plans were being made for the largest worldwide peace meditation ever. But despite all the hoopla that was being made, my harmonies were radically diverging.

My father's death had pushed my delicate biochemistry over the edge. A lover of God and Jesus from the start, I had lost all faith and given up on the powers that be. Confused and lost in grief, I would surely have slipped into clinical depression were it not for one driving obsession: black-belt training.

Three years had passed since I first stepped through the door of Sun Moo Won, a traditional Korean martial arts school in the heart of San Francisco. From the very first class, I was hooked. Six days a week, sometimes seven, I crossed the threshold of the dojang at the crack of dawn, and stopped to bow and greet the day by saying "Hwarang." Warrior training included taekwondo, hapkido, t'ai chi, and Zen meditation. Over the course of those same three years, I watched my father battle gastrointestinal cancer and, ultimately, lose the fight. When, on his deathbed, he expressed concern about my tendency to give up when the going got rough, I vowed, "I promise, Daddy. I'll get my black belt *no matter what.*"

Geralyn Gendreau, MFT, is a yoga lifestyle trainer, martial dance artist, and professional muse. The embodiment of coherent emotion and devotional ecstasy, she is best known for her stage recitations of poetry from two great mystics—Rumi and Hafiz. She is the author of *When I Became God's Lover,* a collection of stories, poems, and essays on the sacred erotic. Both on stage and with clients, she works to ground the light of pure genius to sculpt a more balanced world. Find her on the web at www.themagdalenesect.com.

The following spring, when my black-belt test was only four months away, I decided to go on a vision quest. Here in northern California, vision quests, sweat lodges, fire walks, and ropes courses have replaced mowing the lawn and washing the car as standard weekend fare. On that warm day in May, my friend Susan and I drove to Point Reyes, hiked Bear Valley Trail to the coast at Arch Rock, and then took a north fork to Kellam Beach, where we settled in for the afternoon. Several hours later, as we began to gather our belongings, I decided to take a quick swim. A little bodysurfing seemed just the ticket to cool me off before the five-mile return trek. Always a southern California surfer girl at heart, I sprinted toward the waves.

Now, anyone familiar with the character of the sea off the north coast of California has a deep, body-based respect for incoming waves that someone who grew up south of the Ventura County line cannot truly understand. Until, that is, she meets the north-coast surf firsthand. Or in my case, head first. The crunching sound of my cervical spine being crushed was so loud, I felt certain the moment of my death had arrived. *So that's how it ends* was my only thought. The fact that I could not breathe mattered not at all—death held no fear.

-§-
Divine interventions, as it turns out, actually require human participation.
-§-

As I tumbled beneath the waves, waiting for a tunnel of light to appear, the life I had lived flashed forward all at once. I began to sense, feel, and see the ripple-out effect of my every act as the veil of my encapsulated self-identity lifted. Then—like a sudden alarm—the impact my death would have on my recently widowed mother hit me. When she heard the news, "Your daughter drowned in the ocean this afternoon," she would surely break. My dad had been gone little more than a year. Another such loss would destroy her. *I can't die now!* I thought. An instant later, my head broke the surface.

When Susan pulled me from the surf and dragged my naked body onto the beach, I was alive and breathing, but unable to move. *Oh my God, I'm paralyzed.* A flood of terror hit me with an impact that far exceeded that of the bone-crushing wave.

I lay on the sand, paralyzed. Susan sat near me, terrified. Then came the vision—me, dancing on stage—that ignited my will. *Yes!* cried the voice of my soul. At that very moment, Susan's mind zeroed in on a single overriding thought: *I MUST make her move, or she will never move again.* And with that, she stood up and began to shout, "Crawl, Geri, crawl!"

Why Susan chose that particular word heaven only knows, but thank God heaven does, because that seems to be what makes for miracles. Divine interventions, as it turns out, actually *require* human participation. Something about her screaming the word *crawl...*

Into my state of shock the word dripped, unfurling its magic and pulling me into an extraordinary realm. No longer myself, I had become the first amphibian to emerge from the sea. Feeling nothing but the sand beneath me and a vibrant energy flowing through my body, I writhed in the sand. A doorway opened, allowing my body-mind to link up with the whole of land-based evolution. Pressing my hips into the sand, I felt the wave of my breath travel up my body.

I inched up the beach, following the wave-like pulse moving up my core. From "squirming like a fishy-thing" (Susan's words) I moved to crawling like a lizard. Then I came up on all fours. In my mind's eye, I had morphed into a female tiger. When I reached dry sand, the warmth against my skin snapped me back into the ordinary world. Curling up into a fetal position, I felt like a new babe, fresh from the womb.

That's when it happened. The air became an ocean of liquid, breathing, pulsing love. Everything around me was totally alive. The Infinite Ineffable itself embraced me, seeming to press in on my body from all sides. That's when I heard the words: "Meet the Beloved."

In Search of the Beloved

Many years went by before I could make sense of what happened that day. A decade and a half would pass before I could steadily abide in a state of union with the divine. During those years, I sought the Beloved in many forms. I chased down teachers, sat with saints and gurus, and went on silent meditation retreats. Then I met Jean Liedloff, author of *The Continuum Concept,* and absorbed an evolutionary view of human nature based on Jean's experience with a remote indigenous tribe in the Venezuelan rainforest. Shortly thereafter, I moved to Marin County and all but stopped working in the outer world to work on the inner planes. This continued for almost ten years. During that time, I attended Northern California Dance Collective freestyle events several nights a week and found a new home in my body.

-§-
Day by day, I allow myself to be devoured by a tangible presence that loves me.
-§-

In need of discipline and structure, I became a serious student of yoga, eventually taking up with a left-handed tantrik who showed me the miracle of *shaktipat* and taught me to read the sutras. By then a budding tantrika myself, I fell in with a self-styled sorceress who introduced me to esoteric mystery school teachings. Then came white hot yoga, my "second-birth awakening," and what Saniel Bonder calls

the wake-down-shakedown—a post-awakening personality purge. When I started a relationship with a heart-realized adept in that work, visions of giving birth in ecstasy began to dance in my head. When he decided to end our relationship, the pain, coupled with his touch and understanding, caused a current of bliss—the *amrit nadi*—to open from my heart to my crown.

I kid you not, this is life here in Northern California.

As if all that weren't enough, a spiritual emergency saw me leaping cement walls in a single bound, performing a striptease on the hood of a police car, and landing on my bum in a padded room. But even through the long months of depression that ensued, I danced—it had become my religion.

-§-
The transition from child of God to lover of God gives new meaning to the expression "razor's edge."
-§-

When the Beloved finally called on me a second time, it came in the form of a pillar of beautiful golden energy. I'd been meditating in my bedroom one night when a column of yellowish, shimmering light came down through the ceiling and penetrated the core of my body in an exquisitely personal and intimate way. Unlike my first encounter, this one had a highly erotic quality, prompting my roommate—who was asleep across the hall—to say the next morning, "Sounds like you have a new lover."

Then, in 2001, the Beloved came a third time, this time in the redwood forest near my home at the base of Mount Tamalpais. Overwhelmed with pain and grief after yet another broken love affair, I wandered through the woods, sobbing and crying out—*"Why? Where? Who?"*

Then, all at once, I felt a nudge from the Beloved deep in my core: *I am always near.* And then I heard the words, "You must choose me first." From all around me, the forest resounded with the call. I fell to the ground and kissed the earth, saying, "I do. I do."

In the months that followed, I began to open more and more in surrender to the vast pulsing heart I know as God. Day by day, I allow myself to be devoured by a tangible presence that loves me. "Breath is my mantra. My body is my guru. God is my Lover." These are my living vows. Embodying worship—of the Beloved in the form of man—is both my sacrifice and my devotion. I am forever tasting, as Rumi says in the Coleman Barks translation, "the surprise meal fixed by the lover inside all your other lovers." This, I know as the union I have longed for. With deep gratitude, I daily choose this sacred marriage.

For several years, while I had no steady relationship, the Beloved came to me in the dreamtime as a beautiful Bengal tiger, and we were timeless lovers. With intentional focus, I learned to detach my love-nature from old expectations and ideas, and free myself of inbred Catholic guilt. With the help of many remarkable men—including one extra-special man who did not escape the wheelchair as I did—I forged a new way of being. Today, I stand in awe of the masculine rather than in judgment of any one man's foibles, as much as I am able. And steadily, I see the men around me beginning to look more and more like the gods they are. When my lover—a beautiful man and father of four—took me to Maui last fall, the island goddess, Pele, gave him a spirit-name. Now I call him Tiger.

A psychic friend articulated the path ahead when she said, "We are learning what it is to become a lover to the Beloved." The transition from child of God to lover of God gives new meaning to the expression "razor's edge." When doubts about the veracity of the path arise, I often think of my dear friend, Blake More. Many years ago, while she and I were practicing yoga on my sundeck one afternoon, I said, "I don't have to rely on men for my pleasure anymore. The universe is making love to me all the time!" Being who she is, Blake picked up the clue and became my favorite muse by turning that statement into a lifestyle (see snakelyone.com).

-§-

This is not only a primal hunger, this is a universal one.

-§-

To celebrate becoming a lover to the Beloved and marrying the Divine, I held a wedding ceremony in my redwood grove not long ago. Those in attendance were invited to take their own Inner Marriage vows. Two of my friends have since taken this step in a public way themselves. I'm hoping for a trend.

Venus Talks to Mars: War and Peace Between the Sexes

I've been engaged in a strange contemplation as of late—going bald. Voluntarily letting go of all this blond. Being blond, you see, over-defines me, and I want to know, I really, really want to know who I am beneath it all. I was barely sixteen when I first began to sense the strange power I had just because of the lightness around my head.

These are the opening lines of *Venus Talks to Mars,* a one-woman show performed by two people—my animus, and me. It will be performed with only two stage props: a pole and a set of dumbbells. The pole, around which I will dance and perform a sacred striptease, is a symbol of the masculine Absolute; the dumbbells symbolize—among other things—the part of me that is hopelessly blond.

Although my inner male took up the art of war in the early eighties, it was not until my inner female took up the art of love in the mid nineties that my admittedly loose-cannon personality began to inte-

grate. Today, I work with the Venus archetype on a daily basis, and Venusian love powers have declared their reign over the complaint-ridden woman-scripts that constantly run through my brain.

The subjects I address in *Venus Talks to Mars* are love and desire, loneliness and passion, emptiness and pleasure, and the ever-so-human desire to know God. As Rumi says: "There is a secret medicine given only to those who hurt so hard they can't hope. The hopers would feel slighted if they knew." So much of what we hurt for comes out of a longing that really has no name. I have often wondered, how can my body long so deeply for something it has never known? Endlessly, that's how. Tirelessly. Eternally. Compulsively. Unerringly. For this is not only a primal hunger, this is a universal one, as best I can discern.

The hunger I speak of is the longing for deep relatedness. Total and complete wedded bliss. Union of separate parts, balanced yin and yang, masculine and feminine dancing together—choosing those steps that will serve the greater good for all.

The requisite character for deep relatedness—one that has ceased being ruled by undertones of arrogance and disrespect—is underdeveloped in humans at this point in time. A character that could be distinguished as honorable, humble, attentive, and nurturing rarely has a chance to fully develop in a world that is dominated by competition—a world that encourages, even demands, we become self-important and disassociative in order to survive. Humility has a bad rap in this world, and yet the discovery and maturing into this quality of character is precisely what makes deep and satisfying friendships and lover-partner relationships possible.

-§-

We need all the courage and presence we can muster, to free ourselves from the tyrants of rejection, contempt, and disrespect.

-§-

We so readily blame ourselves, and our loved ones, when relationships fail. What I believe is most important to say—and what I must say to the isolated and confused aspects of myself—is this: Your suffering is not wholly of your own making.

Even within our religions and philosophical traditions, the subject of human relations has been largely overlooked. Our culture has advanced by ignoring certain basic human needs. To that degree, we have waylaid our chances of true fulfillment. In fact, *sensitivity to the intricacies of relatedness is not even considered an intelligence function*—much less the vital form of intelligence it must become if we are to thrive instead of just survive. Our deeper need for relational continuity can no longer be ignored. The interrelatedness of all humanity, and of humanity with all of creation, must emerge as a living reality in our awareness.

I firmly believe we are now in a position to grasp the tail, so to speak, of our own evolution, to wake up from the dream of separation and transform the dysfunctional archetypes currently playing out in the family of man. We need all the courage and presence we can muster, individually and collectively, to free ourselves from the tyrants of rejection, contempt, and disrespect. Only then will our relational intelligence begin to grow swift and strong. Only then will the aspects of each of us that have been trapped in states of arrested development be free to mature. Only then will a deeply loyal relational context, a fertile and honoring ground in which our true nature might flower, emerge in our midst.

My favorite photo of my parents, taken at some point during their courtship, became my favorite precisely because of a certain magical look on Carol and Leo's twenty-three-year-old faces as they gazed in each other's eyes. Having enlarged and framed that photo, which sits even now within my view, I look at it to remind me of the quality of love and presence that gave birth to my very existence. The particular look, one I regard as essential for a level of relaxed well-being, can be recognized as "the look of the Beloved."

Throughout my life, I searched for that look, first in the eyes of my father, and then in the eyes of every significant—or seemingly significant—man I encountered. In the depths of my being, there lived a seed of knowing: *That look* is the quintessential water without which I cannot blossom as a woman. But the look of the Beloved—and its underlying posture, one of deep honor—is uncommon between individuals in this culture. One need only look in the eyes of people on match.com these days to see the deadness so many carry inside, where a vital human rosebush would bloom if only it could.

Too many of us are heartsick, burdened by the paradox of love. We are torn apart by our desperate need for that which seems ever elusive: a full and complete, ultimately satisfying, union with another—a union that sustains. Therein lies the paradox: All things change, and in the end, nothing sustains. Nothing but love, that is. And what if it's true that *love is all there is?* In her seminal book, *Love Without End: Jesus Speaks,* Glenda Green shares these words from the Master's mouth:

> Love opposes nothing, but conquers all… Fear and hatred, and the evils that come from them, are all derivative. Love is primary. Love existed before the universe, and most certainly before the structures of the world. In the beginning

> there was no evil, fear or hatred. There was only One Love… As manifestation began to take shape, free will was extended to every aspect of love… There was even the choice to deny its own nature, if that should be desired. From this last choice all the "weeds" of peril have sprung.
>
> This last choice was a very important gift. For without it you would have been an aspect of love without the power to forward creation… Once love has become your choice as well as your nature, all potential for duality is erased from your life, and you are *given command.*

Recently, during a "rough patch" with Tiger, I began to think perhaps he and I were destined to go our separate ways. Sad as that thought made me feel, I knew nothing could ever touch or change the love we are. Our love will live forever. This did not lessen the pain of letting go, but it did make that eventuality—after all, one of us will one day leave or die—full of light and luminosity. As I focused on love instead of on my fear and pain, I repeated my favorite mantra, "Love powers over all," and prayed throughout a long, lonely night. I got up the next morning and looked in the mirror. Eye to eye with myself, I repeated my spirit-name, Infinity Love Transcendence, over and over until I knew without a doubt that my prayers were answered. And with that, love gave me command.

-§-
I leave the combative phase governed by the war-god Mars and jump valence into the love-drenched phase of Venus.
-§-

In no time at all, I began to see clearly. Tiger has never been anything other than himself. I was the one who suddenly began to turn his every move into a problem. I was the one who backed him into a corner with my annoyance for weeks on end. I was the one who lost touch with the free spirit he fell in love with. He had not hurt me by becoming someone else; I had. With that realization, the rough patch smoothed out, and we began to live in harmony again. Every day I must rededicate myself to the discipline of watching my tongue for those biting comments that subtly, or not so subtly, disrespect my man.

Attending to relationship at this level, I believe, is primarily a woman's responsibility. I call this *neo-feminism.* Neo not only because it is new, but also because this approach makes me, as a woman, "the one"—just like Neo in *The Matrix*—who is responsible.

"Why should the woman be responsible?" you might ask. Because women have the more developed corpus callosum, that plate of nerve fibers that connects the two cerebral hemispheres.

This, I assert, makes women better equipped to make the distinction between arrogance and humility, respect and disrespect, and to take responsibility for the tone of the relationship. I call this process, which involves monitoring not only my razor tongue but also the tone of my voice, "jumping valence" or "phase-shifting." With intentional focus, I leave the combative phase governed by the war-god Mars and jump valence into the love-drenched phase of Venus, the goddess of love and pleasure. Both genders can take up this devotion. Some men are just as sensitive to the distinction as women, and the practice can be learned. Spearheading this aspect of human evolution is a day-to-day task that yields immediate and gorgeous rewards.

For both men and women, it is precisely our capacity to feel and know the pulse of love—and to return to love again and again—that keeps us alive. The hunger for love, and the dream of its fulfillment, is the divine design asserting itself. The passionate desire to know and be known—fully and totally—from flesh and bone to final thought, reaches in and squeezes our soul until we finally take heed. At least it did mine.

Part Eight

The Future of Relationship

Humankind is being led along an evolving course,
through this migration of intelligences,
and though we seem to be sleeping,
there is an inner wakefulness that directs the dream,
and that will eventually startle us back
to the truth of who we are.
~Rumi

Barbara Marx Hubbard: The Suprasexual Revolution

The structure of the patriarchy and the male role, as it has been developed over the last five thousand years, is coming to an end in terms of viability. And the very best men see this. Out of the breakdown of the dominator model, we are seeing the emergence of a new archetype: the feminine cocreator, the evolutionary woman. Building on the pioneering courage of the suffragettes, the next phase began in earnest in the 1960s with the consciousness raising circles and the advent of feminism. Betty Friedan wrote *The Feminine Mystique* and revealed the fact that most women in this culture, in the fifties, had no self-image beyond the age of twenty-one, nor did we have an identity other than wife and mother. This cultural imprint caused such depression, sadness, neurosis, and deep-seated anger that, in those early days, we hardly understood how to express it. With the great awakening of women in the sixties, we took our next step—aiming at equal rights and our identity as women and human beings.

Now, however, we are living through an evolutionary crisis. If we, as a culture, continue to function in the same way, we will see the demise of our life support system itself. This is a huge wake up call. Women are coming into the Third Phase of the woman's movement just as the human species as a whole hits an evolutionary crisis where the dominator structure, if continued, can destroy the future for all our children.

Barbara Marx Hubbard has been a pioneer in positive options for the future of humanity for forty years. A public speaker, author, and social innovator, she is President and Executive Director of the Foundation for Conscious Evolution. She has been instrumental in the founding of many future-oriented organizations, including the World Future Society, New Dimensions Radio, Global Family, Women of Vision In Action, The Foundation for the Future, and the Association for Global New Thought. Among her books are *Emergence* (Hampton Roads, 2001), *Conscious Evolution* (New World Library, 1998), and *The Revelation* (Nataraj, 1995). More information at www.barbaramarxhubbard.com.

At the growing edge of the women's movement there is an evolutionary impulse awakening us to a powerful vision of what must emerge out of this suffering, violence, and unsustainability. We are no longer striving to be equal to men in a dysfunctional world. Rather, we seek to join with men to create a more humane and life-enhancing world.

In this environment of new crises and opportunities in the twenty-first century, a new kind of woman is emerging. She is an evolutionary woman, a feminine cocreator. She senses what is emergent within herself and the world, and seeks to fulfill that greater potential. This new woman is awakened through the heart by Spirit. She wants to express her unique creativity and life purpose for the good of herself and the larger world. She is growing spiritually, and finds that her creativity is pressing her to evolve.

Men and women everywhere are flipping a switch inside. If we are fortunate enough to have a partner whom we can join with creatively in some way, the creativity of each is enlarged exponentially. And that is a great blessing.

The relationship does not have to be an intimate, romantic one. But when it is, the joy of co-creation extends beyond the joy of procreation. I call this the shift from sex, which joins genes to create a baby, to *suprasex*—joining genius to give birth to a larger self, and to a work that contributes to the world. We are moving from procreation toward co-creation—from self-reproduction toward self-evolution and life purpose in terms of work.

-§-

The joy of co-creation extends beyond the joy of procreation.

-§-

As population growth reaches its limit on this Earth and we live longer and longer lives, women *literally* cannot continue to reproduce up to maximum. This triggers a powerful drive that is the life force itself, moving women from the desire to mate—to have children and hold onto a man—to the desire to co-create and join in partnership to express our full creativity. We seek to evolve ourselves through joining, rather than to reproduce ourselves! We want to know our deeper purpose. Within that drive for self-expression and self-evolution, sexuality changes. The main emphasis of sex expands from procreation and recreation toward regeneration. Evolutionary sexuality emerges here.

The intimacy and love of evolutionary sexuality has as its deeper purpose the evolution of the lovers, and the birth of their progeny —that is, their work in the world. Conscious evolution is, simply, *the evolution of evolution*—from unconscious to conscious choice. Even as systems are breaking down, new innovations and creative initiatives are breaking through in every field. Conscious evolution comes about in the noticing, the connecting, and the empowering of that which is emergent. It can be experienced spiritually as the impulse to express the divine within ourselves; and, it is expressed socially as the desire for a life purpose that contributes to the healing of the world.

Women who are consciously evolving want to develop a new pattern of coequal co-creation with men—one that joins us together to deepen our essence, fulfilling more of both partners' potential than is possible when we are separate. This evolutionary sexuality starts to emerge when we seek intimate partners who love us for our initiative, our passion to create, rather than controlling, dominating, or even supporting us, and our children, on the material level. It is essential that these partners are receptive to our power, because conscious evolution is not only personal and social; it is also scientific and technological. In the relationship of coequal co-creators, we aim at wholeness, men balancing their masculine with their feminine, and women doing the same. The relationship of whole being with whole being, beyond dominance or submission, is heralding the evolution of our species itself. For when men and women join to co-create, we see the founding of the new family of humanity, dedicated to co-creating a new world equal to our spiritual, social, and scientific/technological capacities.

I believe that women are leading this shift, partly because of the bioevolution, and partly out of cultural necessity. The men in charge of the world are clearly not capable of handling the problems that are arising. The whole "thinking" layer of Earth, the noosphere, is holding the collective power of science/technology/industry and information systems, right now. These powers, when combined with our spiritual and social initiatives, lead toward a new human and a new world. Of course, the first level of focus has to be on dealing with the immediate crises, such as the environment, poverty, and war. But the far greater opportunity is being presented, at the growing edge of our radical technologies—in biotechnology, nanotechnology, quantum computing, zero-point energy, space development—to transcend the human creature condition altogether.

-§-
When men and women join to co-create, we see the founding of the new family of humanity.
-§-

In *Radical Evolution,* Joel Garreau explains that the human *Homo sapiens sapiens,* as we are now, is moving rapidly either to self-destruct by the misuse of power, or self-evolve by applying that same power in a constructive way. My sense is that the emerging woman, in partnership with the men who love and support her co-creatively, is the key

to relationship shift in our species that can guide that power toward an evolutionary purpose for humanity.

My partner, Sidney, and I have been working deeply with the idea of the evolution of the myth of the Western world. We all know the early part of the myth: the story of Genesis and the punishment, which—from the fundamentalist viewpoint—has a very painful and divisive ending. The mythos of the orthodox Jewish people has them waiting for the messiah. For the fundamentalist Christians, the whole sequence of Armageddon—the Second Coming, the burning in hell of the non-believers—will finally lead to the New Jerusalem through the destruction of the world and all who do not believe in Christ. But from the perspective of the feminine co-creator, the next chapter of the story is not a new Messiah, nor Armageddon; it is the emergence of the whole woman, with her masculine and feminine aspects joined, uniting with the whole man, with his masculine and feminine aspects joined. Whole being coming together with whole being, co-equal cocreators at the Tree of Life, actually learning how to guide the powers given to us by science and technology—powers that we used to project upon the gods.

If we look back to that early Genesis story, we find that this is where the division occurred in the first place. After tasting the fruit of the Tree of Knowledge, Adam and Eve were evidently moving toward the Tree of Life when the Lord God, Yahweh, said, "If they get there, they'll be like us. They'll be immortal!" It was with that threat that we were expelled from the Garden of Eden. The long journey of *Homo sapiens sapiens* began. Gradually, we separated from nature, from each other, and from God. Relentlessly, for the last 40,000 years, we have sought greater power over nature; in self-reflective consciousness, humans have been trying to achieve that god-like power. At this point, through technology, we have the capability to blow up this world, to create new worlds in space—the fact is that we have the powers we used to attribute to gods *now.*

-§-
The fact is that we have the powers we used to attribute to gods *now.*
-§-

Instead of Armageddon, and instead of holding out hope that a messiah will come to save us from ourselves, the evolving myth tells us that Eve is reawakening at this very great point in human history. She is becoming a whole woman, and joining with the whole man, Adam. Her teaching is that we have inherited the powers of co-creation, symbolized by the Tree of Life, and that it is through our own maturation that we can guide these powers toward the evolution of the species. This new myth finds humans becoming co-creators with the divine.

We see this in the changing life cycles of women today. It used to be that women in their younger years were busy having children, tending to their marriages, and, within the last century, holding down outside jobs. We had virtually no positive images of older women, post-menopause. The image of aging was that we were losing our sexuality, our beauty, and our vitality, perhaps grandmothering, preparing for illness and death.

-§-

We have inherited the powers of co-creation, and through our own maturation we can guide these powers toward the evolution of the species.

-§-

But today's woman in this culture is not going to have five to ten children. This liberates a huge amount of creative energy. She is now free to engage in the quest for life purpose, to find meaning beyond traditional roles, a freedom we did not have time for before. Many women in their fifties, sixties, seventies, and eighties are finding that, while the body may be aging, the vitality, spirituality, and creativity are flowing in to fill the space once taken up by traditional "women's work." More women are entering menopause now than at any other point in the history of humanity—and instead of fretting about getting older, they are entering a time of great renewal. I call this *regenopause.*

As Jean Bolen says, feminine creativity is intuitively connected to the whole. We can carry the maternal energy of connectedness forward with us as we pioneer a whole new phase of life, and we can use it to set a context for men as our partners in birthing an emerging world.

If we look back to the original idea that we are created in the image of God and see that we are now finally coming into to that state of god-like power, then what I actually think is happening is that the feminine co-creator is incarnating the creative Word—incarnating the "Father." What we have looked at as our higher selves, or the Christ, or higher being, we are beginning to recognize as our own essence; and, as we begin to incarnate our own higher selves, this "father within the daughter" becomes the co-creative feminine.

This evolution of the feminine is very powerful. The new archetype of the feminine co-creator is different than the Gaian goddess, and different than other versions of the feminine. Gradually, through attention and yearning for higher consciousness, the essential self, the higher self, the God self is coming into our heart and our solar plexus, until the local self, the separated, egoic self, releases its separation and starts to integrate and we become that which we have been seeking. In my book, *Emergence,* I write about how this shift occurred in my own life, the shift of identity from ego to essence, from the local self seeking the divine, to the God-self internalized, educating the local

self. We are incarnating self, and then guiding that self into action in the world.

This consciously evolving woman accepts the power of creativity that the masculine culture has built, that which has come from the patriarchal or father principle in the scientific and technological realms. And she says, "This can be used for the enhancement of life. We can restore the Earth. We can free ourselves from hunger, poverty, and disease. And we can begin the far greater effort to explore the potential of all humans and the universe beyond our planet."

A new cocreative feminine archetype is being born. She is the Goddess of the Noosphere—imbued with universal consciousness, guiding the powers of co-creation in partnership with co-creative men, with the wisdom of nature and the fourteen billion years of evolution awakening in her very blood and bones. This new Goddess, the co-creative, whole Eve, is not only called forth to heal and fix the current, outmoded system; she is called forth to evolve it by tapping into the feminine creativity and sharing that in true partnership. In this way, we participate consciously in our own evolution. Out of the integrity of this partnership, we begin to tune into a higher frequency, which I call the Universal Self, and which is beyond this earthly incarnation.

-§-
The feminine co-creator is incarnating the creative Word.
-§-

We are giving birth within ourselves to a new species, a universal human. This human is, as I said, connected through the heart to the whole of life. She is awakened by Spirit to divine creativity; yearning to expand consciousness to multidimensional realities, we are coming forth as co-creators with God incarnate. And that's the greatest love affair there is—that is the recreation of the world. *This is the suprasexual revolution.*

Laura Uplinger:

A Cosmic Collaboration

In the mid-seventies, a new field was born: prenatal and perinatal psychology. In the past three decades, new findings about conception, pregnancy, birth, and the first months of life have caused old assumptions to fall like leaves in a Canadian autumn. Even at the point in history when science was first taking humans to the moon, we still mistakenly believed that the placenta could protect a fetus from practically everything happening to the mother. Likewise, a newborn was considered a *tabula rasa*—a blank slate.

But science is now revisiting this crucial chapter of our very early beginnings and making discoveries that have mighty implications for the kind of adults we become. Recent discoveries in biochemistry and cell biology have added to these scientific revelations about life before birth. For instance, hormones produced by psychological stresses the pregnant mother endures actually influence placental vascular organization. This is startling and highly motivating news.

In 2001, neonatologist Jean Pierre Relier, editor of the prestigious *Journal of the Neonate,* wrote about the fundamental importance of emotional stability in each of the parents at the time of conception for healthy development of the embryo and placenta. A healthy placenta, in turn, prevents intrauterine growth retardation, prematurity, maternal hypertension, toxemia, and early miscarriage.

Laura Uplinger is an international advocate for conscious relationships and conscious pregnancy. She wrote the script for the 1989 Top Choice Award video, *A Gift for the Unborn Children,* which which combines images of nature with the testimony of experts to reveal the inherent spirituality of pregnancy and birth. She is chairperson for the 2007 international congress of the Association for Pre- and Perinatal Psychology and Health (www.BirthPsychology.com). At twenty-two years of age, Laura Uplinger embarked on a journey of consciousness with Bulgarian spiritual teacher Omraam Mikhaël Aïvanhov, where she studied his remarkable notions of the spiritual power of sexuality.

Thanks to pioneering books such as *The Secret Life of the Unborn Child,* by Thomas Verny, and *The Mind of Your Newborn Baby,* by David Chamberlain, we have become more aware of what goes on psychologically before birth. For the last decade, Dr. Bruce Lipton, a cell biologist, has been deciphering for the lay public recent and exquisite scientific discoveries about the life of our trillions of cells. Especially revealing are Lipton's elucidations as to how our cells take cues from their immediate environment in order to activate—or not, as the case may be—particular functions and specific genes.

From Harvard Medical School, we hear: "What goes on in the womb before you are born is just as important to who you are as your genes." Thanks to recent epigenetic data, it is even possible to infer that the health of a fifty-year-old person may depend more on the way she or he was formed in utero than on diet and exercise habits.

-§-

"The power to create is one of the most divine attributes man possesses. In his exercise of that power, he enacts microcosmically the great macrocosmic drama of creation. The fusion of the male and female organisms is a sacramental enactment of the great drama of the creation of the universe. When it is performed with the motive of pure and mutual love, the two halves of God, as represented in man and woman, are united."

—Geoffrey Hodson, 1929, *The Miracle of Birth*

-§-

Unfortunately, this understanding has not yet reached the general public. In fact, at the dawn of the second millennium, very few people are familiar with the power of prenatal life. I first heard of it in the lectures of the Bulgarian spiritual teacher Omraam Mikhaël Aïvanhov. Nothing of the kind had ever been mentioned in my psychology classes at the university. But sacred traditions have emphasized the crucial importance of conception, pregnancy, birth, and breastfeeding for centuries. Even the Vedic literature, some of the oldest known scripture, makes reference to the importance of the quality of conception.

Few important moments are more empowering, or harbinger more freedom, than the conscious conception of a child. What a momentous freedom to say yes to a cosmic collaboration and welcome the works of life in one's body! Alchemists perceive the sperm as light in liquid state, gold being light made into metal. What a gorgeous image to hold for this miraculous emergence of a human from the union of egg and sperm.

During the months leading to the conception of my child, I was aware that my body was to become a vessel for the making of a new human body. My husband and I sent out a call to the universe—as if posting an ad on a galactic website—stating who we were and what we could offer to a soul who wished to join us. We carried on our daily activities in a mood of solemn expectation and profound surrender: Was a soul going to be drawn to us?

On a clear May morning when the air was full of the scent of spring blossoms, we welcomed the soul of our child as we conceived. "Dear One," I recall saying inwardly, "if we are conceiving your physical body this morning, may you have a vast and luminous life."

The formation of a child in the womb is analogous to the way a fruit grows on a tree. Just as everything matters inside and around that tree, every detail of the life of an expectant mother matters. And for Spirit, matter matters. A European physician from the sixteenth century, Paracelsus, wrote: "Woman is the artist of the imagination, and the child in the womb is the canvas whereon she painteth her pictures." The family of words *image, imagination, magus, matrix, matter, mama,* all contain the root sound *ma,* which means "mother" in Sanskrit.

The formidable period of our formation before birth sets the stage for the way we relate to life. From the teachings of Rudolf Steiner in the early 1900s, we learned that, "During pregnancy, the mother's joy and pleasure are the forces that provide her baby with perfect organs." In 2004, renowned obstetrician Michel Odent demonstrated the same notion in an embryology lesson.

As I am writing these lines, I have in front of me a beautiful painting representing a human fetus in the spiraling shell of a nautilus; above, in silvery letters, I read the following invitation: "Parenting Your Baby Before Birth—Explore the Relationship." Our relationship with our children begins when we start wanting a child and dreaming about bringing a new being into the world. In fact, prenatal parenting sets the tone for the kind of mom or dad we will become, and that tone will be heard throughout the child's life.

Recently, I was delighted to read what a Harvard Professor of Religious Symbology said to the young men of his class: "The next time you find yourself with a woman, look in your heart and see if you cannot approach sex as a mystical, spiritual act. Challenge yourself to find that spark of divinity that man can only achieve through union with the sacred feminine." True, Professor Langdon is only a fictitious character in Dan Brown's *The Da Vinci Code,* but my heart rejoiced to see this important perspective so eloquently spelled out in a runaway bestseller.

Somewhere in the last pages of his seminal book, *How the Irish Saved Civilization,* Thomas Cahill wonders what is germinating the future of our civilization. What shape might human civilization take, I

wonder, if parents would bring renewed consciousness to conception and the early life of a child?

Brazilian psychiatrist and Jungian analyst Eleanor Luzes suggests that our times require the anthropological advent of the *Homo sapiens frater:* individuals capable of altruism, people who cherish and foster brotherhood on Earth. Luzes believes it is imperative for every high school and college around the globe to teach young people how to conceive and raise a child who will grow up to be wise and creative, aware of his or her kinship with all life.

Initiatives like the one launched by childbirth educator Tamara Donn in England gather pregnant women for a beautiful collective experience. In Donn's specially designed Birth Art Café, women meet every week to paint, sculpt, read, or eat croissants and oat cakes while sipping herb tea and chatting. Relaxing music supports and enhances the synergy springing from a circle of joyful bellies teeming with life. Likewise, French Architect Olivier de Rohozinski has created beautiful designs—plans for city parks in which pregnant women can stroll among trees, flowers, and fountains. These special parks include a lodge for expectant mothers to come together and sing, weave, sculpt, and draw, forming their own little cohort and craft village. Imagine a world in which cities all over the planet implemented such plans.

-§-

Few moments are more empowering, or harbinger more freedom, than the conscious conception of a child.

-§-

Even the best socioeconomic and political measures will not be successfully implemented if we go on procreating the unconscious way, ignoring the principles at work in conception, and in a pregnant womb. During pregnancy, a mother gives of her own substance to form her child's organs and psyche. This child will one day walk the Earth expressing peace, wisdom, and generosity—or indifference, rage, and fear. The power to birth a new civilization is the very power nature has given pregnant women. Hope for a brighter future depends on a collective understanding of this, and a collective acceptance of our shared responsibility. Everyone then becomes part of the endeavor. Fathers, families, communities, and nations all rally to support and inspire each and every mother in the monumental adventure of forming in her womb a healthy baby, and raising that child to be centered, intelligent, creative, and caring—a future citizen of the world. In fifty years' time, conscious conception and gestation could indeed redeem our species and change the face of the world.

Kelly Bryson:

The Kite and the String: Freedom and Intimacy

"We are not here to earn God's love, we are here to spend it," according to comic Swami Beyondananda. And what is this God's love that we are here to spend? It is the ecstasy of creative expression—and loving both ourselves and each other—whether through sacred sexual pleasure, the birthing of a book, the planting of a garden, or the raising of a child. It is the bliss, the rapture of surrendering to our urge to merge with creative love. It is enjoying what I think is Goddess's greatest gift to humanity—each other.

How do we enjoy each other? Oh, let me count the ways: seeing each other's spiritual beauty; laughing insanely at a silly joke; finding excuses to play; creating projects together; nurturing friends; touching; viewing physical beauty; intellectual contact; emotional connection; blissful sex; hearing spirit expressed through voices; being present; giving; appreciating others; supporting each other—and on and on.

However, to enjoy each other, we need to recognize and surrender our current coercive, codependent patterns of relating—as well as our current fear-based institutions and traditions—and develop a consciousness of natural giving and receiving. This requires that we develop a new form of spiritual consciousness. It also requires *new micro-cultures* to support that consciousness. As dying sociologist Morrie Schwartz told ABC newsman Ted Koppel, "Our culture does

Kelly Bryson, M.A., MFT, author of *Don't be Nice, Be Real: Balancing Passion for Self with Compassion for Others* (Elite, 2005) has appeared on many TV and radio shows and in national print articles. As well as having a private practice as a therapist, Kelly is a keynote speaker and humorist. He has been a certified trainer for the international Center for Nonviolent Communication for over twenty years, working in global flash points such as Northern Ireland, the Balkans, and the Middle East. He trains, presents, and consults with groups, businesses, churches, and organizations of every description. His website is www.LanguageOfCompassion.com.

not work anymore. We need to create a new one!" But I do not mean to imply that we have to change the world; I have been there, done that, and gotten the T-shirt for indulging in what I call the dark side of compassion. I have felt compelled to help others in order to feel a sense of personal value, playing a role I call the *martyor*—a martyr/savior/warrior.

These new, sophisticated micro-communities have the spiritual consciousness to love us right where we are on the path, without the crazy notion that we should be more evolved, healed, healthy, trim, kind, stable, or motivated than we currently are. By sophisticated, I mean that they have the ability to "hold space" for us—to be a clear mirror, providing wisdom, guidance, and supportive honesty—as we learn to do the "Freedom and Closeness" dance. Relationships offer our primary opportunities for growth and evolution; and because we are each at least as uniquely individual as snowflakes, we need support for discovering and meeting our particularly personal needs within relationships.

-§-
"We are not here to earn God's love, we are here to spend it."
—Swami Beyondananda
-§-

This is, of course, countercultural to the cookie-cutter, codependent, one-size-fits-all template of traditional love or marriage relationships. To the degree that any relationship is tainted by the consciousness of obedience, duty, obligation, buying love, or being good for the sake of external approval, it is doomed to gradually dam the river of love and erotic energy down to a trickle. Traditional marriage vows often say that women will "obey" men and that the couple will stay together no matter what, for better or worse, no matter how sick or bankrupt or miserable they become, until death does them part. This wording is still used in the vast majority of marriages in the western world. Stephen Langton, a Medieval Archbishop of Canterbury, even suggested that a wife should allow herself to be killed before she allows her husband to go sexually unsatisfied, for that might lead him into the great sin of adultery. If a wife is to save her husband from the weeping and wailing of eternal hellfire, she must subjugate her own will to his, and violate her own sacred sexuality. I sometimes joke that in such marriages, I hope that death comes quickly to both parties—for the marriage itself sounds like hell.

Many of the couples I work with, as a licensed marriage therapist, have the following kind of pain going on: The woman is hurt, discouraged, hopeless, and lonely, while the man is angry, frustrated, exhausted, and scared. The woman's unmet need is for empathy, closeness, and a higher quality of intimate conversation. The man's need is for respect, rest, validation of his inherent worth, and to unhook himself from his inner sense of inadequacy and guilt about his partner's pain.

The freedom vs. closeness dance underlies many painful relationships. Many couples spend their whole lives in turmoil about this. But it does not need to be experienced as a conflict. For as Einstein observed, "No problem can be solved from the same level of consciousness that created it." We can look at this freedom vs. closeness dynamic not as a conflict, but as an important, beautiful, playful co-creation. Even though the kite loves its freedom to sail the skies, it still needs the grounding quality of the string in order to function properly. The tension of the string propels the kite to new heights, while the bonding that the string provides protects the kite from getting lost and crashing. It is the dynamic tension between the kite and the string that allows the fulfillment of their different purposes. It is not a conflict to be resolved, but a daring, delightful dance, not a tangle, but a passionate tango, to be continually mastered.

-§-
These new, sophisticated micro-communities love us right where we are, without the crazy notion that we should be more evolved, healed, healthy, trim, kind, stable, or motivated.
-§-

Your community cannot be made up of one single other human being. Your partner cannot meet *all* your needs for freedom and closeness. Without the structure of conscious community, couples inevitably experience great pressure to rely on an A-frame of codependency. As either party tries to take space or follow his or her freedom, the other collapses in an attack of abandonment feelings, and then clings. Of course, this clinging then threatens the other partner's freedom. That is why we need community. Community is like the dance floor. It holds individual autonomy as a primary value. It also values transparency, nonviolence, love, trust, the joy of sacred sexuality, partnership, spirituality, and reverence for nature.

Many summers, I teach at the Zegg intentional community in Germany. This group has found, though long experience, that you cannot resolve the freedom-closeness appearance of conflict in a dyad of just two people. The dyad is too prone to the paralyzing dynamic of polarization, which then creates control battles. Only in a powerful morphogenic field of community energy can sexpeace between couples be achieved. Many in the Zegg community believe that this is also a key to world peace. Sometimes one member of the couple needs a certain quality of empathy that his or her partner just cannot provide. Sometimes there is a certain type of honesty that is needed, one that cannot be received from the partner, but *must* come from an outside community member. It took six weeks of counseling by members of the Zegg Community to get me to hear a particular fact—that my relationship partner cannot give me back my freedom. The reason that she cannot give me my freedom is because she does not possess it in the first place. I do. In my book, *Don't Be Nice, Be Real,* I give other examples of how it "takes a village to raise a relationship"—or the consciousness of an individual. Freedom is the center—and love the circumference—of a healthy relationship.

These integrated micro-communities support the development of holistic spirituality, which begins with both a heavenly consciousness of our free will and an earthly awareness of our interconnectedness. It is very easy for this interconnectedness to get lost in the push-pull polarization of the basic relational unit of society, the couple. It may be that the human being is a tribal or pack animal, like wolves and giraffes, and not like swans, which travel and live in pairs. The strength and security that a tribe provides is essential to preventing the usual codependency in couple relationships. Without this emotional and spiritual security, clinging is inevitable.

-§-
The freedom vs. closeness dance underlies many painful relationships.
-§-

Clinging poisons love. Paul Ferrini describes this dynamic in his book, *Love Without Conditions.*

> Compassion and detachment go hand in hand. You cannot love someone and seek to control him. Only by wanting what is best for him do you offer your brother freedom. And if you do not offer him freedom, you do not offer him love. Every situation in your life provides you with an opportunity to gain greater intimacy and greater freedom. As you love more and more people more and more deeply, you become less attached to them individually. You become attached not to the specific person, but to the love that each one extends to you. This is a movement toward the experience of Divine Love which is beyond the body, indeed beyond form of any kind.

These new communities do not necessarily have physical locations or complex organizational structures, but they do celebrate the divine diversity of bodies, personalities, gender manifestations, spiritual and sexual preferences, varieties of relationship design, and creativity of conscious sexual expression. Often these spontaneous, self-organizing groups are spawned by the spiritual infusion of a particular body of wisdom and creative expression from organizations like Burning Man, Human Awareness Institute (HAI), Nonviolent Communication, Celebrations of Love, and similar forums. These subcultural tribes are necessary to support individual souls in finding and embracing their own unique spiritual and sexual expression in the world. Much of our sexual and relationship behavior has been conditioned by mores, taboos, traditions, and rules created by elite males in cultural and religious leadership roles— and they were influenced by motivations other than empowering others, such as economic security for themselves, and the fear of impotence in the presence of overwhelmingly sexy women.

Esther Hicks, coauthor of *Ask and It Is Given,* jokes about governments creating laws to control people's sexual behavior. She asks: "What if our government decided that it was now changing the law so that we were all required to have at least ten marriage partners, and that each week we had to report to a government office to prove we were abiding by the law?" We would then see how ridiculous it is to have a law telling human beings how they are must love. Any law that tells us how we have to love—one or many, homosexually or heterosexually—violates the most sovereign spiritual principle, that of human autonomy. Every individual has his or her own unique needs for growth as they relate to friendship, love, sexuality, and life partners. During some cycles of development, people may need to be celibate. During others, they may need to have many intense sexual experiences. During yet others, they may require less-intense friendships or love relationships. Other times, they may need a series of partners as they grow and learn. And at others still, they may bond with one life-long partner. The evolution of each soul has its own patterns and needs for experience. These are not governed by the laws of humankind.

-§-

Only in a powerful morphogenic field of community energy can sexpeace between couples be achieved.

-§-

Because of the utter uniqueness of each soul's evolution as it expresses through loving relationships, tolerance becomes more than a nice value; it is a fertilizer absolutely required for our spiritual growth. Neale Donald Walsch, author of *Conversations with God,* wrote, "The decision to stop making each other wrong for what we're doing is going to be a huge turning point in our social evolution. And that's going to happen in the next ten to fifteen years—I'm very clear about that. We're going to stop making each other wrong for our sexual lifestyle choices." He goes on to include our spiritual, political, and other choices, as well.

Unless we are exercise true conscious choice, we are not aligned with the healthy flow of *chi* (life energy) in our bodies, *chit* (or joyful consciousness) in our minds, or love in our hearts. My mentor, Virginia Satir, said, "We need to take the risk of saying our *real* yesses and nos." The symptoms of this lack of alignment with healthy flow

are low sex drive, depression, loss of passion for life, low physical energy, illness, dullness, confusion, addictions, and explosiveness.

One of the most powerful catalysts for this awakening is nonsexual touch. It is healing and nurturing; it can improve self-esteem and ameliorate depression. If every human being belonged to a Touching Tribe, we would all be healthier and happier. As a therapist, it is a joy for me to watch friends and clients come back into the passionate, ecstatic, sweet flow of life. Radiance returns to their faces. Spring returns to their step. Joy returns to their hearts. I have been witness to many miraculous resurrections as people receive the power of compassion. Empathy releases their rage, hurt, and fear, and reopens their hearts. I have witnessed channels being opened to the powerful healing energy of the creative force of life itself: prana, sexual energy, *élan vital.*

-§-
Freedom is the center—and love the circumference—of a healthy relationship.
-§-

One reason we lose connection to our inner voice of choice is that we adapt to our family and community wishes—in order to receive their conditional love. Even our more evolved spiritual communities invite us to listen to parts of ourselves at the expense of our *whole* selves. Riane Eisler, in her book, *Sacred Pleasure,* makes the point this way:

> I think one of the great tragedies of Western religion [and contemporary spirituality] as most of us have known it has been its compartmentalized view of human experience and particularly its elevation of disembodied or, 'spiritual' love over embodied or carnal love.

Traditional religions tell us not to trust our own selfish hearts and to resist the weakness of the flesh. They demonize women, nature, sexuality, recreation, our own emotions, and pleasure. There are, of course, good reasons to ask people not to trust their own inner perceptions—people who are in touch with their own feelings, needs, hearts, and intuition do not make good slaves, soldiers, or religious followers. It is harder to keep such people in line, so fear and guilt tactics are the mainstay of many religions, with threats of eternal, hellish pain inflicted by a scary devil with pitchfork and horns, if we disobey.

There is, by the way, no horned devil mentioned in the Bible. The early Roman Christian church invented it. It came from the image of the bull, with its horns, which Pagans and Nature Worshipers held sacred as a symbol of abundance, potency, sexuality, and life. In the third century, the church took their sacred symbol and used it to demonize the competing religion—and to justify the slaughter of around one million women herbalist-physician-priestesses who still worshiped the feminine aspect of the Goddess, Gaia and nature. This literal demonization of their sacred symbol of sexuality, the bull, takes another interesting form. It has been conflated with the tradition of the cuckold's horns in the slang expression "horny devil." Here, horny does not just mean sexually deprived, lustful, and aroused; in our sexually repressed culture, it also means lascivious and lecherous. This association of sexual energy with the Christian symbol of the incarnation of all that is carnal and evil, the devil, is no accident. If Christian leaders would acknowledge the mistake their religion has been making these last 1,700 years, it might begin to interrupt the dangerous dynamic of denial of this sacred part of ourselves.

I am not going to hold my breath waiting for the apology. No, I am going to breathe deep the fresh air of freedom to create a new church and community that honors both God and Goddess, heavenly and earthly love. This new community not only worsh*ups* toward God, but also worsh*acrosses* toward each other. It values both the group and the individual. It respects both freedom and closeness.

I wonder what it would be like to go to church and make love, not in the pews—but on the altar. I used to feel shame and guilt while making love, imagining that an angry, frowning voyeur God was watching. Now I often experience a sacred, holy presence holding space as I enter that holy of holies, the womb of life, the pulsating heart of the creative life force. I believe that we are all yearning for that experience of wholeness—the wellbeing that flows from feeling ourselves being love and being loved.

Delores Richter of the Zegg community says, "Women are searching for, in a man, what they have lost in the universe." I believe that this is also true of men, but that they are conditioned to not reveal this vulnerable need, which contributes to the abandonment they secretly fear. The possibility of experiencing the presence of the power of the universe, the source of life, is actually available to us. We learn it by allowing our egos to be erased through surrendering to our deep love and lust for our lovers. This experience of the transcendent is transformative, lifting our soul's kite into the numinous knowledge of eternal spiritual wellbeing, while simultaneously plunging our soul's string into the depths of knowing the pleasurable purpose of our physical existence.

To know our spirit while feeling our body, to experience freedom with closeness, togetherness and separateness, to know heaven and earth simultaneously—this is to die, while still being alive. This is the spiritual resurrection, the homecoming, the return of the Goddess to the side of God, the reunion of sex and spirit.

Courtney Arnold:

Beyond the Gender Matrix

In the first days, in the very first days...before anything existed...in the time before the Glittering World...there was no earth, no sea, no sky...from out of the emptiness...a golden cosmic egg...a ball of thread...the seeds of the holy sea...she was created in the image of the unknown...the rainbow serpent...man with a raven's beak...In the beginning was the Word, and the Word was with God, and the Word was God.

Story is a not a thing; it is a force. It has the power to slip between the cracks of mundane experience, and the agency to both reflect and create reality. Through story we learn about our histories and lineages, how to value or dismiss objects, entities, ideas. And we are given a set of guidelines for the behaviors and beliefs that we come to adopt as right and true. Whether we are sitting in a church, a temple, a classroom, at the feet of a village elder, or in front of a television set, the stories we tell and are told teach us who we are, who we might someday become.

The human impulse toward story is universal. Across vast distances of place and time, certain themes and characters—archetypes—have emerged in the story lives of culture after culture. Through these archetypal codes we have tried to translate the ineffable into manageable concepts, symbols onto which we have projected ourselves and the world around us in the attempt to make sense of it all. These stories have waxed and waned, evolved over time, been appropriated, reinterpreted, even driven underground or forced into acceptance

Courtney Kumara Arnold, M.F.A., is a writer, teacher, editor, and Reiki Master. She developed the Creative Writing curriculum for the School of the Art Institute of Chicago's renowned Early College Program, and taught writing and literature at Columbia College Chicago. As a mentor to queer youth, she emphasizes the pivotal role of creativity in claiming identity. Courtney lives in Northern California, where she teaches workshops in energy work and Sacred Writing. Current writing projects include a novel, described as a "contemporary descent myth," and research toward a book on the creative process as sacred/healing practice. For upcoming classes, visit www.sixteenpetals.com.

according to the interests of those who had or wanted power. Like story, our own identities are not static. As the dominant narratives have shifted, so have our perceptions of our individual and collective selves, and the qualities of our relationships to one another and to Spirit.

Over the past few thousand years, the shamanistic worldview, in which humanity is but a minor character in the story of existence, has been largely supplanted by the narrative of mankind as master of his domain. This split is reflected in our outward attempts to subjugate nature, and in our inner suffering of separation from the Divine. To put it plainly, the stories we hold onto have trapped us in a spiritual double bind. We are taught that we are but half of a whole, that fulfillment will come from relationship with another, our opposite or complement. At the same time, we are admonished to transcend the unfortunate state of having a body and mortal attachments, in order to merge with Spirit. On the surface, these two directives can be seen as microcosm and macrocosm: the joy and compromise of a man and a woman coming together in partnership humbly mirroring the dissolution of earthly, individual ego into perfect bliss with the Divine. God is pursued as the Beloved. But, then, God is also to be feared. We are made in the image of God, yet somehow reflect only one part or another on our own. The narrative dysfunction is revealed in the polarity that permeates every level of this estranged state of being. The underlying message is that we are intrinsically different from the Other and, therefore, separated from the state of grace, of wholeness.

-§-
The stories we hold onto have trapped us in a spiritual double bind.
-§-

The estrangement itself is further infused with a binary gender dynamic, to the extent that "the sins of the flesh," submission, and femininity are conflated, while the ideals to which we are to aspire are understood, symbolically or otherwise, to be masculine. In the "civilized" world, the rhythms and cycles of Mother Nature are held at bay by the advancements of science, technology, and "superior," empirical reason.

It is important to remember, however, that this is just story, and only one of many available to us. In order to escape the double-bind of duality and separation from the Divine, we must be willing to question the stories we tell and believe—not only about the way it is out there in the world, but also *within ourselves.* And in questioning the polarity, we must begin by dismantling the poles, first by giving up assumptions of gender as intrinsic or determined by physical sex, and second, by being willing to allow for possibilities outside of, or in between, the strict male/female identity polemic. If we are to have any hope of unity with Spirit, we must re-frame our stories to create space for unity of all Spirit's aspects within ourselves. This is the path of the Spiritual Androgyne.

Concrete, bounded identity feels safe because it gives us control, in the sense that sanctioned roles come with a stock set of rules—"natural" laws that govern our experience of the world. From a limited point of view, prescribed roles keep us safe from the chaos of infinite possibility. But the same is true of a prison cell. If we can muster the courage to broaden our perspective, we see that the boundaries of tidy identity—man, woman, straight, gay, even bi-sexual—do not protect us so much from danger as from challenge and opportunity for spiritual growth.

The nature of the Androgyne is neither the lack of identity, nor the union of dualistic opposites. Rather, it is a nature of staggering breadth, blessed with freedom of play that allows not either/or/both, but all and more. The Androgyne is not alien to other identity types, as traditional roles can all be found within the Androgyne's repertoire, to be tried on and played in at will. The difference lies in non-attachment.

Someone who identifies strictly as female (in the cultural, not the biological sense) can only express *her*self as a woman (or, at best, as a woman in touch with her masculine side), and can only ever experience life on these terms. The Spiritual Androgyne, however, is free to be feminine, at times, or in some ways, and *also* masculine—and can experiment with other possibilities, as well. More importantly, the Androgyne deconstructs the very notion that there are qualities inherent to either biological sex. This is decisively different from the tantric marriage of inner god and goddess. The Spiritual Androgyne is not whole as a result of an integration of opposites, but by virtue of a fearless, far-reaching self-awareness. This is difficult to grasp because our language does not include words to describe alternative states of gender identity—and it is very hard to imagine, much less believe in, that which is not made available to us on the conceptual, linguistic level.

-§-
In order to experience the Divine as true selfhood, we must let go of attachment to any notions of who we are, and unravel.
-§-

This is why language is intensely, innately political. It is also, above all, spiritual. There is no universal word for the Divine, because the Divine is beyond words. Every culture has its terminology for "God," but these Gods tend to be more a reflection of the people, the cultures themselves, than of All That Is. The closest we come as a human race to describing our spiritual source is in the various permutations of the sacred syllable: *om, aum, amen, amin…*

Even the identifier Spiritual Androgyne is limited symbolically. For one thing, the word itself comes from the Greek roots *andro,* a male person, and *gyne,* the female reproductive organ. But more than that, the label gives the idea of a thing without any hint as to the thing's true potential. In order to access the ineffable truth of identity's possibilities, we must be willing to sit with the pleasures and discomforts as the sacred syllable resonates within our own bodies—corporeal *and* subtle.

> COBRA: I'd like to be an acrobat in the *Palace of Wonders.* What should I do to loosen up my joints?
>
> ROSA: Sit down. Place your left foot over the right thigh and the right over the left. Cross your arms behind your back. Grab your left heel with your right hand; the right heel with your left. Look at your navel. And then try to unravel...
>
> —Severo Sarduy, *Cobra*

Identity formation commands the performance of all kinds of austerities: We amputate the unseemly parts of ourselves that do not fit in sanctioned boxes; rebel and face life in the wilderness of the Outsider; bear the incredible burden of our multiple selves, acting different parts in different company. But none of these practices brings us closer to pure, spiritual Self. In order to experience the Divine as true selfhood, we must let go of attachment to any notions of who we are, and unravel. Spiritual Androgyny, then, is not an identity, but a kinetic, energetic state; it is a spectrum, not a point but a field.

-§-
In the face of the void, it is our instinct to create story.
-§-

This is not a feat of conceptual contortion. In fact, the androgynous nature of the universe is revealed in the work of quantum physics. According to Niels Bohr's Copenhagen Interpretation of quantum theory, the state of being of energy itself is entirely dependent upon the assumptions of the perceiver. When we see energy as a particle, it is a particle; when we see it as a wave, it is a wave.

So, we create the reality we believe in and expect to experience. A pattern becomes limiting, self-destructive, when we are so enmeshed with our identity that we are blinded to the possibility of our energy manifesting in any other way, and to the awareness that we are only reflections, refractions of that specific energy's archetype in its infinite potential. In other words, we are particular from the perspective of ego consciousness, but wavelike when free of attachment to concrete identity.

Spiritual Androgyny takes on a sacred aspect when it becomes not only an energetic state, but also a practice through which "our" ego-possessed experience and beliefs can be released and transformed into new expressions of potential. Once restrictions of identity's form and meaning are dissolved and the archetypes are free to manifest in new ways, the grip of attachment is broken; the individual is likewise free to explore new possibilities of experience.

So, we reconsider the boundaries of "male," "female," "homo," and "hetero." But everyday life does not take place on the quantum level. We must exist within tissue and bone, cultures, institutions. We cannot escape 3-D. How do we embrace the Androgyne and put a new identity orientation to practice within the limitations of the day-to-day? We must begin by telling new stories.

To be human is often to be engaged in power struggle. In our culture, this is true on all levels, from politics to professional life to interpersonal relationships. If we are to move beyond the power struggle inherent to polarity, we must begin to question the dominant narratives and the "realities" in which we are entrenched.

We are, as a whole, less faithful to religious stories now than we have been in the past. This is not to say that religion is no longer valid or pertinent to the contemporary Western worldview. Rather, religion now shares sovereignty with other narrative systems. It can be difficult, however, to see contemporary life as bounded by story, because the myths are now very sophisticated and no longer *necessarily* revolve around overt gods, goddesses, monsters, or heroes. Moreover, we often fail to recognize the storied nature of our experience because we tend to equate the idea of story itself with fiction, fantasy—"the untrue." But when we step back from our beliefs and unquestioned assumptions, we see that our consumer culture, politics, even empirical science, are all narrative systems for creating order out of chaos, asserting power over the possibilities. On a foundational level, these story systems are all more or less gendered; and all are couched in a patriarchal narrative structure.

-§-
Pleasure becomes reality-shaking; play, a radical act.
-§-

This is not, or not only, a feminist assertion. Patriarchy is as damaging to men as it is to women. Indeed, it is damaging precisely because it allows for only the limited definitions of "man" and "woman" as available identity options. What's more, the masculine and the feminine are positioned as diametrically opposed—either as halves of a whole or as enemies in the "war of the sexes." But divesting the masculine of its power and shifting to matriarchy is no solution, because the core issue of binary identity would remain unresolved. Instead, we must be willing to transcend the binary by going into the unknown.

In the face of the void, it is our instinct to create story. This is a healthy, self-empowering impulse as long as the stories we tell remain fluid. We have reached a stage in our personal and cultural evolution, however, in which the dominant narrative has calcified to the point of crippling rigidity. It is time to stretch, to breathe. And before evolution can occur within the macrocosm, it must begin with the individual.

Flexibility of story is relatively easy to achieve on the personal level: we call it play. And we can play with the boundaries of self-definition by shifting focus and allowing previously unseen possibilities to emerge. We need not even write new stories to do this—the world's traditions are filled with narratives of transgressive and transformative gender play. Inanna, Sumerian Queen of Heaven and Earth, bestowed high cultic office upon the *kurgarra* and *pili-pili,* her consecrated transgender priests and priestesses. The nineteenth century Indian saint, Sri Ramakrishna, sometimes adopted the dress and mannerisms of Radha, who defied the laws of dharma for the sake of her love for Krishna. The drag queens and kings of the contemporary urban nightclub scene reveal gender to be a form of ritual performance.

-§-

We need to remain mindful of how our play resonates within our core.

-§-

Drag, however, is not for everyone. And the freedom of drag lies in the fact that it is about what we put on—costume, persona—rather than who we are. In order to play with *identity,* we must bring the game to the field of the self. And if we want that play to spill over into the rest of the world, we must locate it in the part of the self that is the point of contact with Other: the body.

So, let us begin with flesh, with fluids. By embodying Spiritual Androgyny in our sexual selves, we can, for moments or for lifetimes, short out programmed identity circuits. Pleasure becomes reality-shaking; play, a radical act. But, as with any radical affront to the safety of established norms, success relies upon our ability to dismantle our stories.

I once found myself in an argument with a born-again Christian about the nature of the feminine. Women, he believed, are naturally inferior to men. Furthermore, he offered as evidence the "fact" that "men are built to penetrate, and women are built to succumb." I pointed out that even biology is a matter of perspective, and that it could be argued that the powerful man is swallowed alive by the woman, only to be expelled in a limp and shriveled state. Because he was unwilling to reconsider his story, this fundamentalist was unable to see that both examples were based upon interpretation. By adopting an attitude of play, however, we are able explore interpretation without getting caught up in a tangle of truths.

Spiritual Androgyny gives us license to play with identity elementally—individually, on the level of the body, as we express our sexual selves, and relationally, as we use our bodies to connect with others. The evolutionary potential of sexuality is available to us whether we choose to make love alone or with a partner. It does not require that we question our personal preferences or attractions, though we are certainly free to do so if that is what we desire. Rather, it provides space in which to relax into the nuances of sexual energetics—degrees of surrender and control, intensity and levity, vocalization, variation, soulfulness and sweat, titillation, tenderness, toys, fantasy, role-play, rhythm, ritual, and beyond.

The ways in which we conceive of our selves, and the selves that we bring into passionate contact with others, if held consciously, have the potential to shift profoundly and, in so doing, profoundly shift the world. This is a very big idea. But we must be careful not to get caught up in the romance and grandiosity, the turn-on of the idea itself. Evolution is not about acts—sexual or otherwise. Nor is it about identity. We can make up pretty stories to validate our own desires. We can create communities and codes of ethics that allow for whatever reality we choose, congratulating ourselves for our awareness and enlightenment, our open mindedness and freedom from guilt or shame. But these stories would likely serve our egos, which are only part of our whole selves.

Expanding our self-concept, and learning to bring the expanded self into contact with another, can be a significant leap of faith in the direction of our own spiritual growth. But in order for identity and sexuality to function as tools of creation, we must acknowledge the tremendous destructive power they can have, as well. And with this awareness, we must be committed to using these tools only with the greatest of respect for ourselves and for others. This means that we need to remain mindful at all times of how our play resonates within our core. Does this attitude or characteristic take me deeper into myself, or is it just an interesting game? Does this kind of contact bring us closer into true intimacy, or is it only physically arousing? By paying attention not only to the moment, but also to the impact of the moment upon our own feelings, tissues, and energy fields, we can come to know ourselves more completely than ever before—not as distinct organisms, but as part of a holistic, living system. The stories that grow organically from this level of knowing will reflect truly androgynous identities, wide enough to encompass the entire spectrum of Spirit.

Spiritual Androgyny—as a path, as an infinite field of possibility—is about neither who we make love with nor how we play, but

about who we become in the process. If we can stretch the boundaries of story enough to transcend rigid identity at the individual level, then we will no longer need to engage in power struggle within our interpersonal relationships. This shift, though intimate in nature, is powerful enough to reverberate within the collective, altering the evolutionary dynamics of the greater human partnership.

The story of polarity, of estrangement from ourselves and from the divine, has given us the gift of a great longing. What we do with that longing, and what new stories will evolve along the way, only *we* can tell.

Barbara Brennan:

Energy Fields in Intimate Relationships

All of us long to know who we are in our true divine center. Our deepest longing is to allow that divine center within us to express in every way. We all have a deep longing to create from our core—from the divinity within us—but what that creation is like will be different for each individual.

Our desires are directly connected to spiritual longing. Whatever you desire, no matter how outrageous or off the wall it may seem, that longing is an expression of what you've come here to do or be. Bringing spirit into matter is how we make Heaven on Earth. That is really what we are here to do. Once that spiritual longing is realized, everything else falls into place.

Perhaps you want a relationship but don't have one. You feel a longing, and you link it to a personal need. But under that personal need is a spiritual longing for communion. Start out by allowing yourself to feel that longing fully. Give yourself full permission to actually feel the loneliness, pain, and negative feelings of wanting a relationship when you don't have one. Let those feelings flow without protecting yourself from their intensity. This will open your heart and create the space inside you for someone to come. Of course, when a relationship does come into your life, you will be faced with more personal process work that needs attention. All the ways you prevent yourself from opening to a relationship will have to be attended to and cleared.

Barbara Brennan, innovator in the field of energy consciousness and former NASA physicist, has been exploring the Human Energy Field and realms of human consciousness for 30 years. Her best-selling books, *Hands of Light* (Bantam, 1988) and *Light Emerging* (Bantam, 1993), are considered classics in the fields of energy work and complementary medicine. The Barbara Brennan School of Healing has educated thousands in Brennan Healing Science—a modality based on the Human Energy-Consciousness System. This holistic work merges High Sense Perception skills with hands-on energy healing techniques to assist individuals with their personal process of healing into optimum health.

Many people long to have a relationship, but do not perceive it as a spiritual longing. They just feel lonely. I encourage them to feel the loneliness instead of cutting themselves off from the feelings. Emptiness can be terrifying. But if you really allow yourself to feel it, out of that emptiness will arise an awareness of how you have kept yourself from having a relationship. If you can begin to perceive that and follow what the new awareness tells you about what you need to do to open yourself, that process will eventually bring a relationship. Looking outside yourself or busily keeping up with match.com, for instance, will not bring you to the needed insight and growth. But if you do the growth piece first, you can go anywhere and attract interesting people.

Most of my work involves studying the human auric field, but I began with a Master's degree in atmospheric physics. I worked with light sensitive devices as a NASA research scientist at Goddard Space Flight Center, NASA's main un-manned satellite center. I worked with an instrument that was flown on the Nimbus II weather satellite. It measured light in the infra-red, visible, and ultraviolet wave lengths that come from the earth. I applied those techniques to analyze auras, but rather than use a physical instrument, I used my high sense perception, or clairvoyance. I was training to become a bio-energetic therapist when I began to perceive the human energy field, or aura. Over a period of fifteen years, my high sense perception developed to a higher degree of accuracy. I also used my scientific background to interpret how my perceptions worked and then applied what I was learning to teach other people.

-§-
Our desires are directly connected to spiritual longing.
-§-

By studying the human energy field (HEF), you can perceive how every decision and everything that we experience in life affects the body. Every thought and feeling a person has shows in their aura. The way we deal with our life experiences, how we react to negative experiences in our lives, all are reflected in the aura.

The HEF has a specific pattern of health. When we distort our energy fields, this distortion has a direct and immediate effect on the physical body. The effect might be slight and unnoticeable at first, but if we make a habit of reacting in a negative way to situations, the habitual reaction will eventually show in the physical body and cause a physical disturbance.

The HEF is the foundation of the body. The field precedes the body, rather than the body preceding the field. The field, in fact, creates the body. That is why hands-on healing works. Think about it—if the energy that keeps us alive is coming from the cells of the body and we put a little energy in the cells, will it do much? On the other hand, if the energy field forms the structure and it is there *before* the cell... So if we address what's wrong with the structure, what will happen? A skilled healer can repair the structure of the field and teach the client how to maintain the healthy structure. Then the physical body will respond in kind. We work from the structure that gives rise to the body, rather than work directly on the body itself.

Another interesting thing to think about is that the HEF is bigger than the physical body.

In other words, your body is actually *in* your auric field rather the way we often think—"I am in my body."

Anyone can learn to expand their regular senses to perceive the aura. When you expand the senses, they begin to differentiate. For example, there is a big difference between the experience of love and the experience of feelings. They are actually discrete and separate senses in the world of the HEF. When the ordinary senses expand in this way, you begin to learn that, in fact, *perception serves awareness.* You can become aware of the HEF just as you become aware of anything else in your world.

In my school, we work on expanding the senses of touch, vision, emotional feelings, the feeling of love and understanding something. We also work with the auditory sense, receiving sounds or words of information. How you learn is by practicing.

There are three basic kinds of human energy field *interactions* that people use in relationship. They are the three ways we exchange energy and consciousness. The most common interaction exchange we use is through bio-plasmic streamers. They are the arcs of energy-consciousness we send back and forth to each other. Imagine something like the physical world plasma, such as a lightening strike, only a higher vibration, flowing between people in an arc. This arc contains the energy-consciousness of the interaction; it can have positive or negative intention. This occurs long-distance as well as close-up. It can also travel through time.

-§-
Under that personal need is a spiritual longing for communion.
-§-

Another way we exchange energy and consciousness is through harmonic inductance. This is not unlike what happens when you hit a tuning fork and another one begins to vibrate and make a sound. Many people have this experience when they get close to somebody who has a very high frequency, meditating at the foot of a guru, for example. If you sit in a room with a spiritual master, you will often perceive very strong energy moving through you.

The third way is through relational cords that connect people who have been linked with each other at one time or another. The cords connect through each person's chakras. The deeper and more intimate the relationship, the more substantial the cord connection. The cords do not dissolve, not even at death—once connected, always connected. People who die are still connected to you and the cords are still in place unless you tear them out. This happens quite often and people don't always know what they have done. It can happen in the process of mourning, for instance, or in the process of divorce. This is very unhealthy. Healing must be done to reconnect the cords and heal them. Even if you didn't like the relationship. When healed they become cords of love.

-§-
People who die are still connected to you and the cords are still in place. This is healthy. Don't tear them out.
-§-

A great deal of information flows through the cords. When a parent dies, for example, the cords are still connected and energy consciousness flows through the cords to surviving family members through the cords, provided the person will allow it. A parent will go to the children or spouse and actually pour love and information into that person through the cord.

I observed a when a woman who worked with me in the office three days after her mother had died. I saw her deceased mother come into the room and feed her information through the relational cords—the information was her mother's condensed wisdom of an entire lifetime. This happens quite often when a parent dies. It is a gift, and it causes pain in the person who left the physical world if that gift is not received. Many times we tend to break or stop that flow. We honor our ancestors when we allow them to share this remarkable gift with us by allowing their presence to be felt and opening to receive it.

One of my books, *Light Emerging,* asks, "What are your true needs? Here is how to allow the feelings and the longings for those real needs to fill your being so that they can be fulfilled. First, make a list—what you wish to create for yourself. Keep it simple and profound. As you make the visualization clear, do not it send it up to your guides, as if we will give it down to you, but rather, seed it deeply into the core of your being so that it can emerge from your inner fountain." Life has a brilliant way of bringing us to the exact spiritual work we need to do so that we can center more and more in our core and allow that core to express in the world.

Dawson Church:

Igniting the Passion-Field

You live in a gingerbread cottage in a lush forest, where the sweetness of nature assaults your senses at every turn. Birds sing in your yard. Deer wander across your lawn, secure in the knowledge that here, everything is safe.

Your water supply is a crystal-clear pond in your back yard, fed by an underground spring. Visitors to your idyllic cottage agree that this is the most wonderful liquid they have ever tasted. The water is so clear that not a streak mars any part of the pond's perfection. It is so still that not an eddy disturbs its surface.

One day you wake up feeling ill, sickened by something you ate a long time ago. You know you're going to throw up. Where do you choose to do that? In the spring? Of course not!

Yet that's precisely what almost every couple does with their relationship. The power of two people's energy fields combining creates a third field. This field is the energy body of the relationship. Kept clear and clean, like the crystal spring, it is a source of inspiration for every couple around them. When used as a garbage dump for old angers and disappointments, the couple's energy field becomes a polluted cesspit full of ancient, regurgitated, fossilized resentments.

Forbearance and Nourishment

Cultivating a beautiful energy field as a couple requires two acts of consciousness. The first, *nourishment,* means pouring words, ges-

Dawson Church, Ph.D., has edited or authored over 200 books. He is a co-founder of Aslan Publishing, a former CEO of Atrium Publisher's Group, and current publisher of Elite Books. During a long publishing career he has worked with many best-selling authors, as well as developing the careers of unknowns. He is passionately interested in emerging psychological and medical techniques that can yield fast and radical cures (see www.SoulMedicineInstitute.com); his recent books on the subject are *The Genie in Your Genes* (Elite, 2007) and *Soul Medicine* (Elite, 2006). See www.AuthorsPublishing.com.

tures, actions, and thoughts of goodwill into your reservoir, filling it to the brim with clear, loving energy. When you're feeling strong, happy, and relaxed, and your heart is overflowing with goodwill, nourishing your relationship is easy. When you're not feeling good, a second act of consciousness is required, and that's *forbearance.*

Forbearance is an old-fashioned word that deserves to be dusted off and put back in the twenty-first-century lexicon, along with fortitude, restraint, and reticence. In *Soul Medicine,* an ambitious survey of the field of energy medicine that I coauthored with pioneering neurosurgeon Norm Shealy, M.D., Ph.D., we identify intention as a crucial pillar of health. Intention doesn't mean "having good intentions," those paving stones of the road to hell, while acting out the same old, same old, same old scripts we're so comfortable with. Intention means holding a vision of what you want that is *so powerful that it conditions every thought, word, and action.* When your intention is strong, you can summon up forbearance—even when you are tempted to drop bombs into your boudoir, instead of bonbons.

-§-
A reliable set of couple skills provides the building blocks for a gorgeous shared energy structure.
-§-

Initially, creating beauty is not spontaneous. It takes work. It may require a great deal of effort to stop your mouth from saying that negative thing (forbearance). It might require unaccustomed mental acuity to remember to bring your wife flowers each week (nourishment). You feel grouchy—so you express love anyway. A beautiful relationship is not an accident of nature; it's a work of art, in which every stroke is painted with the brush of intention.

Energy Fields Condition Matter

Powerful loving intentions, held in consciousness, bring the gift of health to our bodies. For *we are energy beings giving rise to a physical body,* not the other way around. For a long time, scientists thought that the physical body gave rise to its energy field, or in the jargon of academia, that "consciousness is an epiphenomenon of matter."

But no more. Quantum physicist Ervin Laslo, Ph.D., says, "Matter is vanishing as a fundamental feature of reality, retreating before energy; and continuous fields are replacing discrete particles as the basic elements of an energy-bathed universe." Early in the twentieth century, noting the direction in which research was trending, English physicist James Jeans exclaimed, "The stream of knowledge is heading towards a non-mechanical reality; the universe begins to look more like a great thought than a great machine." Energy fields are not an abstraction. They are at the foundation of physical matter. Just because you can't see them, that doesn't mean that they aren't affecting your relationship every day. When you become aware of your energy fields, you can begin to use them consciously to create the relationship you desire.

Even the expression of DNA in genes follows energy. Experimental scientific evidence is accumulating for what's called *epigenetic control*—the control of genes from outside the cell. The old dogma that genes control your personal characteristics is rapidly crumbling; we're discovering that genes get turned on and off by the environments in which they exist. Those include the chemical environment, the neural environment, and—most importantly—the energetic environment. Of these, the energetic environment sends signals the fastest. Cell biologist Bruce Lipton, Ph.D., author of the best-selling book *The Biology of Belief,* says that, "The laws of quantum physics, not Newtonian laws, control a molecule's life-generating movements... Energetic signaling mechanisms such as electromagnetic frequencies are a hundred times more efficient in relaying environmental information than physical signals such as hormones, neurotransmitters, growth factors, etc." The cascade of biochemicals conditioning your cells is the result of your energy field, and the quality of your energy field is under your conscious control. "When someone has a sudden shift of belief," he states, "it can radically change the epigenetics, which means that the same genetic code will now be interpreted completely differently—this could be the difference between cancer and remission." Or a relationship pool that is full of slime, and one that sparkles with love.

-§-

When you become aware of your energy fields, you can use them to consciously create the relationship you desire.

-§-

You are literally turning genes on or off in your body through the quality of your interactions with your partner, and through the shared energy field that the two of you create. This is not metaphysical speculation; it is scientific fact. Leading researcher James Oschman, Ph.D., author of the authoritative book *Energy Medicine,* says: "In the past it had been thought that the genes give rise to proteins that then spontaneously assemble into the living structures that carry out living processes, including consciousness. In the emerging quantum model, it is the action of quantum coherence that organizes the parts into living structures, and it is the action of quantum coherence that gives rise to consciousness as a distributed and emergent property of the assembled parts." Or, in the words of researcher Karl Maret, M.D., "The genome is plastic and resembles constantly rewritten software code rather than being fixed hardware that you inherit at birth." A robust energy field, conducive to health, is produced by loving thoughts and actions in a well-nourished energy

system. A polluted energy field, in which one or both partners feel free to dump the accumulated weight of past disappointments, also affects your health—like a toxic injection. "Your thoughts create your reality" is not a metaphysical platitude; it is a certainty rooted in quantum physics and the latest medical science. Intention is a sacred stone dropped into the well of consciousness, rippling out to create patterns in the quantum universe that reflect and reinforce itself.

-§-
When two people are each in alignment with their own souls, they are naturally in alignment with each other.
-§-

Because energy fields are invisible, it is tempting to imagine that they can be ignored. *Can't I plop just this one little resentment into the field?* you may wonder. *Can't I express just this tiny piece of ill-will?* you ask yourself, or think, *Surely that bit of anger won't have too big an effect—and I feel such urgency about expressing it!*

The bad *and* the good news is that energy systems are a matrix. When you affect one part of a matrix, it affects the whole. Small resentments can have big effects, just as, in fractal mathematics, a butterfly flapping its wings in Singapore can tip the balance of global climate just enough to produce a hurricane in Florida. Small kindnesses can also tip the whole energy balance. If your first waking word to your spouse has always been grouchy, making a different choice can set the tone for the whole day.

Try this experiment: Think of the face of your beloved. Make it the purest soul-face you can imagine, rather than the stubbly, unkempt, puffy-eyed zombie that might stare out at you from the pillow beside you each morning. Imagine your beloved's soul-face surrounded by a pink field of beautiful, glowing energy. Feel the beauty of this soul that is with you on your relationship journey. Whatever your partner's behavior, the soul still shines—that's what attracted you to this person in the first place.

Every moment that you choose to speak to your partner at that soul level, looking at that fresh, radiant soul-face rather than at the A.M. gargoyle presenting itself to your physical eyes, you begin to shift the whole relationship onto that soul plane. If you've had just four soul-seconds with him in the last ten years, and four hundred million miserable seconds, the accumulated weight of misery is pretty hard to shift. The relationship is like a battlefield strewn with four hundred million tattered, rotting corpses—and just a handful of dancing ballerinas. Cultivating the ballerina moments to the point where they outnumber the corpses is going to take consistent consciousness.

Consciousness is key. When we act consciously, choosing kind and loving words, we create a lovely energy environment. When we speak unconsciously, out of old programming, we produce the same god-awful, scorched-earth battleground we've produced through all the other unconscious words we've spoken. We're creating either way. Why not use consciousness to create something beautiful in our lives, our relationships, and our bodies?

Energy fields aren't an abstraction; they're the place from which material reality springs. When you treat your relationship's energy field with this kind of respect, knowing that you're setting up a good or a bad relationship through the quality of your consciousness, you can no more dump your old resentments into your field than you would vomit into your drinking water.

Self-Focus

Two broken people can't produce a fixed relationship. No amount of trying to fix your relationship is going to work as long as you remain wounded yourself. When you remove your focus from your relationship partner, and shift it instead to your higher self, you do your relationship partner the greatest favor imaginable. When you seek to bring yourself into impeccable alignment with your soul, and you begin to express from that soul-source, you radiate the qualities of divinity into the world around you, including into the relationship.

When two people are each in alignment with their own souls, they are naturally in alignment with each other, because all souls are naturally in alignment with the Great Soul. When two individuals shift their focus from creating effects in their shared space, to creating peace in their individual spaces, the shared space automatically becomes redolent with peace. The Great Soul part of you is always in complete agreement with the Great Soul part of your partner, no matter how deep the feud between your personalities might be. When you line yourself up with your own Great Soul, you find yourself in natural harmonious relationship with that part of your partner.

-§-
Breathe, and your soul breathes with you.
-§-

It seems like a paradox that you build a wonderful relationship by removing your focus from the relationship, and focusing completely on yourself. Yet this shift in focus is exactly what is required to bring healing, love, and peace into the shared space.

Here's a simple test to refocus yourself: before you speak, think, or act, just breathe. Take a deep breath, and feel the calm place inside yourself. If you are unable to take a breath, or to feel your calm center, if you feel a pressing sense of urgency forcing you to speak right now, then you know that you are connected to a wounded inner place.

When you unplug your thoughts and actions from your soul-source, and instead plug them into those wounded voices, then your words and actions convey the energy of the wound back out into your relationship. This reinforces the wound experience. It brings past wounding right into the present.

If, instead, you breathe, feel the calm place, and speak and act from there, you convey healing into the present. The healing present you are then creating also reaches back to soothe and heal the past wounds. You replace your experience of wounding with the experience of healing. When you create a healing space in your relationship many times a day, you reinforce the felt experience of healing throughout your energy body and your neural physiology, replacing the felt experience of living a wound.

Those wounds need love. They are old hurts crying out for healing. They are coming into our present experience not to be drivers of our present thoughts and feelings, but in order to be healed. As we make the choice to remain in our calm center, we are pouring our love into those old hurts, giving them the healing and solace they crave. Each moment is a brick we are laying in the house of our lives. By making the choice to lay bricks of love and joy, we steadily build a beautiful structure. Brick by brick, we build the house of healing and peace in place of the house of fear and anguish we built when our behavior was controlled by those old wounds. From this secure foundation, we can love those wounds all the way through to healing.

-§-
The first step on the path to divine relationship requires the intention of only one partner.
-§-

This takes enormous determination. When our unhealed voices are screaming, when we cannot breathe because we feel such urgency and pressure to speak, to scream, to cry, it seems impossible that we might choose instead to slow down, find our breath, and speak from our calm center. The pressure of the wound feels so urgent that not expressing it feels like death. It's as if every cell is being picked up and turned in the direction of wound expression.

It takes a strong person to resist the urge, to make the choice to breathe and stay calm instead. If we do not resist the urge, and we express the wound, we reinforce the wounding in our relationship. And sometimes it takes producing continued destruction in our relationships to waken us to the necessity for change. Yet our souls are patient. They are always there, accessible, waiting for that moment when we are open to making another choice. The choice is just one breath away. Breathe, and your soul breathes with you.

Your partner is not responsible for your happiness or peace. Your partner is not even ten percent responsible for your enlightenment. If you believe that your partner must change—even one percent—in order for you to be happy or enlightened, you have simply handed one percent of your power over to somebody else, and delayed the day of your happiness accordingly.

Self-Reinforcing Fields

Many people are so damaged, they have had so many traumatic experiences of relationship, starting in the womb, that their embedded model of relationship is like a black hole in space, with a gravity so strong that it sucks anything within orbital range remorselessly into its void. It requires intention of steel to counteract our habits. Yet the payoff is huge. If you maintain your intention, a marvelous thing happens: One day, you reach critical mass. You begin to create beauty spontaneously.

When two individual energy fields collude, they produce a third field. When a person I adore walks into the room, something mysterious about that person's field makes me calmer, more focused, and happier. The interaction of the two sets of vibrations creates a shared field that conditions the fields of both individuals. When enough loving actions are fed into this reservoir of energy, a magical moment of spontaneous combustion occurs. The passion-field is ignited. Just as, in the presence of a saint, the disciple feels the energy and becomes saintly, the shared love-field of a couple can begin to overwhelm the negative tendencies and behaviors of the individual partners for as long as the partners maintain their strong intention.

Once you've created a morphogenic field full of love and goodwill, it becomes self-reinforcing. Like a huge, clear reservoir, it overpowers the occasional splash of ink. It can accommodate the occasional bad day, low biorhythm, sideways remark, hormonal shift, impatient gesture, act of andropausal amnesia—and remain intact. You wake up in the morning feeling out of sorts, but when you turn to see the face of your beloved on the pillow next to you, the sweetness of the field overpowers all your tendencies toward grouchiness. You then act in accordance with love. That's a self-reinforcing energy field. It is a state of grace that loves the grinchiness out of you.

Practicing Intention

The characteristics of energy fields provide both challenges and opportunities. Imagine a karate master, crouched like a coiled tiger on the mat of the dojo, senses at peak alertness, as she prepares to

fend off three attackers simultaneously. One slip of consciousness, and she's defeated. Like the martial arts master, moving with practiced impeccability through her routines, we must practice the *marital arts* with the same degree of precision if we are to get good at them. Getting good at both forbearance and nourishment requires devotion. Like thugs attacking a master, the subterranean world of our subconscious programming throws adversaries into our consciousness every day, challenging our commitment to gorgeous couple energy. That's the challenge.

Here's the opportunity: These old habits are not trying to destroy us; they're simply testing the strength of our intention and the purity of our consciousness, providing us with opportunities to sharpen our marital arts skills. Energy without structure lacks a framework for expression. We need both the fire of love and the structure of technique. Without technique, even the greatest of love energies has no forum for expression. You may have the potential to be the world's greatest violinist, but unless you learn to play the violin, your potential remains unexpressed. And when the world's greatest violinist is stressed or upset, and the magic isn't flowing as usual, she still has technique to fall back on. Learning a reliable set of couple skills, and practicing them before you're in an emergency, provides the building blocks for a gorgeous shared energy structure. You'll find some of the most effective techniques at www.SoulMedicineInstitute.com, along with links to detailed instructions for each. Once the structure is built, you can play in and out of techniques as you choose whatever is most useful and enjoyable for you.

When your thoughts, words, and actions are plugged into your soul's reality, that reality then flows through you to create beauty all around you. The energy of your soul then has an outlet into the relationship. And when soul-energy starts to flow into the relationship, the relationship is kissed by the breath of God. When the wave-form of God's breath is being breathed by two people into a relationship, the third wave created by the two divine breaths is so powerful that it has the potential to transform everyone in the vicinity of the divine couple. That's the power of a robust passion-field.

Cultivating that passion-field takes intention and consciousness. Saving it from harm requires forbearance. Yet, when you combine those principles and ignite the passion-field, your relationship becomes a beacon of transformation for the community around you. One brain and body plugged into God is powerful; two or more plugged in, and participating together in the co-creative dance of the universe, are unstoppable. By creating divine relationship together, we bring heaven to earth.